子連れ狼

LONE
WOLF
AND
CUB

子連れ狼

story
KAZUO KOIKE

art
GOSEKI KOJIMA

DARK HORSE COMICS

translation
DANA LEWIS

lettering & retouch
DIGITAL CHAMELEON

cover artwork
FRANK MILLER with **LYNN VARLEY**

publisher
MIKE RICHARDSON

editors
MIKE HANSEN and **DAN HARRIS**

assistant editor
TIM ERVIN-GORE

consulting editor
TOREN SMITH for **STUDIO PROTEUS**

book design
DARIN FABRICK

art director
MARK COX

Published by Dark Horse Comics, Inc. in association
with MegaHouse and Koike Shoin Publishing Company.

Dark Horse Comics, Inc.
10956 SE Main Street, Milwaukie, OR 97222
www.darkhorse.com

First edition: September 2000
ISBN: 1-56971-503-3

5 7 9 10 8 6

Printed in Canada

To find a comics shop in your area, call the
Comic Shop Locator Service toll-free at 1-888-266-4226

THE GATELESS BARRIER

子連れ狼

By KAZUO KOIKE
& GOSEKI KOJIMA

VOLUME
2

A NOTE TO READERS

Lone Wolf and Cub is famous for its carefully researched re-creation of Edo-Period Japan. To preserve the flavor of the work, we have chosen to retain many Edo-Period terms that have no direct equivalents in English. Japanese is written in a mix of Chinese ideograms and a syllabic writing system, resulting in numerous synonyms. In the glossary, you may encounter words with multiple meanings. These are words written with Chinese ideograms that are pronounced the same but carry different meanings. A Japanese reader seeing the different ideograms would know instantly which meaning it is, but these synonyms can cause confusion when Japanese is spelled out in our alphabet. *O-yurushi o* (please forgive us)!

LONE WOLF AND CUB

子連れ狼

TABLE OF CONTENTS

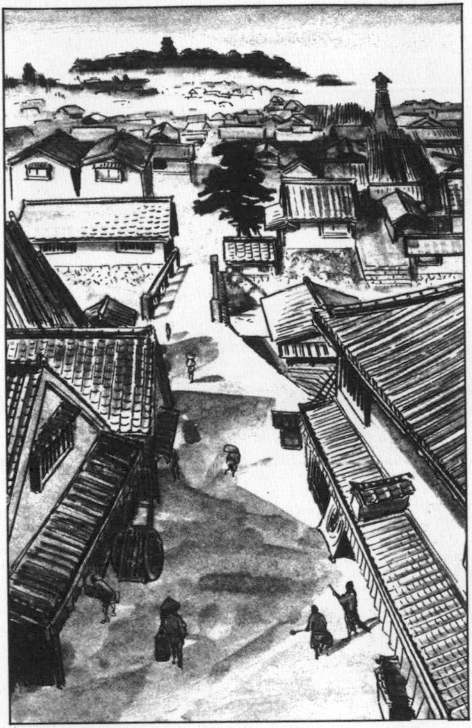

the tenth

Red Cat

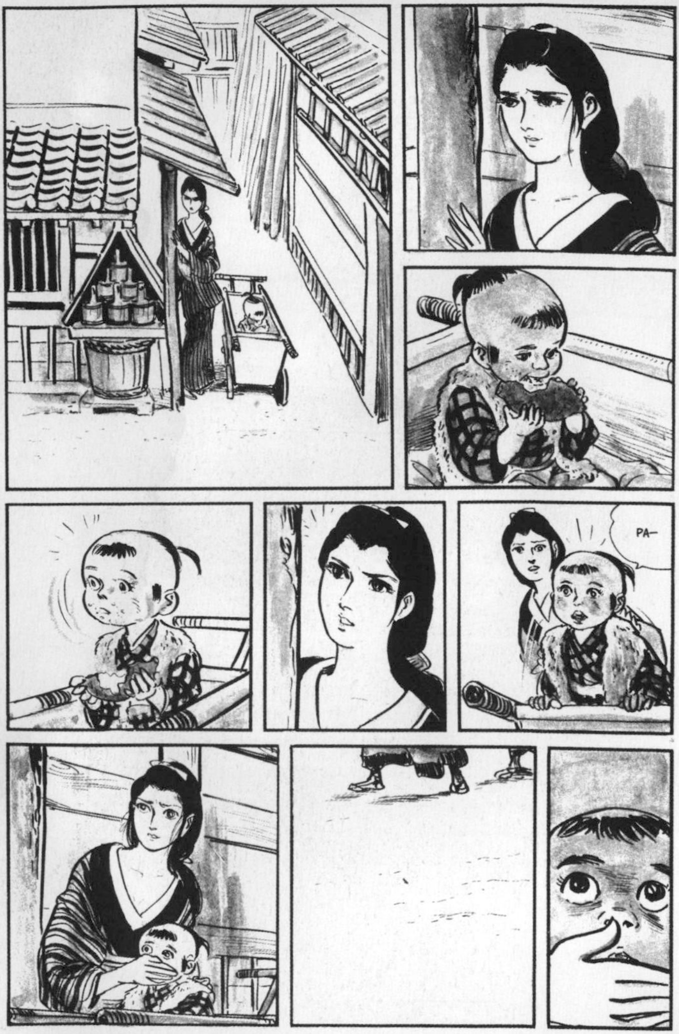
PA—

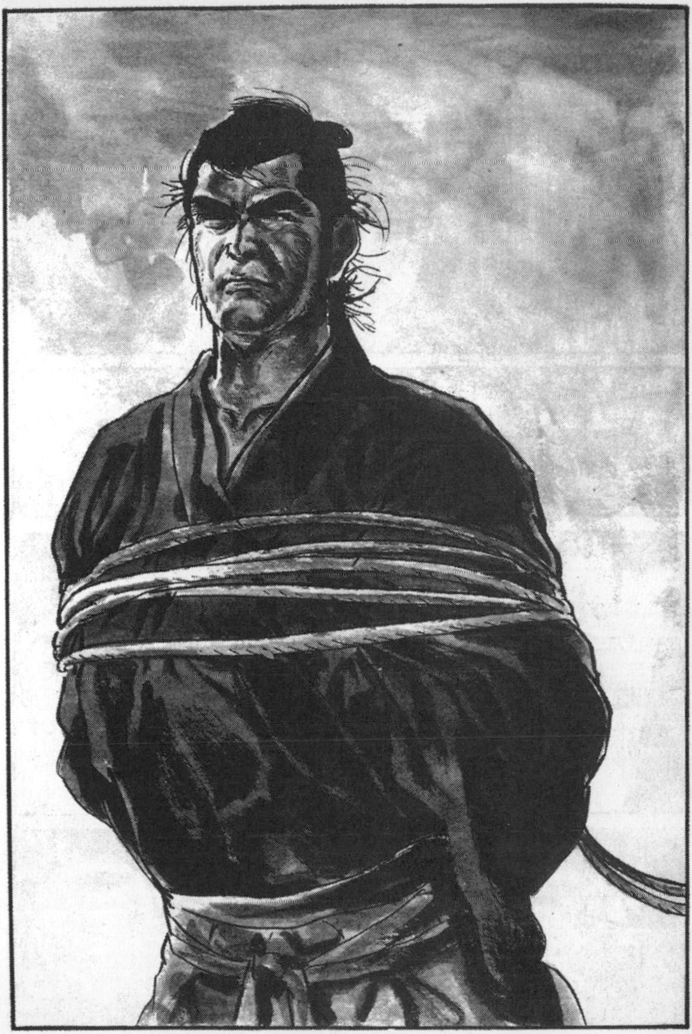

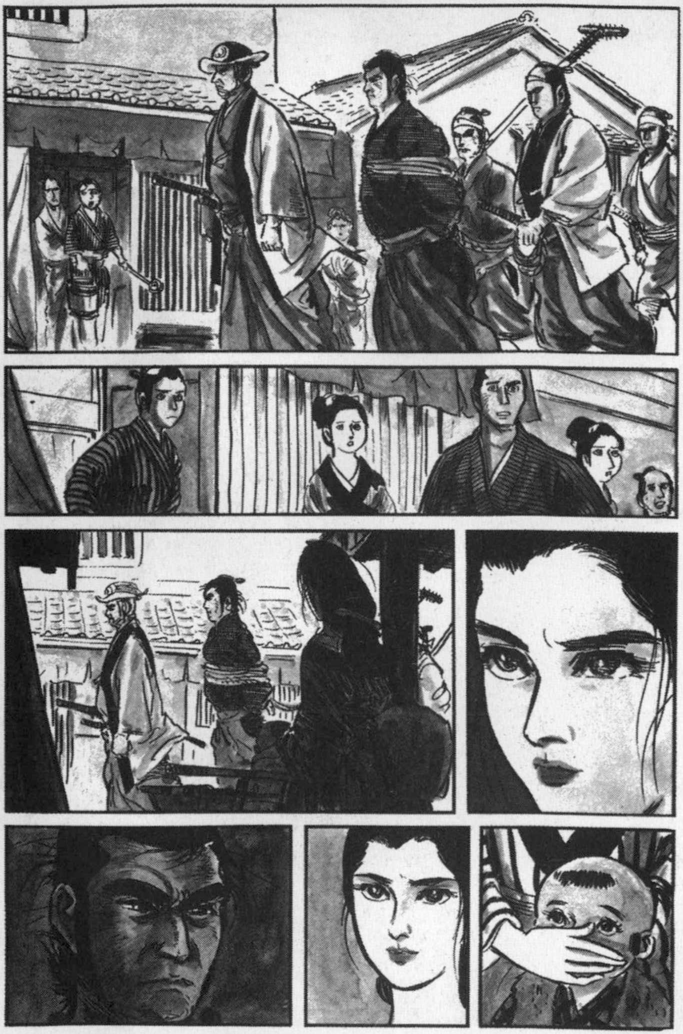

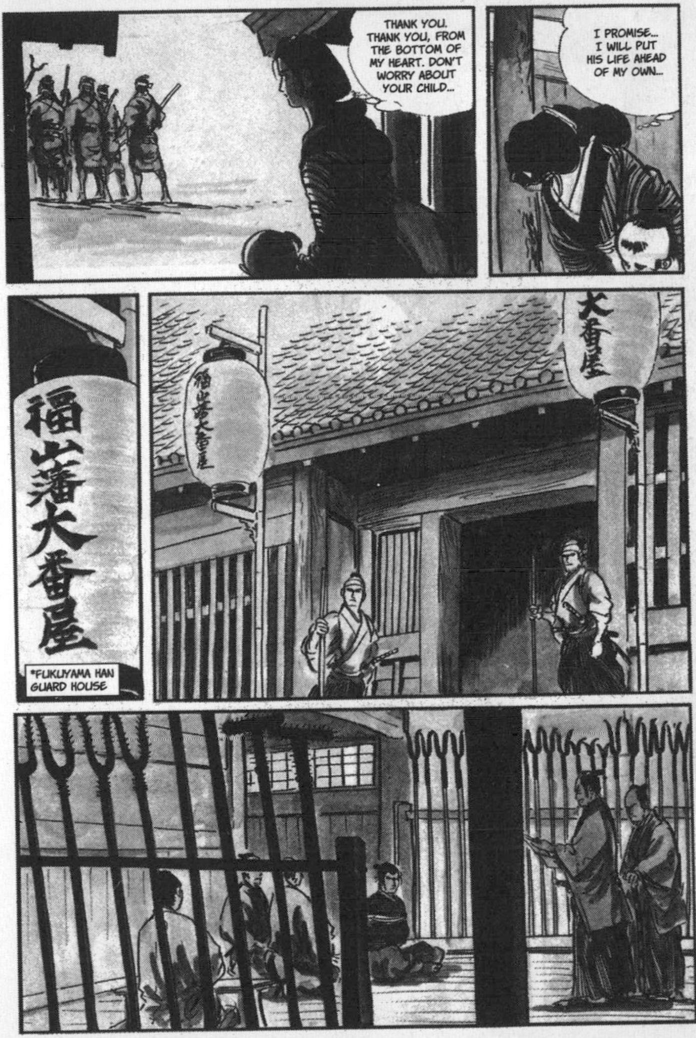
THANK YOU. THANK YOU, FROM THE BOTTOM OF MY HEART. DON'T WORRY ABOUT YOUR CHILD...
I PROMISE... I WILL PUT HIS LIFE AHEAD OF MY OWN...
福山藩大番屋
*FUKUYAMA HAN GUARD HOUSE
大番屋

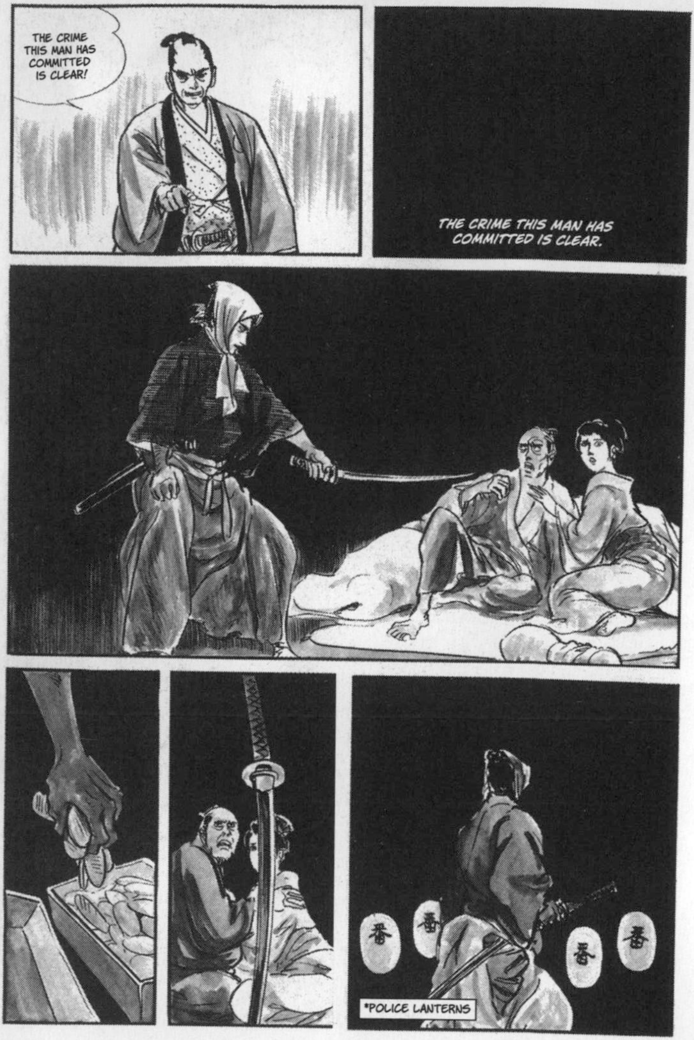
THE CRIME THIS MAN HAS COMMITTED IS CLEAR!
THE CRIME THIS MAN HAS COMMITTED IS CLEAR.
番
番
番
番
*POLICE LANTERNS

LAY DOWN YOUR WEAPON!

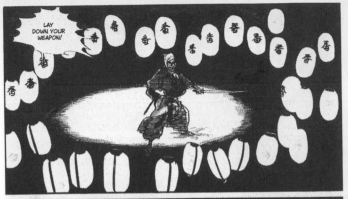

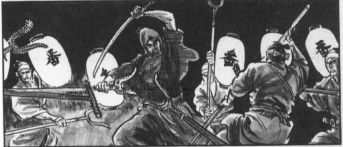

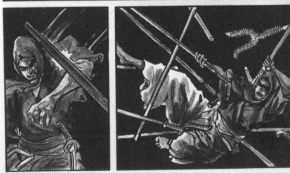

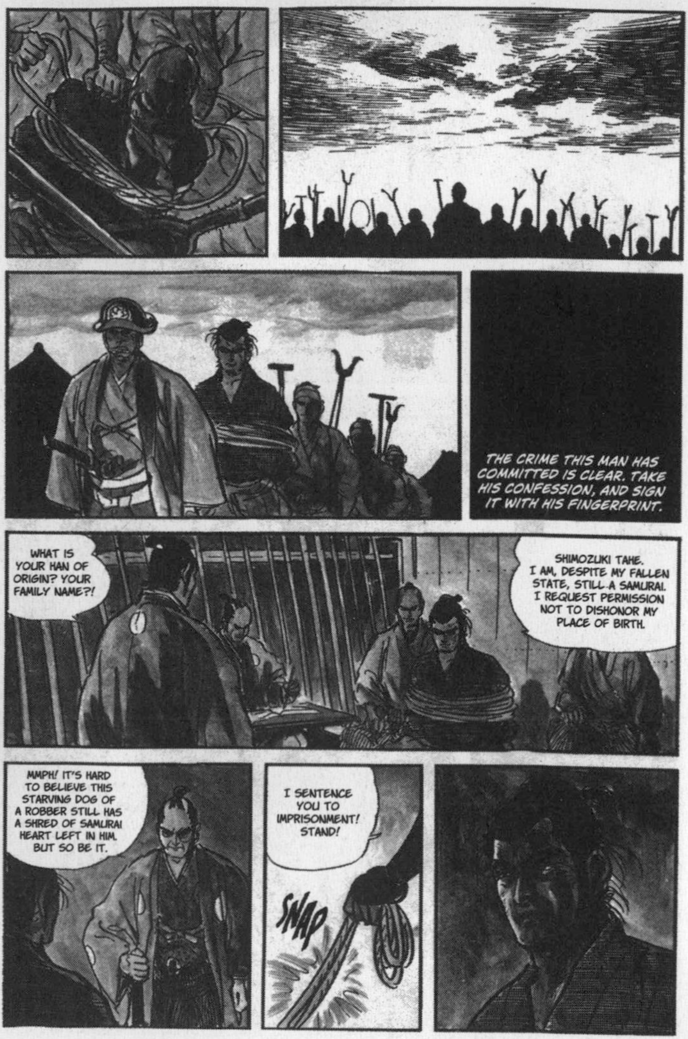
THE CRIME THIS MAN HAS COMMITTED IS CLEAR. TAKE HIS CONFESSION, AND SIGN IT WITH HIS FINGERPRINT.
WHAT IS YOUR HAN OF ORIGIN? YOUR FAMILY NAME?!
SHIMOZUKI TAHE. I AM, DESPITE MY FALLEN STATE, STILL A SAMURAI. I REQUEST PERMISSION NOT TO DISHONOR MY PLACE OF BIRTH.
MMPH! IT'S HARD TO BELIEVE THIS STARVING DOG OF A ROBBER STILL HAS A SHRED OF SAMURAI HEART LEFT IN HIM. BUT SO BE IT.
I SENTENCE YOU TO IMPRISONMENT! STAND!
SNAP

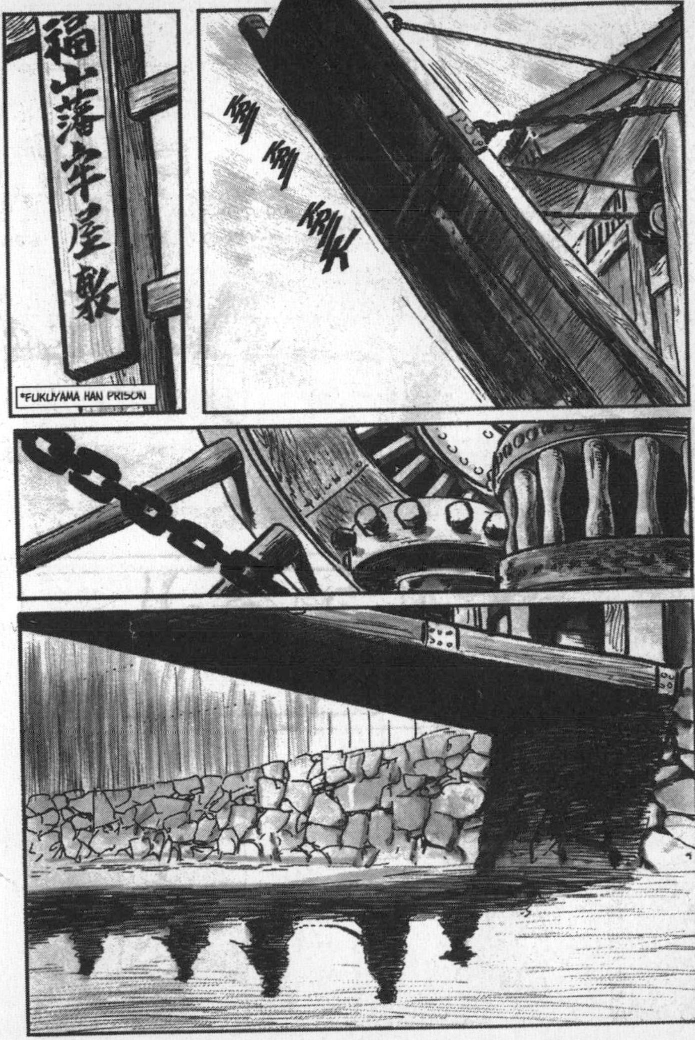
福山藩牢屋敷
*FUKUYAMA HAN PRISON

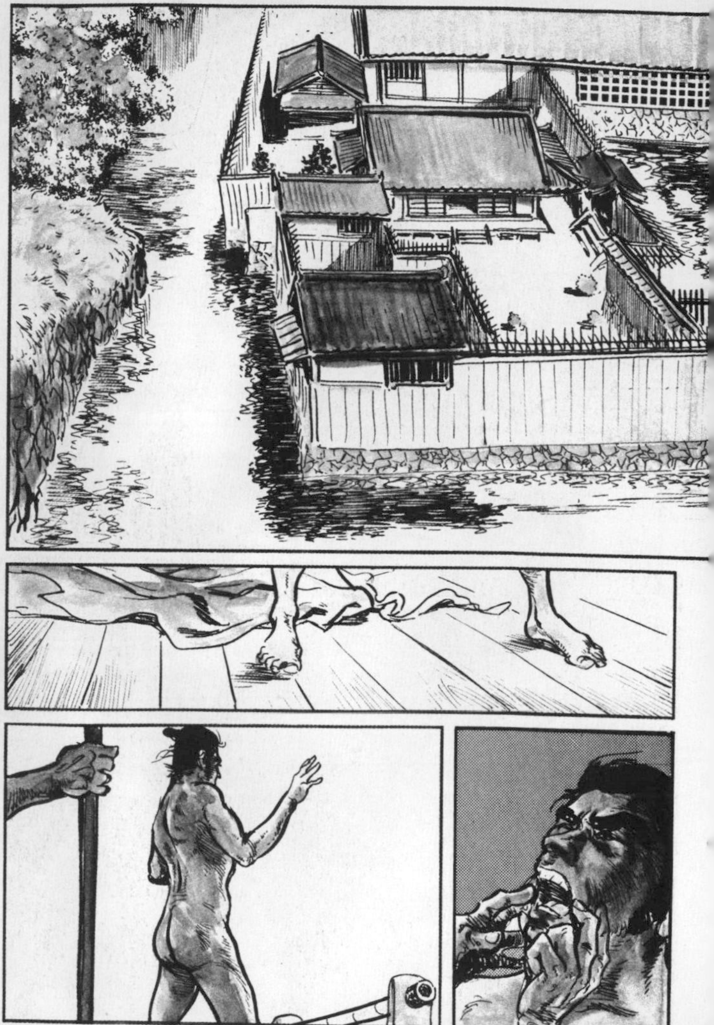

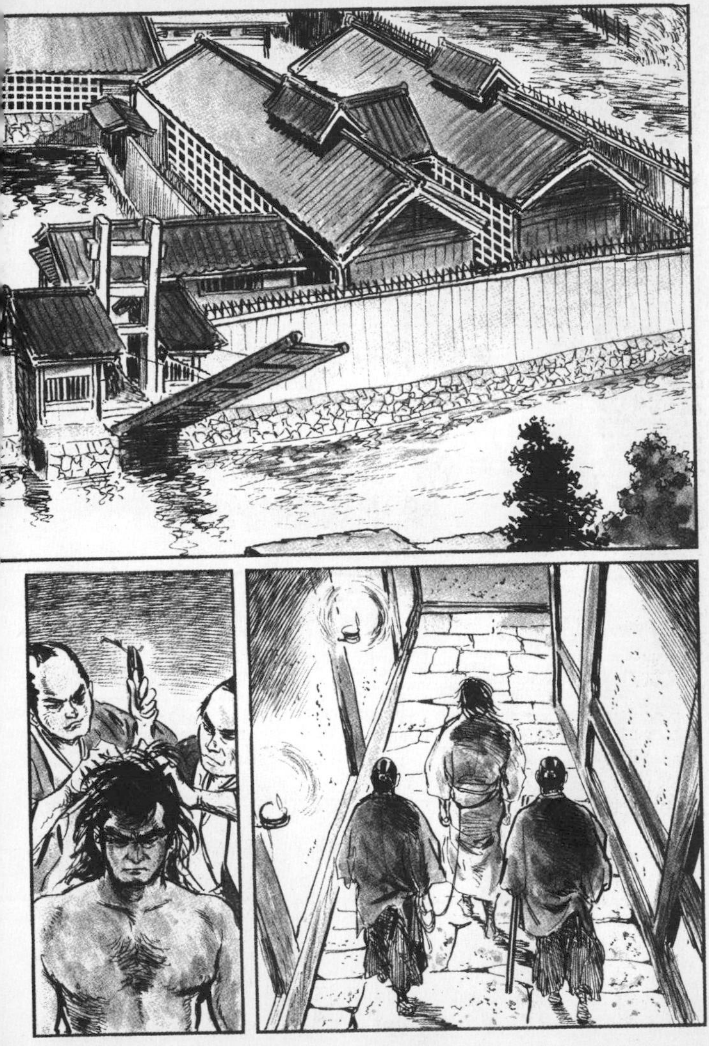

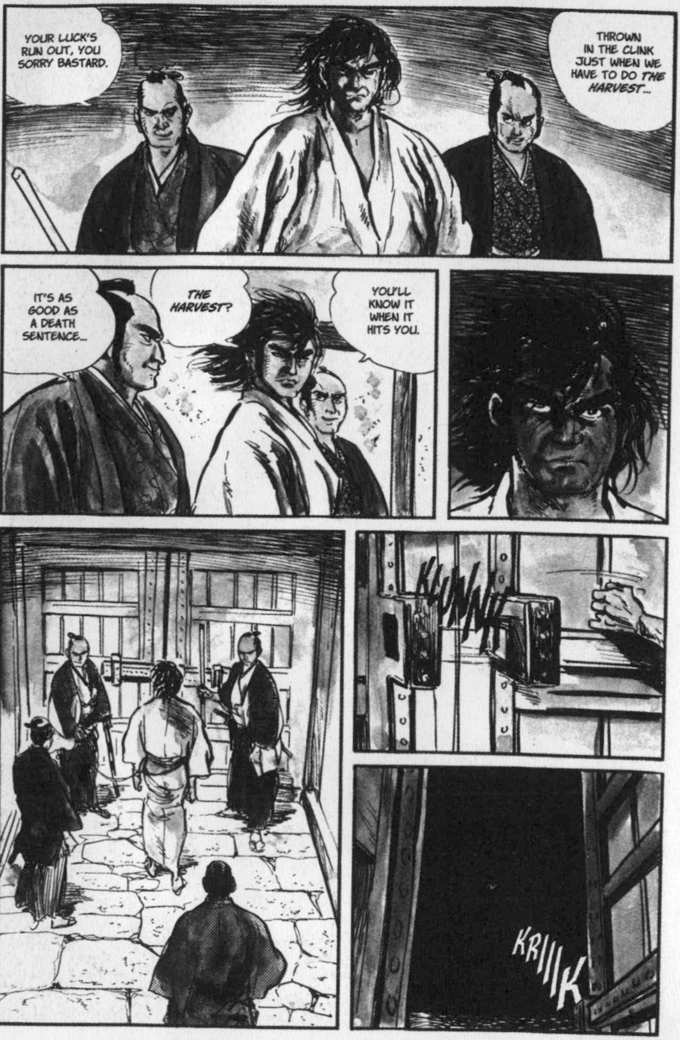
YOUR LUCK'S RUN OUT, YOU SORRY BASTARD.
THROWN IN THE CLINK JUST WHEN WE HAVE TO DO THE HARVEST...
IT'S AS GOOD AS A DEATH SENTENCE...
THE HARVEST?
YOU'LL KNOW IT WHEN IT HITS YOU.
KLUNNK
KRIIIK

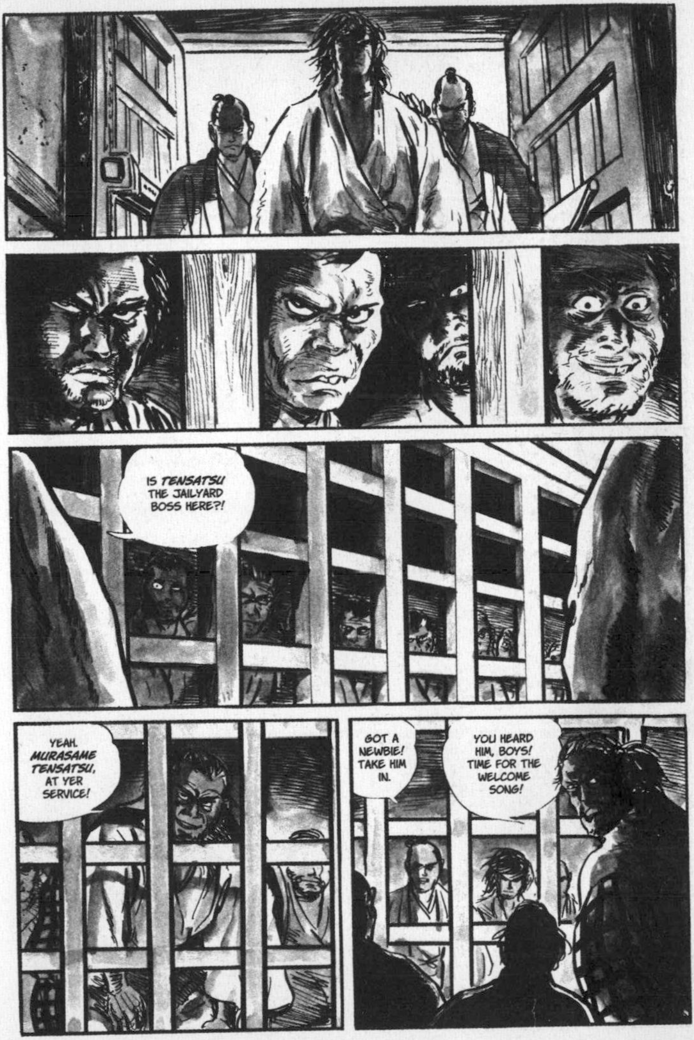
IS TENSATSU THE JAILYARD BOSS HERE?!
YEAH. MURASAME TENSATSU, AT YER SERVICE!
GOT A NEWBIE! TAKE HIM IN.
YOU HEARD HIM, BOYS! TIME FOR THE WELCOME SONG!

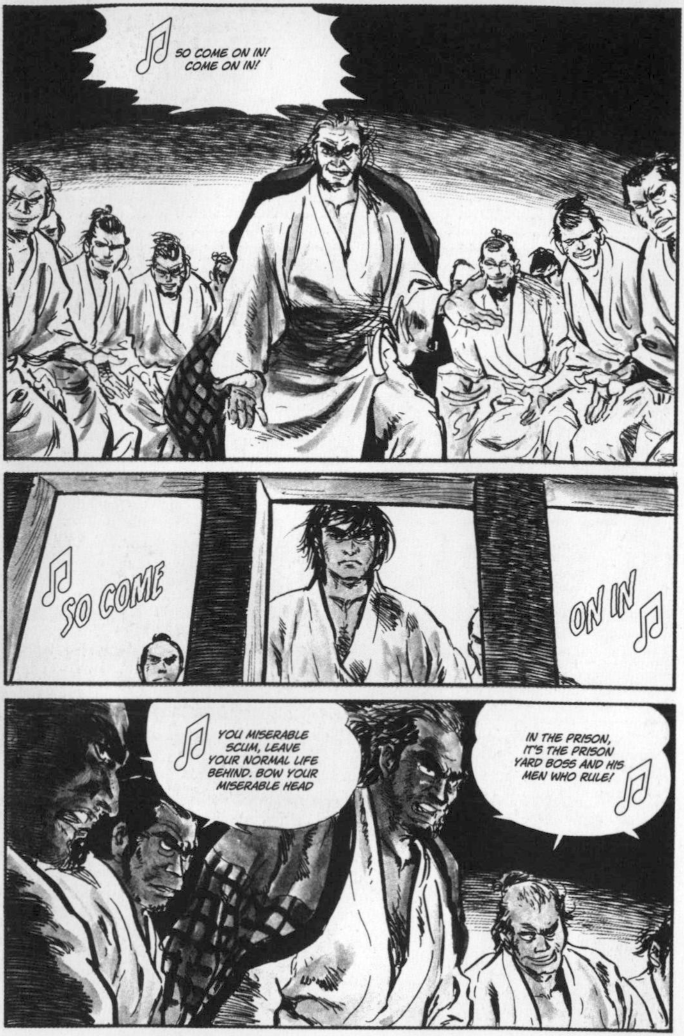
SO COME ON IN! COME ON IN!
SO COME
ON IN
YOU MISERABLE SCUM, LEAVE YOUR NORMAL LIFE BEHIND. BOW YOUR MISERABLE HEAD
IN THE PRISON, IT'S THE PRISON YARD BOSS AND HIS MEN WHO RULE!

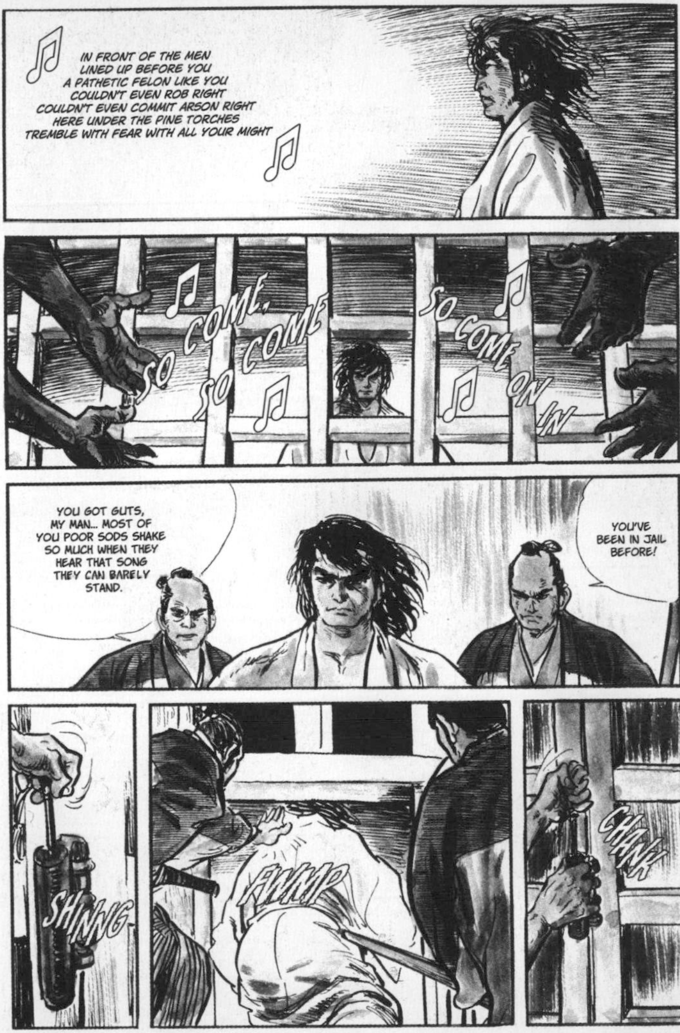
IN FRONT OF THE MEN
LINED UP BEFORE YOU
A PATHETIC FELON LIKE YOU
COULDN'T EVEN ROB RIGHT
COULDN'T EVEN COMMIT ARSON RIGHT
HERE UNDER THE PINE TORCHES
TREMBLE WITH FEAR WITH ALL YOUR MIGHT
SO COME, SO COME
SO COME ON IN
YOU GOT GUTS, MY MAN... MOST OF YOU POOR SODS SHAKE SO MUCH WHEN THEY HEAR THAT SONG THEY CAN BARELY STAND.
YOU'VE BEEN IN JAIL BEFORE!
SHING
FWMP
CHANK

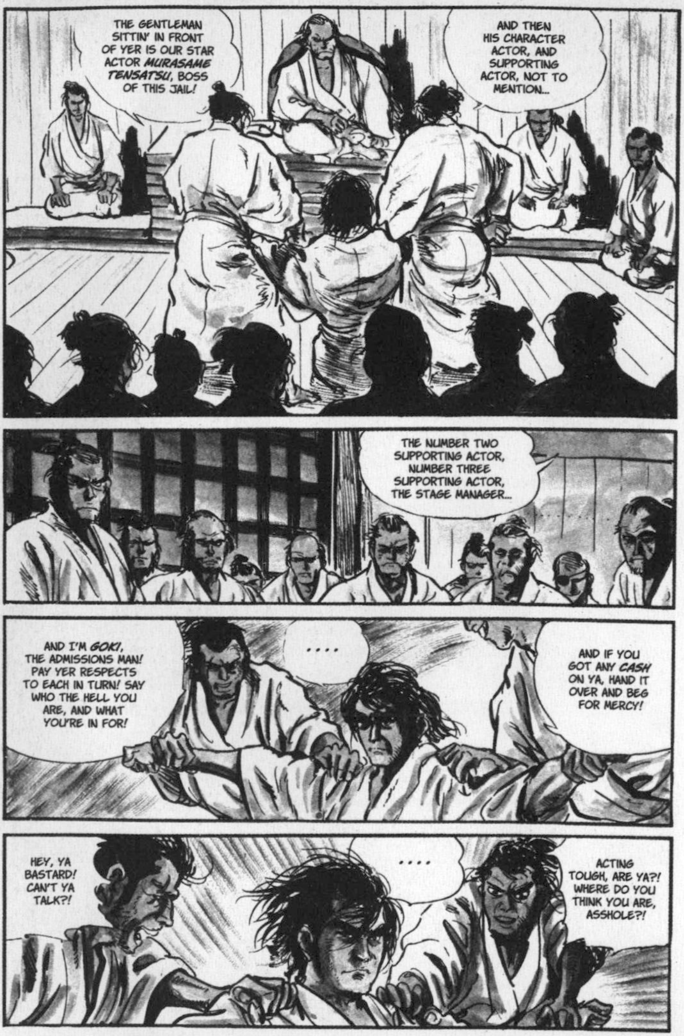
THE GENTLEMAN SITTIN' IN FRONT OF YER IS OUR STAR ACTOR MURASAME TENSATSU, BOSS OF THIS JAIL!
AND THEN HIS CHARACTER ACTOR, AND SUPPORTING ACTOR, NOT TO MENTION...
THE NUMBER TWO SUPPORTING ACTOR, NUMBER THREE SUPPORTING ACTOR, THE STAGE MANAGER...
AND I'M GOKI, THE ADMISSIONS MAN! PAY YER RESPECTS TO EACH IN TURN! SAY WHO THE HELL YOU ARE, AND WHAT YOU'RE IN FOR!
....
AND IF YOU GOT ANY CASH ON YA, HAND IT OVER AND BEG FOR MERCY!
HEY, YA BASTARD! CAN'T YA TALK?!
....
ACTING TOUGH, ARE YA?! WHERE DO YOU THINK YOU ARE, ASSHOLE?!

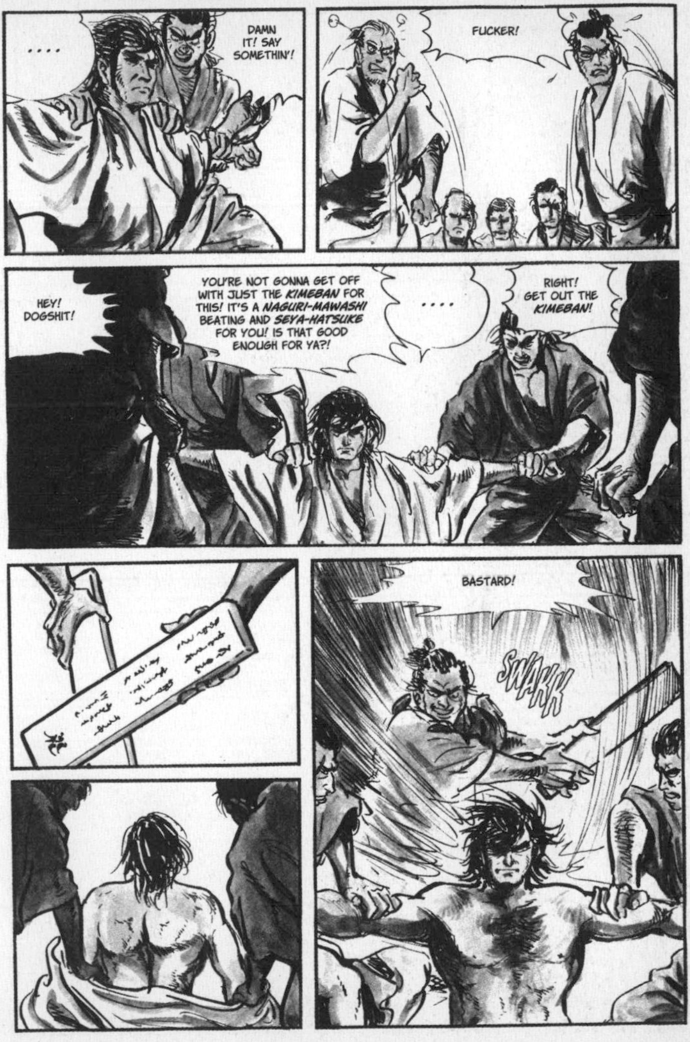
....
DAMN IT! SAY SOMETHIN'!
FUCKER!
HEY! DOGSHIT!
YOU'RE NOT GONNA GET OFF WITH JUST THE KIMEBAN FOR THIS! IT'S A NAGURI-MAWASHI BEATING AND SEYA-HATSUKE FOR YOU! IS THAT GOOD ENOUGH FOR YA?!
....
RIGHT! GET OUT THE KIMEBAN!
BASTARD!
SWAKK

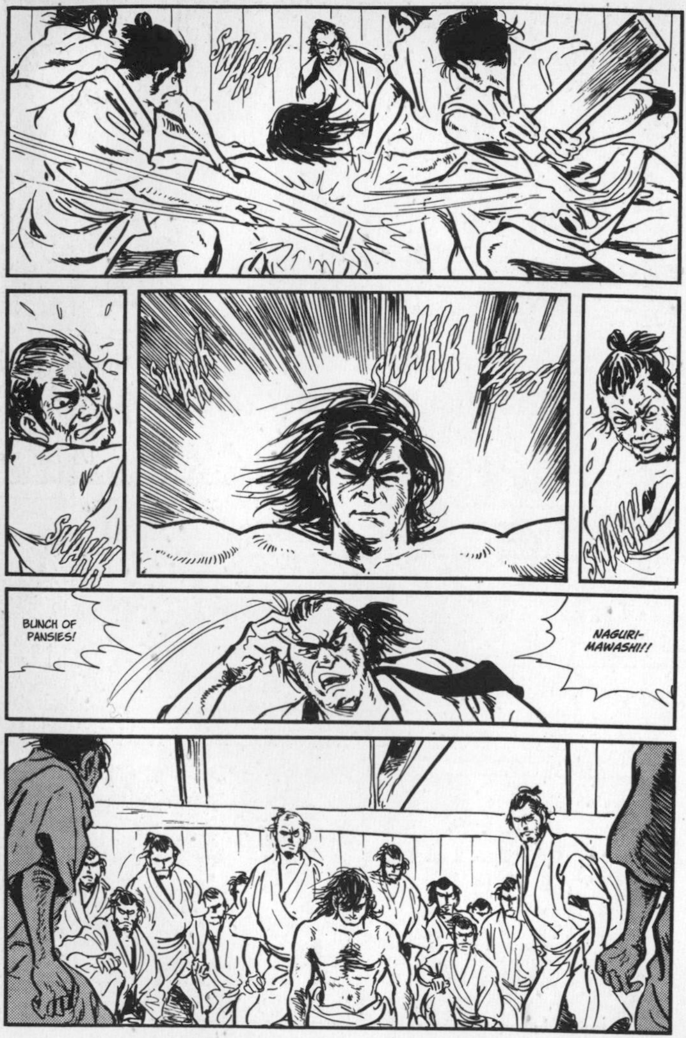
SWAKK
SWAKK
SWAKK
SWAKK
SWAKK
SWAKK
BUNCH OF PANSIES!
NAGURI-MAWASHI!!

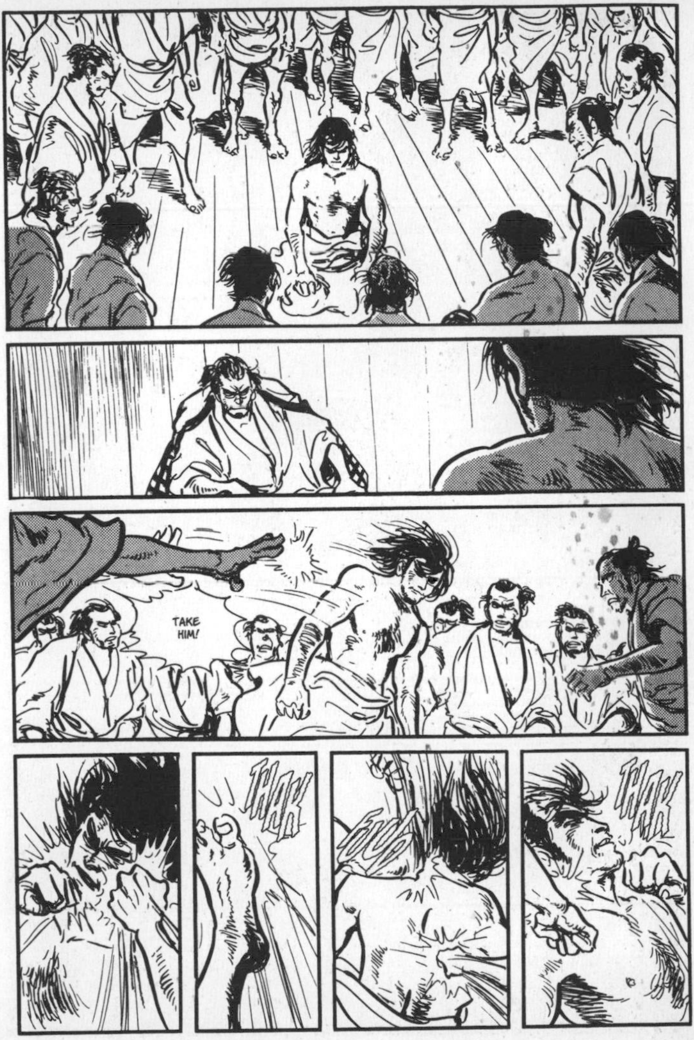

TAKE HIM!
THAK
THAK

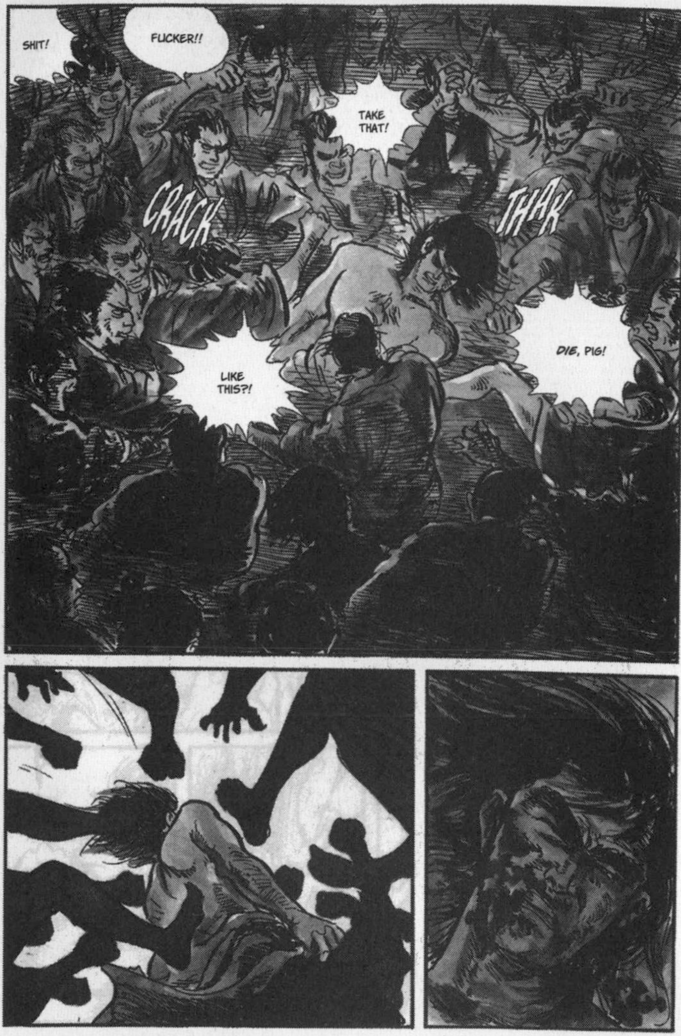
SHIT!
FUCKER!!
TAKE THAT!
CRACK
THAK
LIKE THIS?!
DIE, PIG!

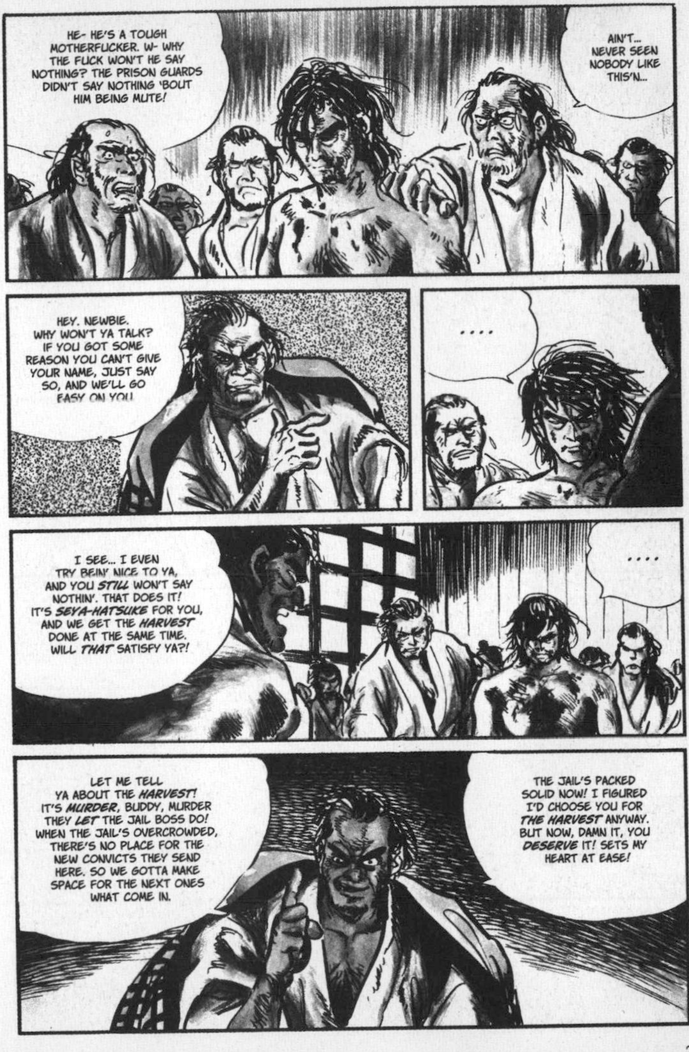
HE- HE'S A TOUGH MOTHERFUCKER. W- WHY THE FUCK WON'T HE SAY NOTHING? THE PRISON GUARDS DIDN'T SAY NOTHING 'BOUT HIM BEING MUTE!
AIN'T... NEVER SEEN NOBODY LIKE THIS'N...
HEY. NEWBIE. WHY WON'T YA TALK? IF YOU GOT SOME REASON YOU CAN'T GIVE YOUR NAME, JUST SAY SO, AND WE'LL GO EASY ON YOU.
....
I SEE... I EVEN TRY BEIN' NICE TO YA, AND YOU *STILL* WON'T SAY NOTHIN'. THAT DOES IT! IT'S *SEYA-HATSUKE* FOR YOU, AND WE GET THE *HARVEST* DONE AT THE SAME TIME. WILL *THAT* SATISFY YA?!
....
LET ME TELL YA ABOUT THE *HARVEST*! IT'S *MURDER*, BUDDY, MURDER THEY *LET* THE JAIL BOSS DO! WHEN THE JAIL'S OVERCROWDED, THERE'S NO PLACE FOR THE NEW CONVICTS THEY SEND HERE. SO WE GOTTA MAKE SPACE FOR THE NEXT ONES WHAT COME IN.
THE JAIL'S PACKED SOLID NOW! I FIGURED I'D CHOOSE YOU FOR *THE HARVEST* ANYWAY. BUT NOW, DAMN IT, YOU *DESERVE* IT! SETS MY HEART AT EASE!

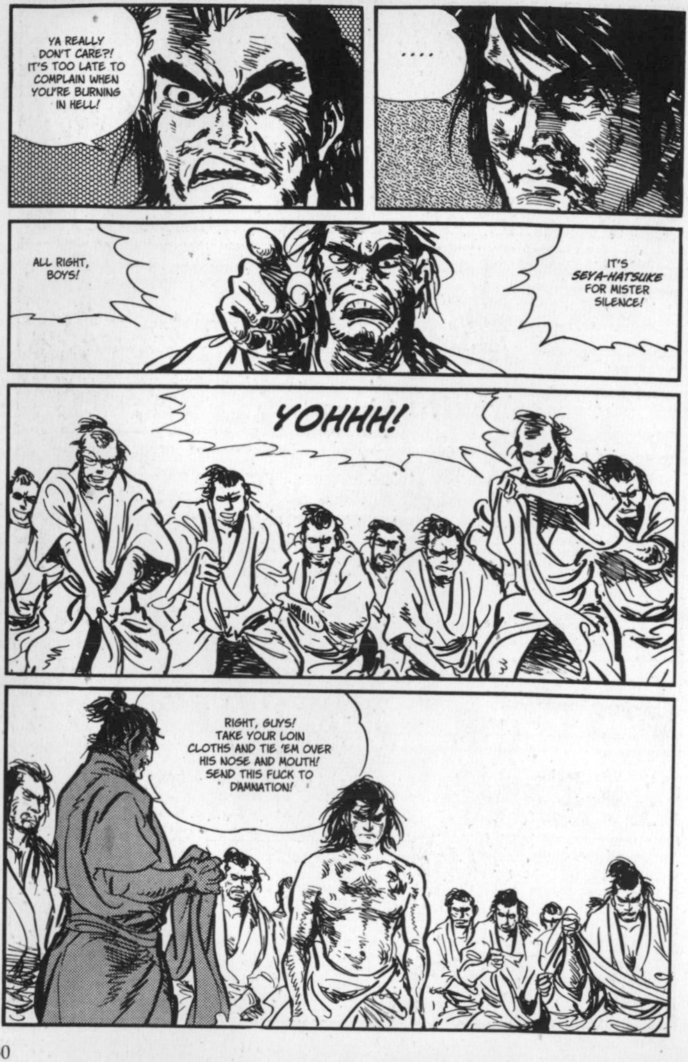
YA REALLY DON'T CARE?! IT'S TOO LATE TO COMPLAIN WHEN YOU'RE BURNING IN HELL!
....
ALL RIGHT, BOYS!
IT'S SEYA-HATSUKE FOR MISTER SILENCE!
YOHHH!
RIGHT, GUYS! TAKE YOUR LOIN CLOTHS AND TIE 'EM OVER HIS NOSE AND MOUTH! SEND THIS FUCK TO DAMNATION!

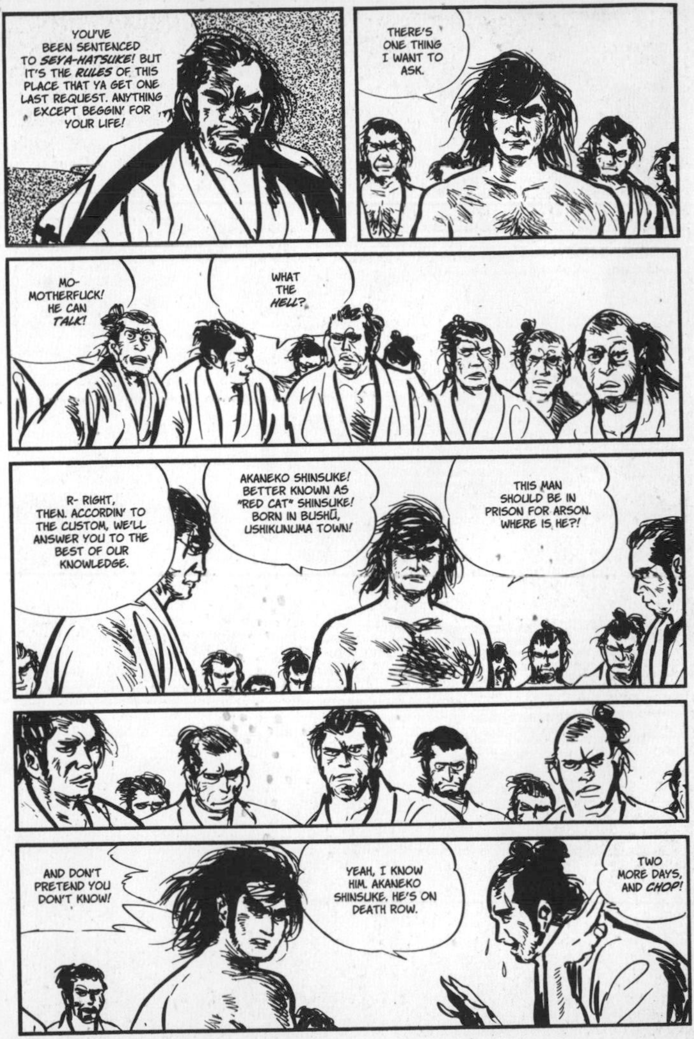
YOU'VE BEEN SENTENCED TO SEYA-HATSUKE! BUT IT'S THE RULES OF THIS PLACE THAT YA GET ONE LAST REQUEST. ANYTHING EXCEPT BEGGIN' FOR YOUR LIFE!
THERE'S ONE THING I WANT TO ASK.
MO- MOTHERFUCK! HE CAN TALK!
WHAT THE HELL?
R- RIGHT, THEN. ACCORDIN' TO THE CUSTOM, WE'LL ANSWER YOU TO THE BEST OF OUR KNOWLEDGE.
AKANEKO SHINSUKE! BETTER KNOWN AS "RED CAT" SHINSUKE! BORN IN BUSHŪ, USHIKUNUMA TOWN!
THIS MAN SHOULD BE IN PRISON FOR ARSON. WHERE IS HE?!
AND DON'T PRETEND YOU DON'T KNOW!
YEAH, I KNOW HIM. AKANEKO SHINSUKE. HE'S ON DEATH ROW.
TWO MORE DAYS, AND CHOP!

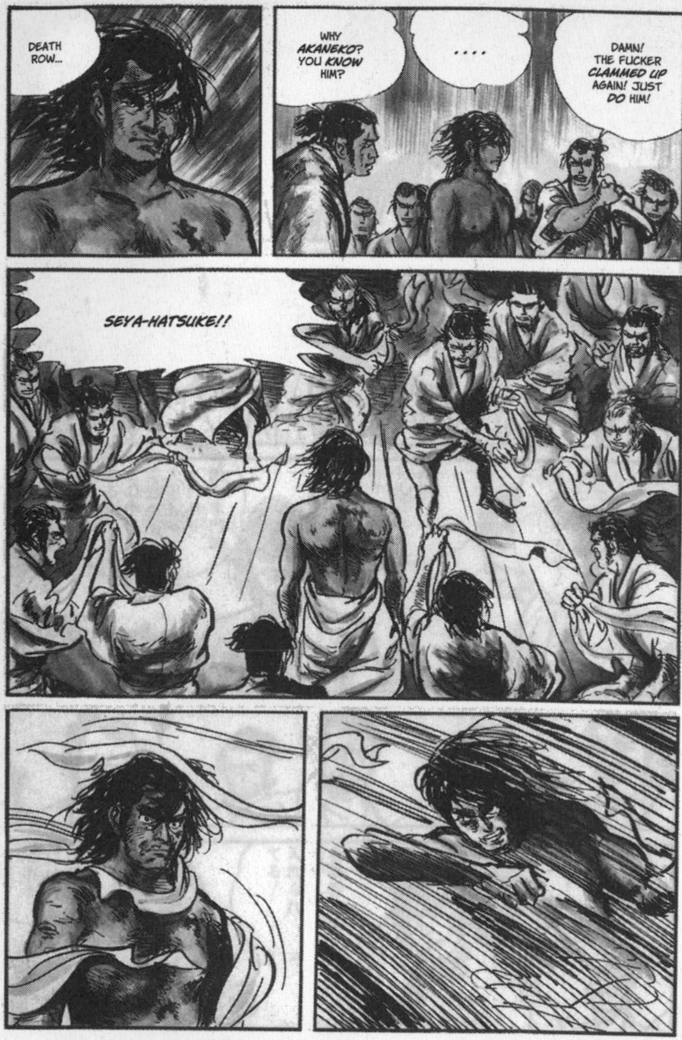
DEATH ROW...
WHY AKANEKO? YOU KNOW HIM?
....
DAMN! THE FUCKER CLAMMED UP AGAIN! JUST DO HIM!
SEYA-HATSUKE!!

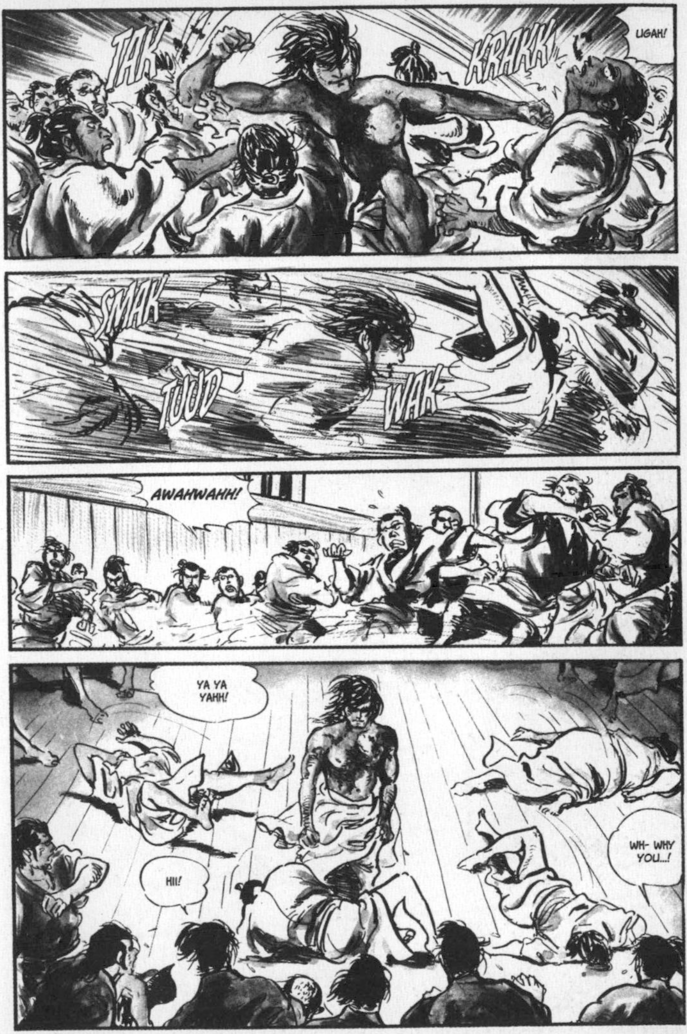
TAK
KRAKK
UGAH!
SMAK
TUUD
WAK
AWAHWAHH!
YA YA YAHH!
HII!
WH- WHY YOU...!

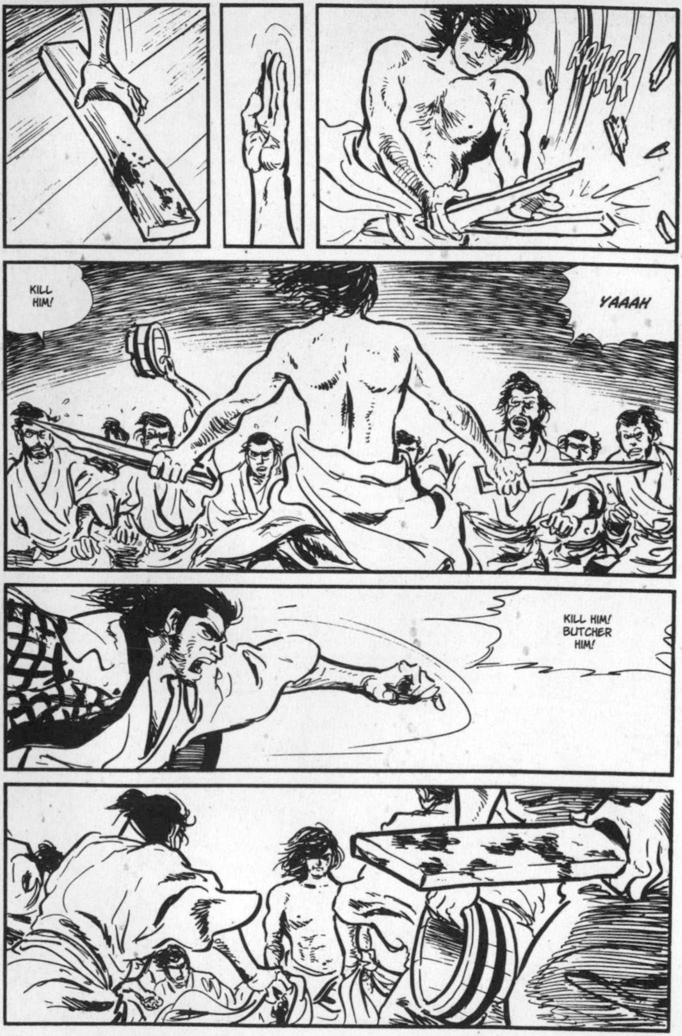
KRAKK
KILL HIM!
YAAAH
KILL HIM! BUTCHER HIM!

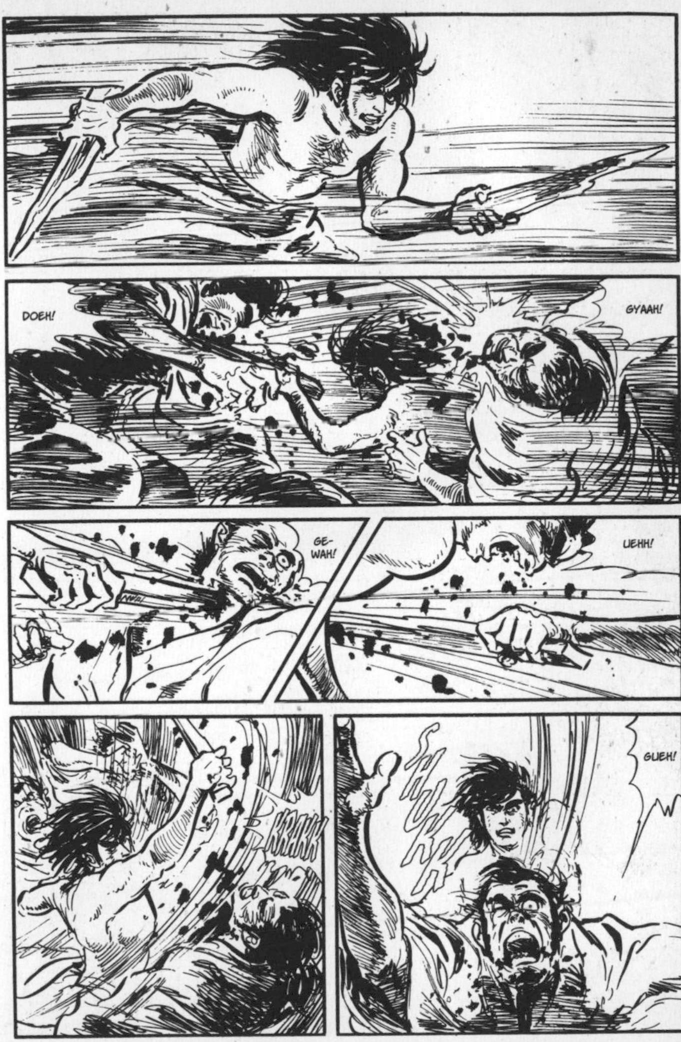
DOEH!
GYAAH!
GE-WAH!
UEHH!
KRAKK
GUEH!

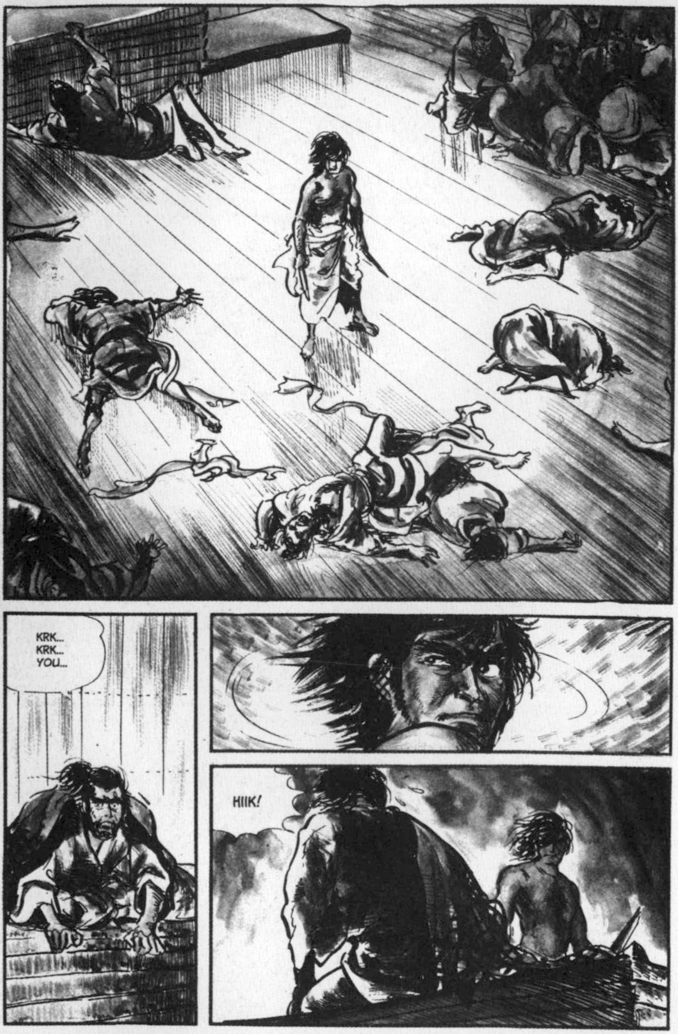
KRK...
KRK...
YOU...
HIIK!

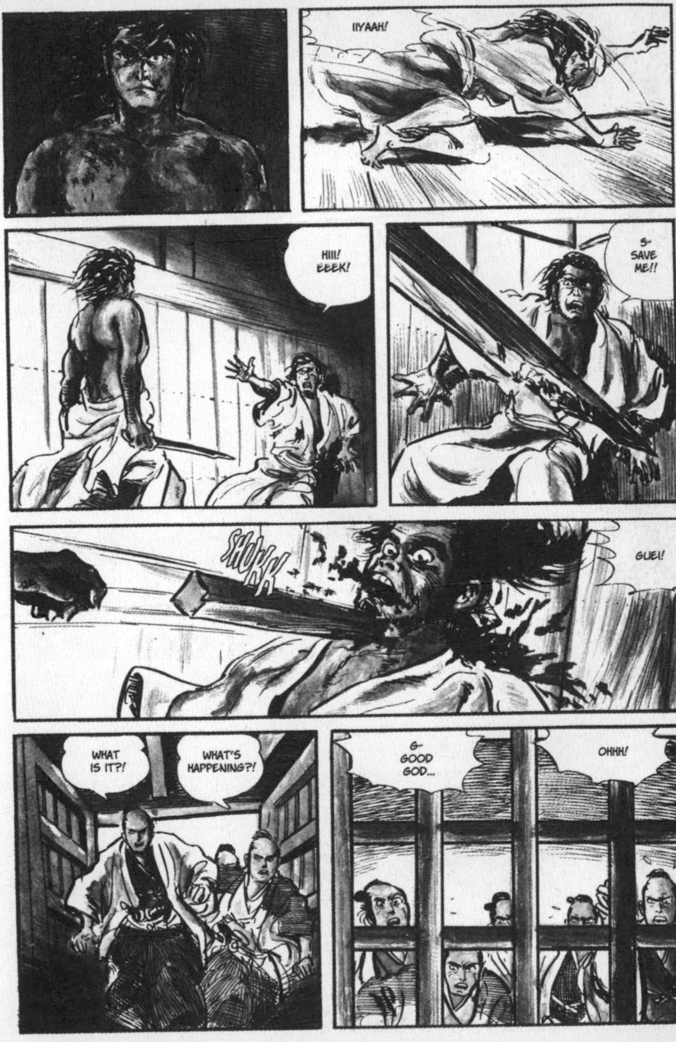
IIYAAH!
HIII! EEEK!
S-SAVE ME!!
SHUKK
GUEI!
WHAT IS IT?!
WHAT'S HAPPENING?!
G-GOOD GOD...
OHHH!

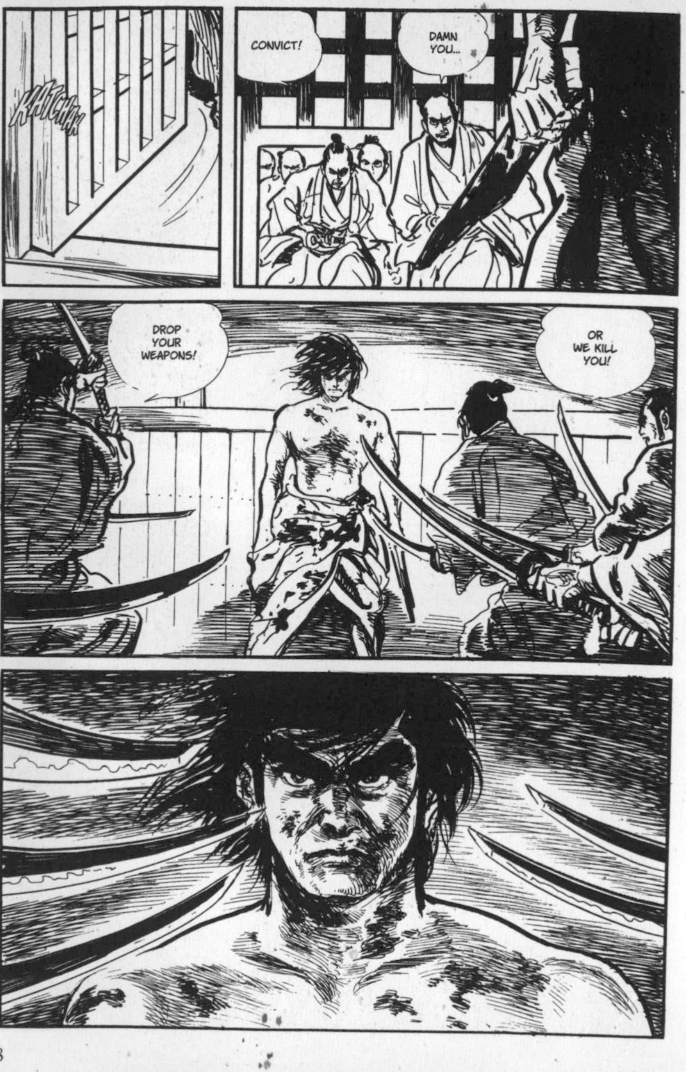
KATCHAK
CONVICT!
DAMN YOU...
DROP YOUR WEAPONS!
OR WE KILL YOU!

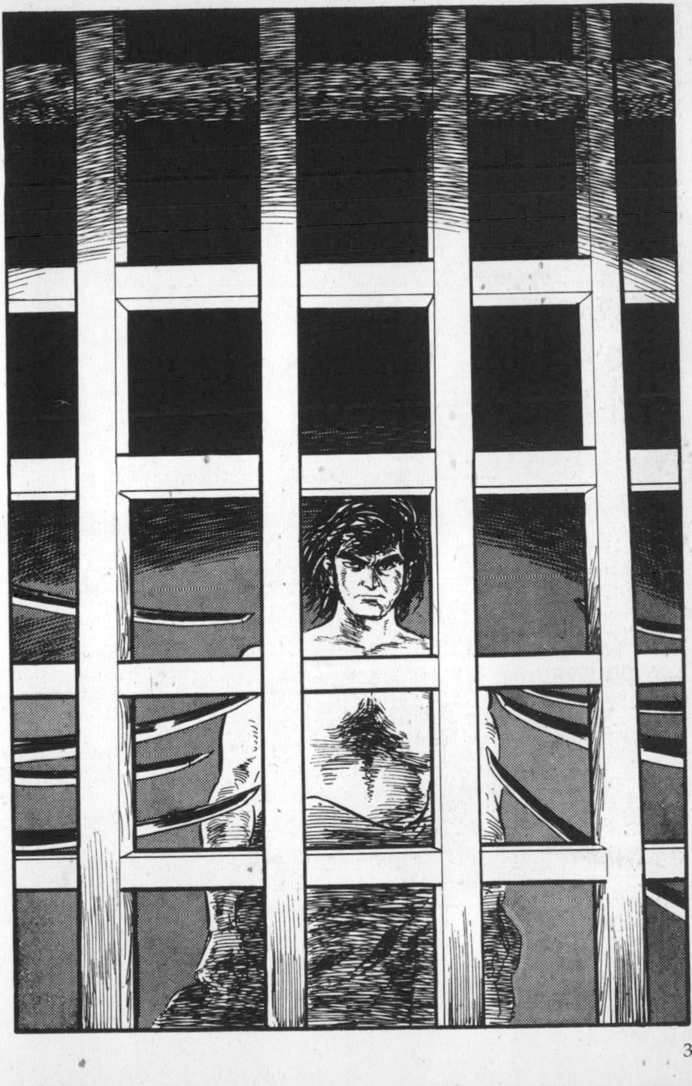

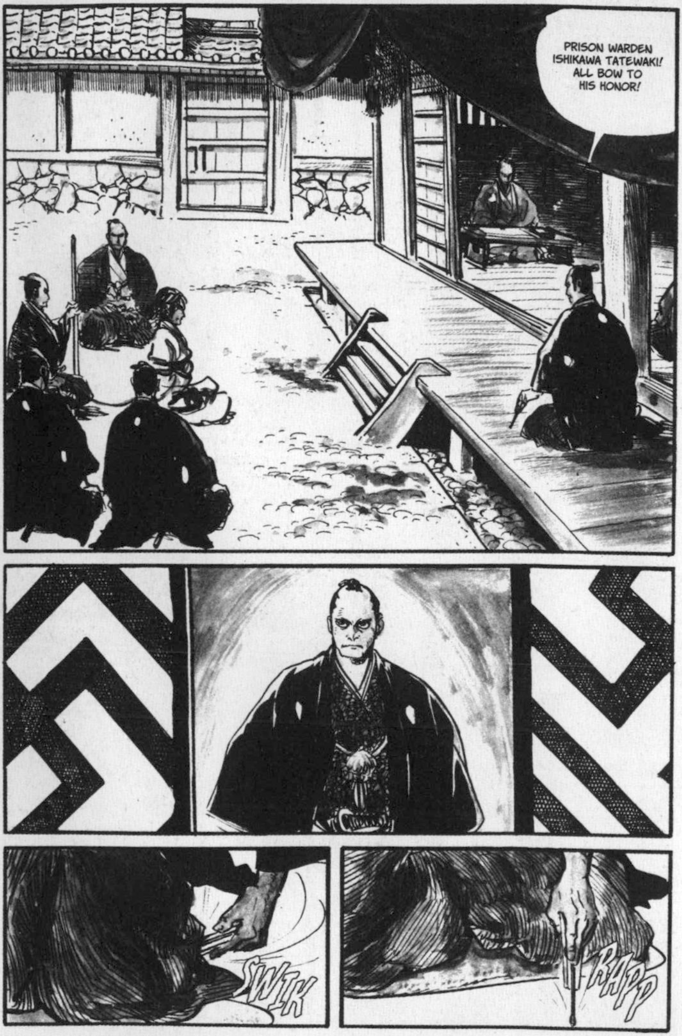
PRISON WARDEN ISHIKAWA TATEWAKI! ALL BOW TO HIS HONOR!
SWIK
FRAPP

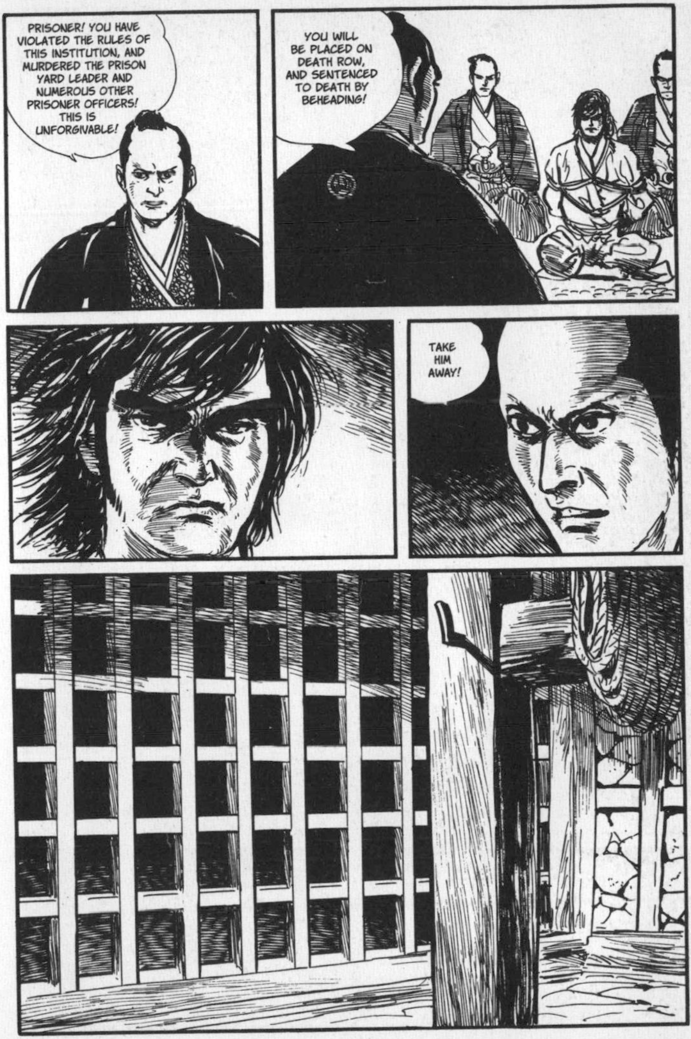
PRISONER! YOU HAVE VIOLATED THE RULES OF THIS INSTITUTION, AND MURDERED THE PRISON YARD LEADER AND NUMEROUS OTHER PRISONER OFFICERS! THIS IS UNFORGIVABLE!
YOU WILL BE PLACED ON DEATH ROW, AND SENTENCED TO DEATH BY BEHEADING!
TAKE HIM AWAY!

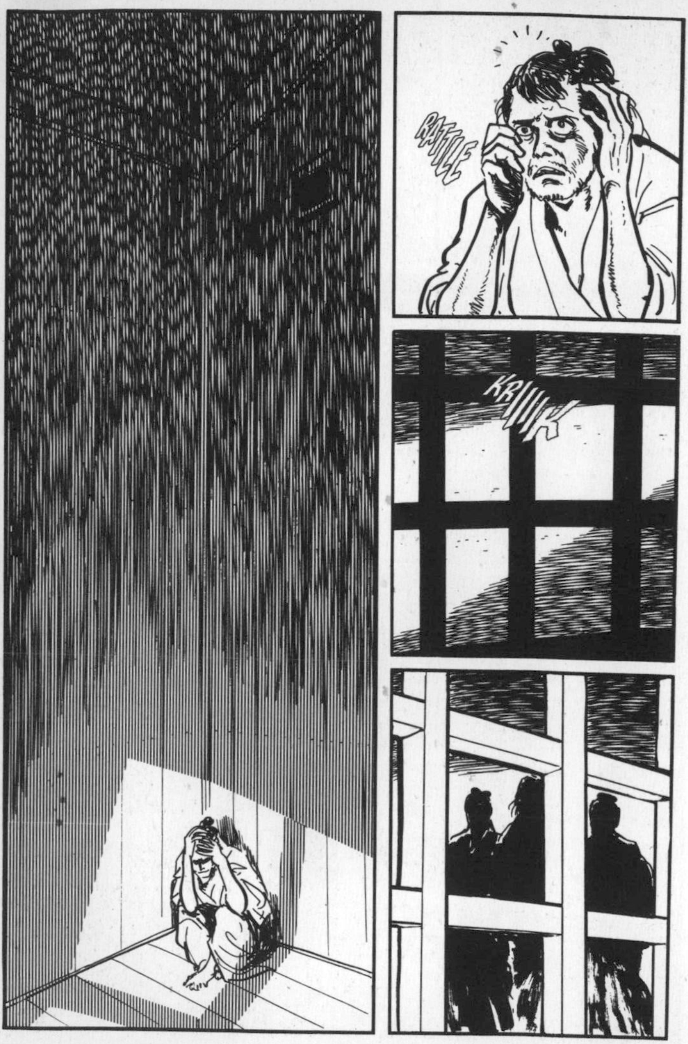
RATTLE
KRIIIK

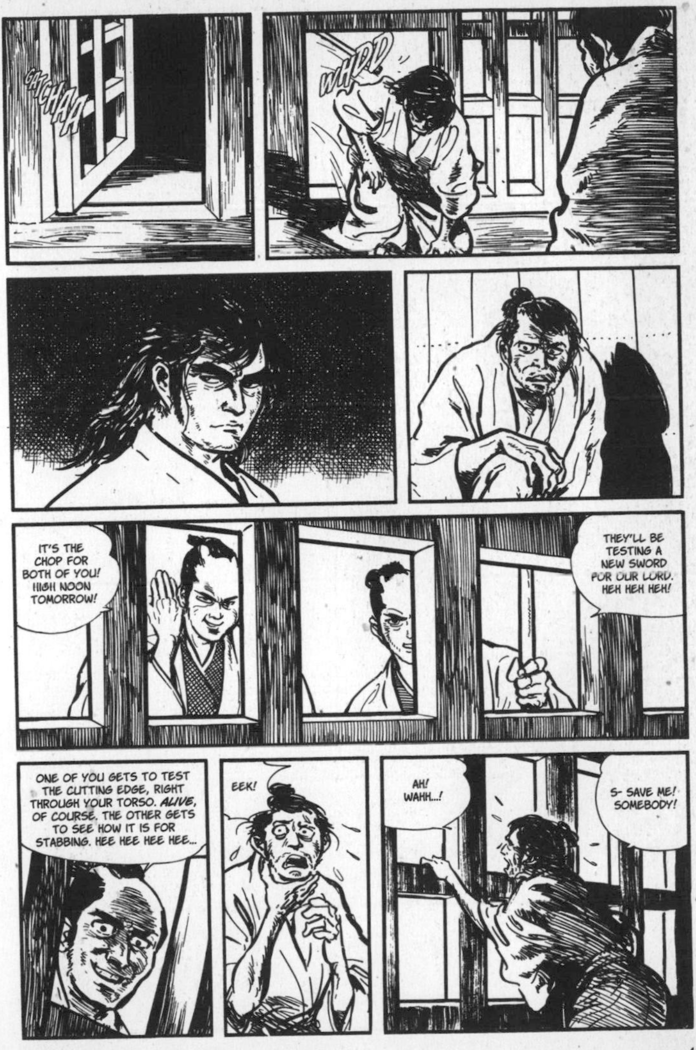
GACHAA
WHPD
IT'S THE CHOP FOR BOTH OF YOU! HIGH NOON TOMORROW!
THEY'LL BE TESTING A NEW SWORD FOR OUR LORD. HEH HEH HEH!
ONE OF YOU GETS TO TEST THE CUTTING EDGE, RIGHT THROUGH YOUR TORSO. *ALIVE*, OF COURSE. THE OTHER GETS TO SEE HOW IT IS FOR STABBING. HEE HEE HEE HEE...
EEK!
AH! WAHH...!
S- SAVE ME! SOMEBODY!

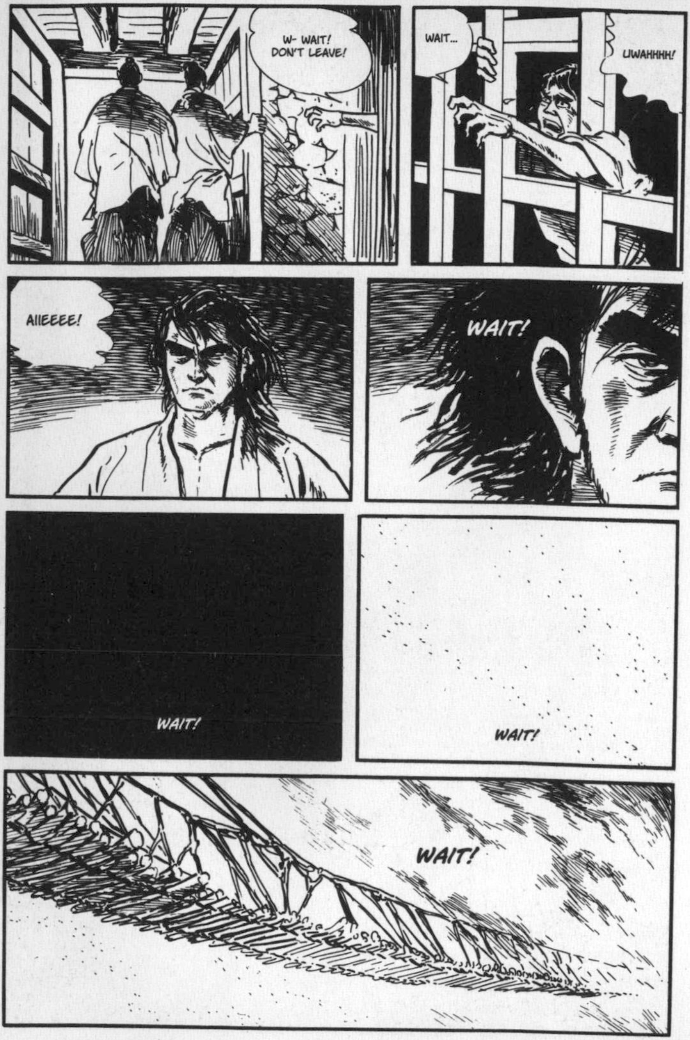
W- WAIT! DON'T LEAVE!
WAIT...
UWAHHHH!
AIIEEEE!
WAIT!
WAIT!
WAIT!
WAIT!

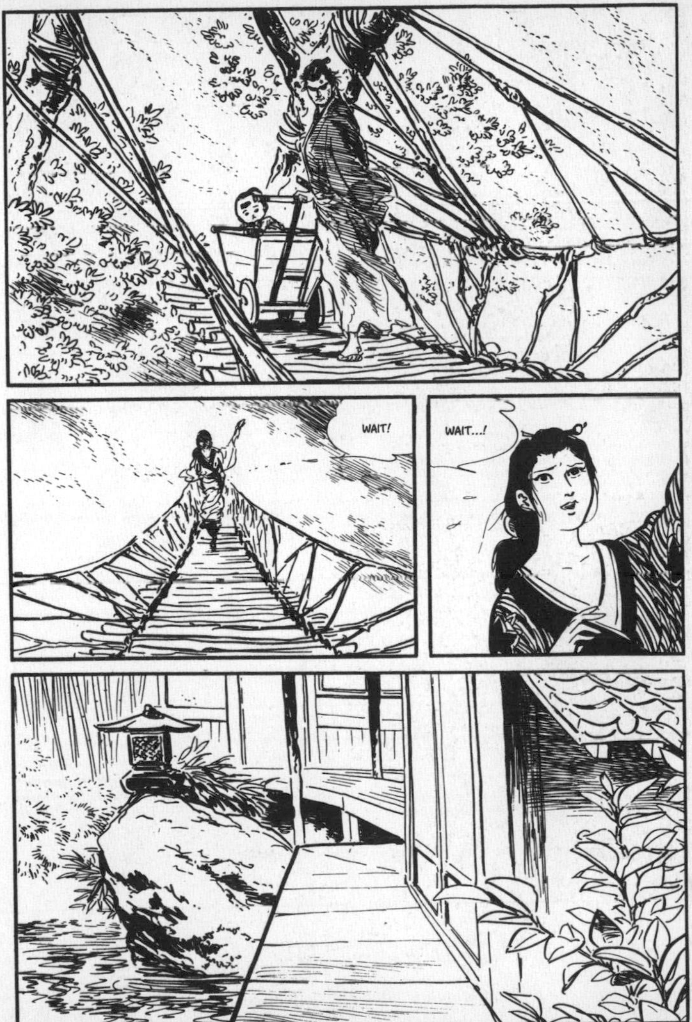
WAIT!
WAIT...!

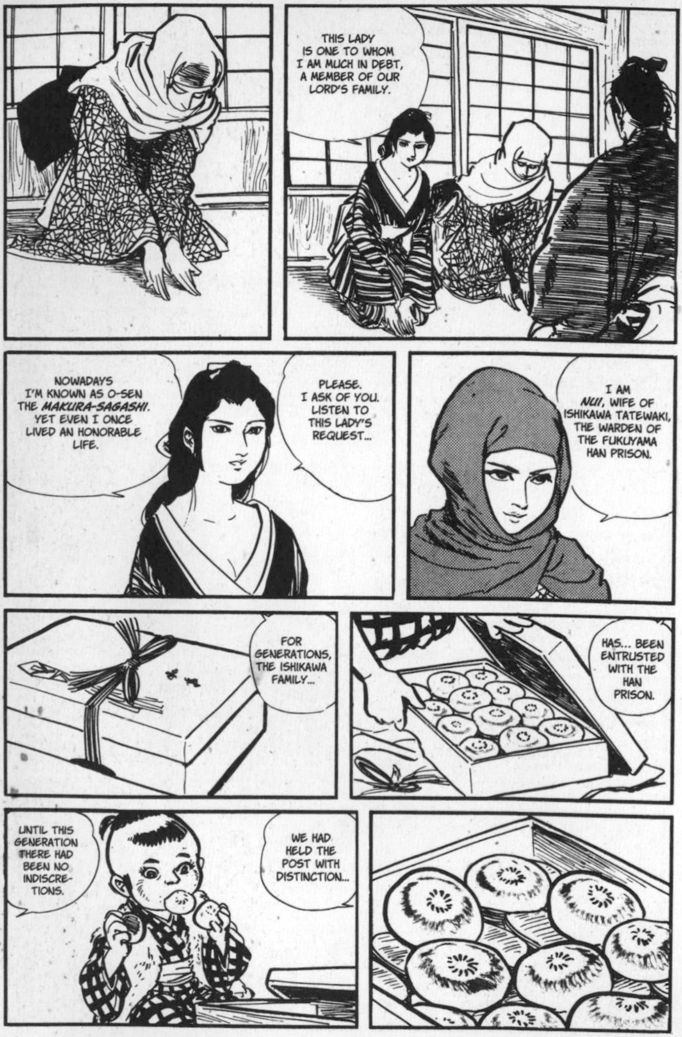
THIS LADY IS ONE TO WHOM I AM MUCH IN DEBT, A MEMBER OF OUR LORD'S FAMILY.
NOWADAYS I'M KNOWN AS O-SEN THE *MAKURA-SAGASHI*. YET EVEN I ONCE LIVED AN HONORABLE LIFE.
PLEASE. I ASK OF YOU. LISTEN TO THIS LADY'S REQUEST...
I AM *NUI*, WIFE OF ISHIKAWA TATEWAKI, THE WARDEN OF THE FUKUYAMA HAN PRISON.
FOR GENERATIONS, THE ISHIKAWA FAMILY...
HAS... BEEN ENTRUSTED WITH THE HAN PRISON.
UNTIL THIS GENERATION THERE HAD BEEN NO INDISCRE-TIONS.
WE HAD HELD THE POST WITH DISTINCTION...

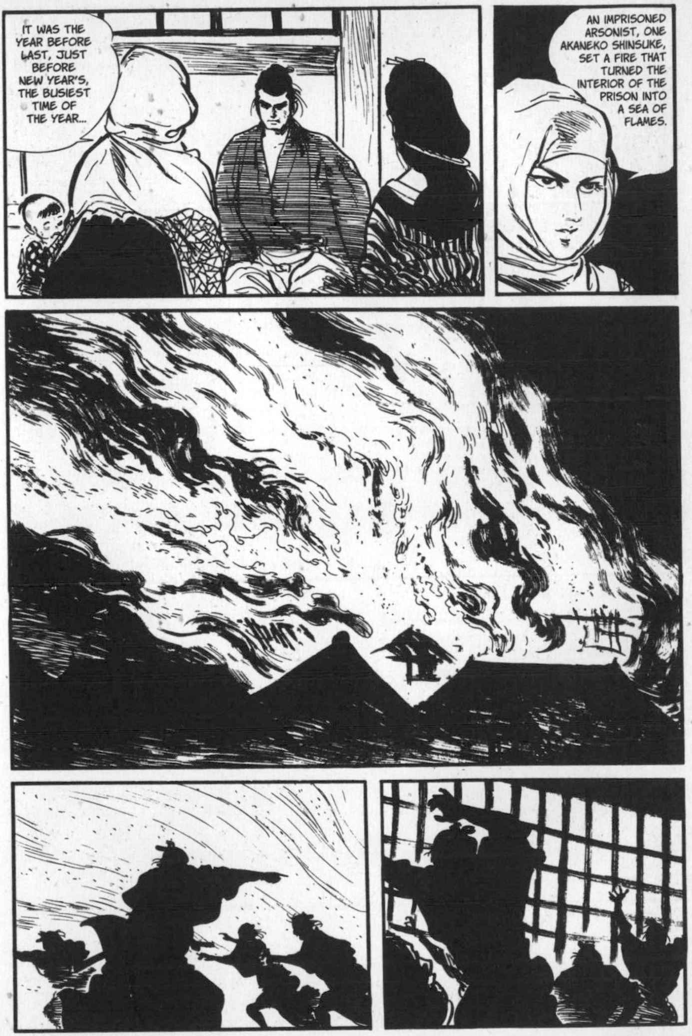
IT WAS THE YEAR BEFORE LAST, JUST BEFORE NEW YEAR'S, THE BUSIEST TIME OF THE YEAR...
AN IMPRISONED ARSONIST, ONE AKANEKO SHINSUKE, SET A FIRE THAT TURNED THE INTERIOR OF THE PRISON INTO A SEA OF FLAMES.

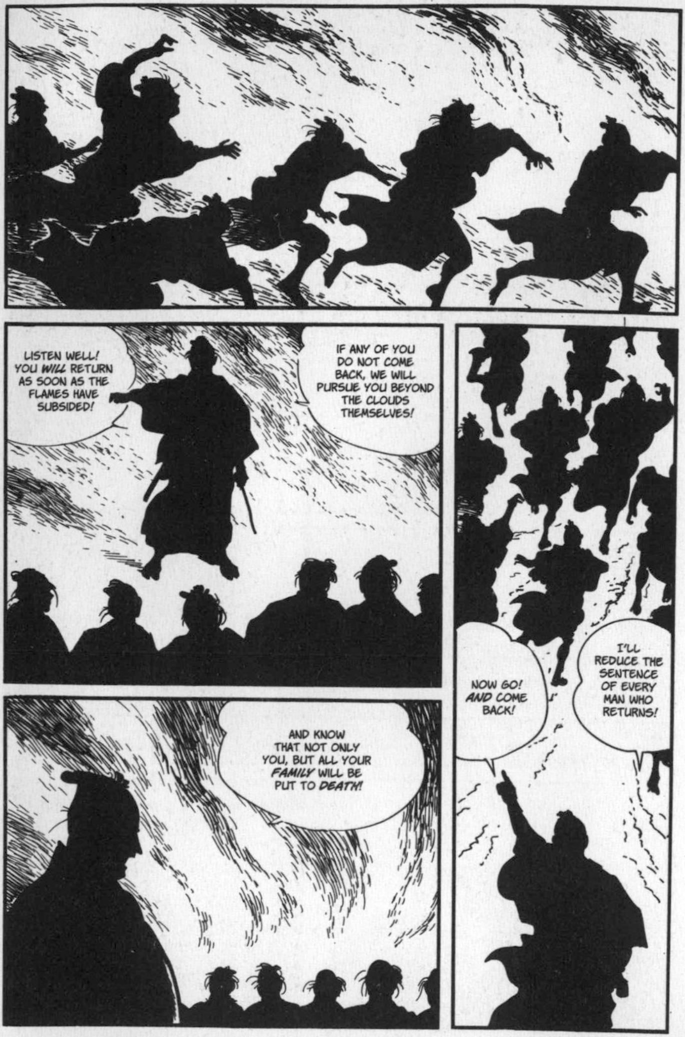
LISTEN WELL! YOU WILL RETURN AS SOON AS THE FLAMES HAVE SUBSIDED!
IF ANY OF YOU DO NOT COME BACK, WE WILL PURSUE YOU BEYOND THE CLOUDS THEMSELVES!
AND KNOW THAT NOT ONLY YOU, BUT ALL YOUR FAMILY WILL BE PUT TO DEATH!
NOW GO! AND COME BACK!
I'LL REDUCE THE SENTENCE OF EVERY MAN WHO RETURNS!

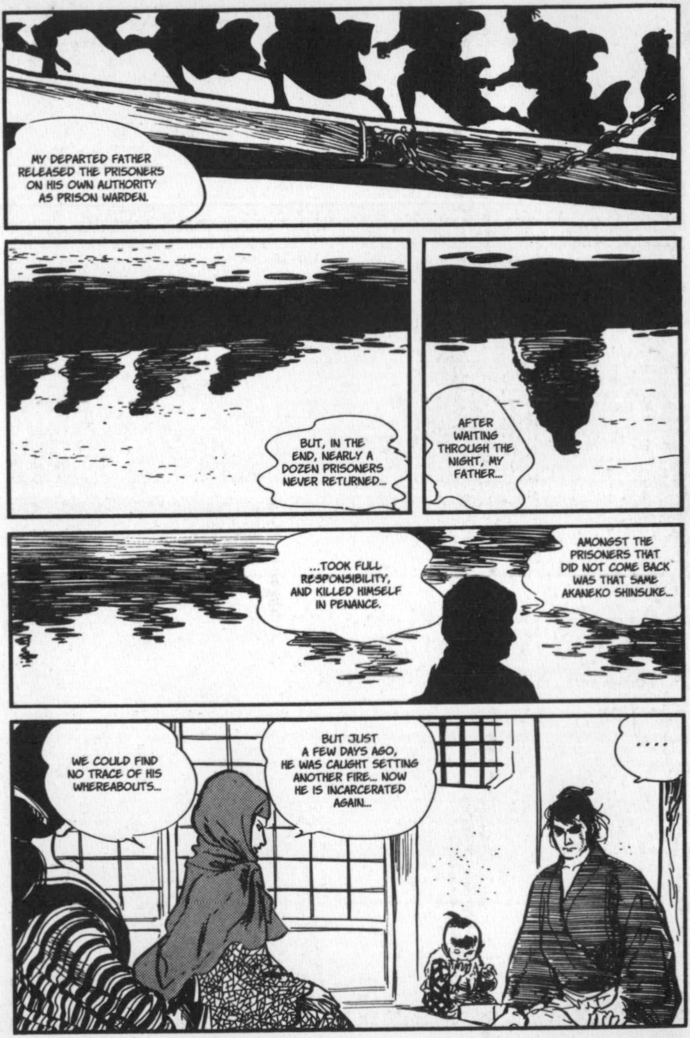
MY DEPARTED FATHER RELEASED THE PRISONERS ON HIS OWN AUTHORITY AS PRISON WARDEN.
BUT, IN THE END, NEARLY A DOZEN PRISONERS NEVER RETURNED...
AFTER WAITING THROUGH THE NIGHT, MY FATHER...
...TOOK FULL RESPONSIBILITY, AND KILLED HIMSELF IN PENANCE.
AMONGST THE PRISONERS THAT DID NOT COME BACK WAS THAT SAME AKANEKO SHINSUKE...
WE COULD FIND NO TRACE OF HIS WHEREABOUTS...
BUT JUST A FEW DAYS AGO, HE WAS CAUGHT SETTING ANOTHER FIRE... NOW HE IS INCARCERATED AGAIN...
....

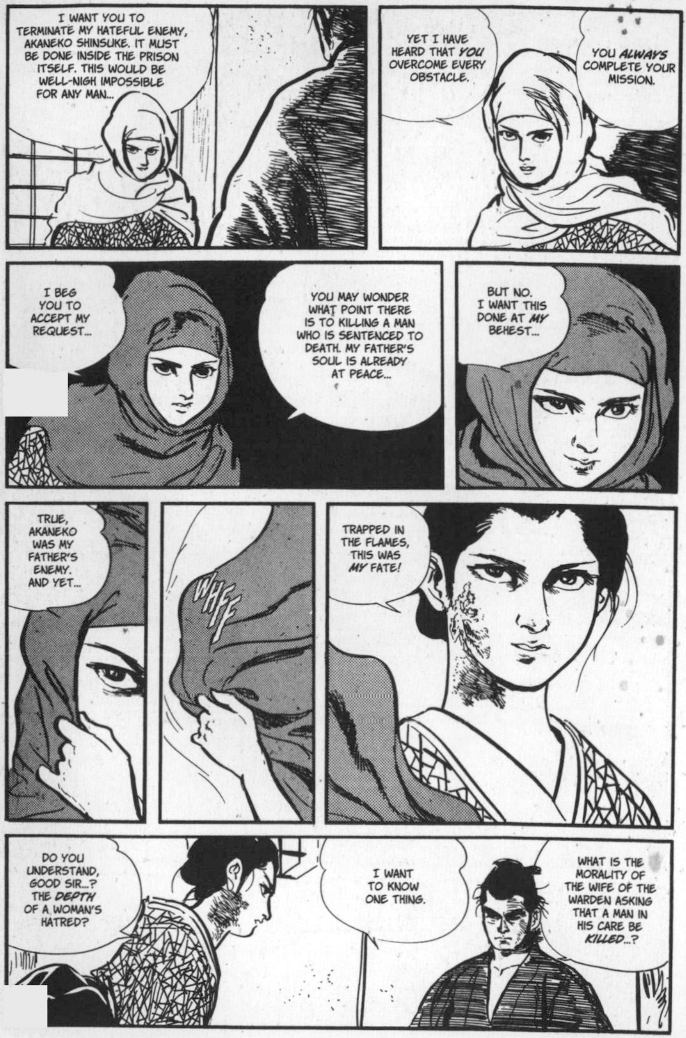
I WANT YOU TO TERMINATE MY HATEFUL ENEMY, AKANEKO SHINSUKE. IT MUST BE DONE INSIDE THE PRISON ITSELF. THIS WOULD BE WELL-NIGH IMPOSSIBLE FOR ANY MAN...
YET I HAVE HEARD THAT YOU OVERCOME EVERY OBSTACLE.
YOU ALWAYS COMPLETE YOUR MISSION.
I BEG YOU TO ACCEPT MY REQUEST...
YOU MAY WONDER WHAT POINT THERE IS TO KILLING A MAN WHO IS SENTENCED TO DEATH. MY FATHER'S SOUL IS ALREADY AT PEACE...
BUT NO. I WANT THIS DONE AT MY BEHEST...
TRUE, AKANEKO WAS MY FATHER'S ENEMY. AND YET...
WHFF
TRAPPED IN THE FLAMES, THIS WAS MY FATE!
DO YOU UNDERSTAND, GOOD SIR...? THE DEPTH OF A WOMAN'S HATRED?
I WANT TO KNOW ONE THING.
WHAT IS THE MORALITY OF THE WIFE OF THE WARDEN ASKING THAT A MAN IN HIS CARE BE KILLED...?

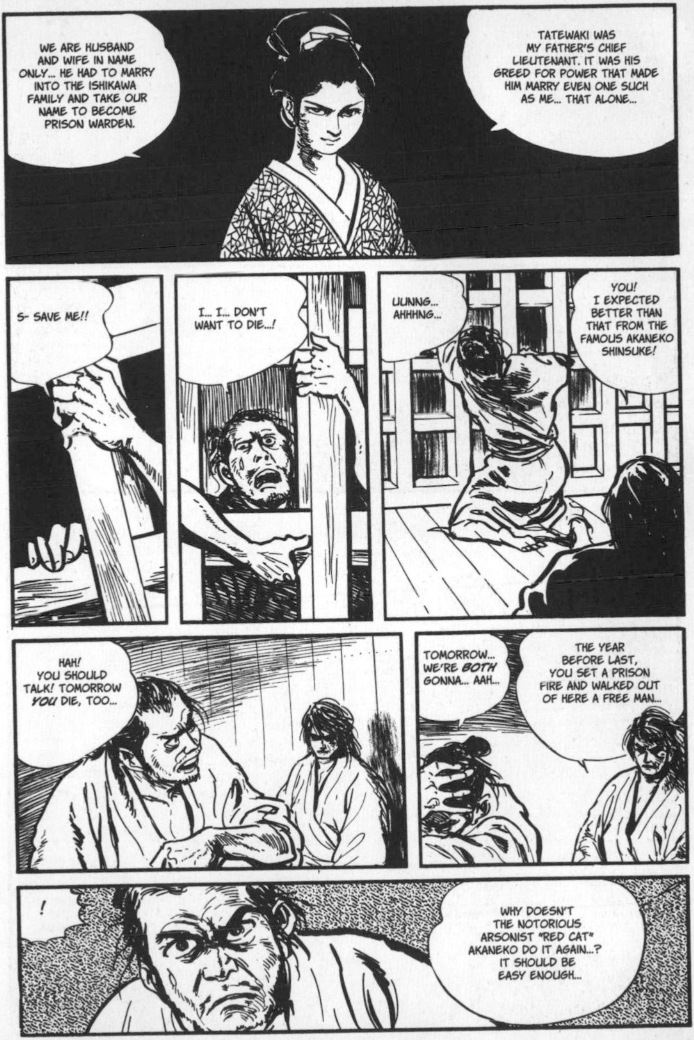
WE ARE HUSBAND AND WIFE IN NAME ONLY... HE HAD TO MARRY INTO THE ISHIKAWA FAMILY AND TAKE OUR NAME TO BECOME PRISON WARDEN.
TATEWAKI WAS MY FATHER'S CHIEF LIEUTENANT. IT WAS HIS GREED FOR POWER THAT MADE HIM MARRY EVEN ONE SUCH AS ME... THAT ALONE...
S- SAVE ME!!
I... I... DON'T WANT TO DIE...!
UUNNG... AHHHNG...
YOU! I EXPECTED BETTER THAN THAT FROM THE FAMOUS AKANEKO SHINSUKE!
HAH! YOU SHOULD TALK! TOMORROW *YOU* DIE, TOO...
TOMORROW... WE'RE *BOTH* GONNA... AAH...
THE YEAR BEFORE LAST, YOU SET A PRISON FIRE AND WALKED OUT OF HERE A FREE MAN...
!
WHY DOESN'T THE NOTORIOUS ARSONIST "RED CAT" AKANEKO DO IT AGAIN...? IT SHOULD BE EASY ENOUGH...

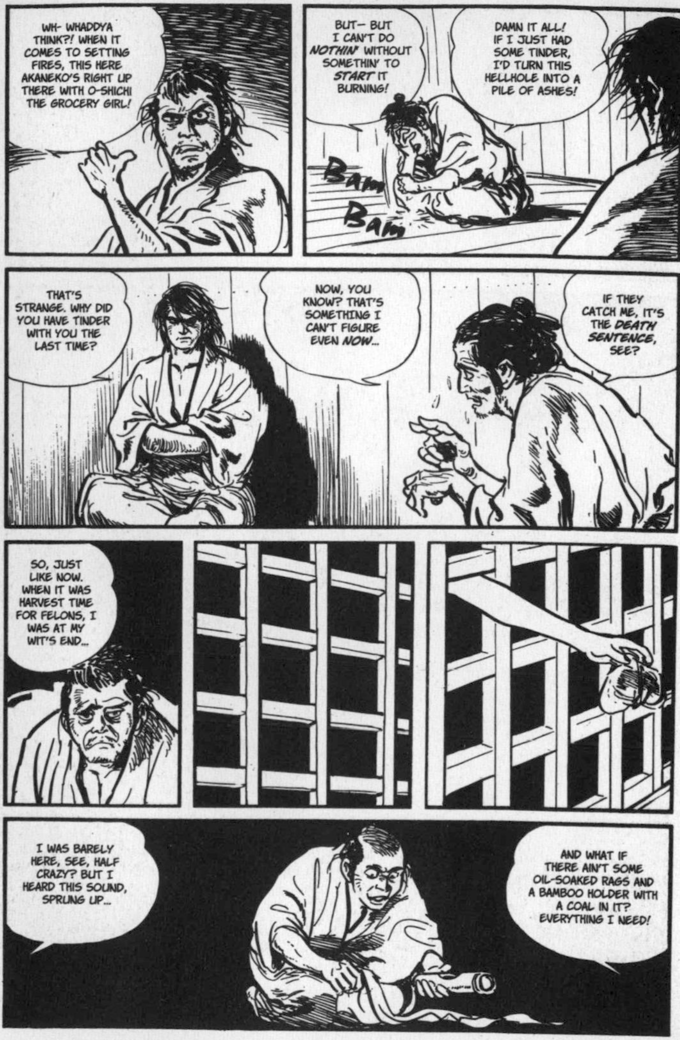
WH- WHADDYA THINK?! WHEN IT COMES TO SETTING FIRES, THIS HERE AKANEKO'S RIGHT UP THERE WITH O-SHICHI THE GROCERY GIRL!
BUT— BUT I CAN'T DO *NOTHIN'* WITHOUT SOMETHIN' TO *START* IT BURNING!
DAMN IT ALL! IF I JUST HAD SOME TINDER, I'D TURN THIS HELLHOLE INTO A PILE OF ASHES!
BAM BAM
THAT'S STRANGE. WHY DID YOU HAVE TINDER WITH YOU THE LAST TIME?
NOW, YOU KNOW? THAT'S SOMETHING I CAN'T FIGURE EVEN *NOW*...
IF THEY CATCH ME, IT'S THE *DEATH SENTENCE*, SEE?
SO, JUST LIKE NOW. WHEN IT WAS HARVEST TIME FOR FELONS, I WAS AT MY WIT'S END...
I WAS BARELY HERE, SEE, HALF CRAZY? BUT I HEARD THIS SOUND, SPRUNG UP...
AND WHAT IF THERE AIN'T SOME OIL-SOAKED RAGS AND A BAMBOO HOLDER WITH A COAL IN IT? EVERYTHING I NEED!

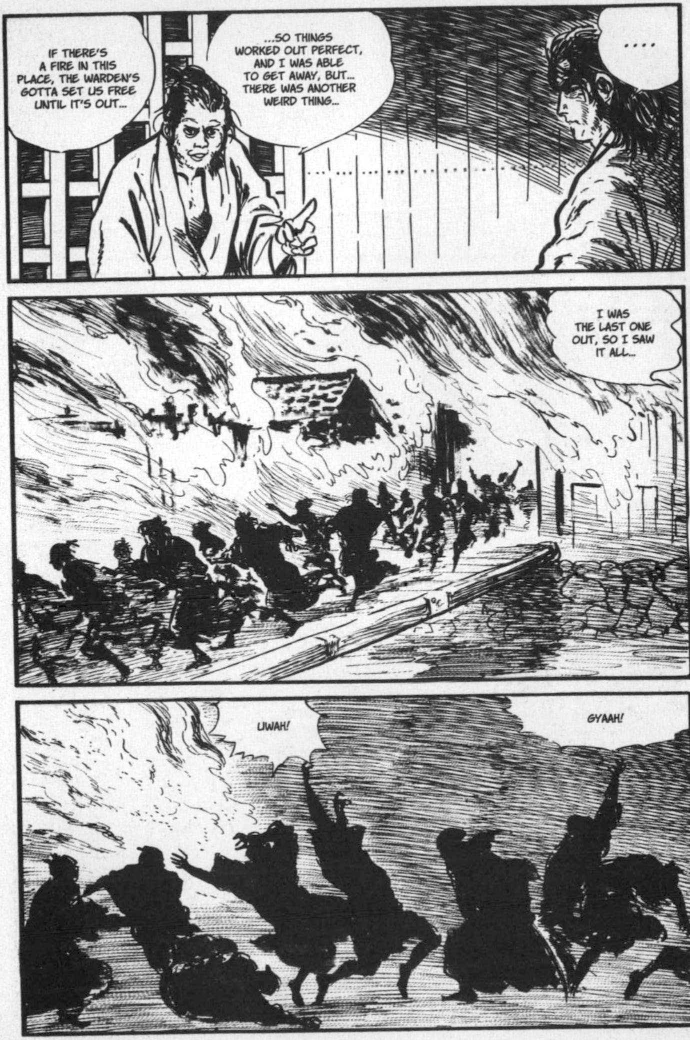
IF THERE'S A FIRE IN THIS PLACE, THE WARDEN'S GOTTA SET US FREE UNTIL IT'S OUT...
...SO THINGS WORKED OUT PERFECT, AND I WAS ABLE TO GET AWAY, BUT... THERE WAS ANOTHER WEIRD THING...
....
I WAS THE LAST ONE OUT, SO I SAW IT ALL...
UWAH!
GYAAH!

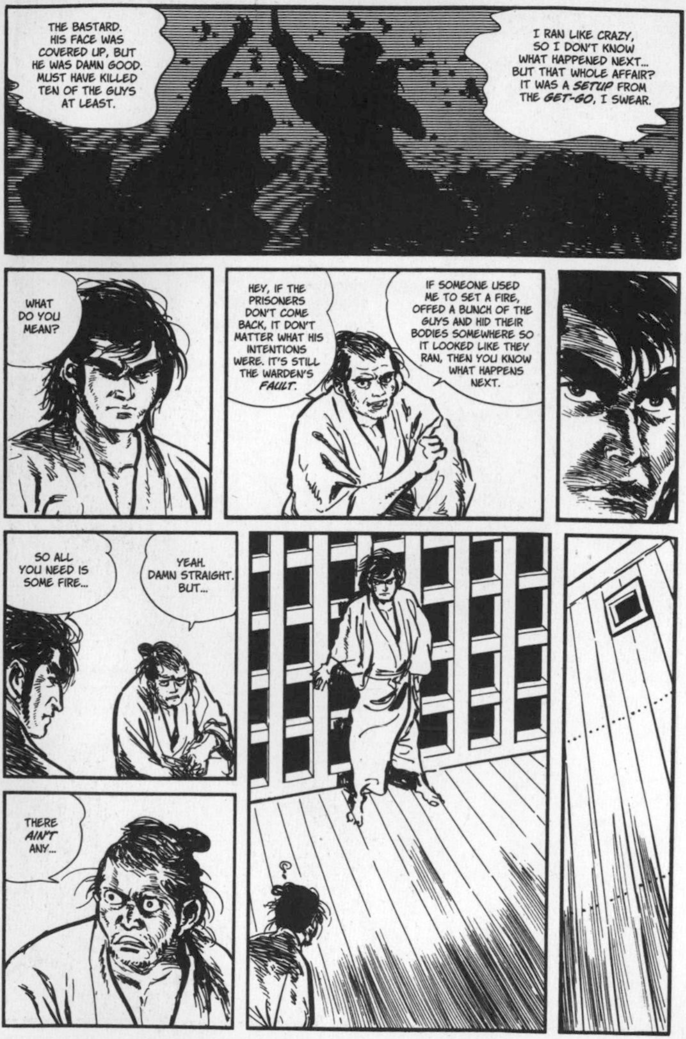
THE BASTARD. HIS FACE WAS COVERED UP, BUT HE WAS DAMN GOOD. MUST HAVE KILLED TEN OF THE GUYS AT LEAST.
I RAN LIKE CRAZY, SO I DON'T KNOW WHAT HAPPENED NEXT... BUT THAT WHOLE AFFAIR? IT WAS A *SETUP* FROM THE *GET-GO*, I SWEAR.
WHAT DO YOU MEAN?
HEY, IF THE PRISONERS DON'T COME BACK, IT DON'T MATTER WHAT HIS INTENTIONS WERE. IT'S STILL THE WARDEN'S *FAULT*.
IF SOMEONE USED ME TO SET A FIRE, OFFED A BUNCH OF THE GUYS AND HID THEIR BODIES SOMEWHERE SO IT LOOKED LIKE THEY RAN, THEN YOU KNOW WHAT HAPPENS NEXT.
SO ALL YOU NEED IS SOME FIRE...
YEAH. DAMN STRAIGHT. BUT...
THERE *AIN'T* ANY...
?

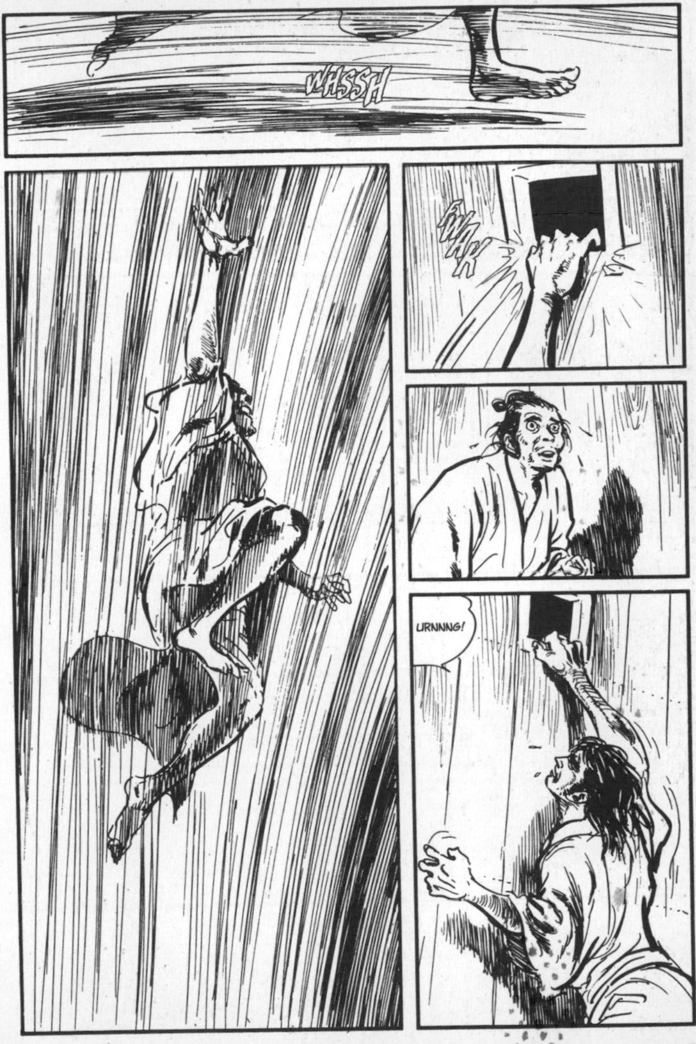
WHSSH
FWAK
URNNNG!

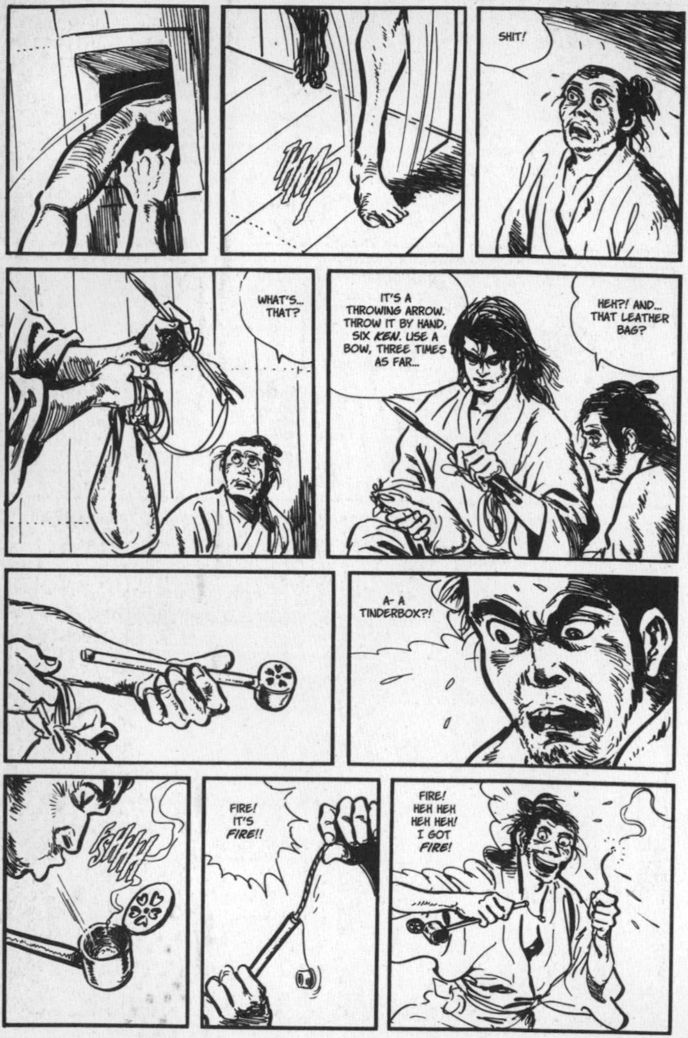
THP
SHIT!
WHAT'S... THAT?
IT'S A THROWING ARROW. THROW IT BY HAND, SIX *KEN*. USE A BOW, THREE TIMES AS FAR...
HEH?! AND... THAT LEATHER BAG?
A- A TINDERBOX?!
FIRE! IT'S *FIRE*!!
FIRE! HEH HEH HEH HEH! I GOT *FIRE*!

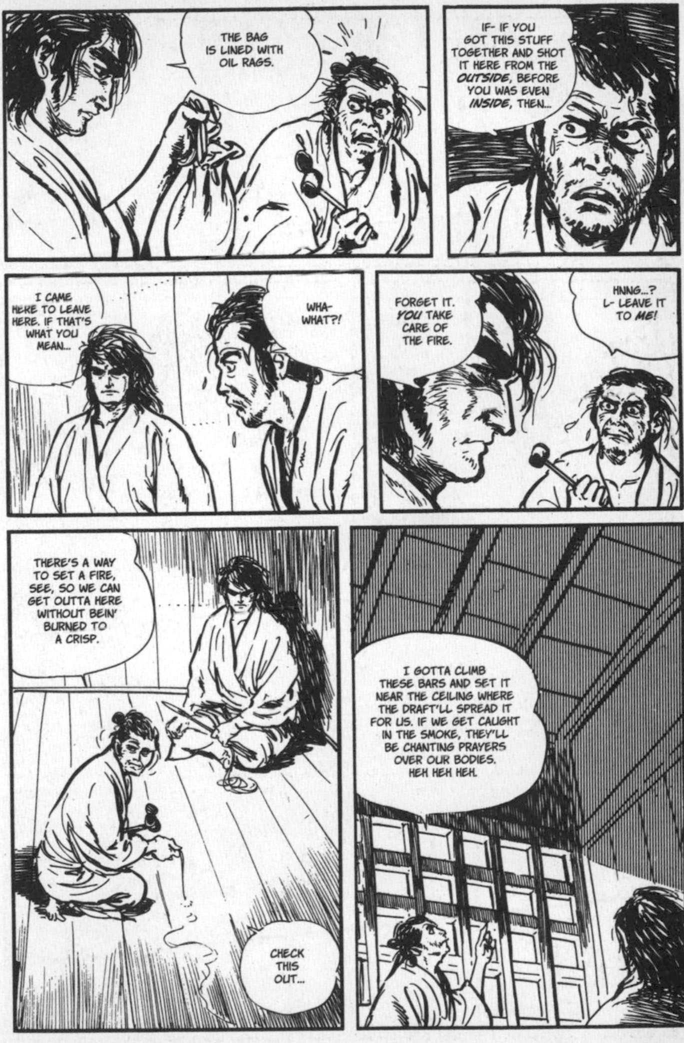
THE BAG IS LINED WITH OIL RAGS.
IF- IF YOU GOT THIS STUFF TOGETHER AND SHOT IT HERE FROM THE *OUTSIDE*, BEFORE YOU WAS EVEN *INSIDE*, THEN...
I CAME HERE TO LEAVE HERE. IF THAT'S WHAT YOU MEAN...
WHA- WHAT?!
FORGET IT. *YOU* TAKE CARE OF THE FIRE.
HNNG...? L- LEAVE IT TO *ME*!
THERE'S A WAY TO SET A FIRE, SEE, SO WE CAN GET OUTTA HERE WITHOUT BEIN' BURNED TO A CRISP.
CHECK THIS OUT...
I GOTTA CLIMB THESE BARS AND SET IT NEAR THE CEILING WHERE THE DRAFT'LL SPREAD IT FOR US. IF WE GET CAUGHT IN THE SMOKE, THEY'LL BE CHANTING PRAYERS OVER OUR BODIES. HEH HEH HEH.

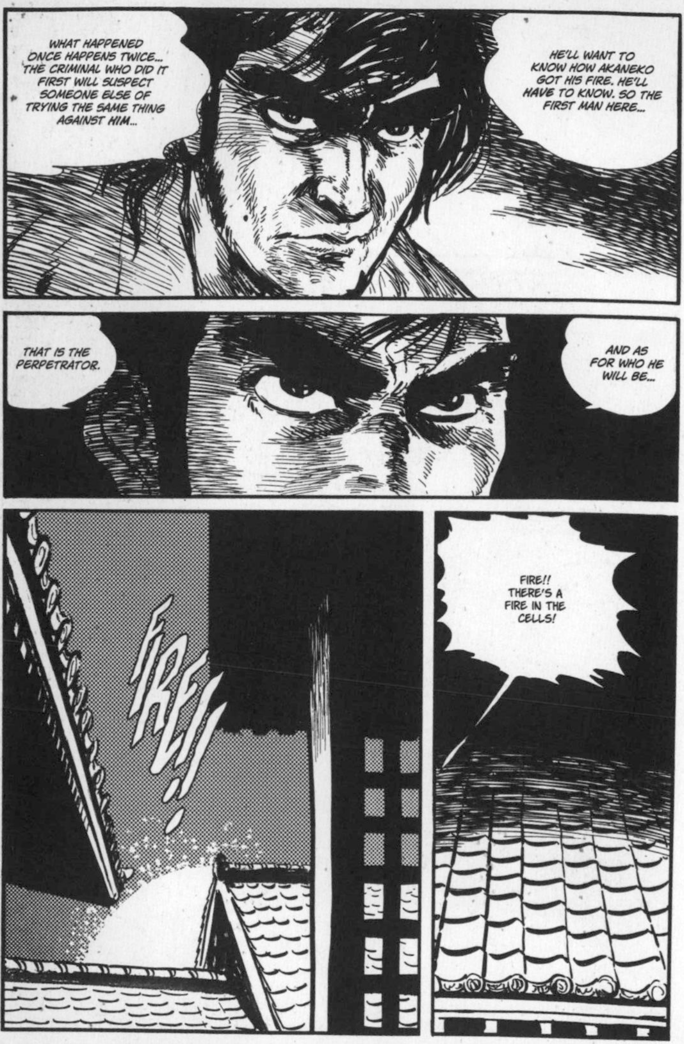
WHAT HAPPENED ONCE HAPPENS TWICE... THE CRIMINAL WHO DID IT FIRST WILL SUSPECT SOMEONE ELSE OF TRYING THE SAME THING AGAINST HIM...
HE'LL WANT TO KNOW HOW AKANEKO GOT HIS FIRE. HE'LL HAVE TO KNOW. SO THE FIRST MAN HERE...
THAT IS THE PERPETRATOR.
AND AS FOR WHO HE WILL BE...
FIRE!!
FIRE!! THERE'S A FIRE IN THE CELLS!

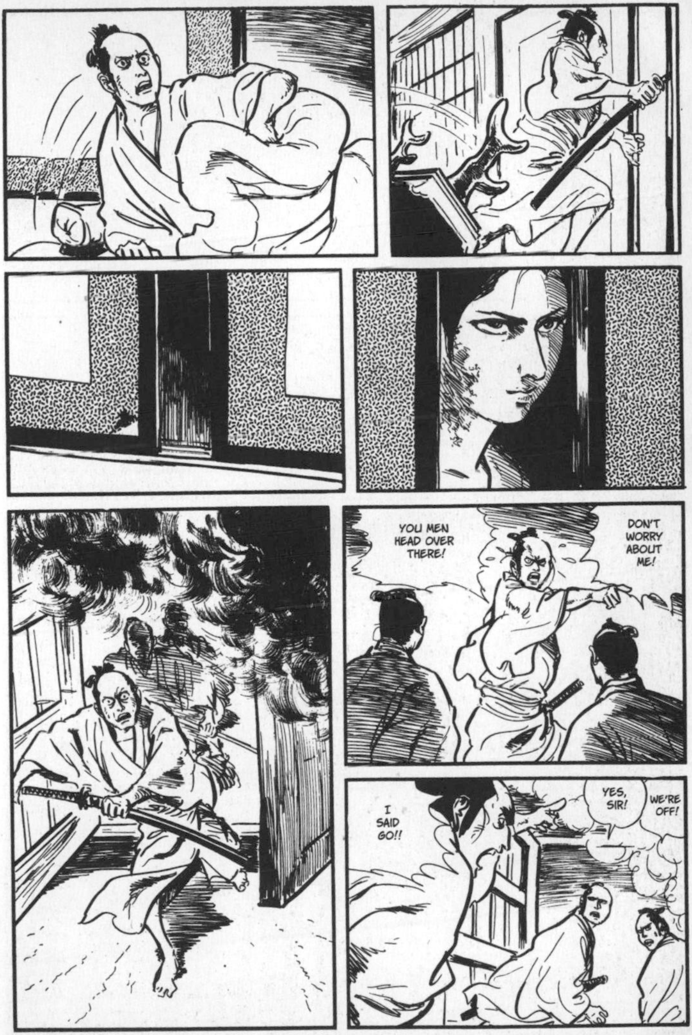
YOU MEN HEAD OVER THERE!
DON'T WORRY ABOUT ME!
I SAID GO!!
YES, SIR!
WE'RE OFF!

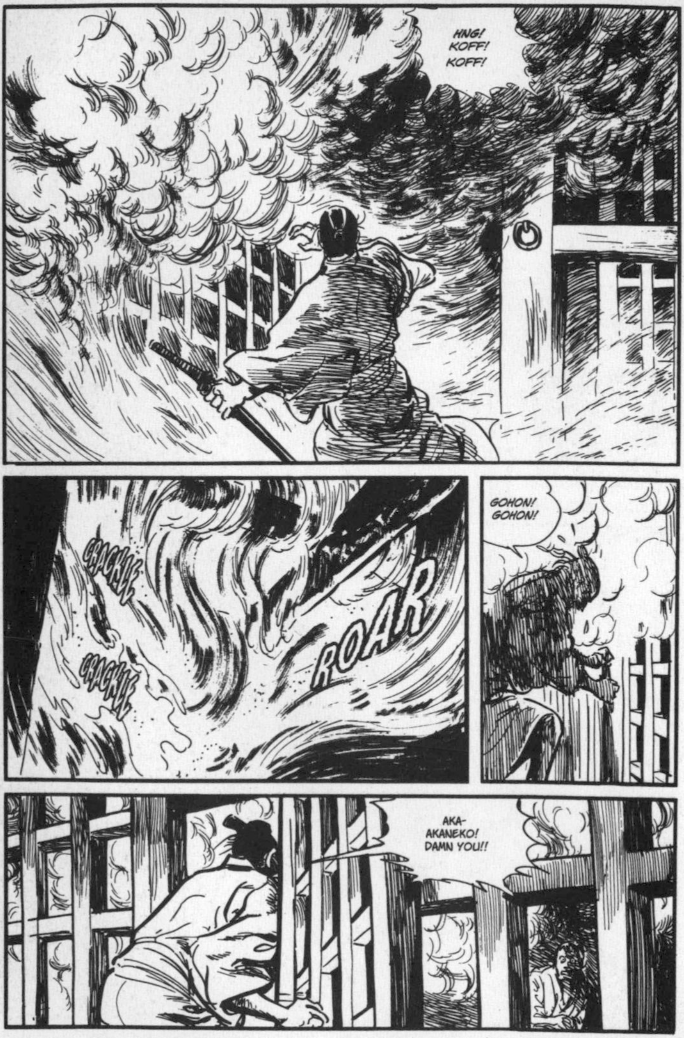
HNG! KOFF! KOFF!
CRACKLE
CRACKLE
ROAR
GOHON! GOHON!
AKA- AKANEKO! DAMN YOU!!

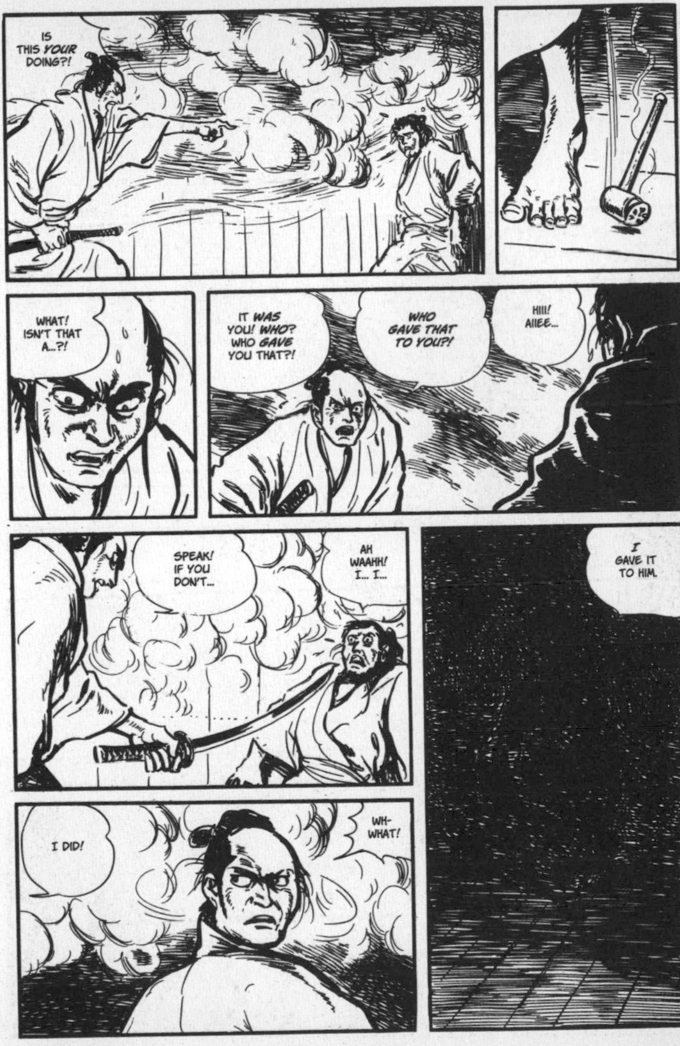
IS THIS *YOUR* DOING?!
WHAT! ISN'T THAT A...?!
IT *WAS* YOU! *WHO?* WHO *GAVE* YOU THAT?!
WHO GAVE THAT TO YOU?!
HIII! AIIEE...
SPEAK! IF YOU DON'T...
AH WAAHH! I... I...
I DID!
WH-WHAT!
I GAVE IT TO HIM.

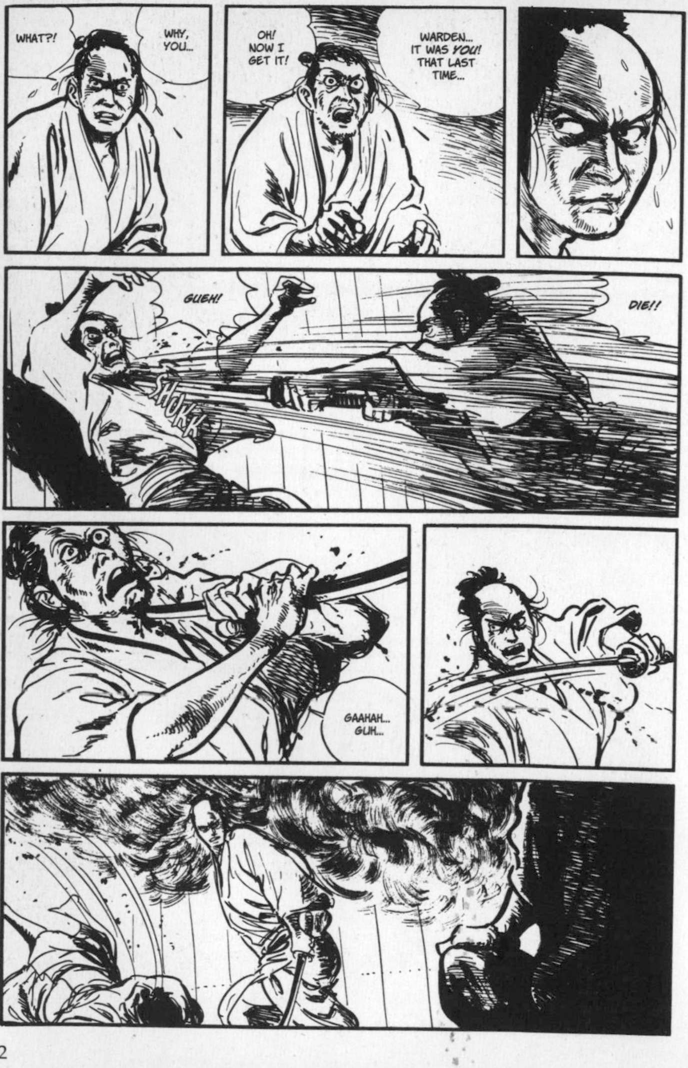
WHAT?!
WHY, YOU...
OH! NOW I GET IT!
WARDEN... IT WAS *YOU!* THAT LAST TIME...
GUEH!
DIE!!
SHUKK
GAAHAH... GUH...

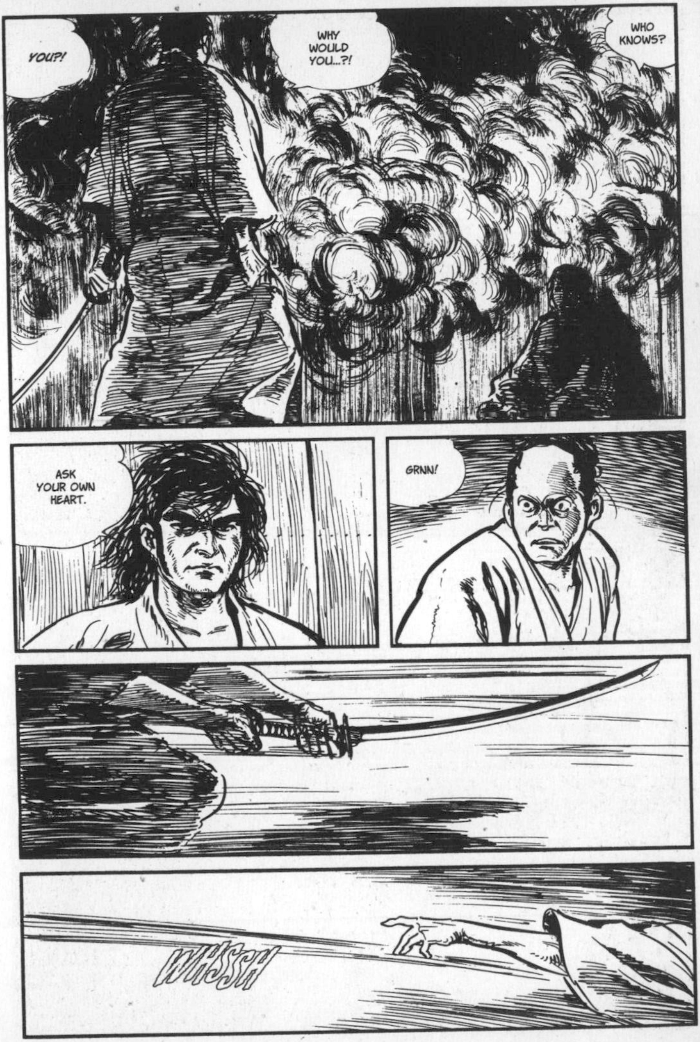
YOU?!
WHY WOULD YOU...?!
WHO KNOWS?
ASK YOUR OWN HEART.
GRNN!
WHSSH

SHAKK

URGGK...

EHKK...

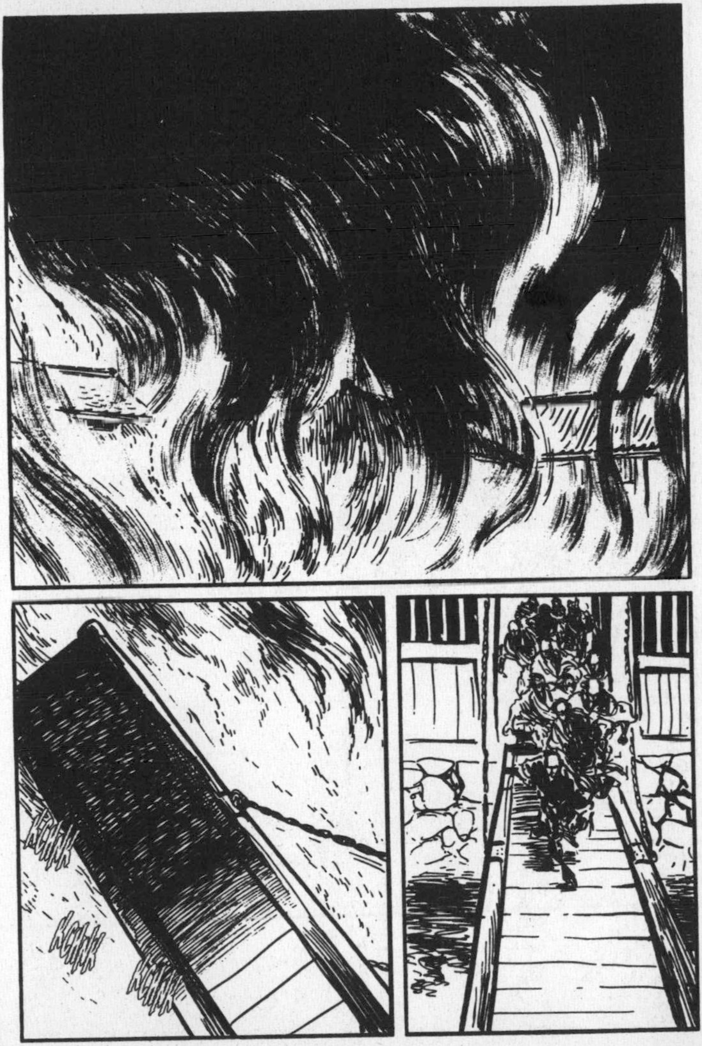
KCHK
KCHK
KCHK

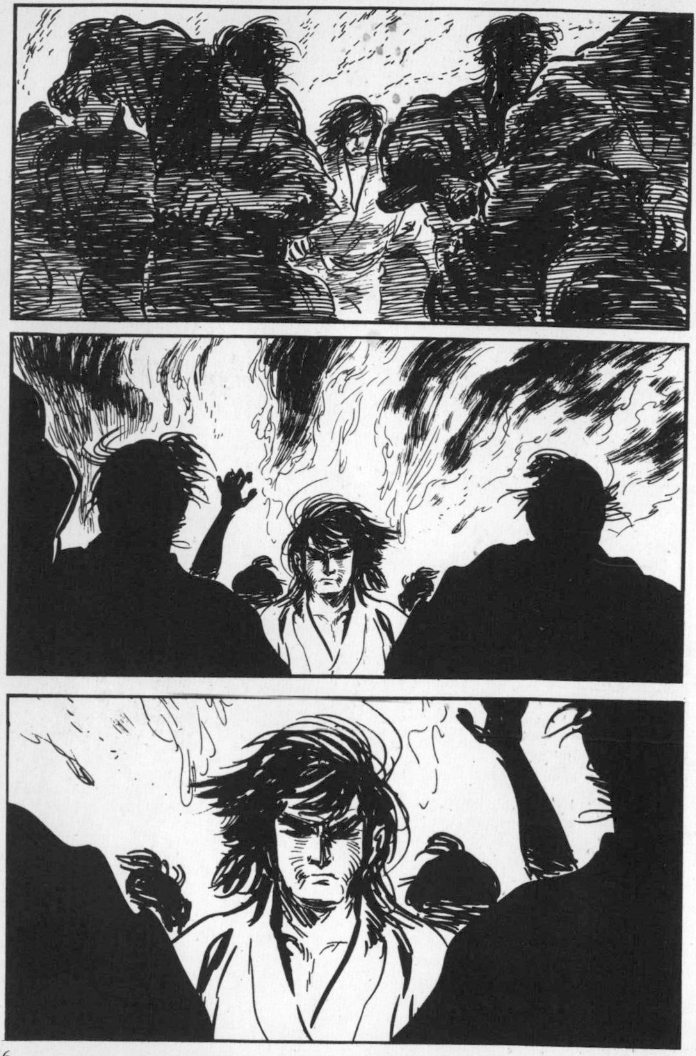

the eleventh

The Coming of the Cold

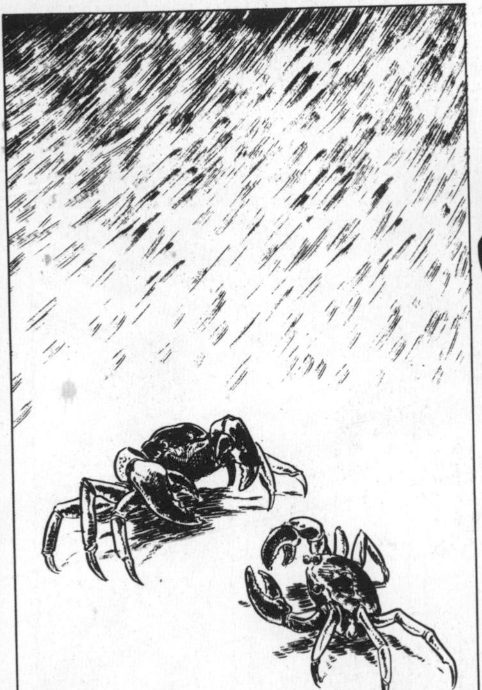

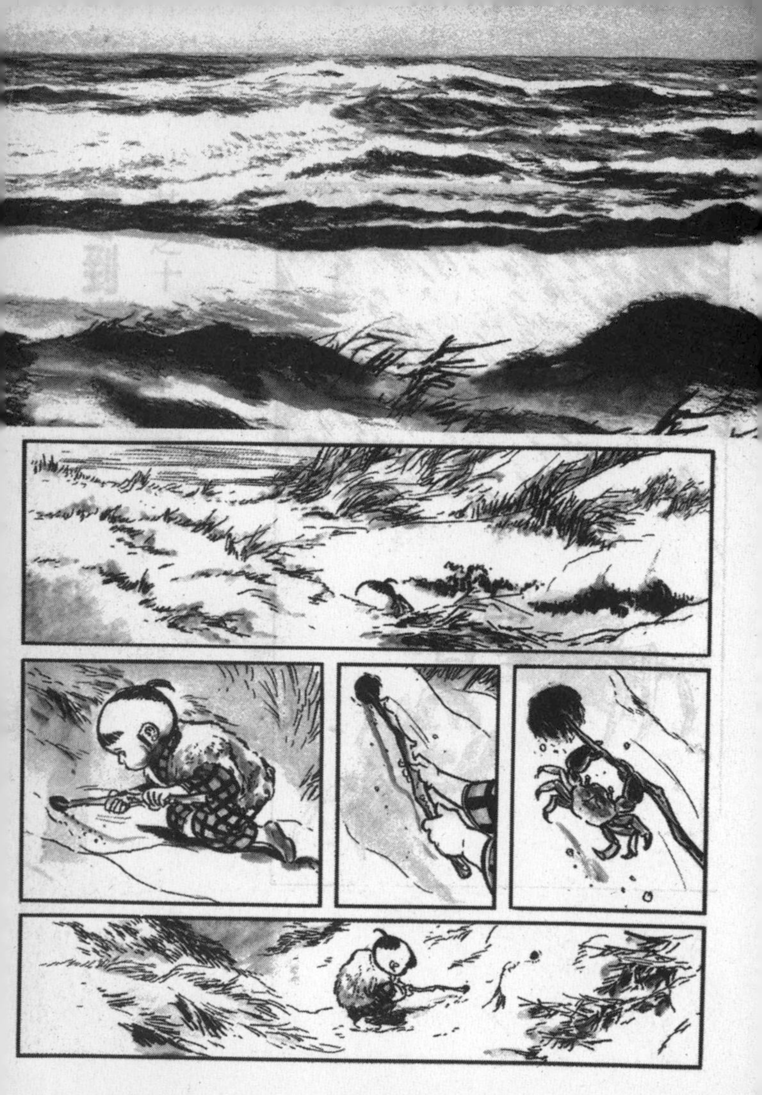

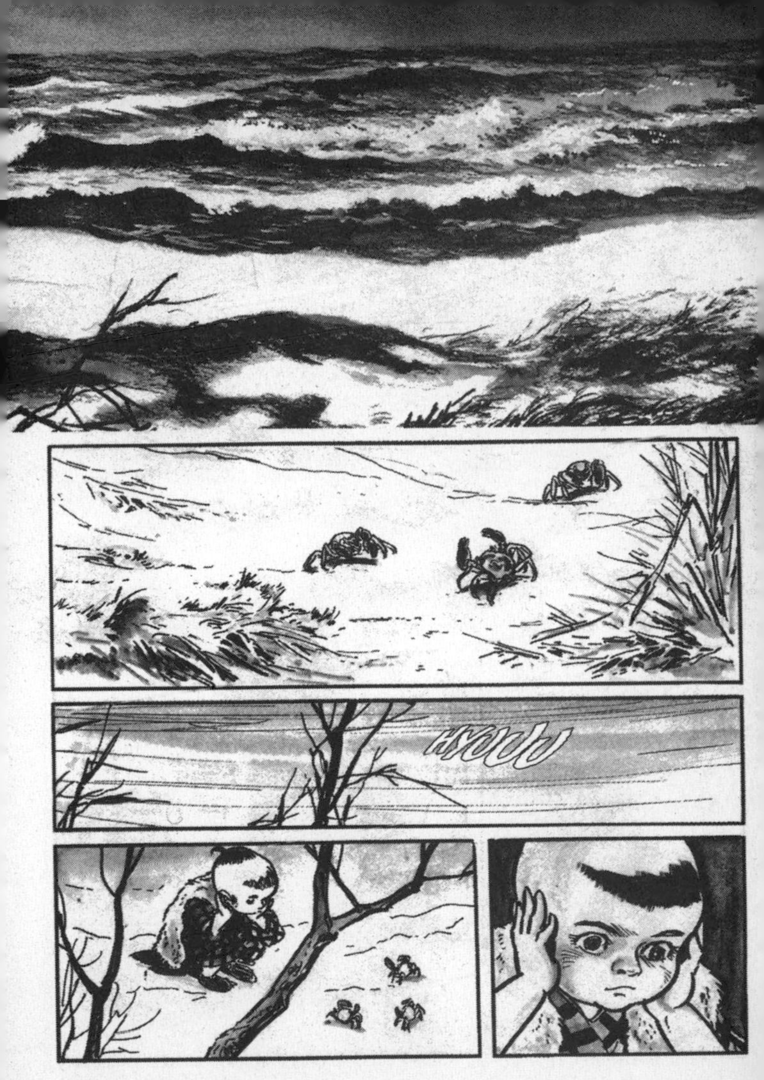
HYUUU

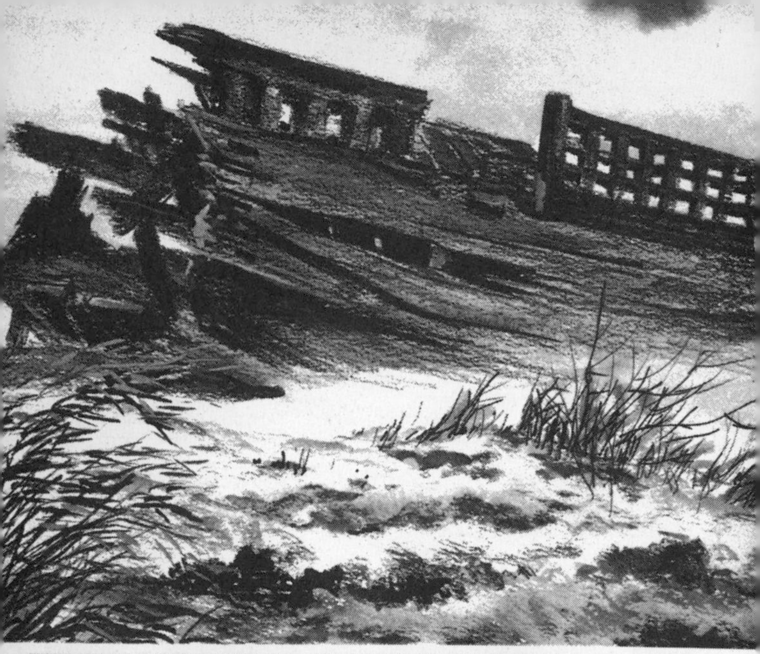

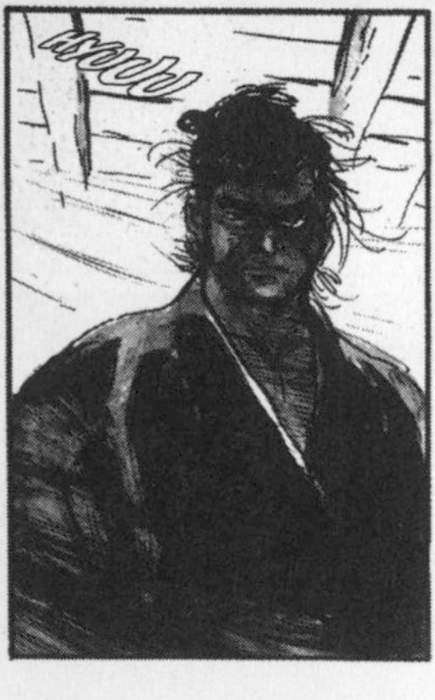
HYUUU

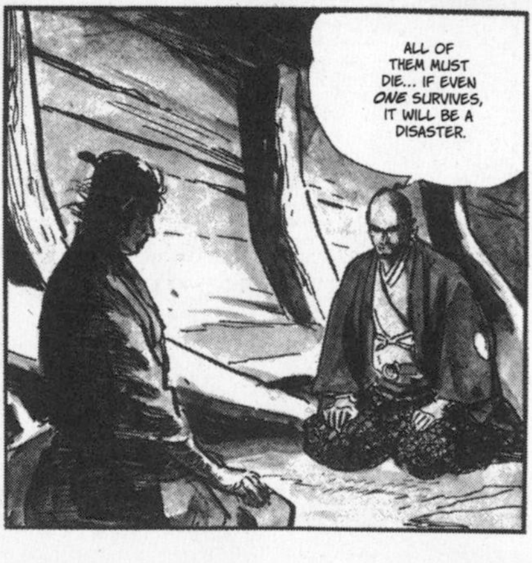
ALL OF THEM MUST DIE... IF EVEN *ONE* SURVIVES, IT WILL BE A DISASTER.

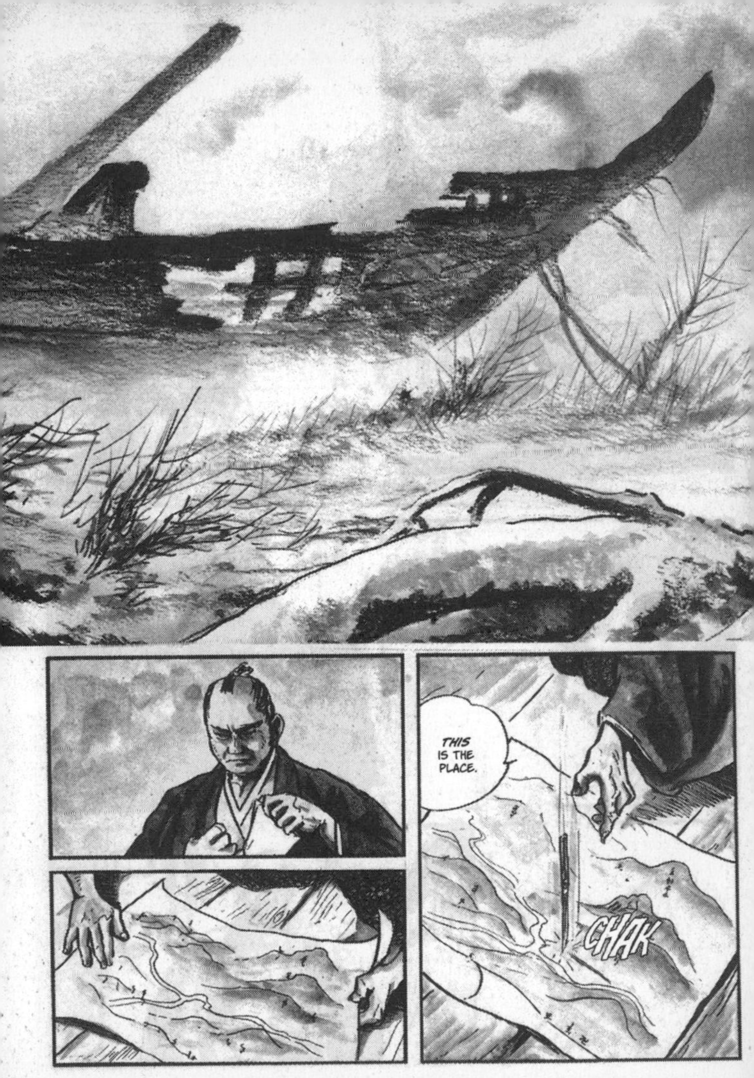
THIS IS THE PLACE.
CHAK

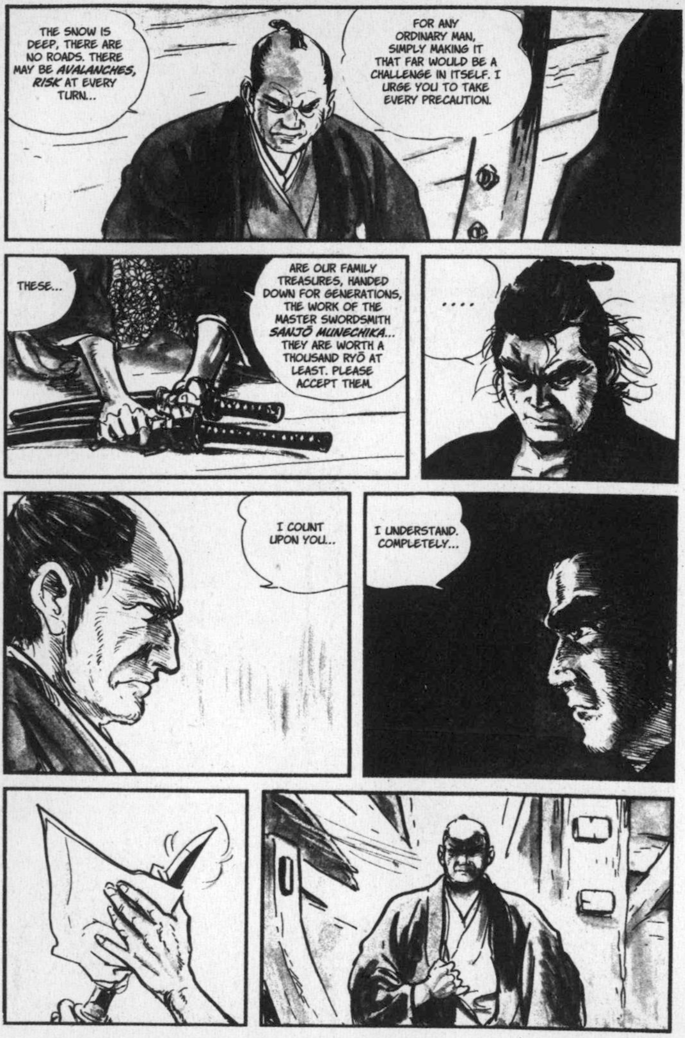
THE SNOW IS DEEP, THERE ARE NO ROADS. THERE MAY BE *AVALANCHES, RISK* AT EVERY TURN...
FOR ANY ORDINARY MAN, SIMPLY MAKING IT THAT FAR WOULD BE A CHALLENGE IN ITSELF. I URGE YOU TO TAKE EVERY PRECAUTION.
THESE...
ARE OUR FAMILY TREASURES, HANDED DOWN FOR GENERATIONS, THE WORK OF THE MASTER SWORDSMITH *SANJŌ MUNECHIKA*... THEY ARE WORTH A THOUSAND RYŌ AT LEAST. PLEASE ACCEPT THEM.
....
I COUNT UPON YOU...
I UNDERSTAND. COMPLETELY...

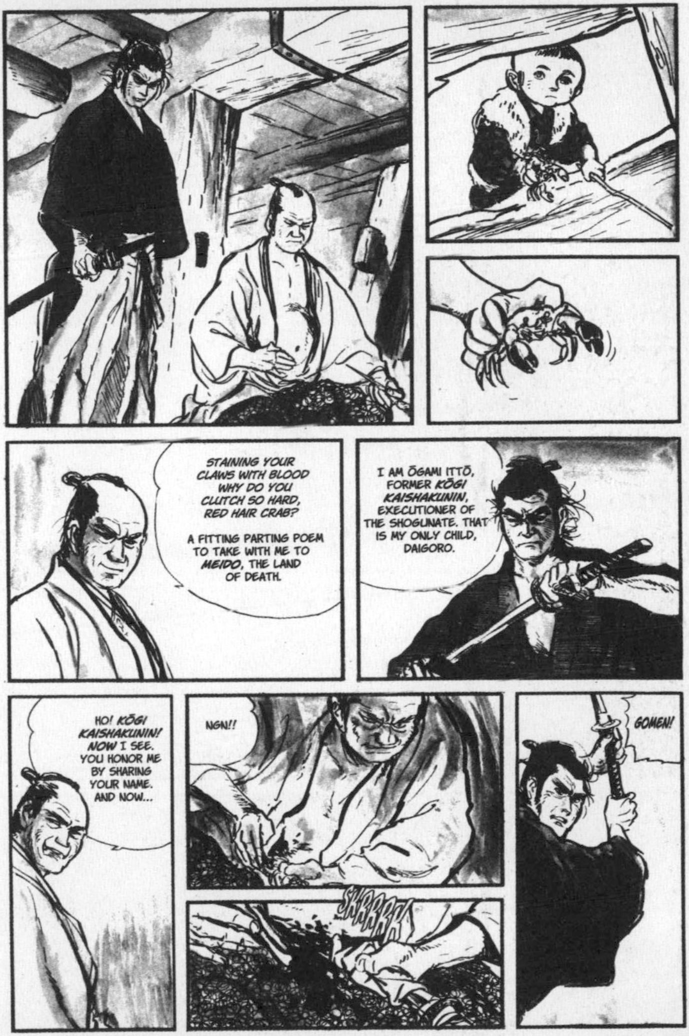
STAINING YOUR CLAWS WITH BLOOD WHY DO YOU CLUTCH SO HARD, RED HAIR CRAB?
A FITTING PARTING POEM TO TAKE WITH ME TO MEIDO, THE LAND OF DEATH.
I AM ŌGAMI ITTŌ, FORMER KŌGI KAISHAKUNIN, EXECUTIONER OF THE SHOGUNATE. THAT IS MY ONLY CHILD, DAIGORO.
HO! KŌGI KAISHAKUNIN! NOW I SEE. YOU HONOR ME BY SHARING YOUR NAME. AND NOW...
NGN!!
SKRRRK
GOMEN!

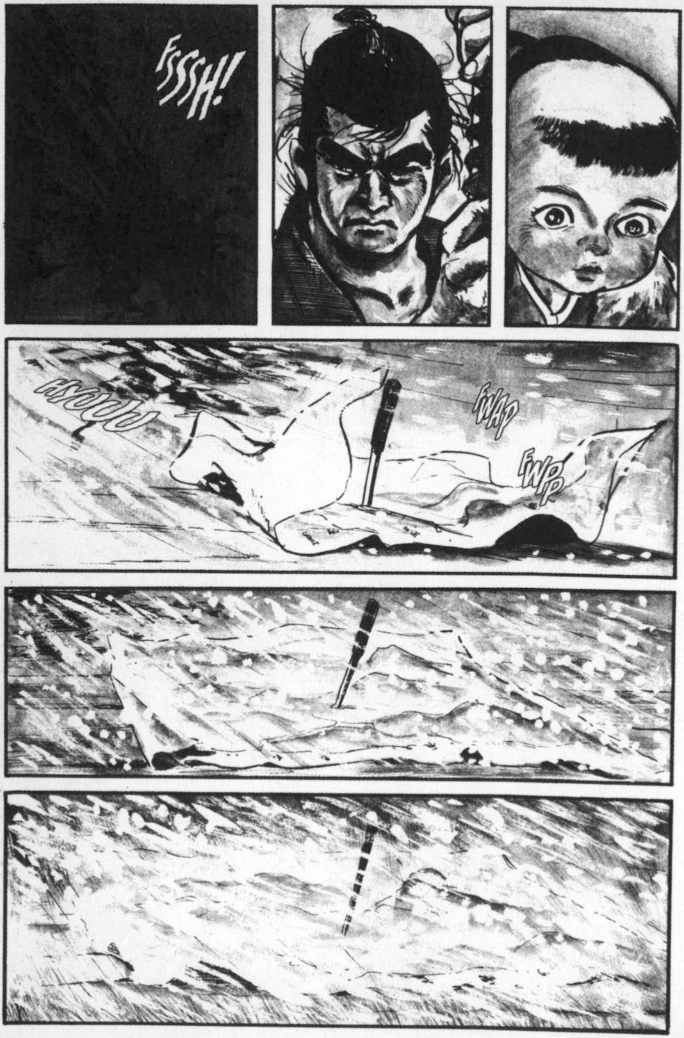
FSSSH!
HYUUUU
FWAP
FWPP

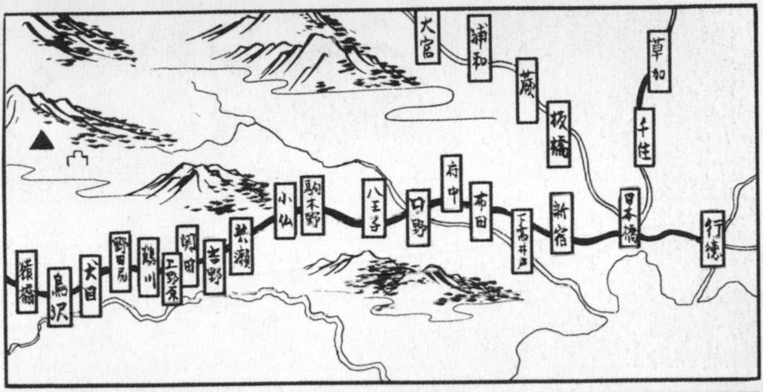
猿橋
鳥沢
犬目
野田尻
鶴川
上野原
関田
吉野
与瀬
小仏
駒木野
八王子
日野
府中
布田
下高井戸
新宿
大宮
浦和
蕨
板橋
日本橋
草加
千住
行徳
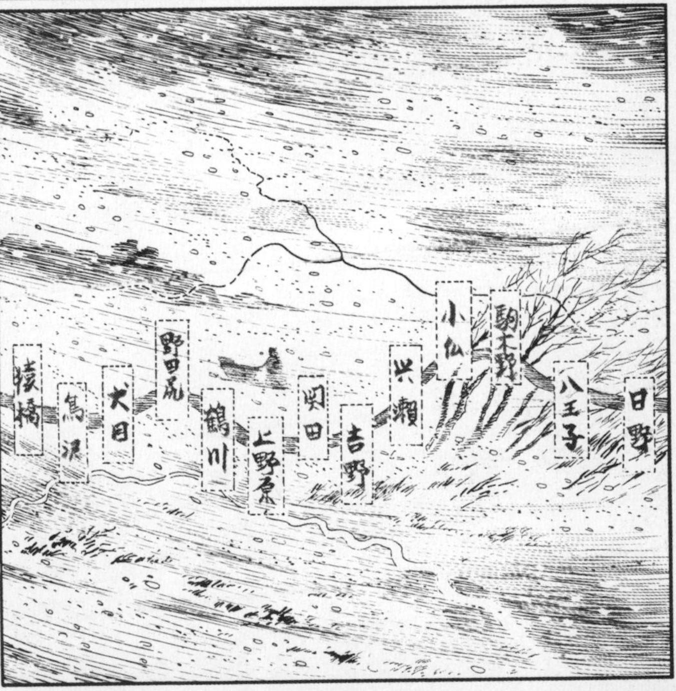
猿橋
鳥沢
犬目
野田尻
鶴川
上野原
関田
吉野
与瀬
小仏
駒木野
八王子
日野

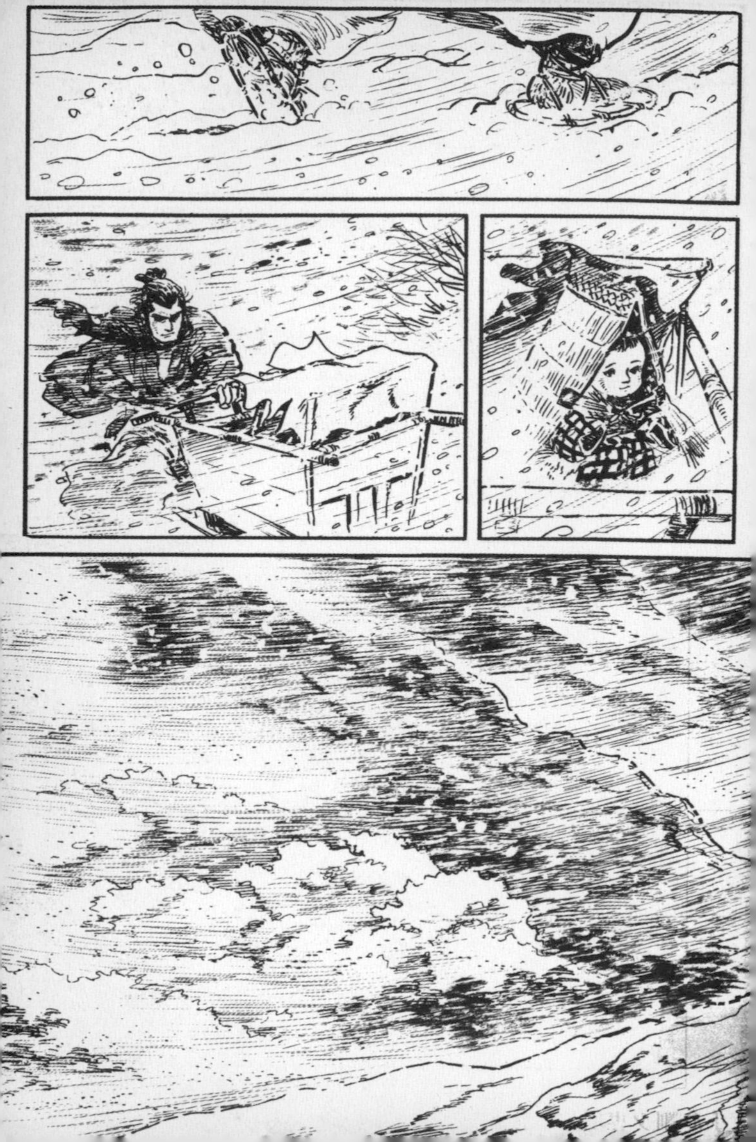

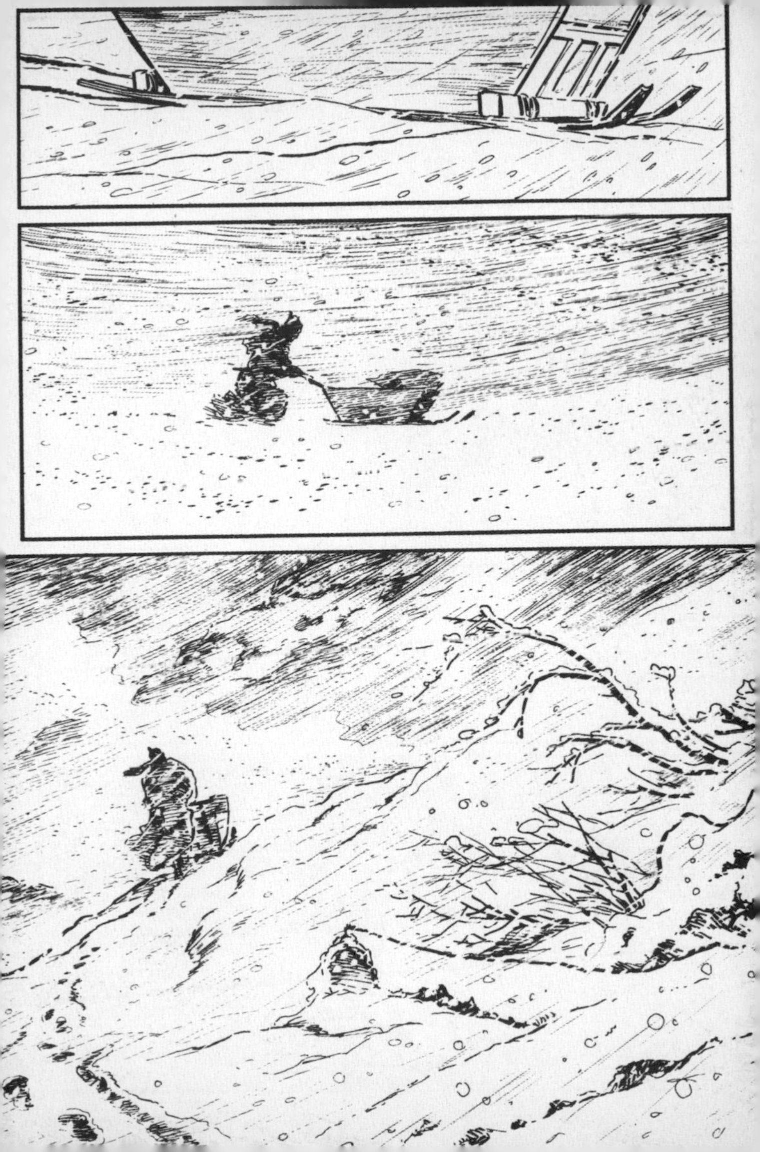

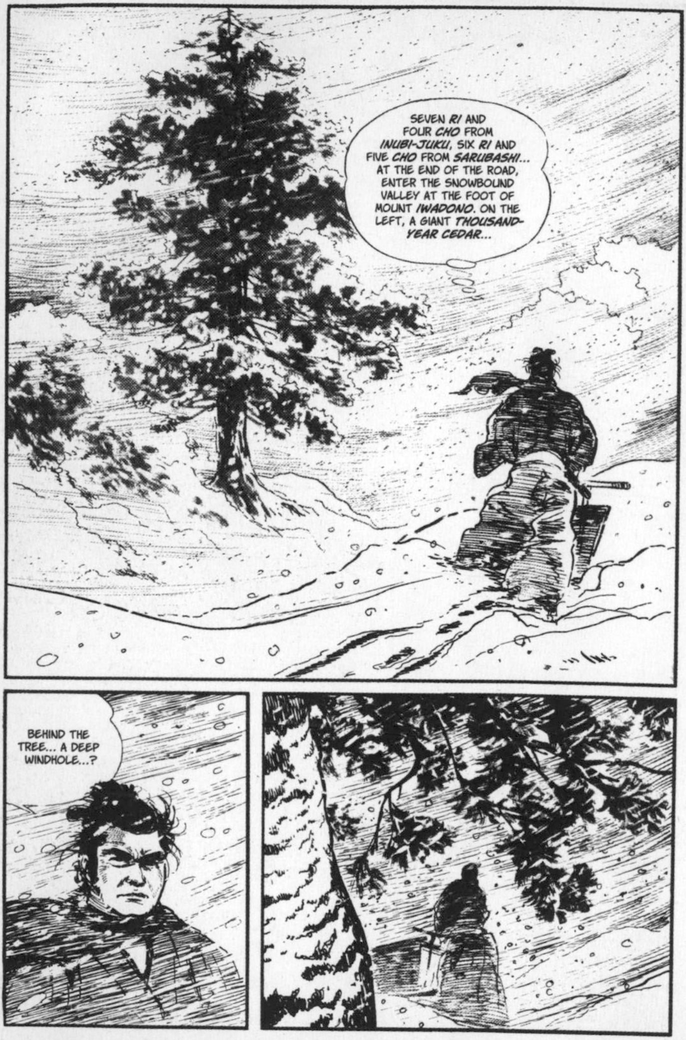
SEVEN *RI* AND FOUR *CHO* FROM *INUBI-JUKU*, SIX *RI* AND FIVE *CHO* FROM *SARUBASHI*... AT THE END OF THE ROAD, ENTER THE SNOWBOUND VALLEY AT THE FOOT OF MOUNT *IWADONO*. ON THE LEFT, A GIANT *THOUSAND-YEAR CEDAR*...
BEHIND THE TREE... A DEEP WINDHOLE...?

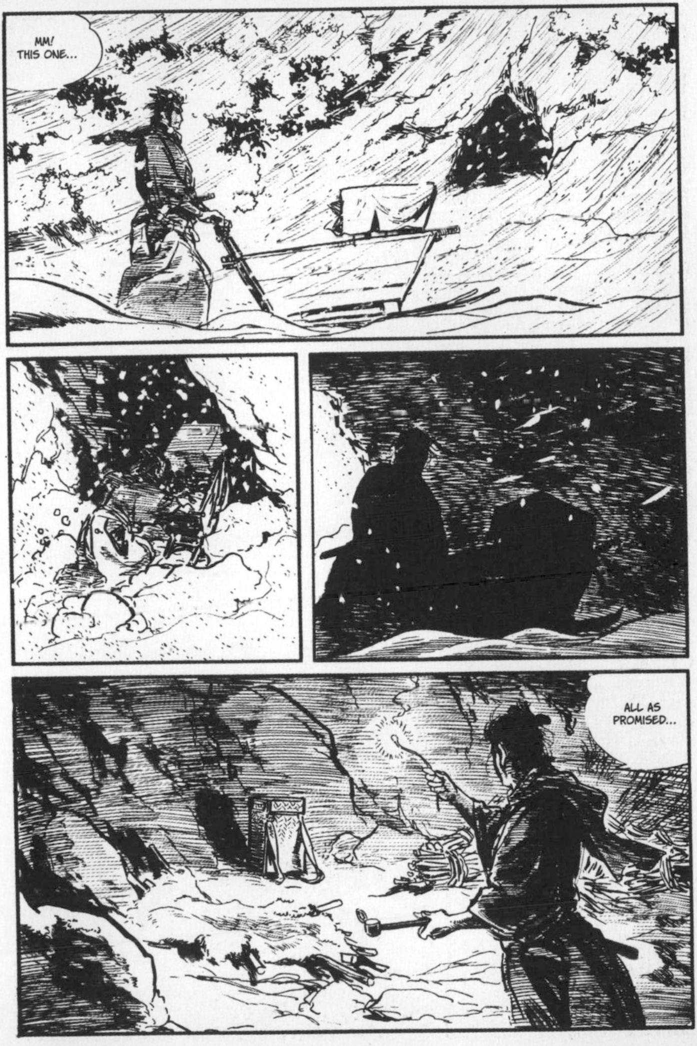
MM! THIS ONE...
ALL AS PROMISED...

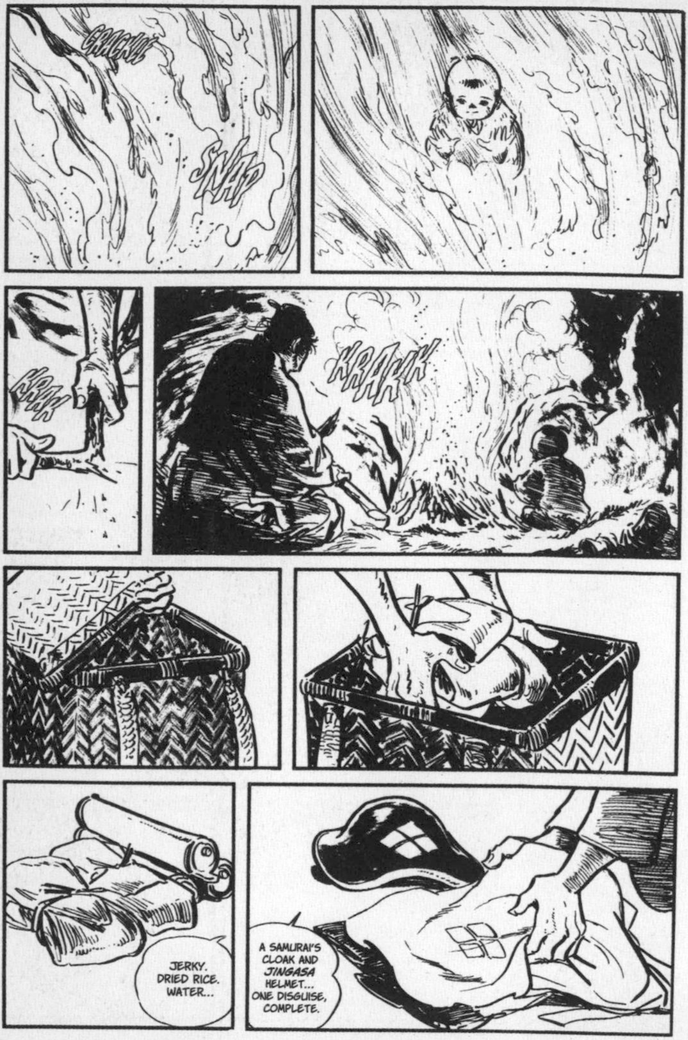
CRACKLE
SNAP
KRAK
KRAAK
JERKY. DRIED RICE. WATER...
A SAMURAI'S CLOAK AND *JINGASA* HELMET... ONE DISGUISE, COMPLETE.

THIS SHOULD LAST... FIVE DAYS...?

DAIGORO! YOU WILL WAIT FOR FATHER HERE!

UHN!

IF YOU GET HUNGRY, EAT JERKY AND DRY RICE.

IF YOU GET THIRSTY, DRINK WATER FROM THESE BAMBOO PIPES.

UHN.

PEE AND POTTY OVER THERE.

UHN.

NO MATTER WHAT HAPPENS, YOU MUST NOT GO OUTSIDE! IF FATHER DOES NOT RETURN, YOU ALSO DIE!

IF YOU DO NOT CRY EVEN WHEN HUNGRY, IF YOU ENDURE EVEN WHEN COLD, IF YOU WAIT PATIENTLY, YOU, TOO, CAN DIE.

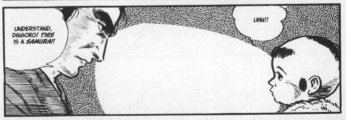

UNDERSTAND, DAIGORO! THIS IS A *SAMURAI*!

UHN!!

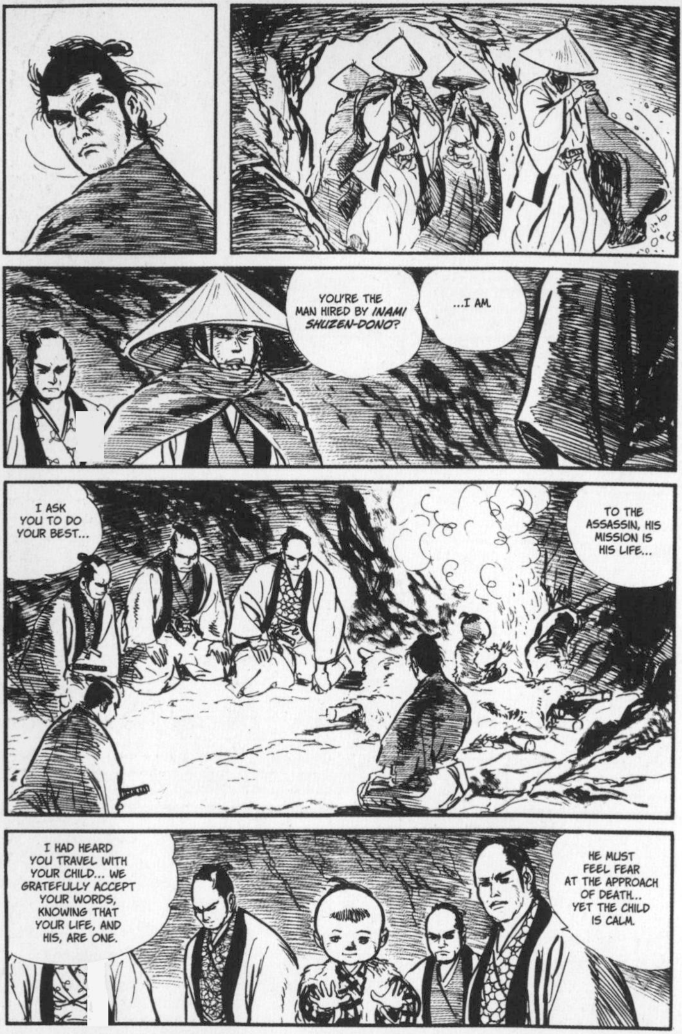
YOU'RE THE MAN HIRED BY *INAMI SHUZEN-DONO*?
...I AM.
I ASK YOU TO DO YOUR BEST...
TO THE ASSASSIN, HIS MISSION IS HIS LIFE...
I HAD HEARD YOU TRAVEL WITH YOUR CHILD... WE GRATEFULLY ACCEPT YOUR WORDS, KNOWING THAT YOUR LIFE, AND HIS, ARE ONE.
HE MUST FEEL FEAR AT THE APPROACH OF DEATH.. YET THE CHILD IS CALM.

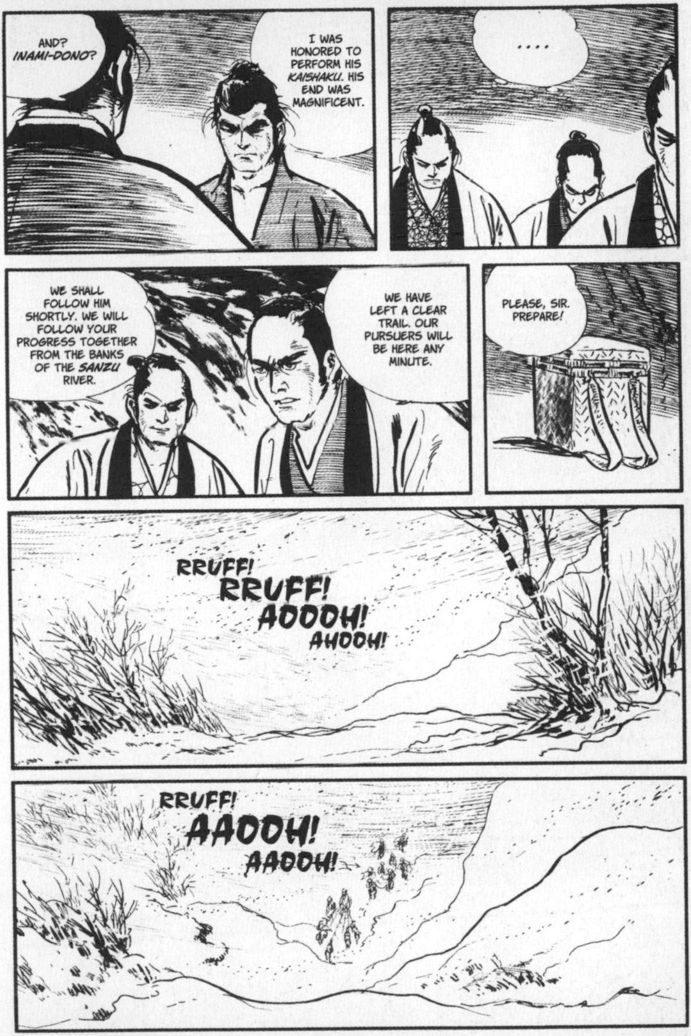
AND? *INAMI-DONO?*
I WAS HONORED TO PERFORM HIS *KAISHAKU*. HIS END WAS MAGNIFICENT.
....
WE SHALL FOLLOW HIM SHORTLY. WE WILL FOLLOW YOUR PROGRESS TOGETHER FROM THE BANKS OF THE *SANZU* RIVER.
WE HAVE LEFT A CLEAR TRAIL. OUR PURSUERS WILL BE HERE ANY MINUTE.
PLEASE, SIR. PREPARE!
RRUFF!
RRUFF!
AOOOH!
AHOOH!
RRUFF!
AAOOH!
AAOOH!

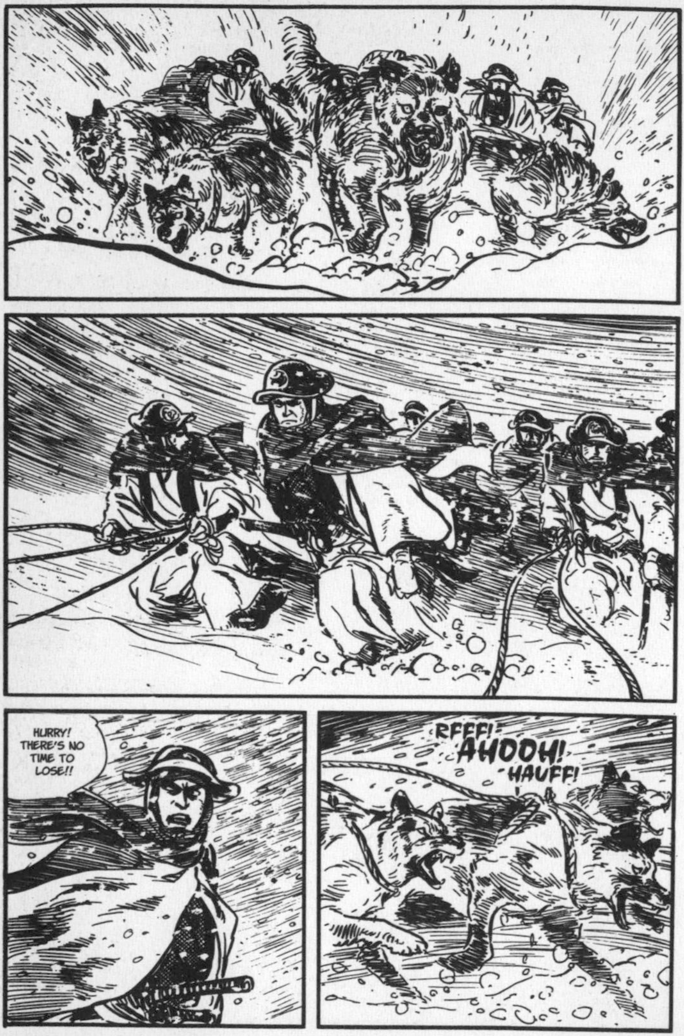
HURRY! THERE'S NO TIME TO LOSE!!
RFFF!
AHOOH!
HAUFF!

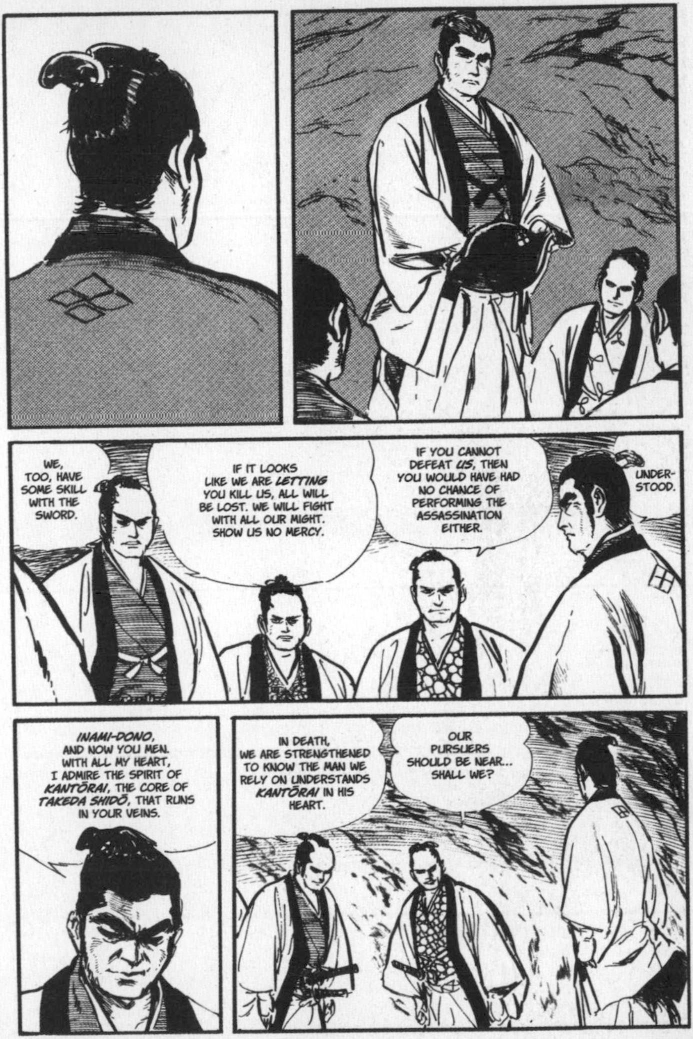
WE, TOO, HAVE SOME SKILL WITH THE SWORD.
IF IT LOOKS LIKE WE ARE *LETTING* YOU KILL US, ALL WILL BE LOST. WE WILL FIGHT WITH ALL OUR MIGHT. SHOW US NO MERCY.
IF YOU CANNOT DEFEAT *US*, THEN YOU WOULD HAVE HAD NO CHANCE OF PERFORMING THE ASSASSINATION EITHER.
UNDER-STOOD.
INAMI-DONO, AND NOW YOU MEN. WITH ALL MY HEART, I ADMIRE THE SPIRIT OF *KANTŌRAI*, THE CORE OF *TAKEDA SHIDŌ*, THAT RUNS IN YOUR VEINS.
IN DEATH, WE ARE STRENGTHENED TO KNOW THE MAN WE RELY ON UNDERSTANDS *KANTŌRAI* IN HIS HEART.
OUR PURSUERS SHOULD BE NEAR... SHALL WE?

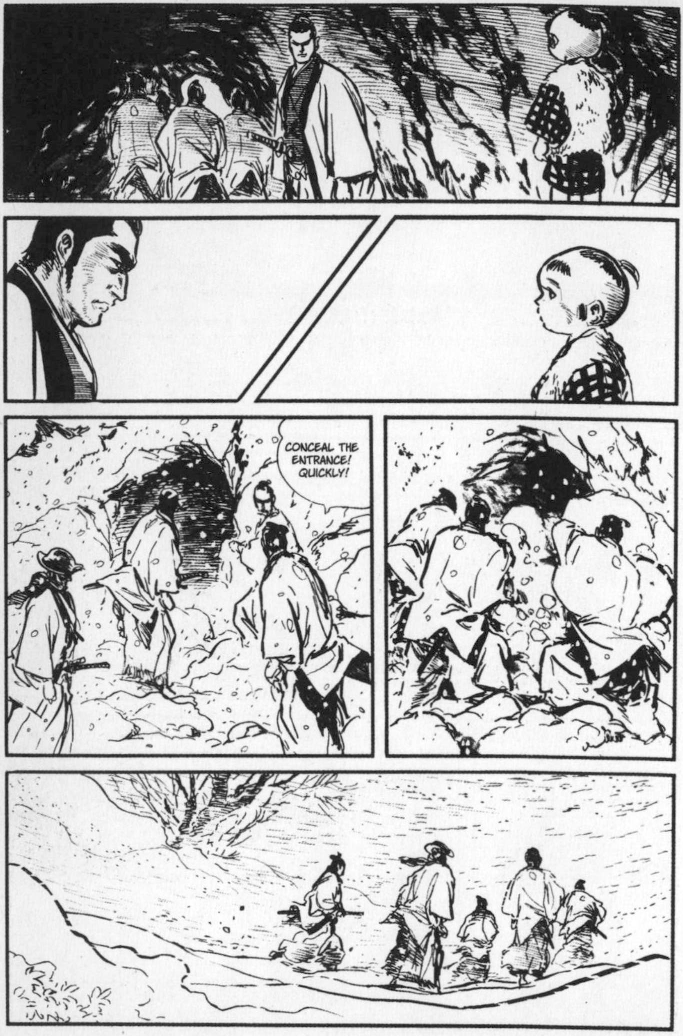
CONCEAL THE ENTRANCE! QUICKLY!

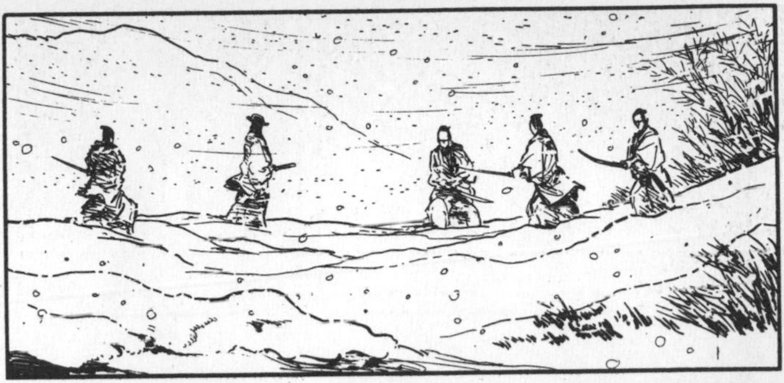
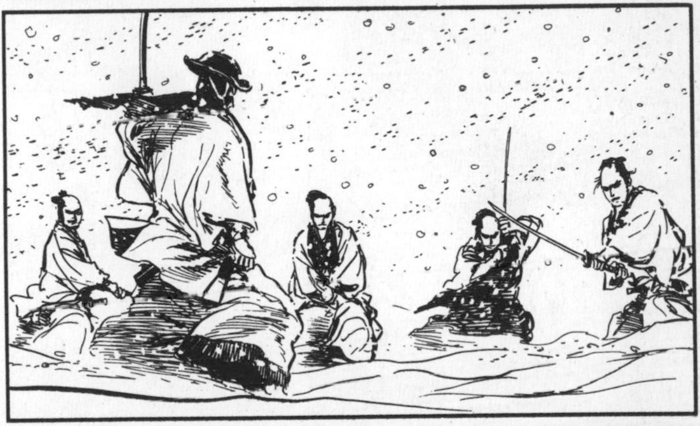
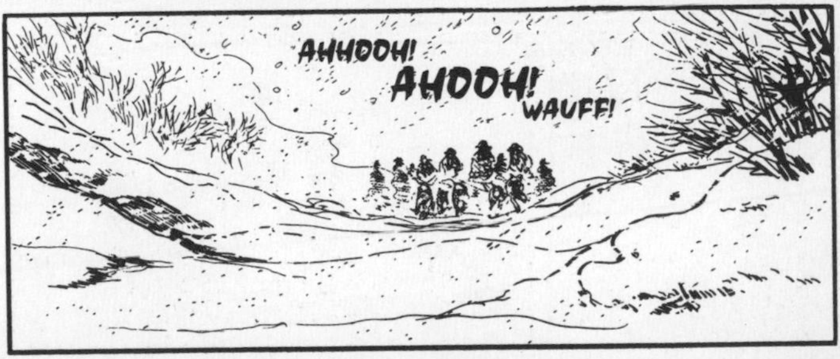
AHHOOH!
AHOOH!
WAUFF!

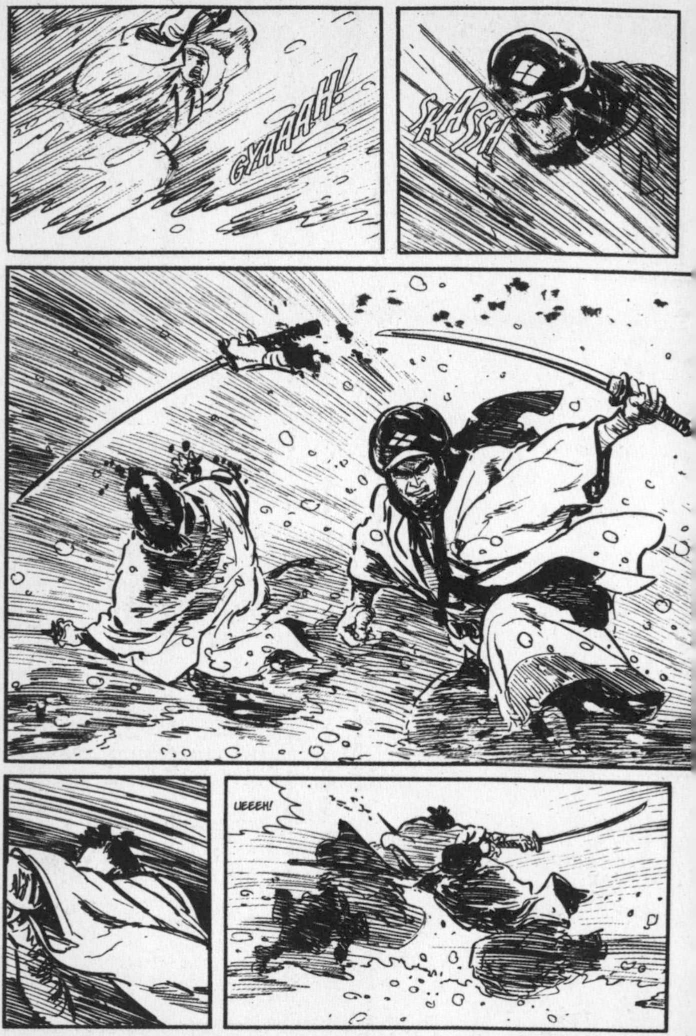
GYAAAH!
SKASSH
UEEEH!

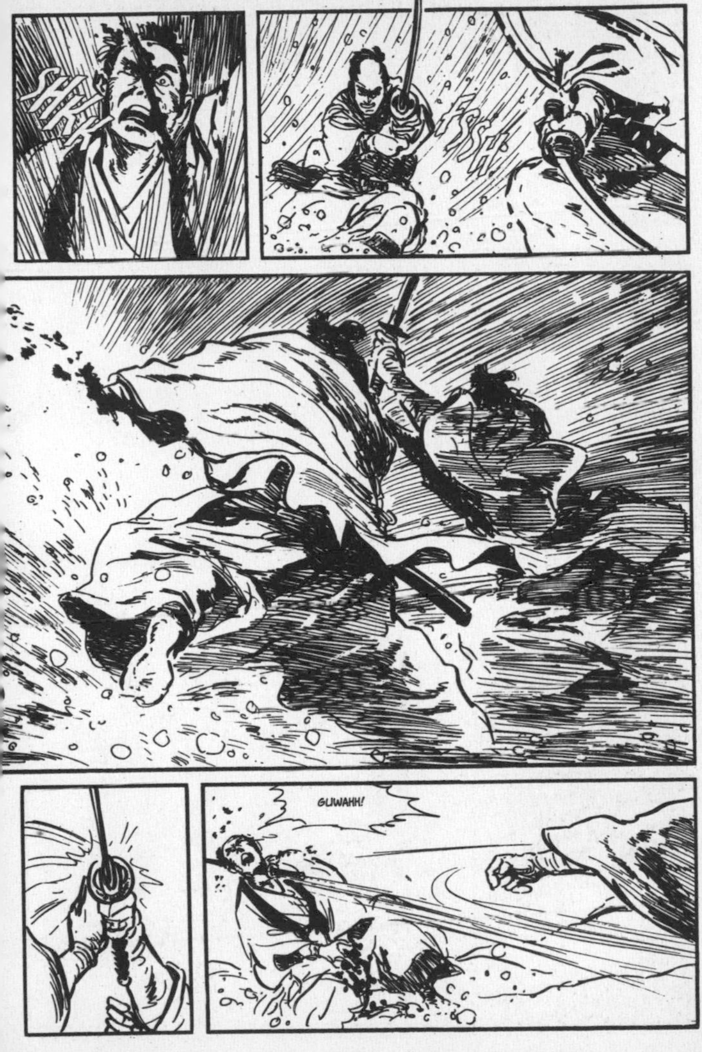
SHK
FSH
GUWAHH!

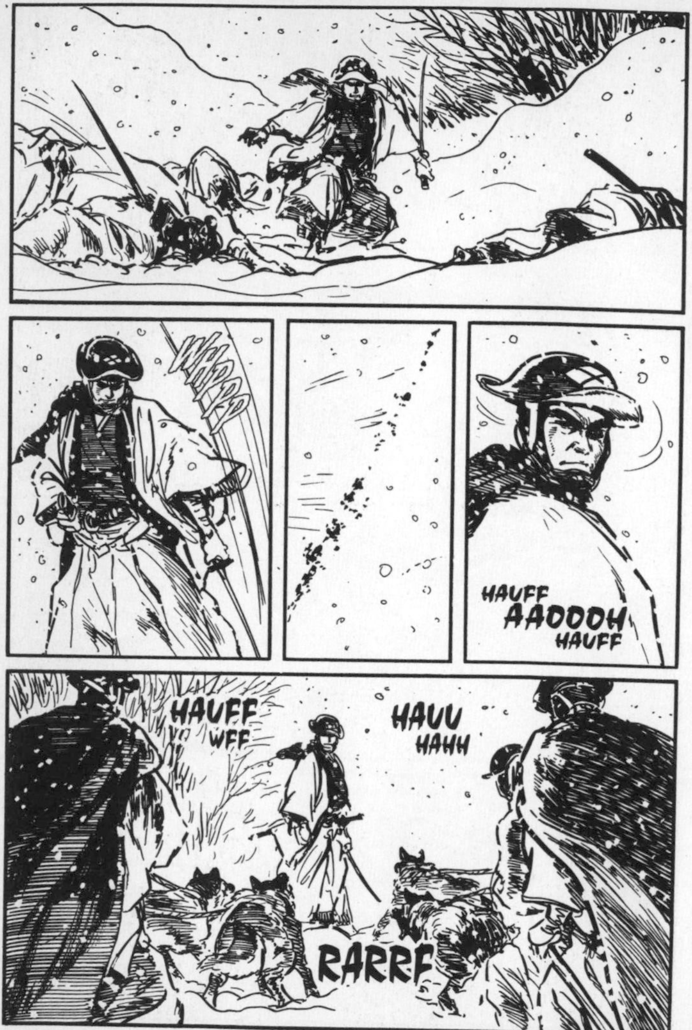
HAUFF
AAOOOH
HAUFF
HAUFF
WFF
HAUU
HAHH
RARRF

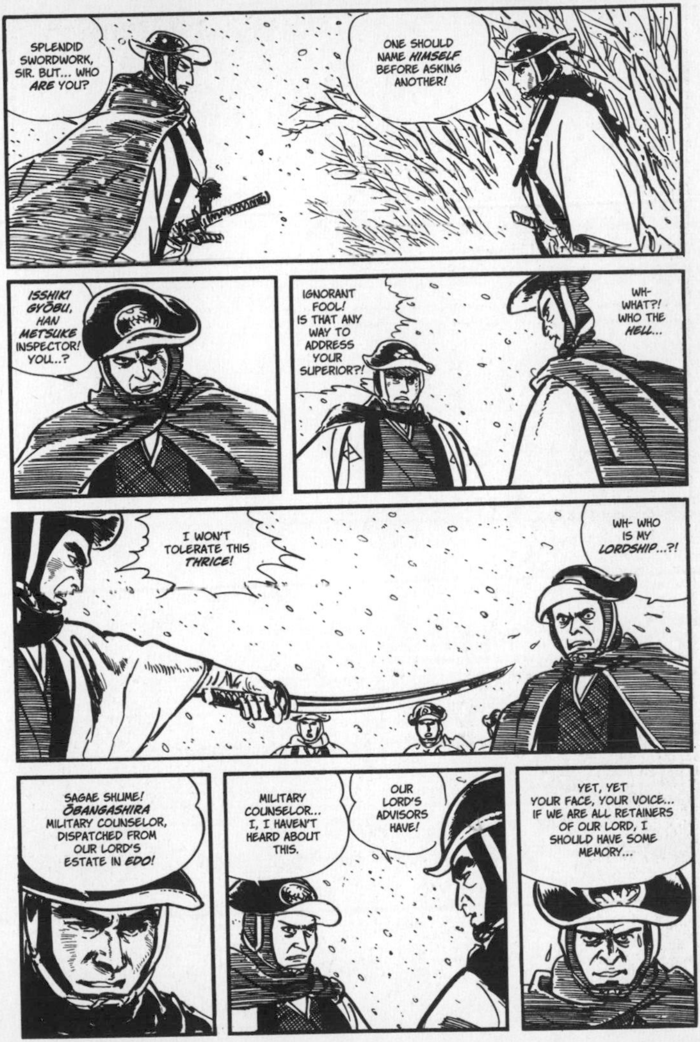
SPLENDID SWORDWORK, SIR. BUT... WHO *ARE* YOU?
ONE SHOULD NAME *HIMSELF* BEFORE ASKING ANOTHER!
ISSHIKI GYŌBU, HAN METSUKE INSPECTOR! YOU...?
IGNORANT FOOL! IS THAT ANY WAY TO ADDRESS YOUR SUPERIOR?!
WH- WHAT?! WHO THE *HELL*...
I WON'T TOLERATE THIS *THRICE*!
WH- WHO IS MY *LORDSHIP*...?!
SAGAE SHUME! *ŌBANGASHIRA* MILITARY COUNSELOR, DISPATCHED FROM OUR LORD'S ESTATE IN *EDO*!
MILITARY COUNSELOR... I, I HAVEN'T HEARD ABOUT THIS.
OUR LORD'S ADVISORS HAVE!
YET, YET YOUR FACE, YOUR VOICE... IF WE ARE ALL RETAINERS OF OUR LORD, I SHOULD HAVE SOME MEMORY...

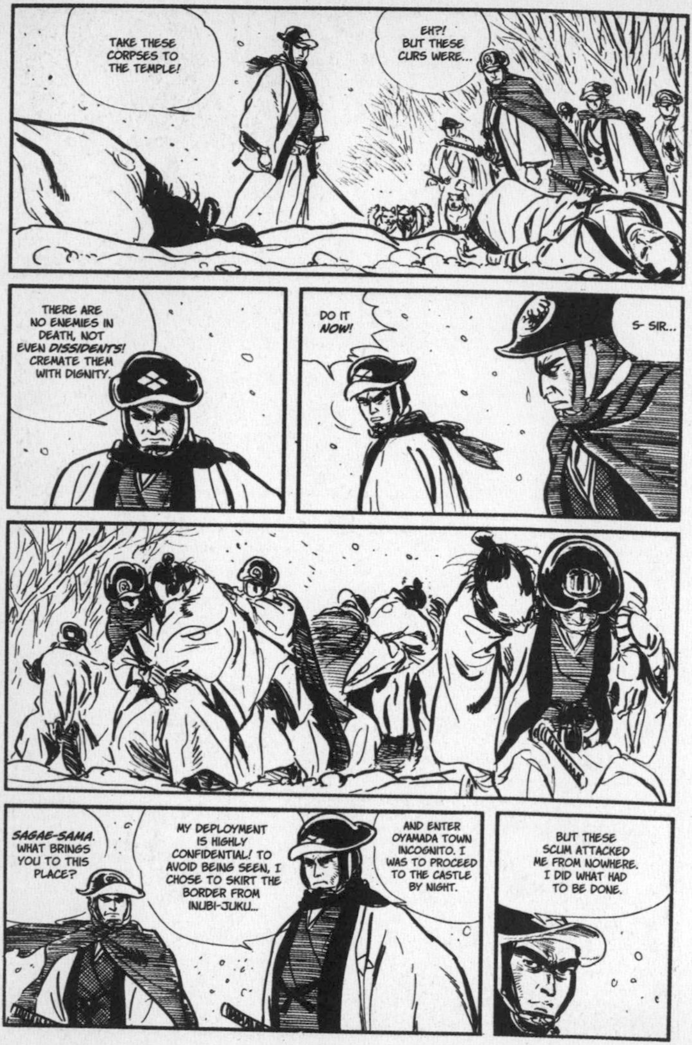
TAKE THESE CORPSES TO THE TEMPLE!
EH?! BUT THESE CURS WERE...
THERE ARE NO ENEMIES IN DEATH, NOT EVEN *DISSIDENTS!* CREMATE THEM WITH DIGNITY.
DO IT *NOW!*
S- SIR...
SAGAE-SAMA. WHAT BRINGS YOU TO THIS PLACE?
MY DEPLOYMENT IS HIGHLY CONFIDENTIAL! TO AVOID BEING SEEN, I CHOSE TO SKIRT THE BORDER FROM INUBI-JUKU...
AND ENTER OYAMADA TOWN INCOGNITO. I WAS TO PROCEED TO THE CASTLE BY NIGHT.
BUT THESE SCUM ATTACKED ME FROM NOWHERE. I DID WHAT HAD TO BE DONE.

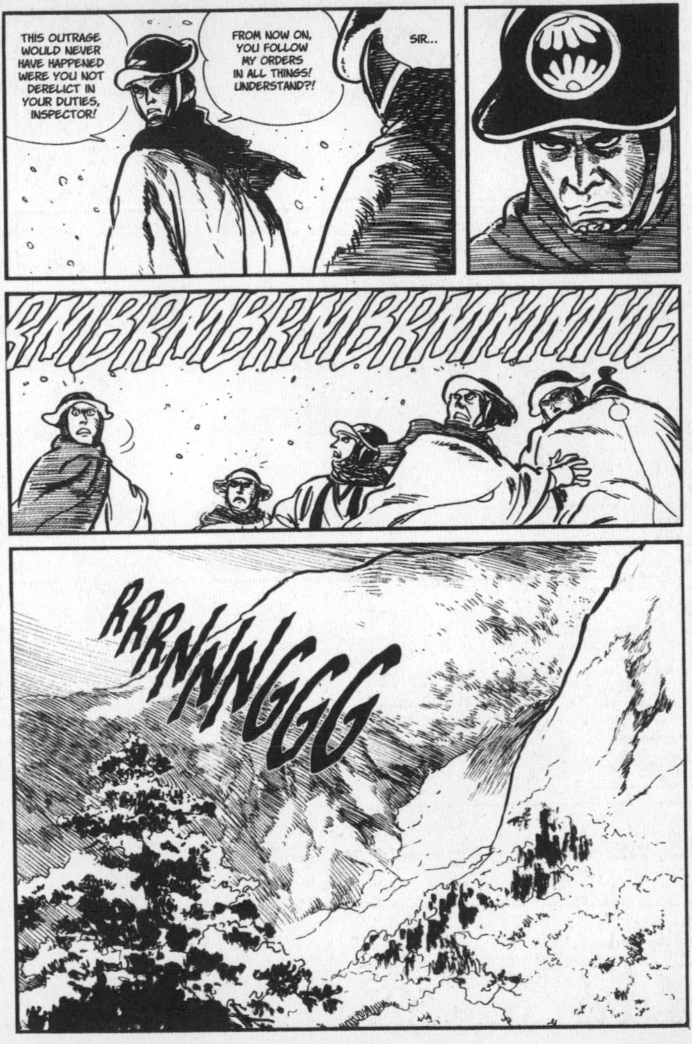
THIS OUTRAGE WOULD NEVER HAVE HAPPENED WERE YOU NOT DERELICT IN YOUR DUTIES, INSPECTOR!
FROM NOW ON, YOU FOLLOW MY ORDERS IN ALL THINGS! UNDERSTAND?!
SIR...
BRRMBRRMBRRMBRRMMMMMMMB
RRRNNNGGG

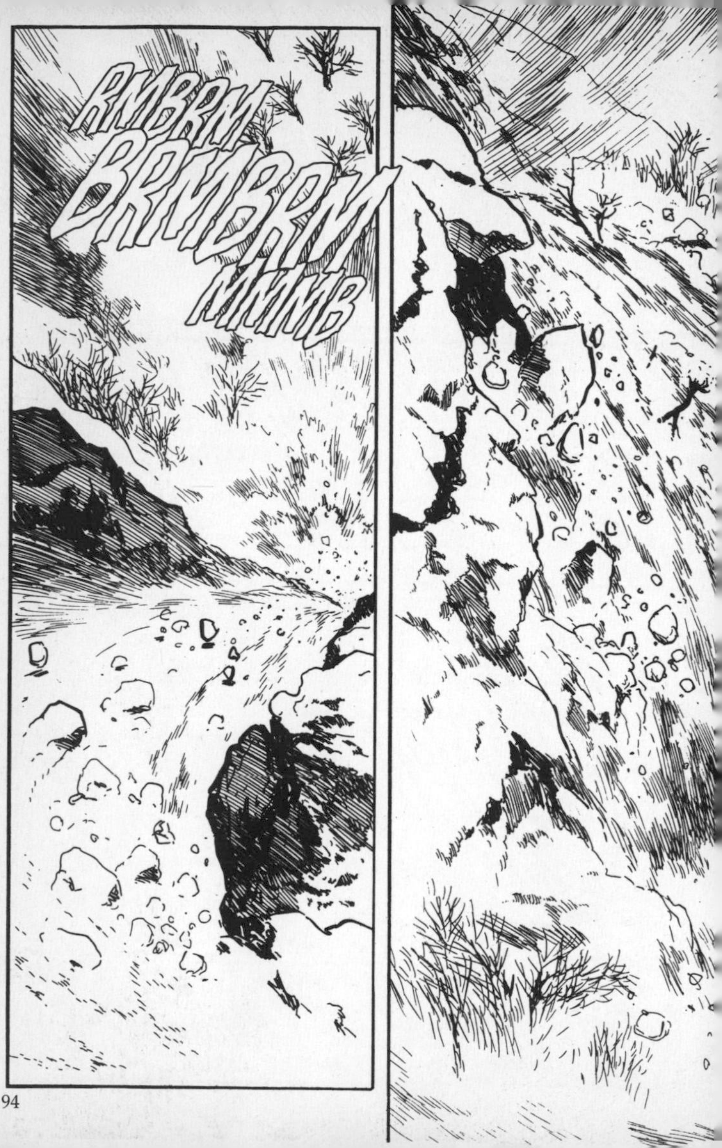
RMBRM
BRMBRM
MMMB

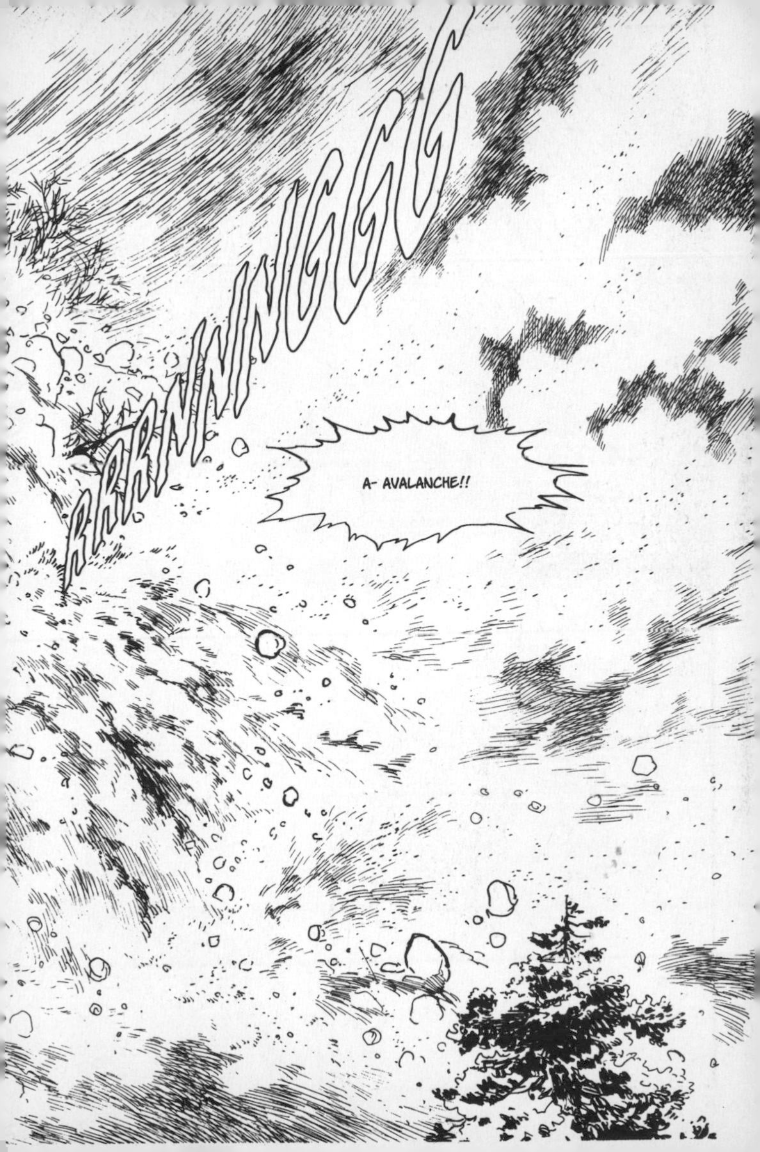
RRRNNNGGG
A- AVALANCHE!!

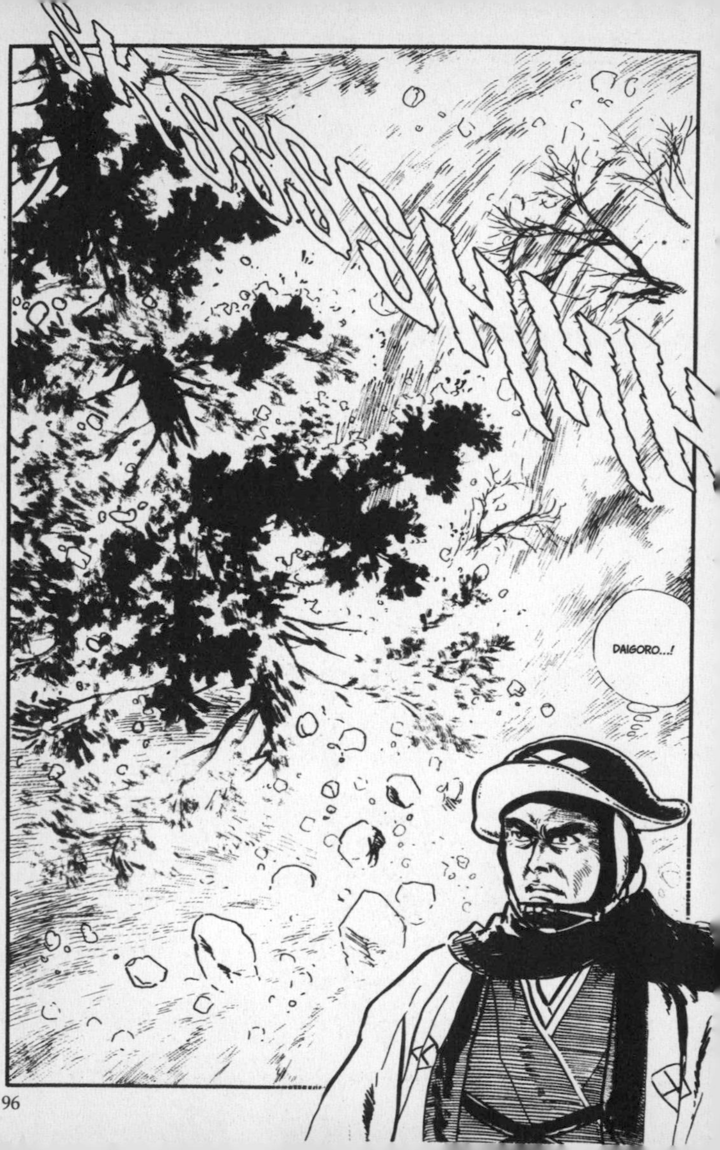
DAIGORO...!

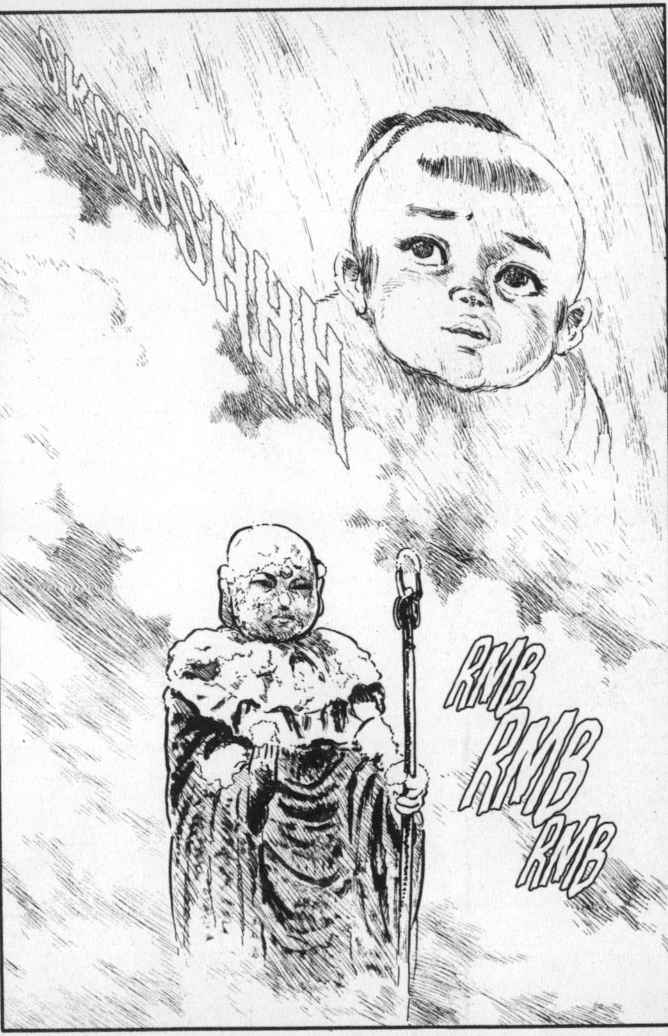
SHOOOSHHH
RMB
RMB
RMB

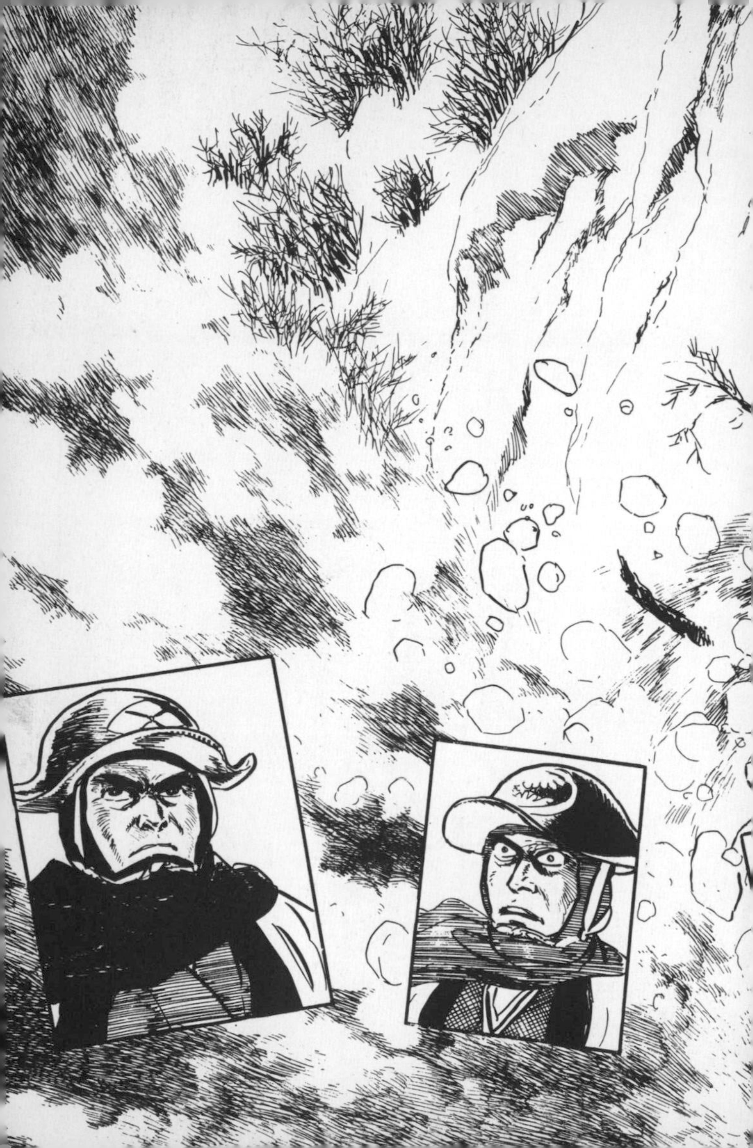

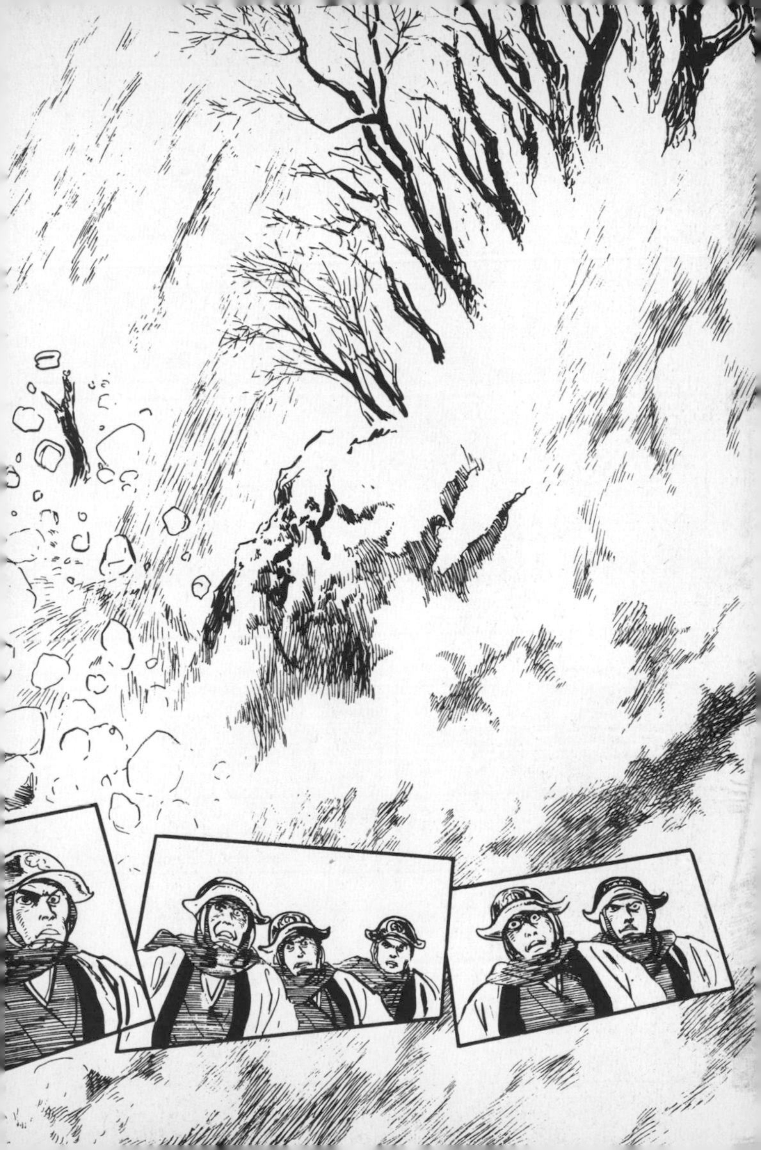

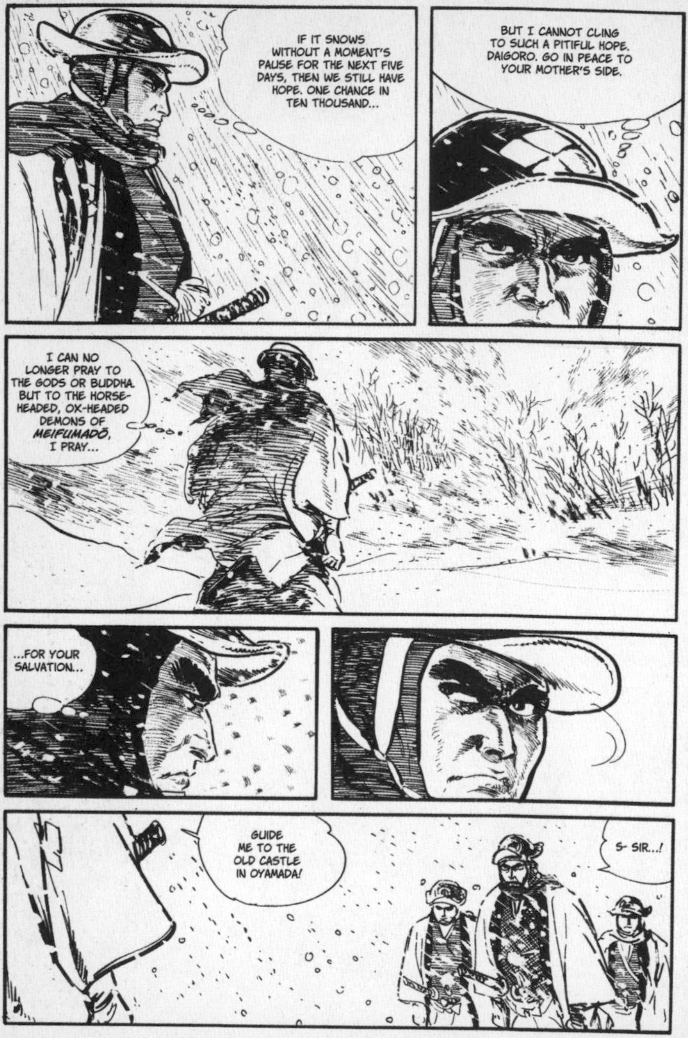
IF IT SNOWS WITHOUT A MOMENT'S PAUSE FOR THE NEXT FIVE DAYS, THEN WE STILL HAVE HOPE. ONE CHANCE IN TEN THOUSAND...
BUT I CANNOT CLING TO SUCH A PITIFUL HOPE. DAIGORO. GO IN PEACE TO YOUR MOTHER'S SIDE.
I CAN NO LONGER PRAY TO THE GODS OR BUDDHA. BUT TO THE HORSE-HEADED, OX-HEADED DEMONS OF *MEIFUMADŌ*, I PRAY...
...FOR YOUR SALVATION...
GUIDE ME TO THE OLD CASTLE IN OYAMADA!
S- SIR...!

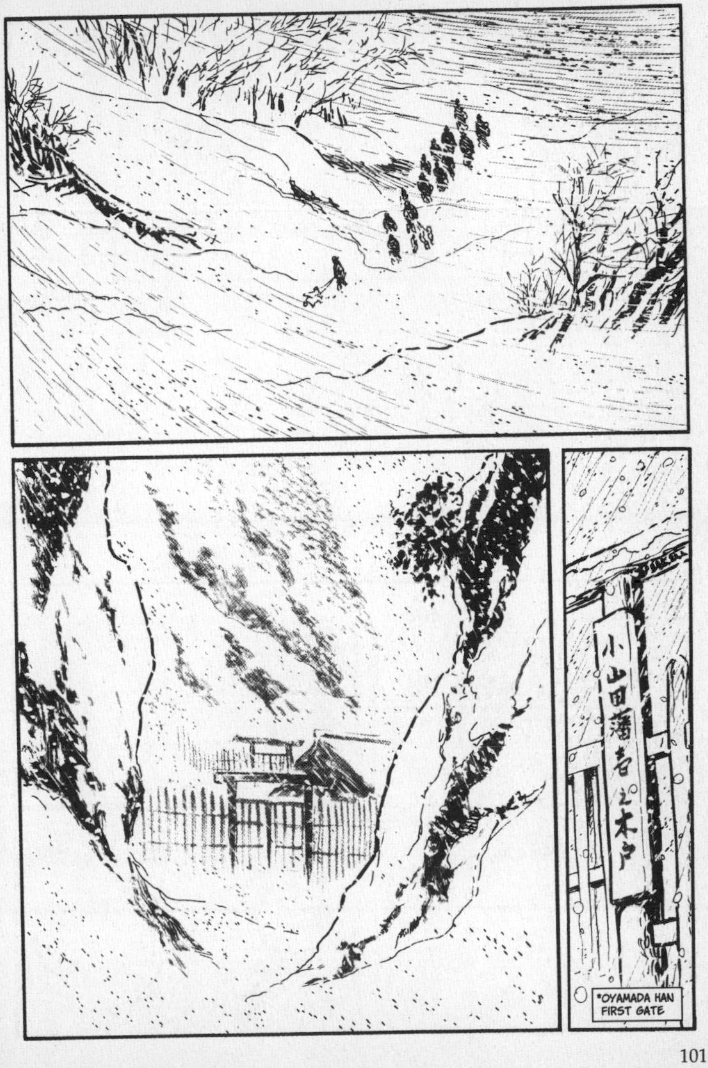
小山田藩壱之木戸
*OYAMADA HAN FIRST GATE

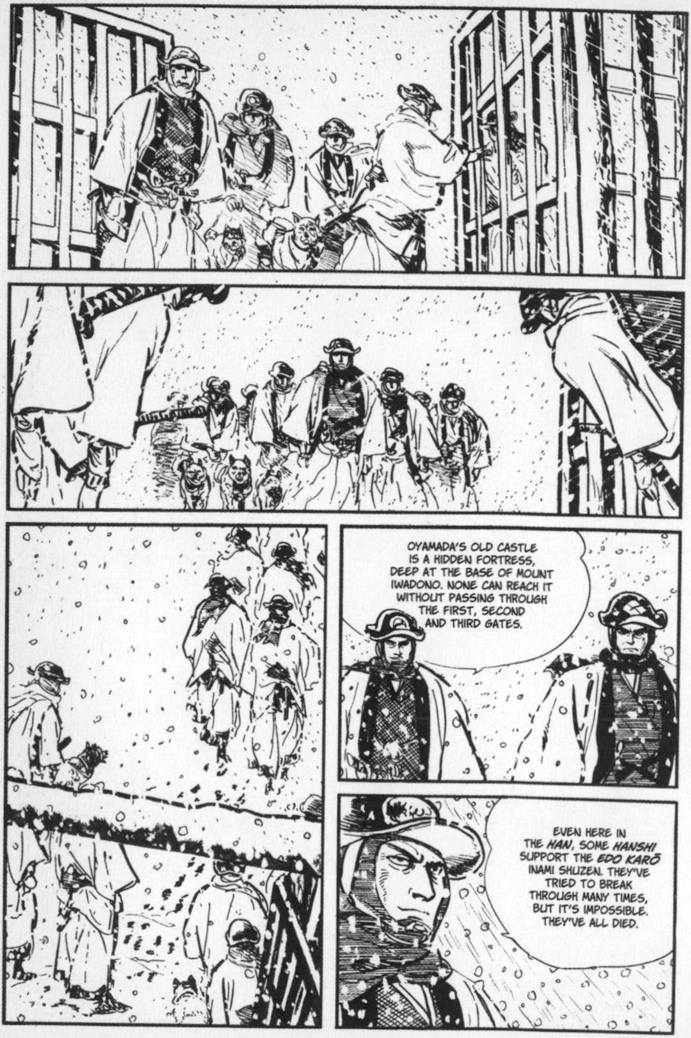
OYAMADA'S OLD CASTLE IS A HIDDEN FORTRESS, DEEP AT THE BASE OF MOUNT IWADONO. NONE CAN REACH IT WITHOUT PASSING THROUGH THE FIRST, SECOND AND THIRD GATES.
EVEN HERE IN THE *HAN*, SOME *HANSHI* SUPPORT THE *EDO KARŌ* INAMI SHUZEN. THEY'VE TRIED TO BREAK THROUGH MANY TIMES, BUT IT'S IMPOSSIBLE. THEY'VE ALL DIED.

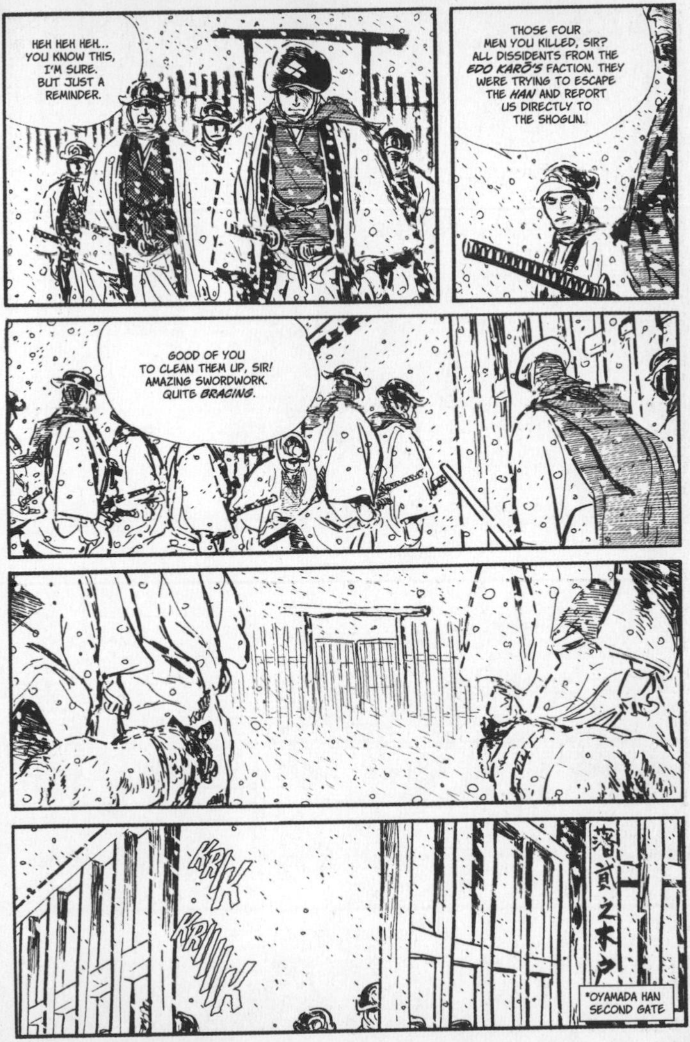
HEH HEH HEH... YOU KNOW THIS, I'M SURE. BUT JUST A REMINDER.
THOSE FOUR MEN YOU KILLED, SIR? ALL DISSIDENTS FROM THE EDO KARŌ'S FACTION. THEY WERE TRYING TO ESCAPE THE HAN AND REPORT US DIRECTLY TO THE SHOGUN.
GOOD OF YOU TO CLEAN THEM UP, SIR! AMAZING SWORDWORK. QUITE BRACING.
KRIK
KRIIIK
*OYAMADA HAN SECOND GATE

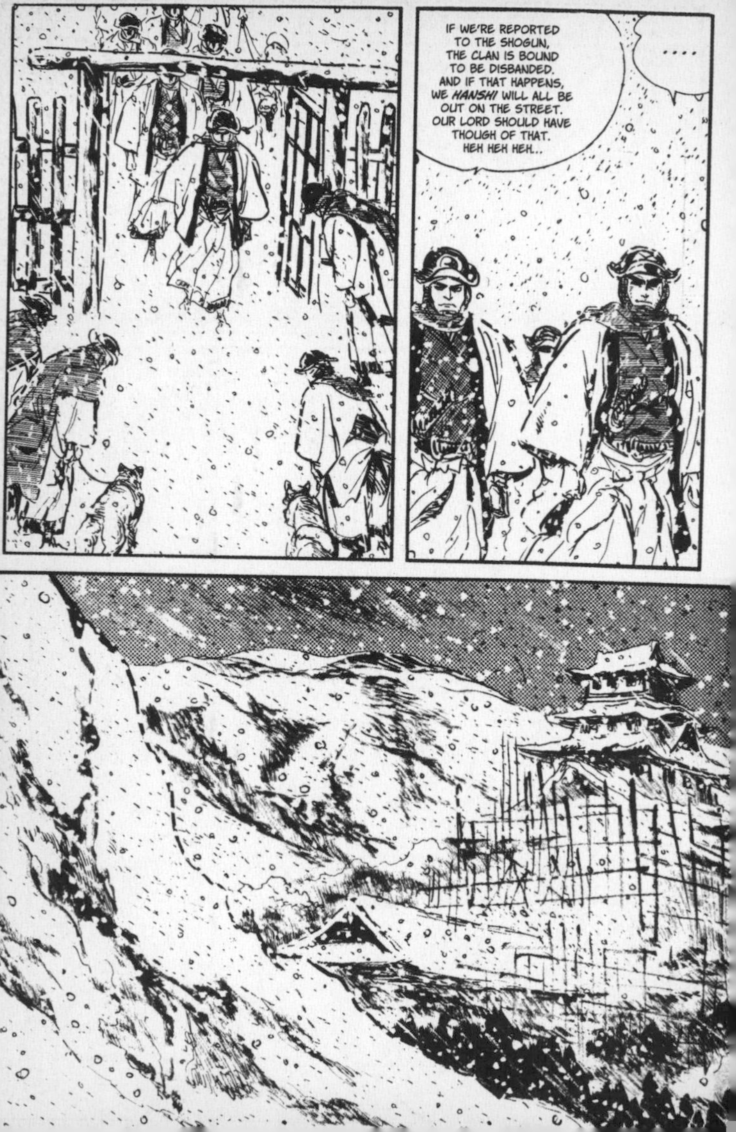
IF WE'RE REPORTED TO THE SHOGUN, THE CLAN IS BOUND TO BE DISBANDED. AND IF THAT HAPPENS, WE *HANSHI* WILL ALL BE OUT ON THE STREET. OUR LORD SHOULD HAVE THOUGH OF THAT. HEH HEH HEH...
....

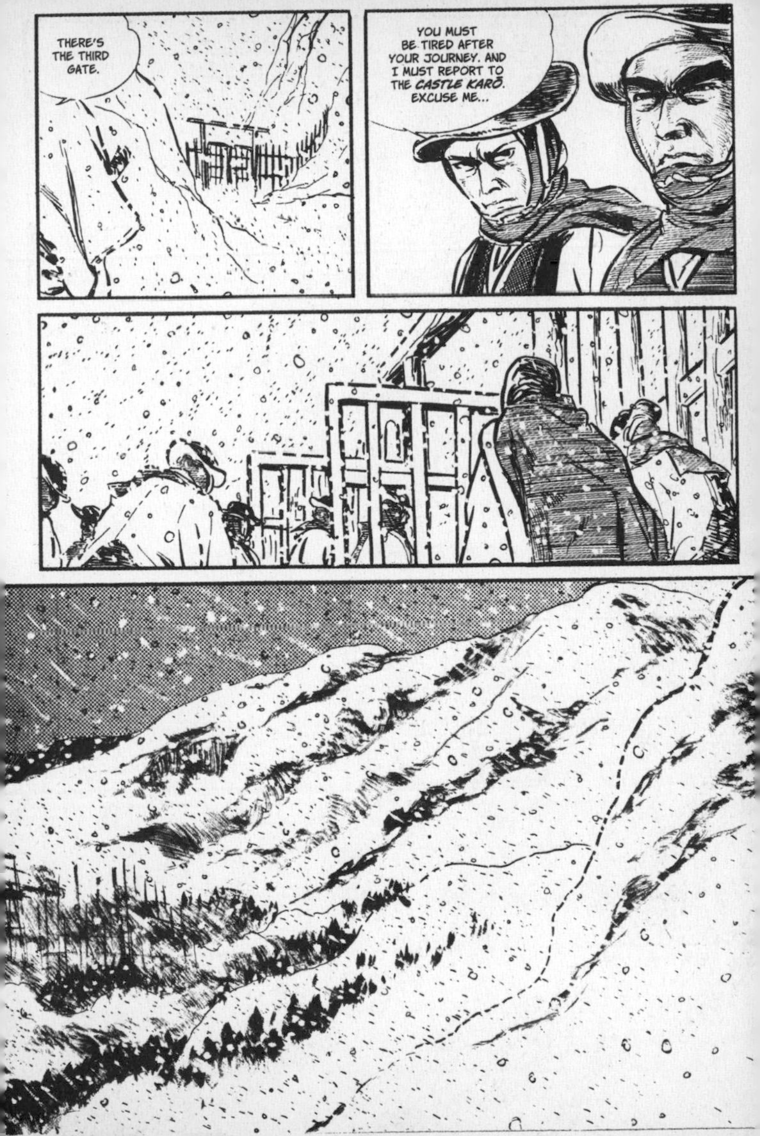
THERE'S THE THIRD GATE.
YOU MUST BE TIRED AFTER YOUR JOURNEY. AND I MUST REPORT TO THE *CASTLE KARŌ*. EXCUSE ME...

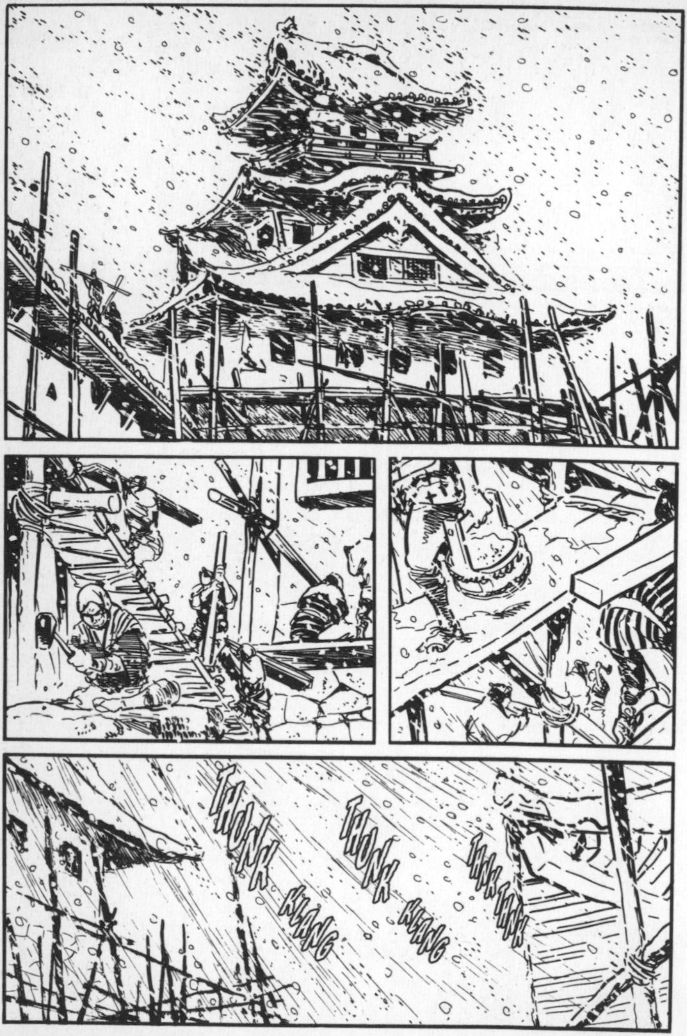
THUNK
KLANG
THUNK
KLANG
TINK TINK

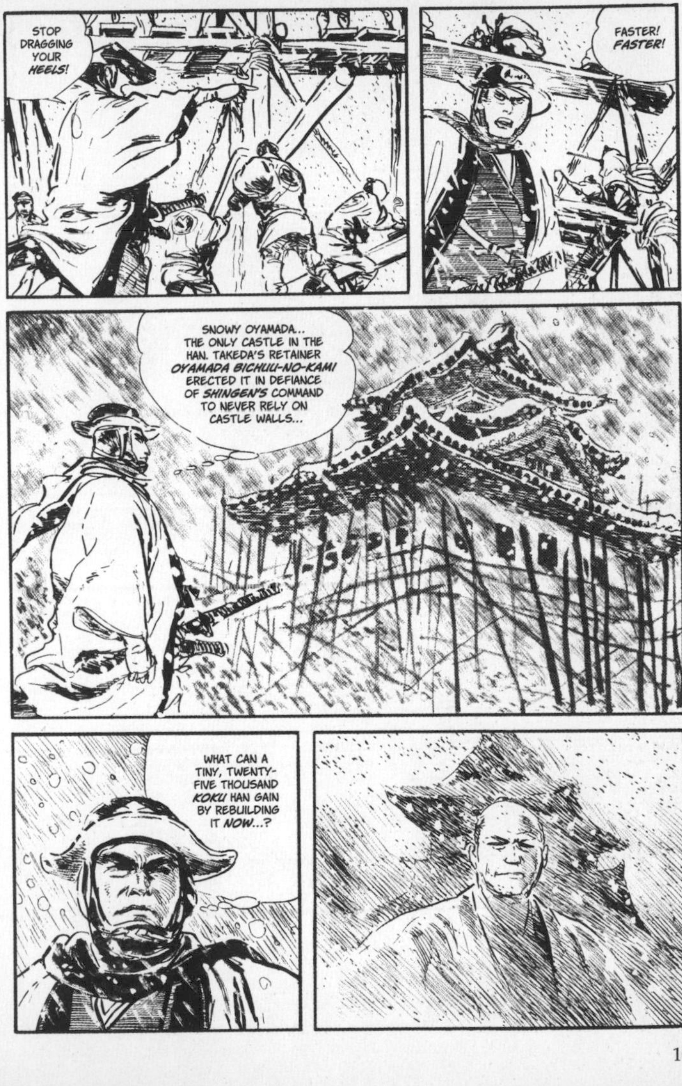
STOP DRAGGING YOUR *HEELS!*
FASTER! *FASTER!*
SNOWY OYAMADA... THE ONLY CASTLE IN THE HAN. TAKEDA'S RETAINER *OYAMADA BICHUU-NO-KAMI* ERECTED IT IN DEFIANCE OF *SHINGEN'S* COMMAND TO NEVER RELY ON CASTLE WALLS...
WHAT CAN A TINY, TWENTY-FIVE THOUSAND *KOKU* HAN GAIN BY REBUILDING IT *NOW*...?

ALMOST ALL OF *KŌSHŪ* IS *TENRYŌ* LAND BELONGING TO THE SHOGUN HIMSELF, CONTROLLED BY THE SHOGUN'S *KŌSHŪ* MAGISTRATE... OUR LORD'S CLAN, GRANTED A MERE HANDFUL OF THAT LAND, ARE *JINYA* BATTLEFIELD *DAIMYŌ*, FORBIDDEN TO HAVE A CASTLE OF THEIR OWN...

YET EVEN HERE IN THE LAND OF *TAKEDA SHINGEN* THERE WAS ALREADY A CASTLE, LEFT BY OUR ANCESTORS. OUR RETIRED *DAIMYŌ*, LORD *ICHIŌ*, DECIDED TO REBUILD IT FOR HIS PERSONAL RESIDENCE.

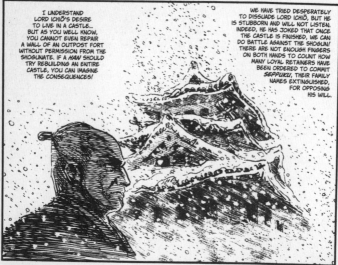

I UNDERSTAND LORD ICHIŌ'S DESIRE TO LIVE IN A CASTLE... BUT AS YOU WELL KNOW, YOU CANNOT EVEN REPAIR A WALL OF AN OUTPOST FORT WITHOUT PERMISSION FROM THE SHOGUNATE. IF A *HAN* SHOULD TRY REBUILDING AN ENTIRE CASTLE, YOU CAN IMAGINE THE CONSEQUENCES!

WE HAVE TRIED DESPERATELY TO DISSUADE LORD ICHIŌ, BUT HE IS STUBBORN AND WILL NOT LISTEN. INDEED, HE HAS JOKED THAT ONCE THE CASTLE IS FINISHED, WE CAN DO BATTLE AGAINST THE SHOGUN! THERE ARE NOT ENOUGH FINGERS ON BOTH HANDS TO COUNT HOW MANY LOYAL RETAINERS HAVE BEEN ORDERED TO COMMIT *SEPPUKU*, THEIR FAMILY NAMES EXTINGUISHED, FOR OPPOSING HIS WILL.

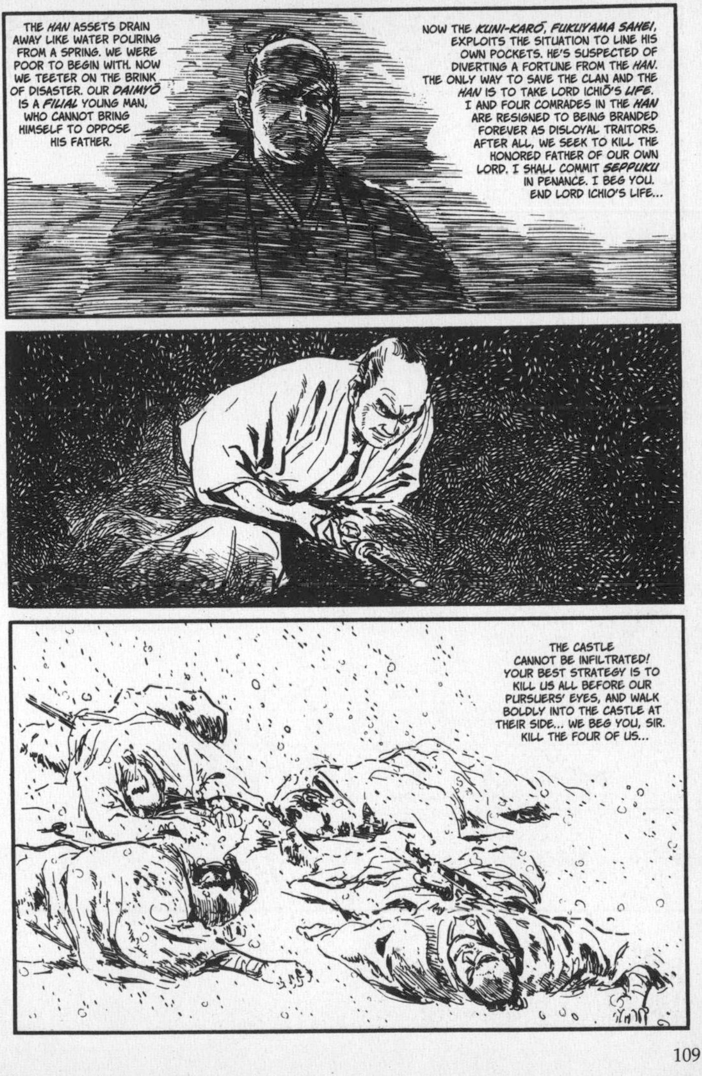
THE HAN ASSETS DRAIN AWAY LIKE WATER POURING FROM A SPRING. WE WERE POOR TO BEGIN WITH. NOW WE TEETER ON THE BRINK OF DISASTER. OUR DAIMYŌ IS A FILIAL YOUNG MAN, WHO CANNOT BRING HIMSELF TO OPPOSE HIS FATHER.
NOW THE KUNI-KARŌ, FUKUYAMA SAHEI, EXPLOITS THE SITUATION TO LINE HIS OWN POCKETS. HE'S SUSPECTED OF DIVERTING A FORTUNE FROM THE HAN. THE ONLY WAY TO SAVE THE CLAN AND THE HAN IS TO TAKE LORD ICHIŌ'S LIFE. I AND FOUR COMRADES IN THE HAN ARE RESIGNED TO BEING BRANDED FOREVER AS DISLOYAL TRAITORS. AFTER ALL, WE SEEK TO KILL THE HONORED FATHER OF OUR OWN LORD. I SHALL COMMIT SEPPUKU IN PENANCE. I BEG YOU. END LORD ICHIO'S LIFE...
THE CASTLE CANNOT BE INFILTRATED! YOUR BEST STRATEGY IS TO KILL US ALL BEFORE OUR PURSUERS' EYES, AND WALK BOLDLY INTO THE CASTLE AT THEIR SIDE... WE BEG YOU, SIR. KILL THE FOUR OF US...

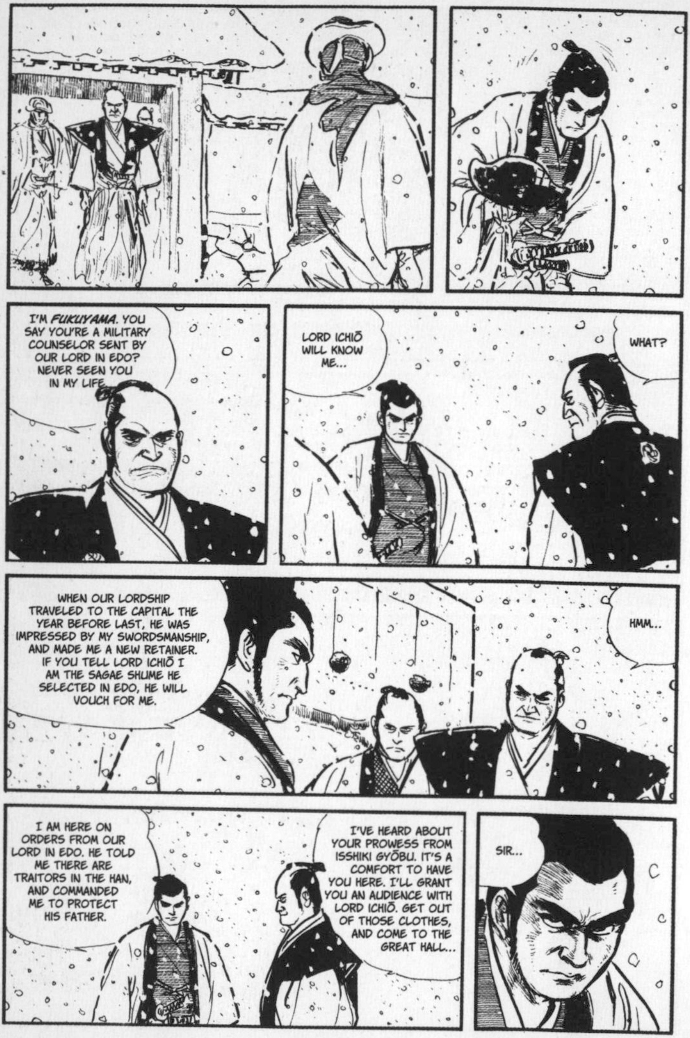

I'M FUKUYAMA. YOU SAY YOU'RE A MILITARY COUNSELOR SENT BY OUR LORD IN EDO? NEVER SEEN YOU IN MY LIFE.
LORD ICHIŌ WILL KNOW ME...
WHAT?
WHEN OUR LORDSHIP TRAVELED TO THE CAPITAL THE YEAR BEFORE LAST, HE WAS IMPRESSED BY MY SWORDSMANSHIP, AND MADE ME A NEW RETAINER. IF YOU TELL LORD ICHIŌ I AM THE SAGAE SHUME HE SELECTED IN EDO, HE WILL VOUCH FOR ME.
HMM...
I AM HERE ON ORDERS FROM OUR LORD IN EDO. HE TOLD ME THERE ARE TRAITORS IN THE HAN, AND COMMANDED ME TO PROTECT HIS FATHER.
I'VE HEARD ABOUT YOUR PROWESS FROM ISSHIKI GYŌBU. IT'S A COMFORT TO HAVE YOU HERE. I'LL GRANT YOU AN AUDIENCE WITH LORD ICHIŌ. GET OUT OF THOSE CLOTHES, AND COME TO THE GREAT HALL...
SIR...

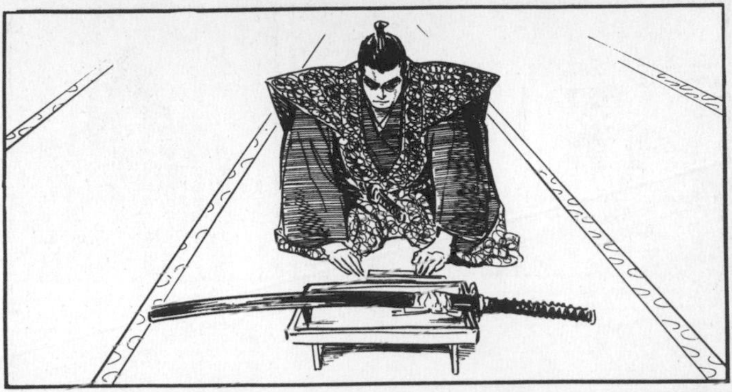
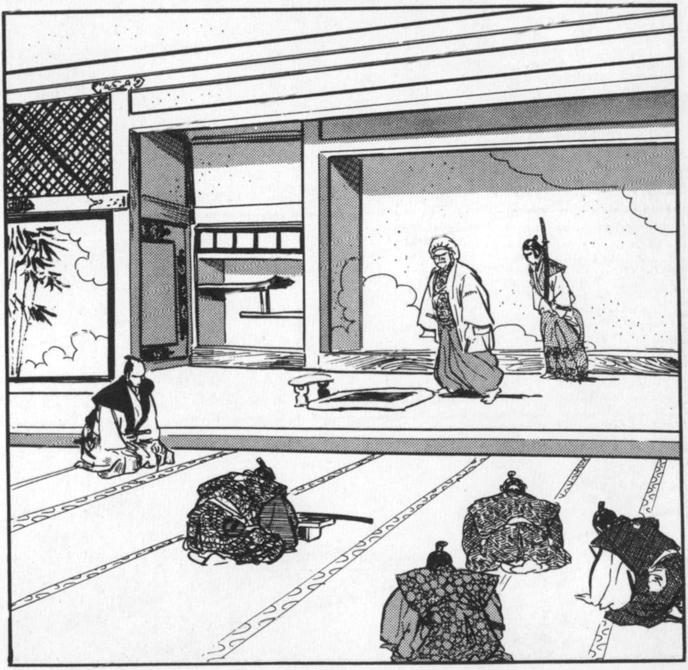

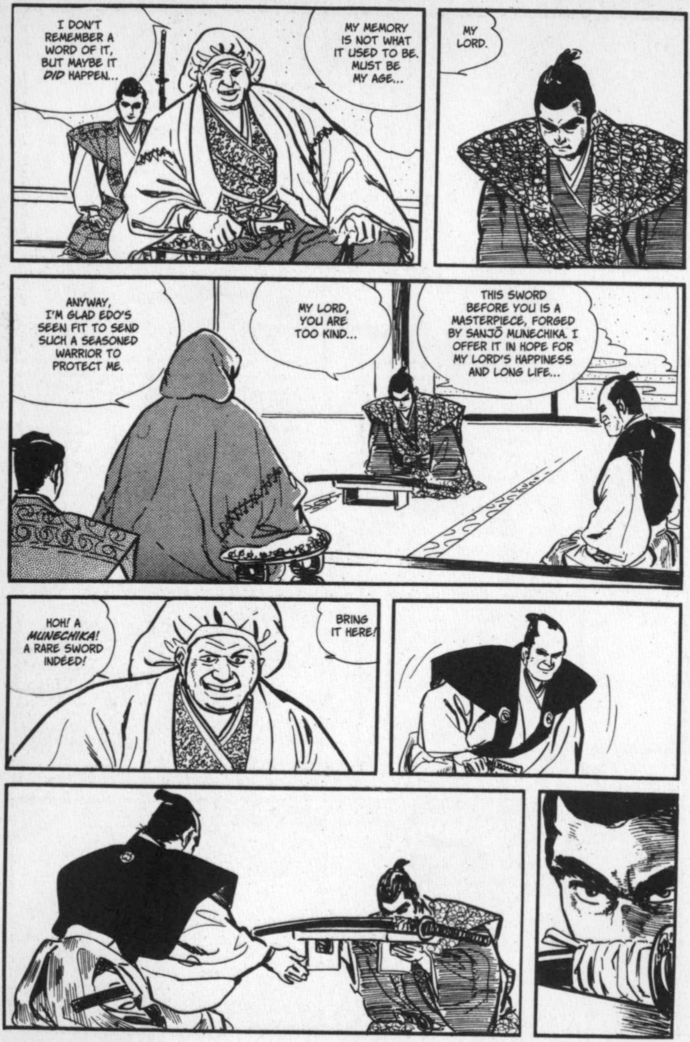
I DON'T REMEMBER A WORD OF IT, BUT MAYBE IT *DID* HAPPEN...
MY MEMORY IS NOT WHAT IT USED TO BE. MUST BE MY AGE...
MY LORD.
ANYWAY, I'M GLAD EDO'S SEEN FIT TO SEND SUCH A SEASONED WARRIOR TO PROTECT ME.
MY LORD, YOU ARE TOO KIND...
THIS SWORD BEFORE YOU IS A MASTERPIECE, FORGED BY SANJŌ MUNECHIKA. I OFFER IT IN HOPE FOR MY LORD'S HAPPINESS AND LONG LIFE...
HOH! A *MUNECHIKA!* A RARE SWORD INDEED!
BRING IT HERE!

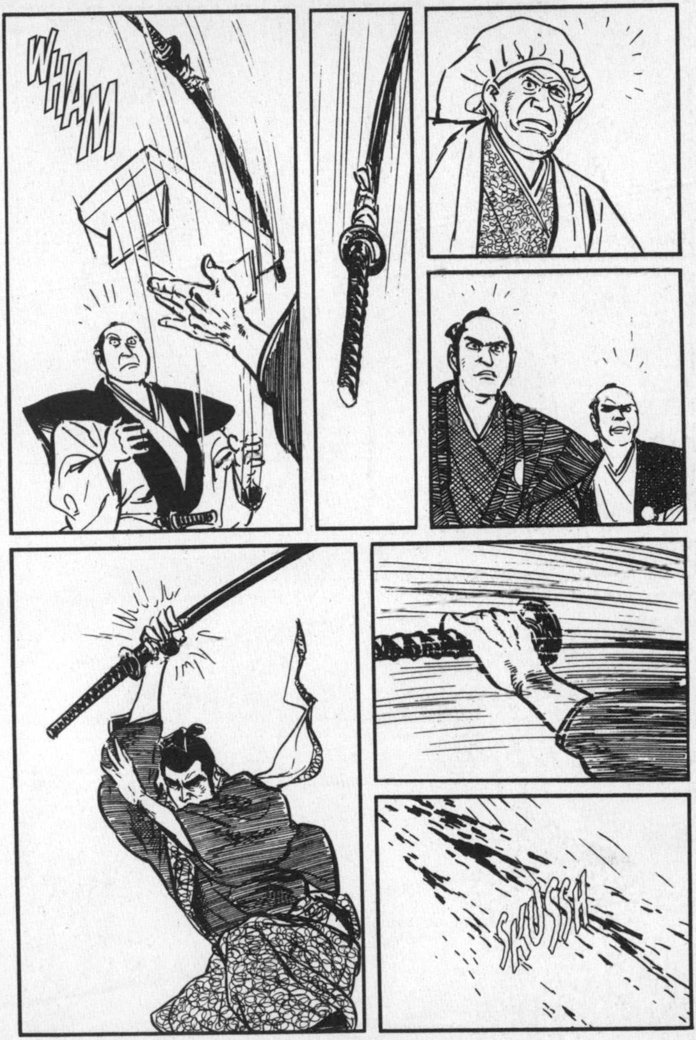
WHAM
SKUSSH

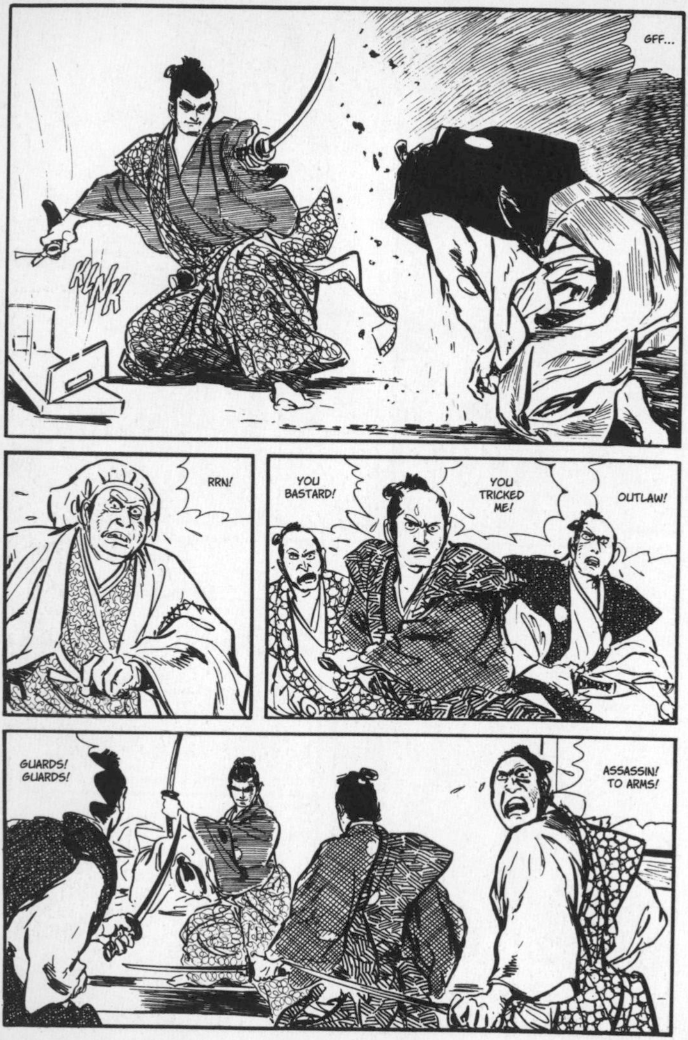
GFF...
KLINK
RRN!
YOU BASTARD!
YOU TRICKED ME!
OUTLAW!
GUARDS! GUARDS!
ASSASSIN! TO ARMS!

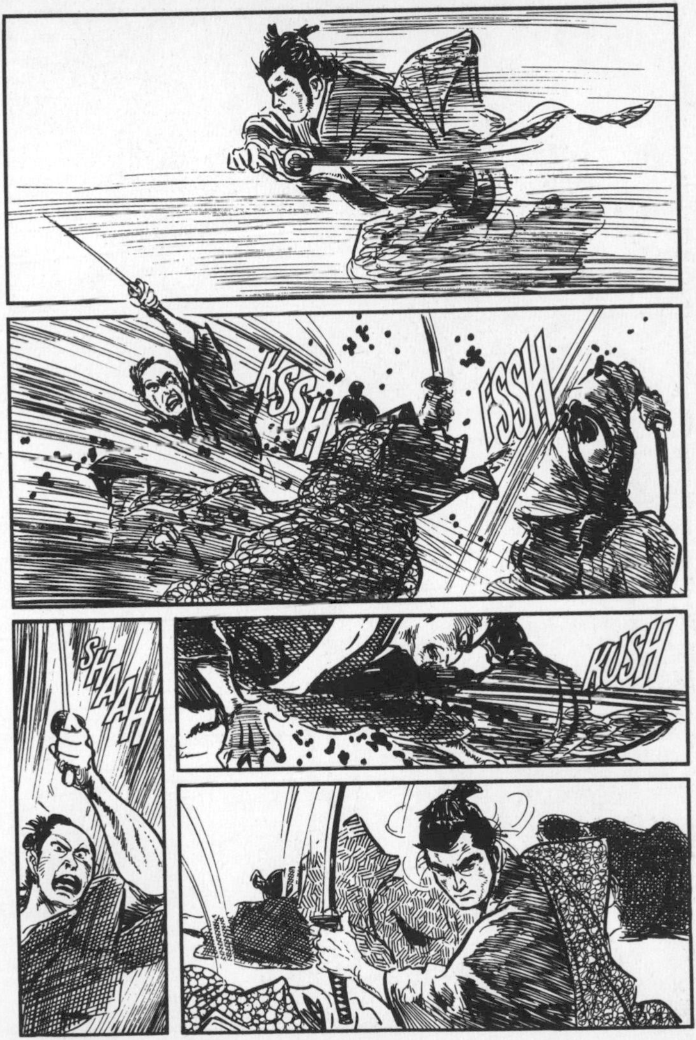
KSSH
FSSH
SHAAH
KUSH

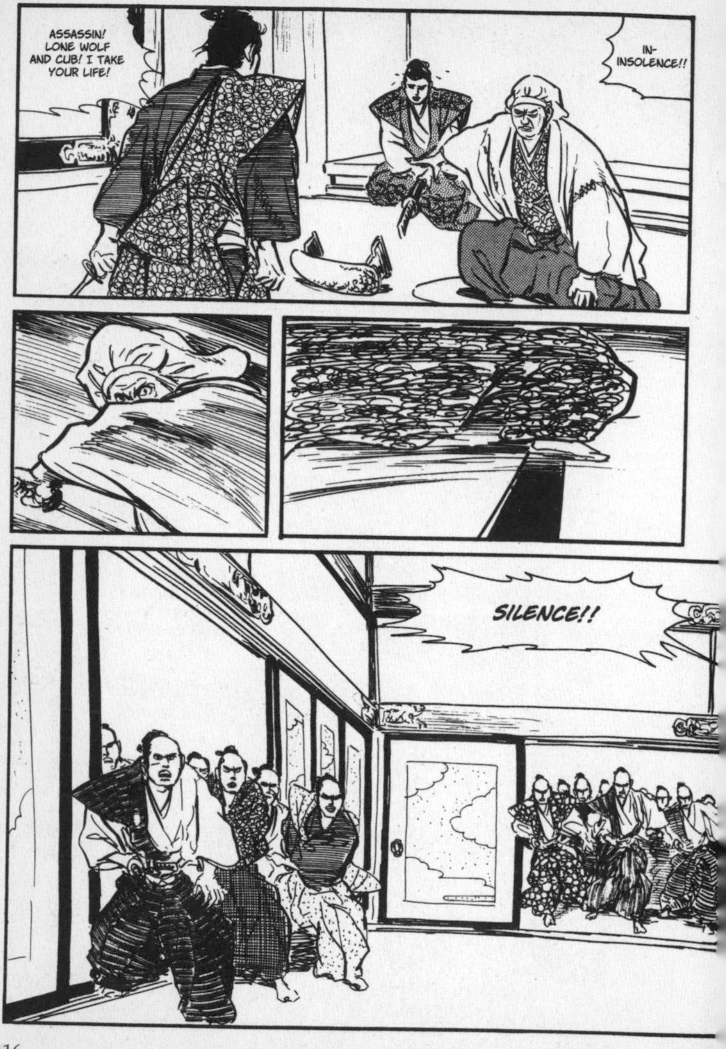
ASSASSIN! LONE WOLF AND CUB! I TAKE YOUR LIFE!
IN-INSOLENCE!!
SILENCE!!

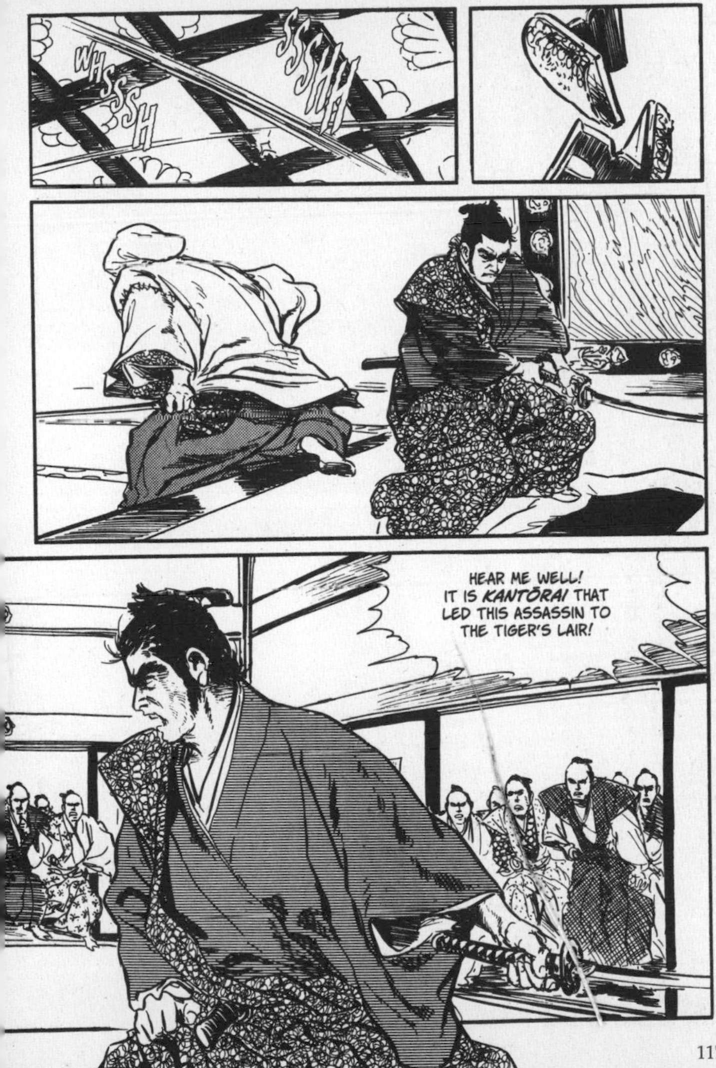
WHSSH
SSSH
HEAR ME WELL! IT IS KANTŌRAI THAT LED THIS ASSASSIN TO THE TIGER'S LAIR!

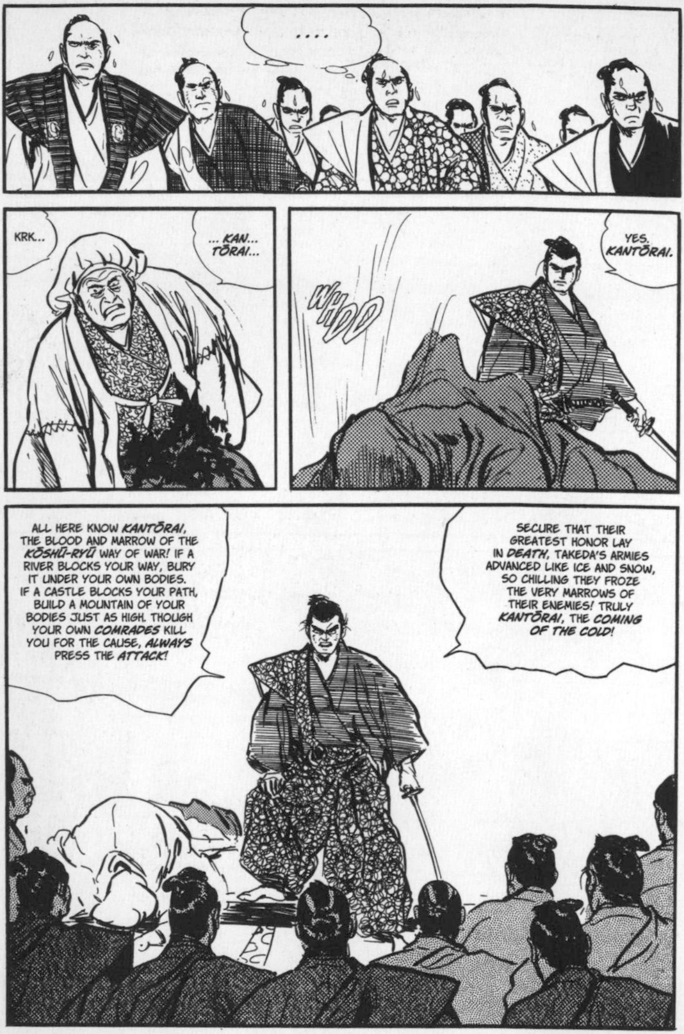
....
KRK...
... KAN... TŌRAI...
WHOO
YES. KANTŌRAI.
ALL HERE KNOW KANTŌRAI, THE BLOOD AND MARROW OF THE KŌSHŪ-RYŪ WAY OF WAR! IF A RIVER BLOCKS YOUR WAY, BURY IT UNDER YOUR OWN BODIES. IF A CASTLE BLOCKS YOUR PATH, BUILD A MOUNTAIN OF YOUR BODIES JUST AS HIGH. THOUGH YOUR OWN COMRADES KILL YOU FOR THE CAUSE, ALWAYS PRESS THE ATTACK!
SECURE THAT THEIR GREATEST HONOR LAY IN DEATH, TAKEDA'S ARMIES ADVANCED LIKE ICE AND SNOW, SO CHILLING THEY FROZE THE VERY MARROWS OF THEIR ENEMIES! TRULY KANTŌRAI, THE COMING OF THE COLD!

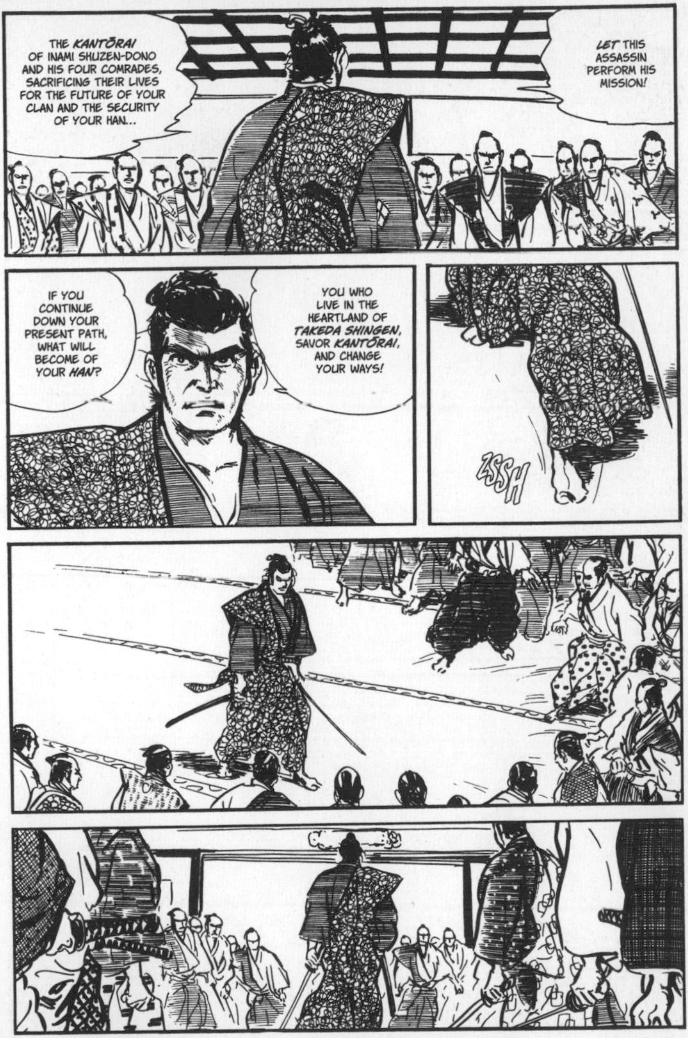
THE *KANTŌRAI* OF INAMI SHUZEN-DONO AND HIS FOUR COMRADES, SACRIFICING THEIR LIVES FOR THE FUTURE OF YOUR CLAN AND THE SECURITY OF YOUR HAN...
LET THIS ASSASSIN PERFORM HIS MISSION!
IF YOU CONTINUE DOWN YOUR PRESENT PATH, WHAT WILL BECOME OF YOUR *HAN*?
YOU WHO LIVE IN THE HEARTLAND OF *TAKEDA SHINGEN*, SAVOR *KANTŌRAI*, AND CHANGE YOUR WAYS!
ZSSH

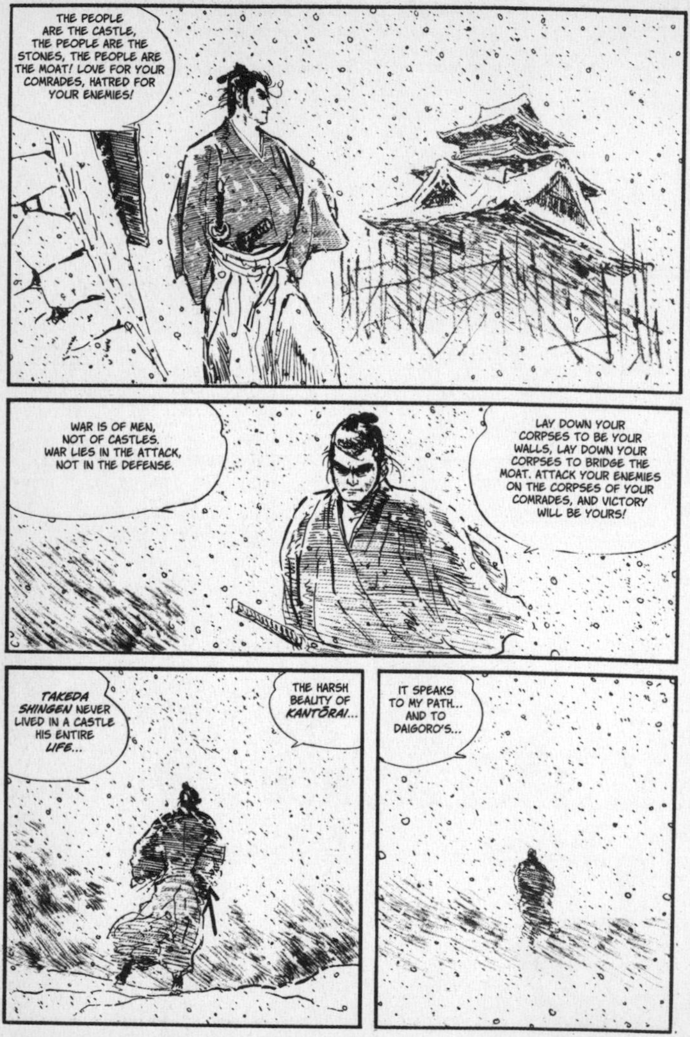
THE PEOPLE ARE THE CASTLE, THE PEOPLE ARE THE STONES, THE PEOPLE ARE THE MOAT! LOVE FOR YOUR COMRADES, HATRED FOR YOUR ENEMIES!
WAR IS OF MEN, NOT OF CASTLES. WAR LIES IN THE ATTACK, NOT IN THE DEFENSE.
LAY DOWN YOUR CORPSES TO BE YOUR WALLS, LAY DOWN YOUR CORPSES TO BRIDGE THE MOAT. ATTACK YOUR ENEMIES ON THE CORPSES OF YOUR COMRADES, AND VICTORY WILL BE YOURS!
TAKEDA SHINGEN NEVER LIVED IN A CASTLE HIS ENTIRE *LIFE*...
THE HARSH BEAUTY OF *KANTŌRAI*...
IT SPEAKS TO MY PATH... AND TO DAIGORO'S...

PERHAPS OGAMI'S
PRAYERS TO
MEIFUMADO
HAD BEEN HEARD...
FOR FIVE DAYS
AND NIGHTS, IT
SNOWED WITH-
OUT PAUSE.

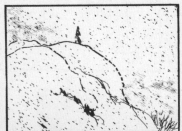

121

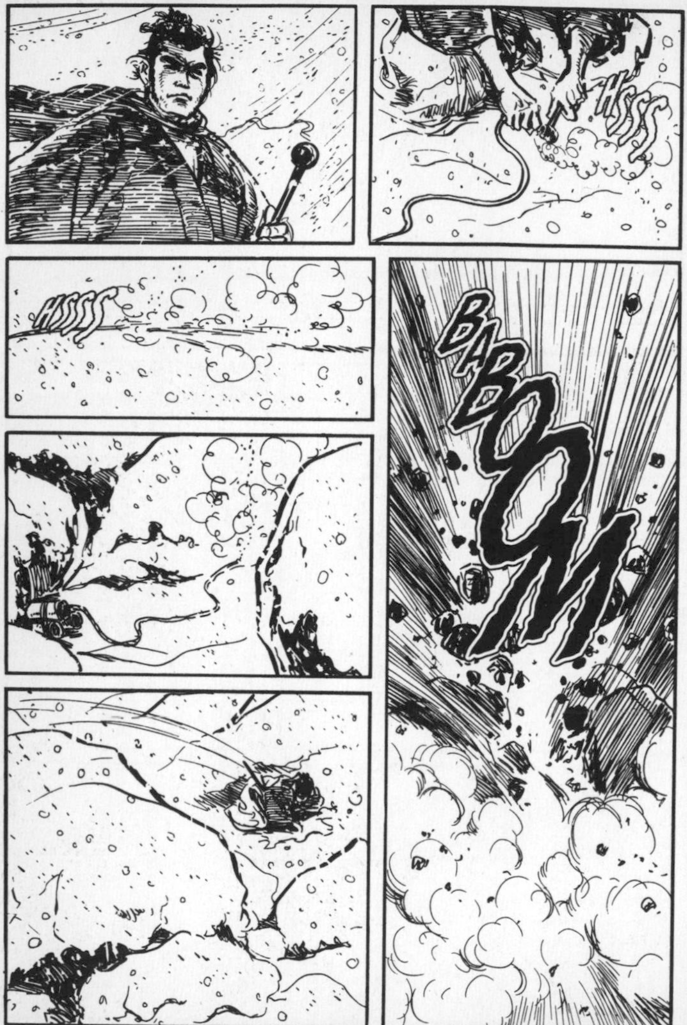
HSSS
HSSS
BADOOM

RMBRMB

WITH FIVE DAYS OF SNOWFALL, I CAN TRIGGER A LARGER AVALANCHE THAN THE FIRST...

RMBRM BRMBRM BRMB

IF THE SECOND AVALANCHE IS LARGER, IT SHOULD PUSH ASIDE THE SNOW LEFT BY THE FIRST AVALANCHE, AND RUN FURTHER DOWN THE SLOPE...

ONE CHANCE IN TEN THOUSAND. BUT IF THE DEMONS OF HELL ARE WITH US...

123

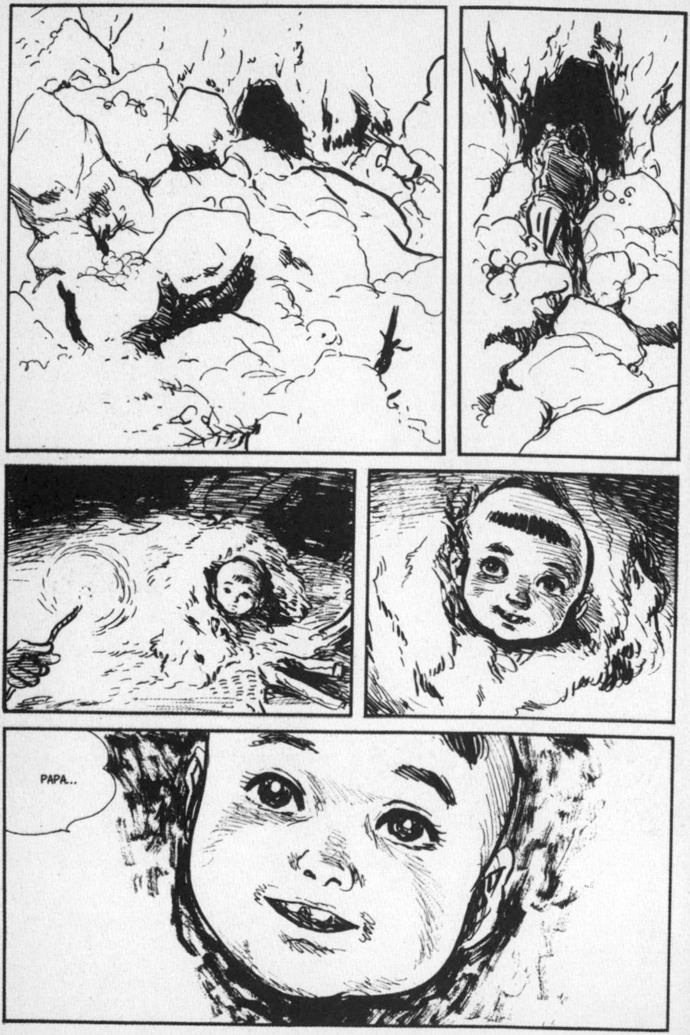
PAPA..

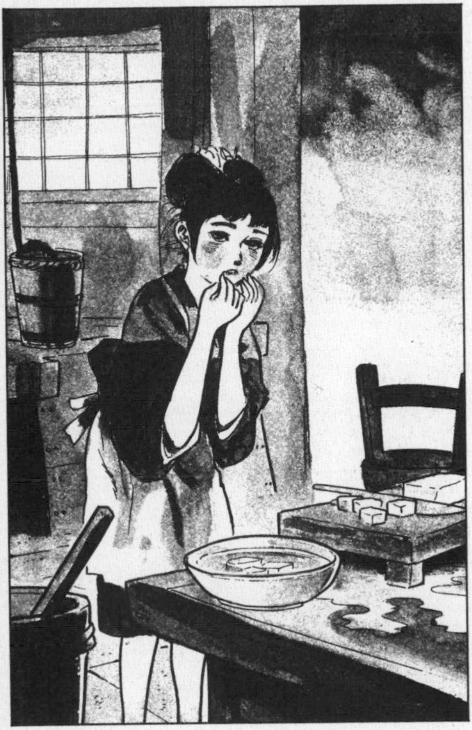

the twelfth

Tragic O-Sue

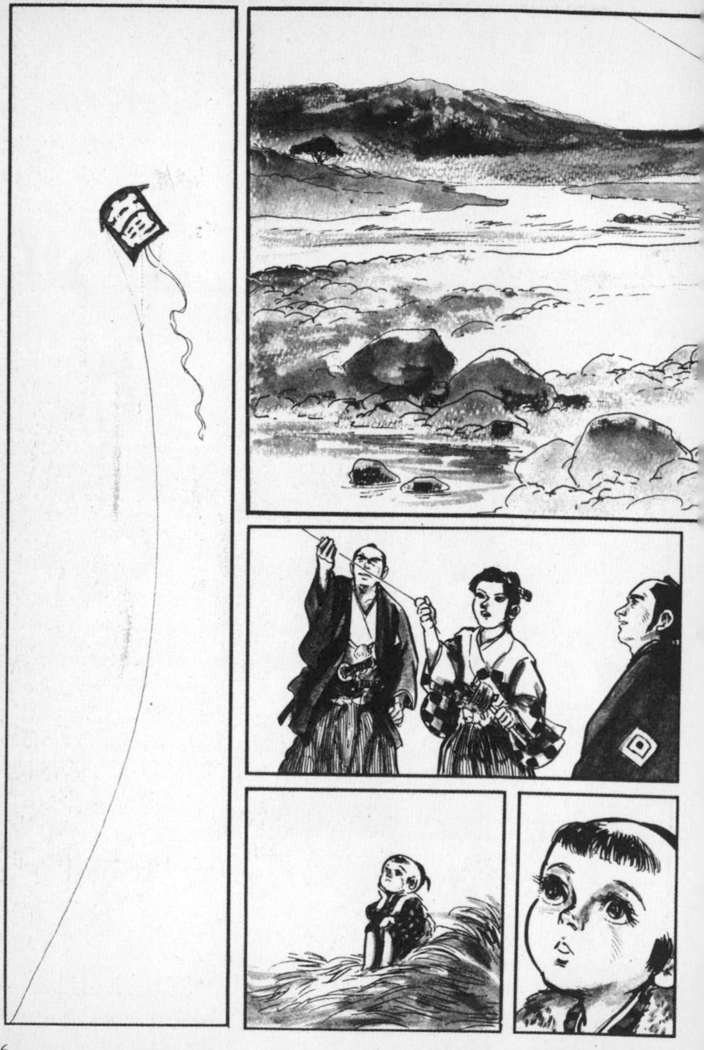

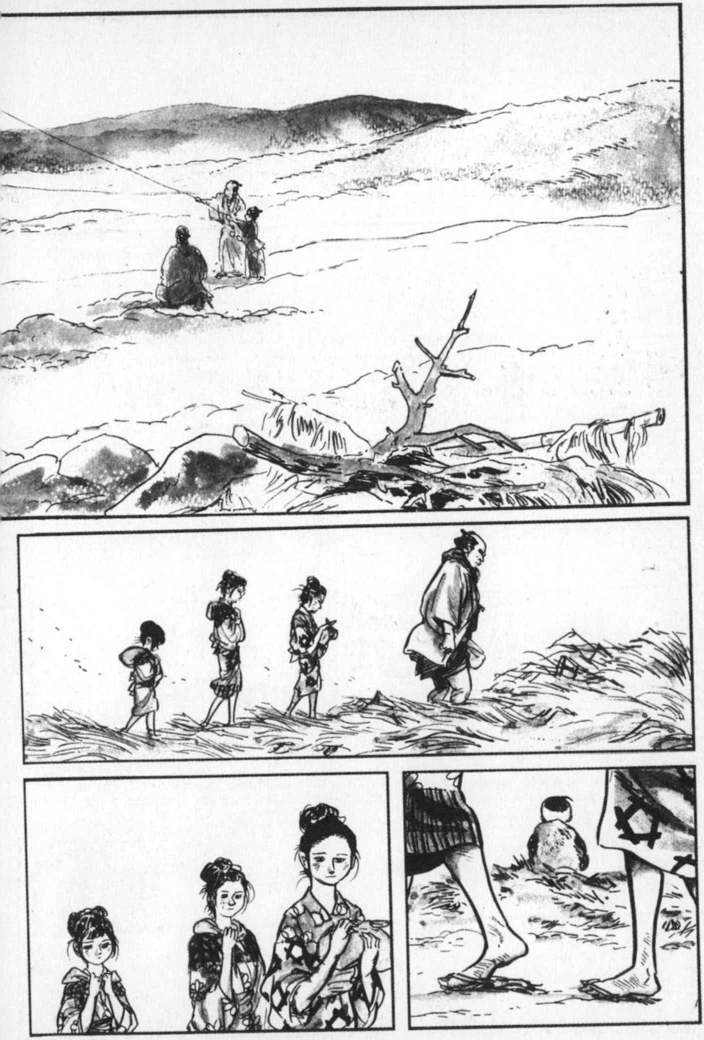

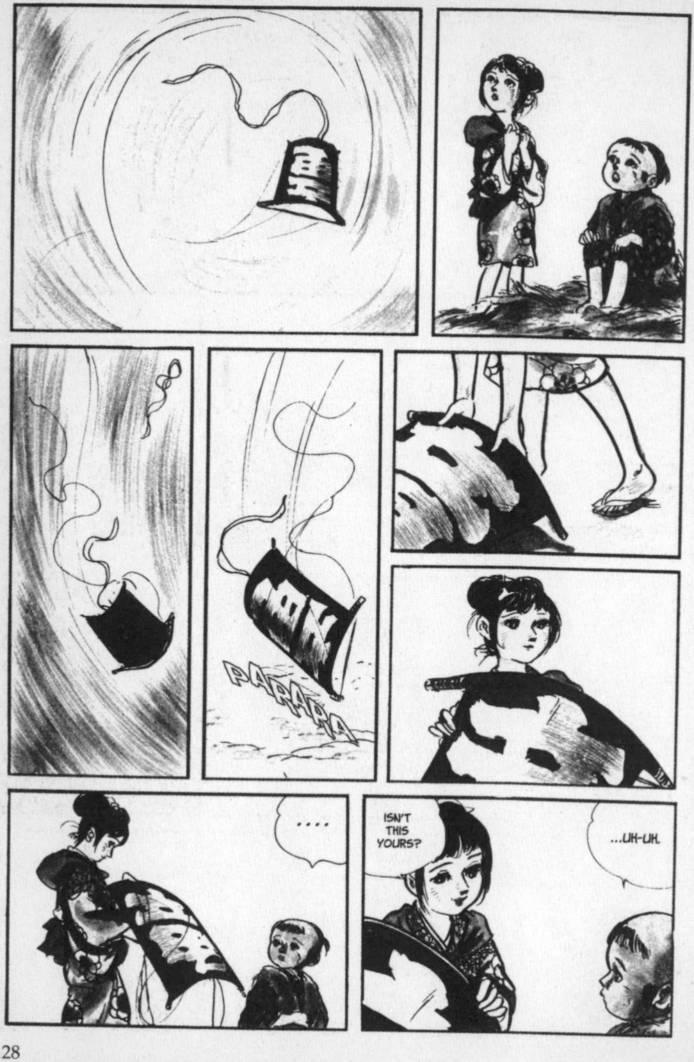
PAPARA
...UH-UH.
ISN'T THIS YOURS?
....

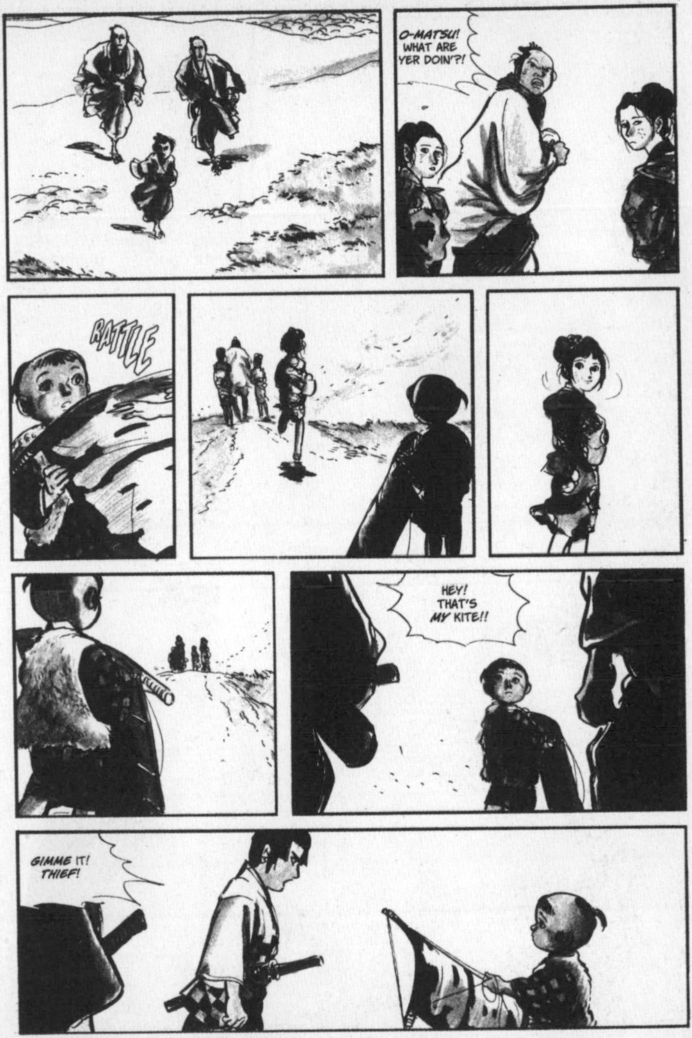

O-MATSU! WHAT ARE YER DOIN'?!
RATTLE
HEY! THAT'S MY KITE!!
GIMME IT! THIEF!

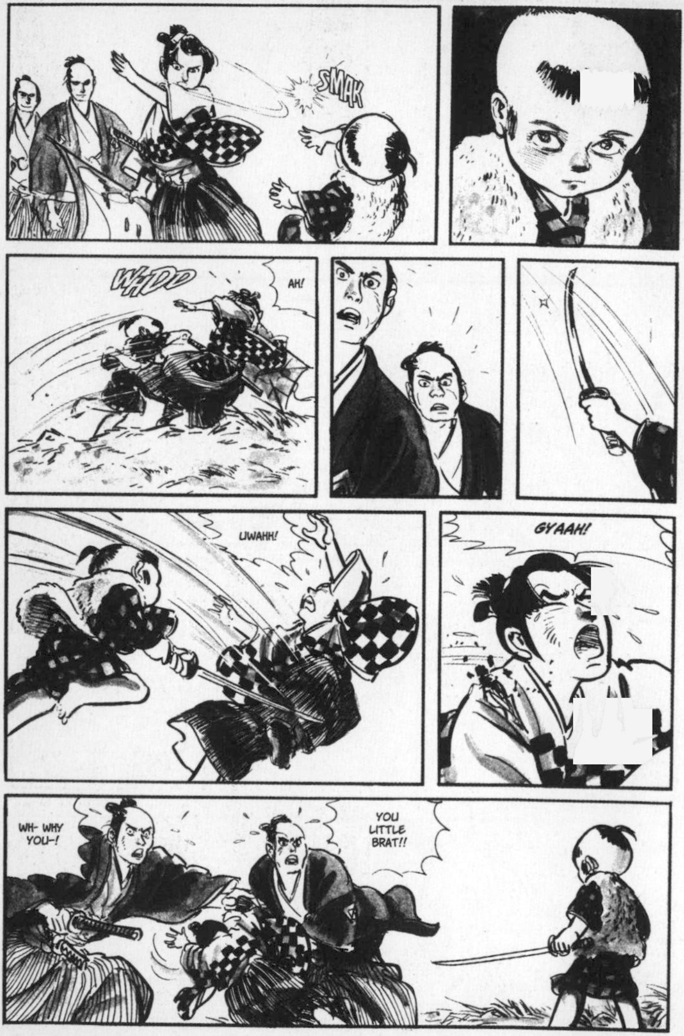
SMAK
WHDD
AH!
UWAHH!
GYAAH!
WH- WHY YOU-!
YOU LITTLE BRAT!!

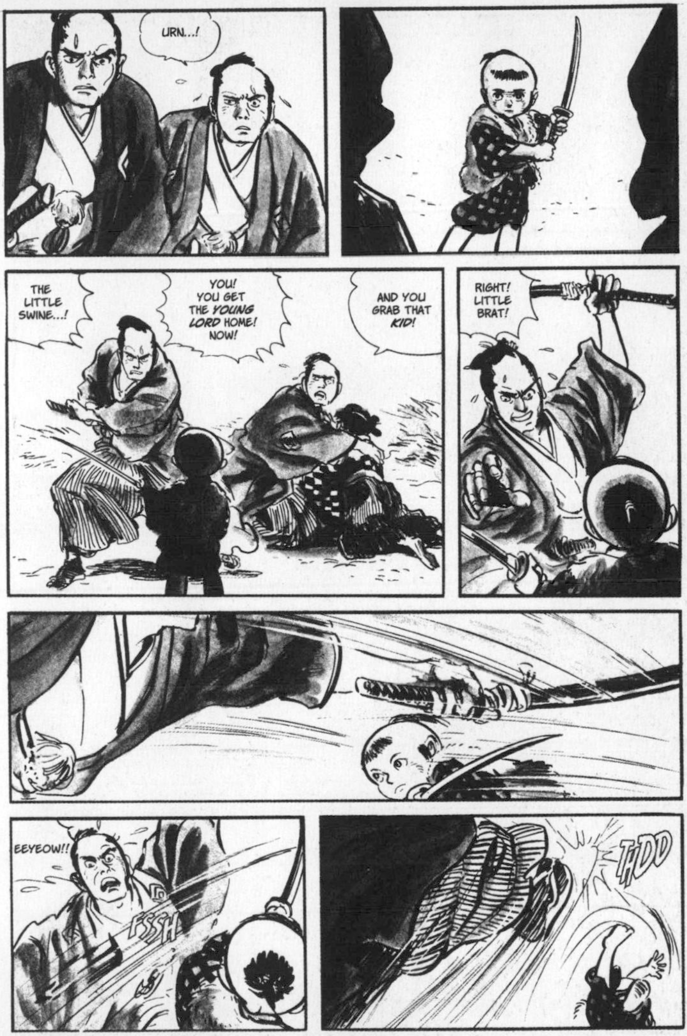
URN...!
THE LITTLE SWINE...!
YOU! YOU GET THE *YOUNG LORD* HOME! NOW!
AND YOU GRAB THAT *KID*!
RIGHT! LITTLE BRAT!
EEYEOW!!
FSSH
THDD

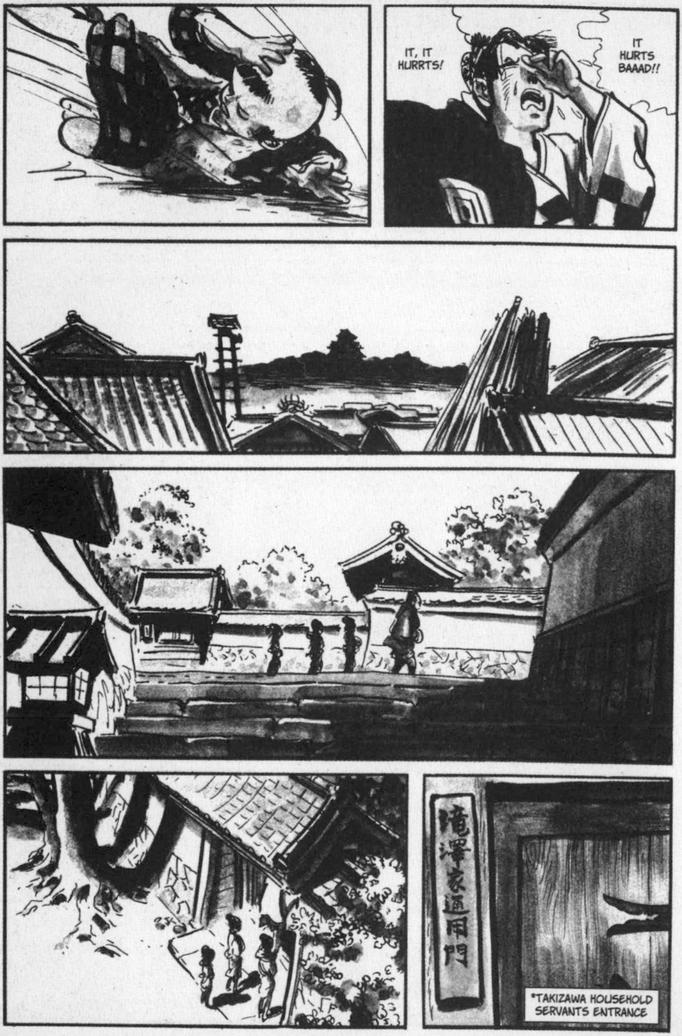
IT, IT HURRTS!
IT HURTS BAAAD!!
滝澤家通用門
*TAKIZAWA HOUSEHOLD SERVANTS ENTRANCE

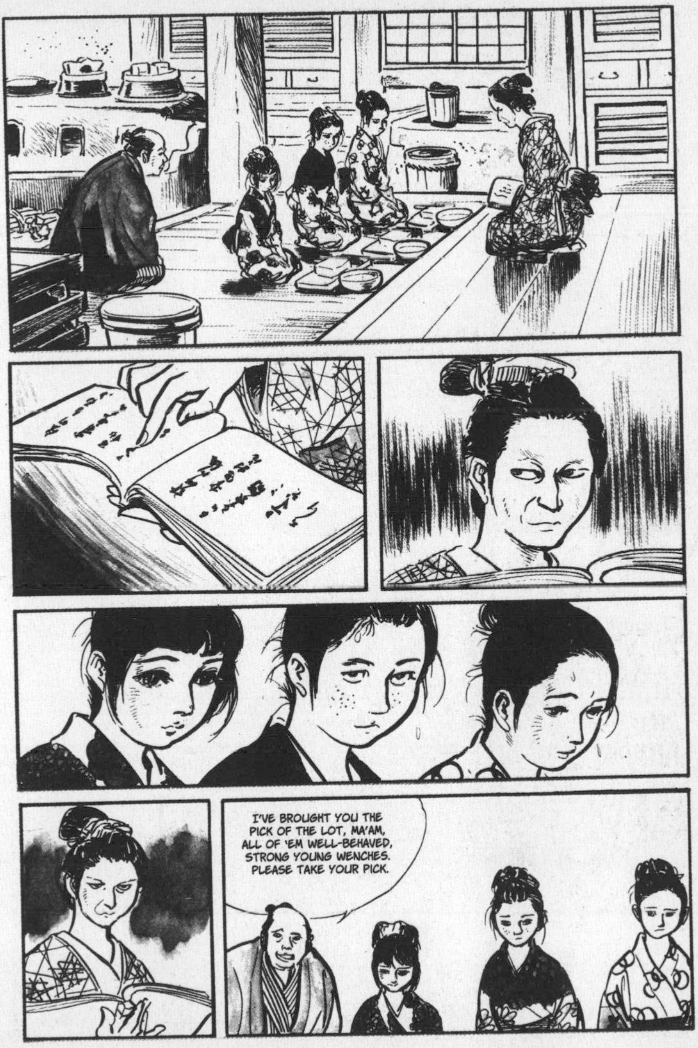
I'VE BROUGHT YOU THE PICK OF THE LOT, MA'AM, ALL OF 'EM WELL-BEHAVED, STRONG YOUNG WENCHES. PLEASE TAKE YOUR PICK.

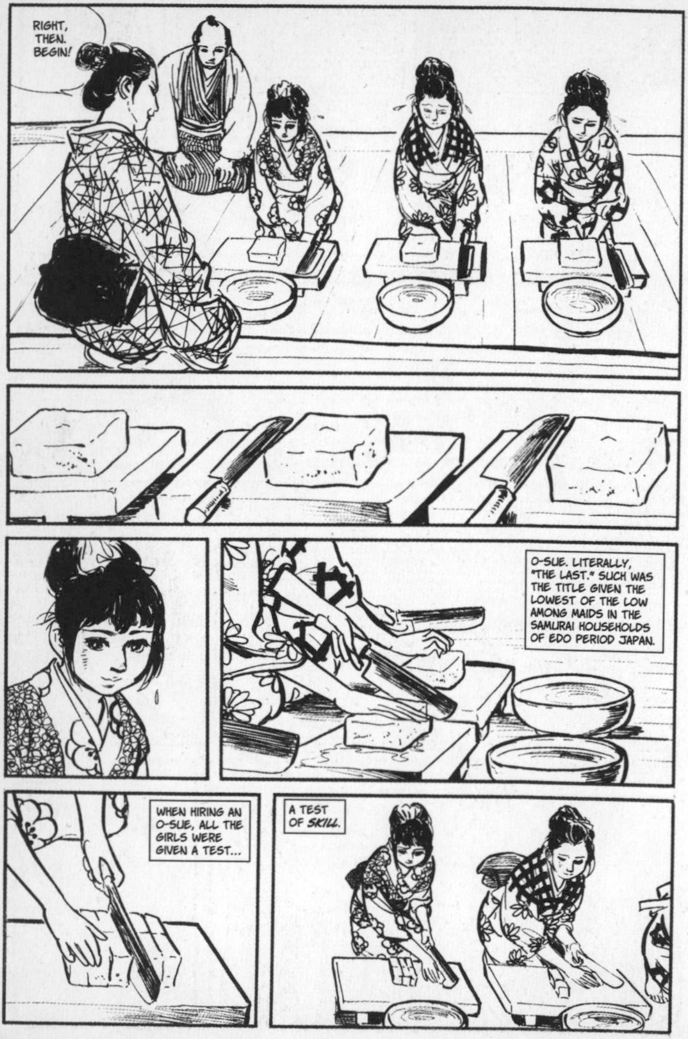
RIGHT, THEN. BEGIN!
O-SUE. LITERALLY, "THE LAST." SUCH WAS THE TITLE GIVEN THE LOWEST OF THE LOW AMONG MAIDS IN THE SAMURAI HOUSEHOLDS OF EDO PERIOD JAPAN.
WHEN HIRING AN O-SUE, ALL THE GIRLS WERE GIVEN A TEST...
A TEST OF *SKILL.*

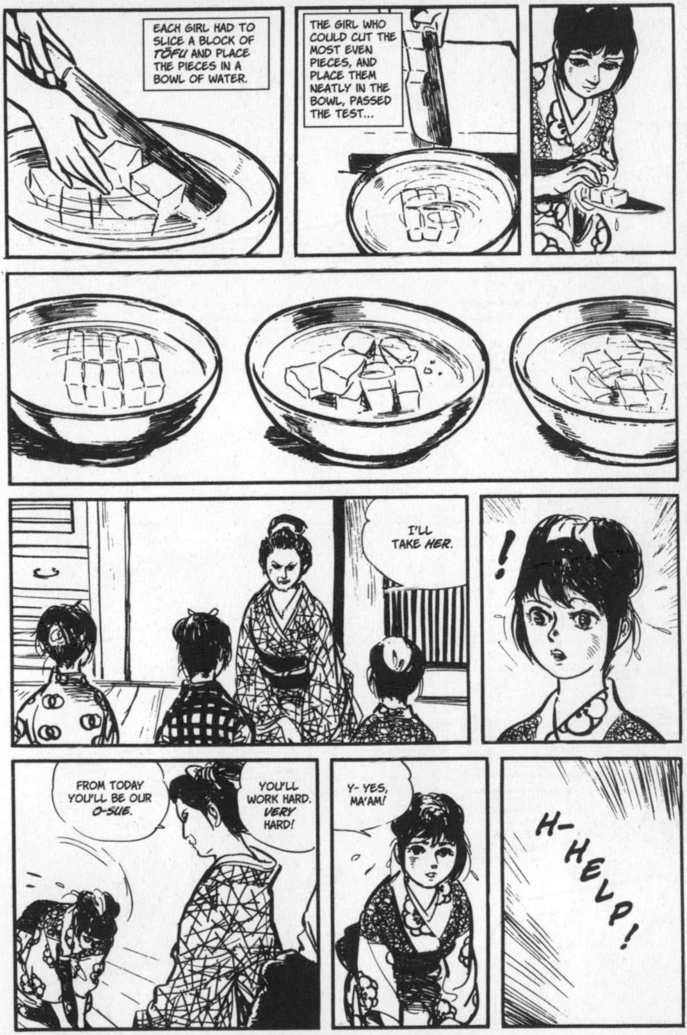
EACH GIRL HAD TO SLICE A BLOCK OF TŌFU AND PLACE THE PIECES IN A BOWL OF WATER.
THE GIRL WHO COULD CUT THE MOST EVEN PIECES, AND PLACE THEM NEATLY IN THE BOWL, PASSED THE TEST...
I'LL TAKE HER.
!
FROM TODAY YOU'LL BE OUR O-SUE.
YOU'LL WORK HARD. VERY HARD!
Y- YES, MA'AM!
H-HELP!

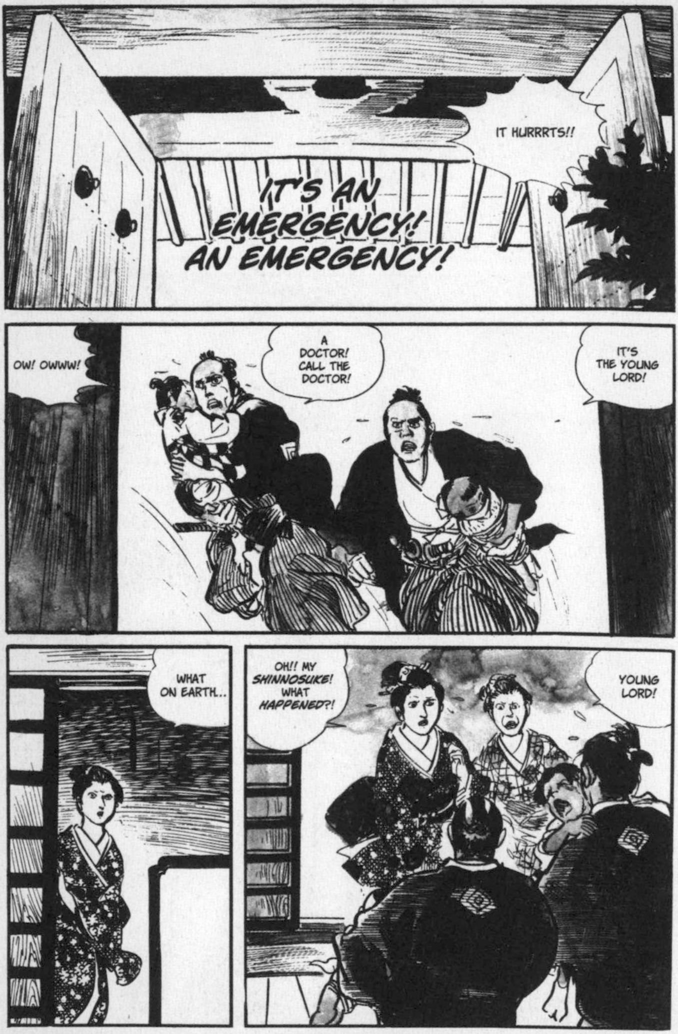
IT HURRRTS!!
IT'S AN EMERGENCY! AN EMERGENCY!
OW! OWWW!
A DOCTOR! CALL THE DOCTOR!
IT'S THE YOUNG LORD!
WHAT ON EARTH...
OH!! MY *SHINNOSUKE!* WHAT *HAPPENED?!*
YOUNG LORD!

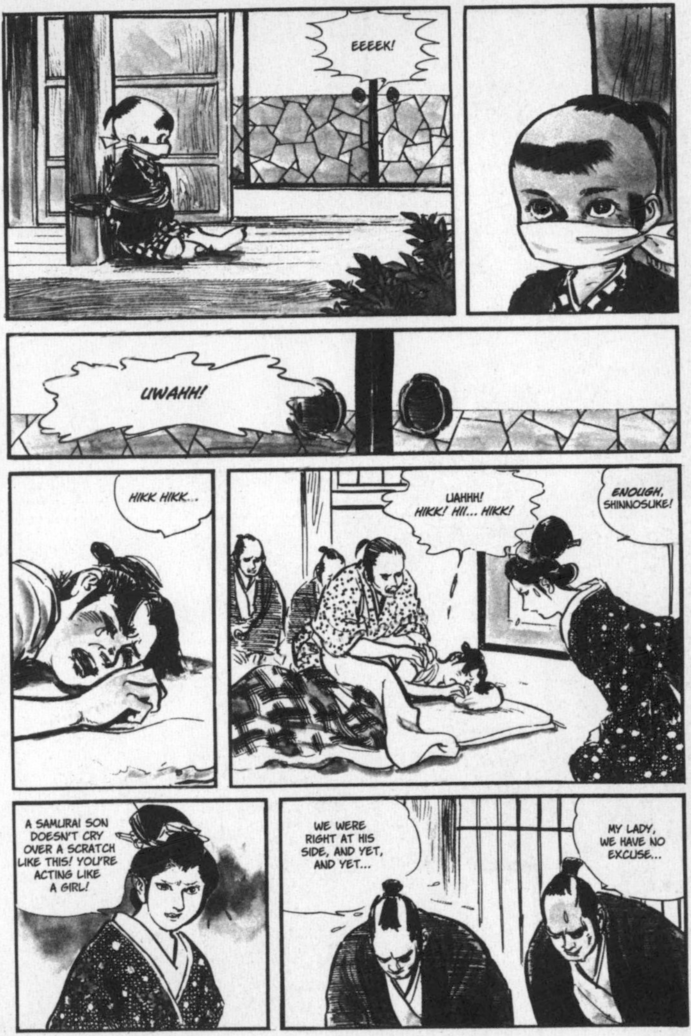
EEEEK!
UWAHH!
HIKK HIKK...
UAHHH! HIKK! HII... HIKK!
ENOUGH, SHINNOSUKE!
A SAMURAI SON DOESN'T CRY OVER A SCRATCH LIKE THIS! YOU'RE ACTING LIKE A GIRL!
WE WERE RIGHT AT HIS SIDE, AND YET, AND YET...
MY LADY, WE HAVE NO EXCUSE...

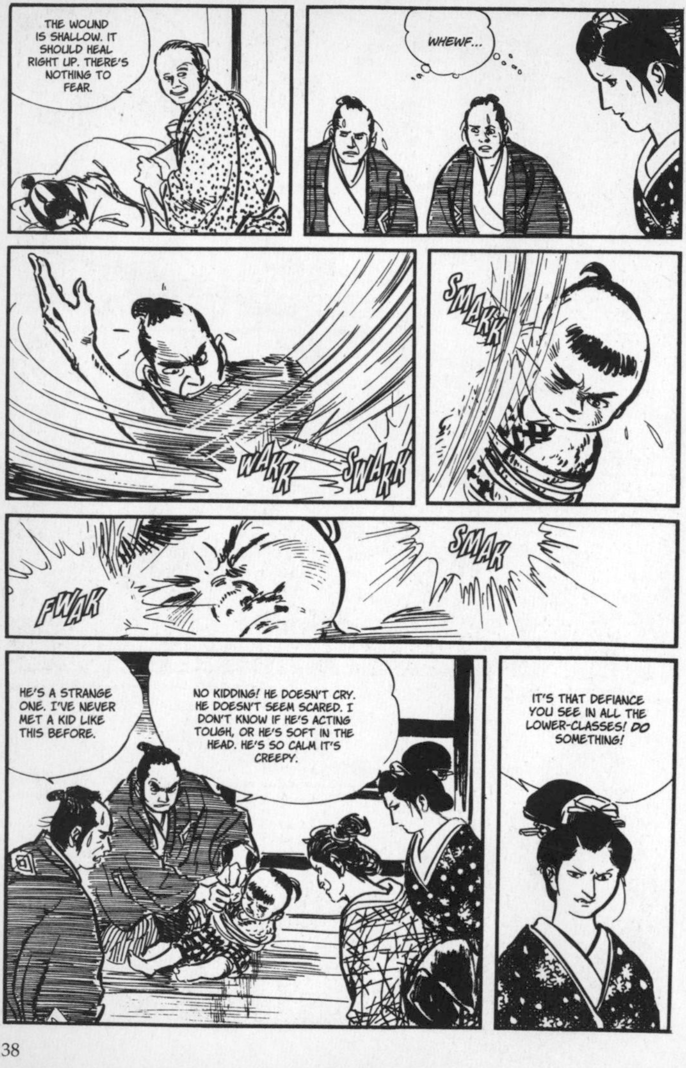
THE WOUND IS SHALLOW. IT SHOULD HEAL RIGHT UP. THERE'S NOTHING TO FEAR.
WHEWF...
WAKK
SWAKK
SMAKK
FWAK
SMAK
HE'S A STRANGE ONE. I'VE NEVER MET A KID LIKE THIS BEFORE.
NO KIDDING! HE DOESN'T CRY. HE DOESN'T SEEM SCARED. I DON'T KNOW IF HE'S ACTING TOUGH, OR HE'S SOFT IN THE HEAD. HE'S SO CALM IT'S CREEPY.
IT'S THAT DEFIANCE YOU SEE IN ALL THE LOWER-CLASSES! DO SOMETHING!

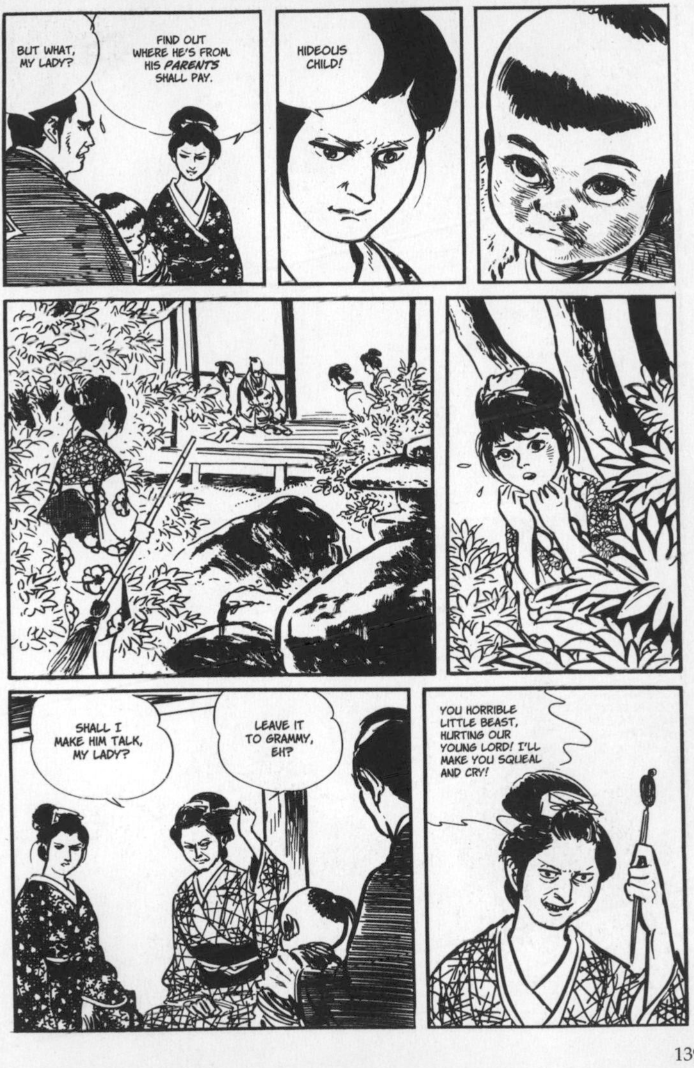
BUT WHAT, MY LADY?
FIND OUT WHERE HE'S FROM. HIS *PARENTS* SHALL PAY.
HIDEOUS CHILD!
SHALL I MAKE HIM TALK, MY LADY?
LEAVE IT TO GRAMMY, EH?
YOU HORRIBLE LITTLE BEAST, HURTING OUR YOUNG LORD! I'LL MAKE YOU SQUEAL AND CRY!

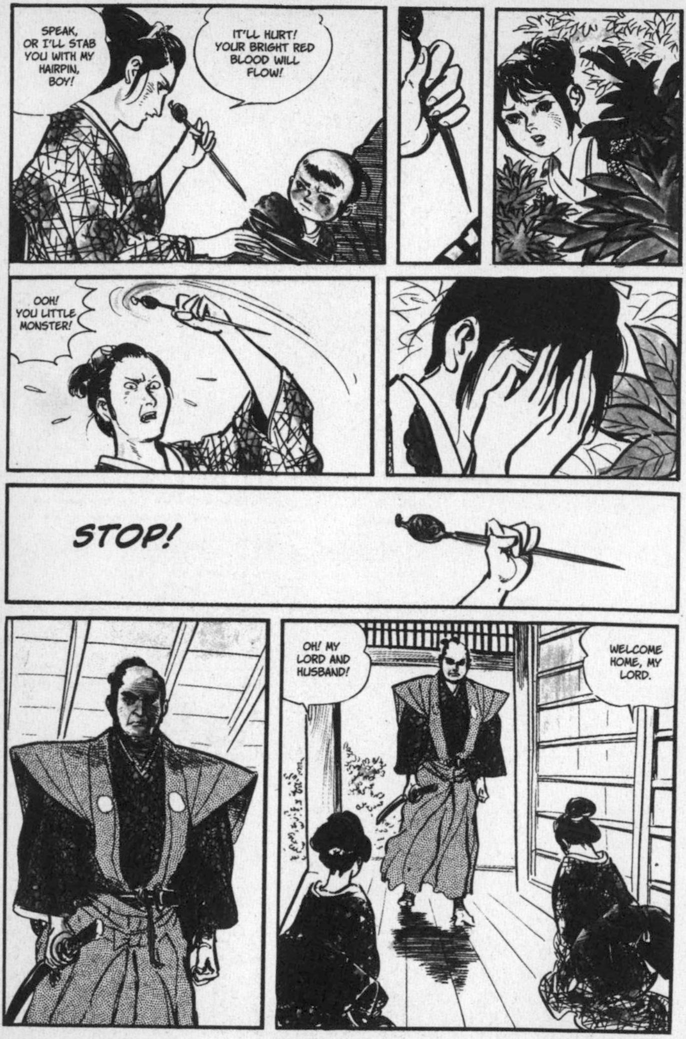
SPEAK, OR I'LL STAB YOU WITH MY HAIRPIN, BOY!
IT'LL HURT! YOUR BRIGHT RED BLOOD WILL FLOW!
OOH! YOU LITTLE MONSTER!
STOP!
OH! MY LORD AND HUSBAND!
WELCOME HOME, MY LORD.

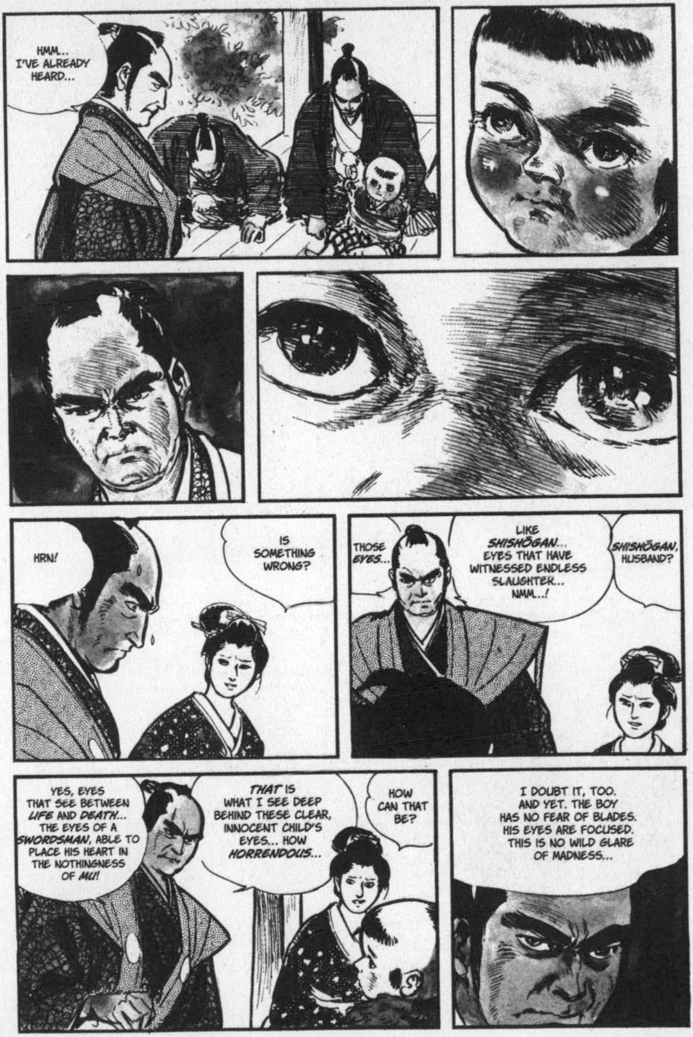
HMM... I'VE ALREADY HEARD...
HRN!
IS SOMETHING WRONG?
THOSE EYES...
LIKE SHISHŌGAN... EYES THAT HAVE WITNESSED ENDLESS SLAUGHTER... NMM...!
SHISHŌGAN, HUSBAND?
YES, EYES THAT SEE BETWEEN LIFE AND DEATH... THE EYES OF A SWORDSMAN, ABLE TO PLACE HIS HEART IN THE NOTHINGNESS OF MU!
THAT IS WHAT I SEE DEEP BEHIND THESE CLEAR, INNOCENT CHILD'S EYES... HOW HORRENDOUS...
HOW CAN THAT BE?
I DOUBT IT, TOO. AND YET. THE BOY HAS NO FEAR OF BLADES. HIS EYES ARE FOCUSED. THIS IS NO WILD GLARE OF MADNESS...

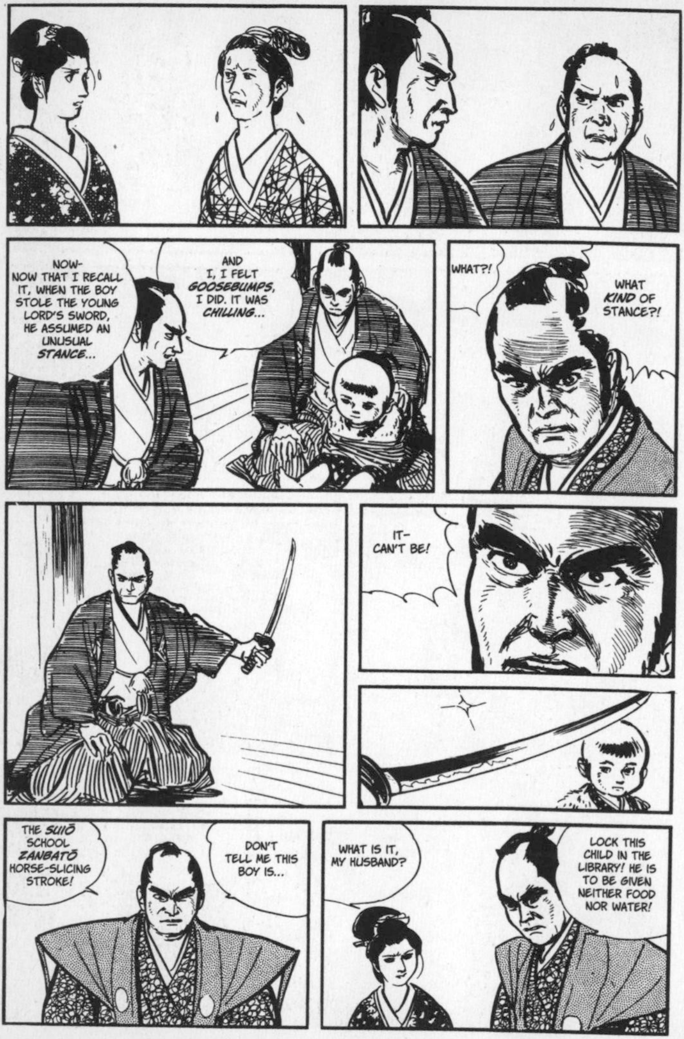
NOW- NOW THAT I RECALL IT, WHEN THE BOY STOLE THE YOUNG LORD'S SWORD, HE ASSUMED AN UNUSUAL *STANCE*...
AND I, I FELT *GOOSEBUMPS*, I DID. IT WAS *CHILLING*...
WHAT?!
WHAT *KIND* OF STANCE?!
IT- CAN'T BE!
THE *SUIŌ* SCHOOL *ZANBATŌ* HORSE-SLICING STROKE!
DON'T TELL ME THIS BOY IS...
WHAT IS IT, MY HUSBAND?
LOCK THIS CHILD IN THE LIBRARY! HE IS TO BE GIVEN NEITHER FOOD NOR WATER!

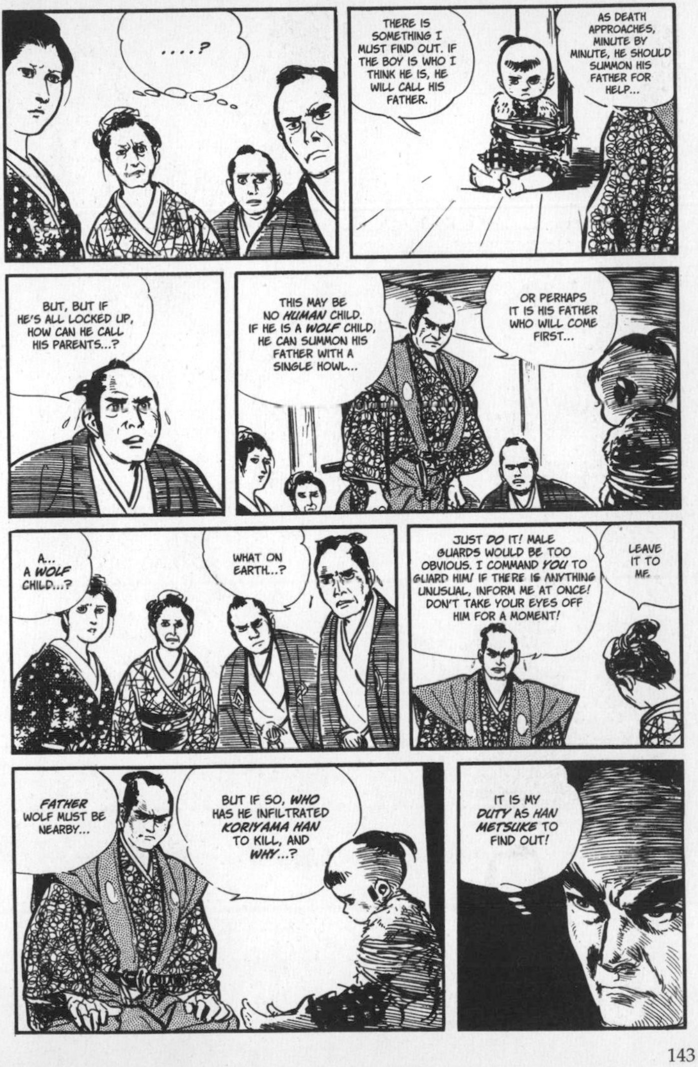
....?
THERE IS SOMETHING I MUST FIND OUT. IF THE BOY IS WHO I THINK HE IS, HE WILL CALL HIS FATHER.
AS DEATH APPROACHES, MINUTE BY MINUTE, HE SHOULD SUMMON HIS FATHER FOR HELP...
BUT, BUT IF HE'S ALL LOCKED UP, HOW CAN HE CALL HIS PARENTS...?
THIS MAY BE NO HUMAN CHILD. IF HE IS A WOLF CHILD, HE CAN SUMMON HIS FATHER WITH A SINGLE HOWL...
OR PERHAPS IT IS HIS FATHER WHO WILL COME FIRST...
A... A WOLF CHILD...?
WHAT ON EARTH...?
JUST DO IT! MALE GUARDS WOULD BE TOO OBVIOUS. I COMMAND YOU TO GUARD HIM! IF THERE IS ANYTHING UNUSUAL, INFORM ME AT ONCE! DON'T TAKE YOUR EYES OFF HIM FOR A MOMENT!
LEAVE IT TO ME.
FATHER WOLF MUST BE NEARBY...
BUT IF SO, WHO HAS HE INFILTRATED KORIYAMA HAN TO KILL, AND WHY...?
IT IS MY DUTY AS HAN METSUKE TO FIND OUT!

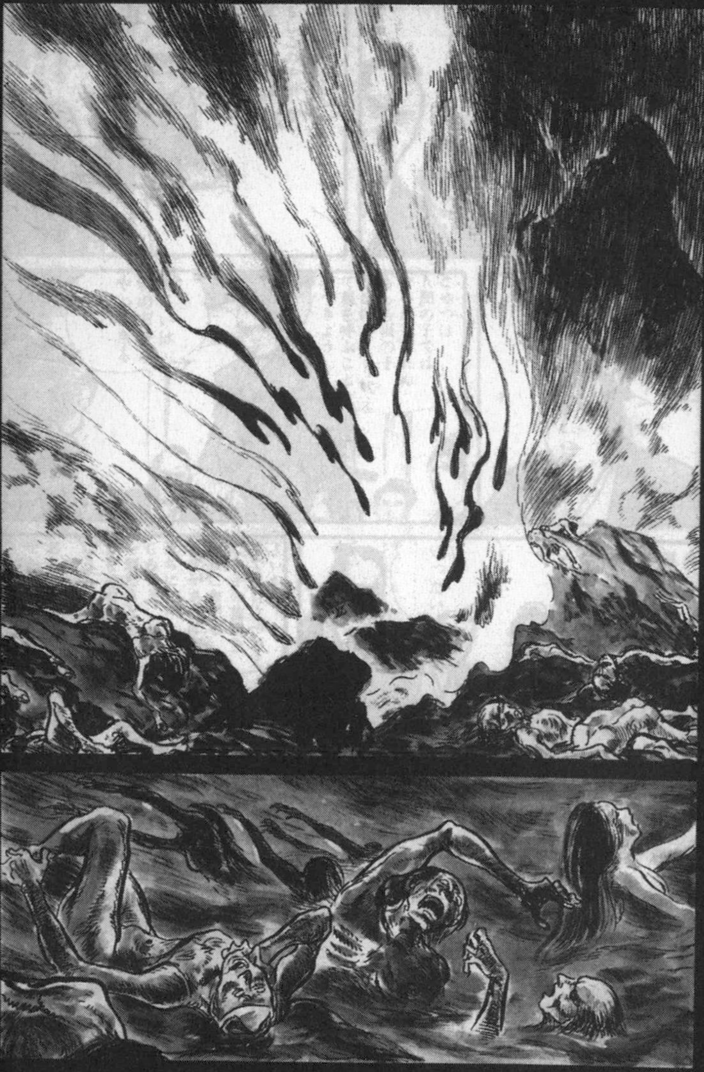

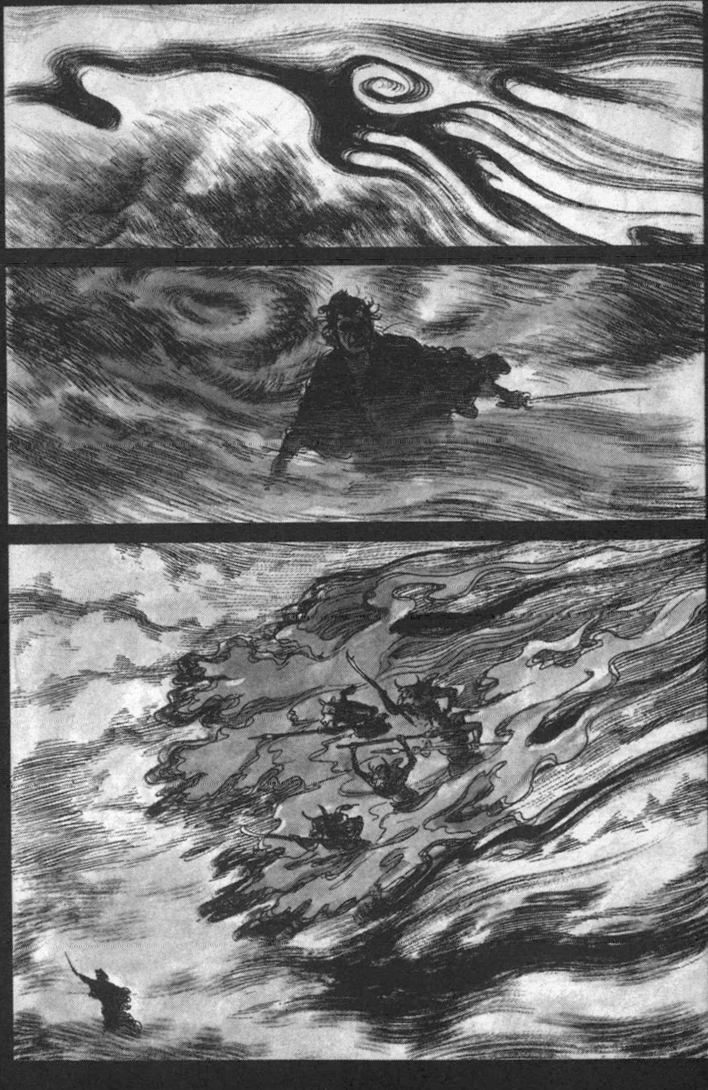

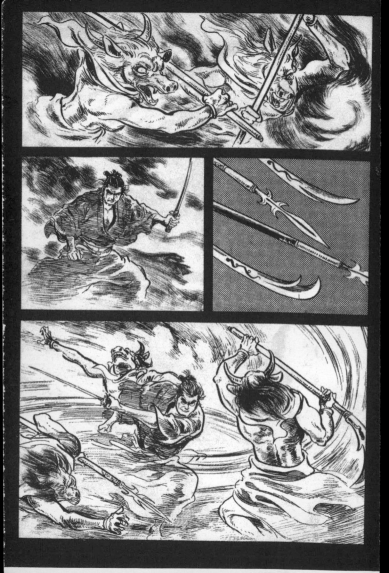

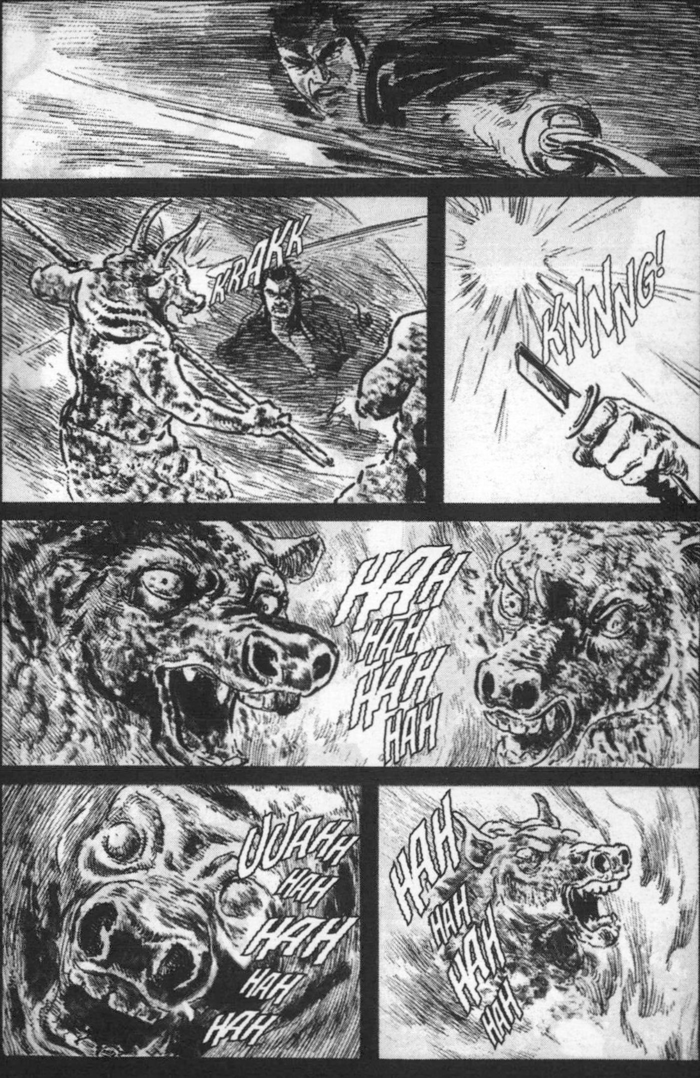
KRAKK
KNNNG!
HAH HAH HAH HAH
UUAHH HAH HAH HAH HAH
HAH HAH HAH HAH

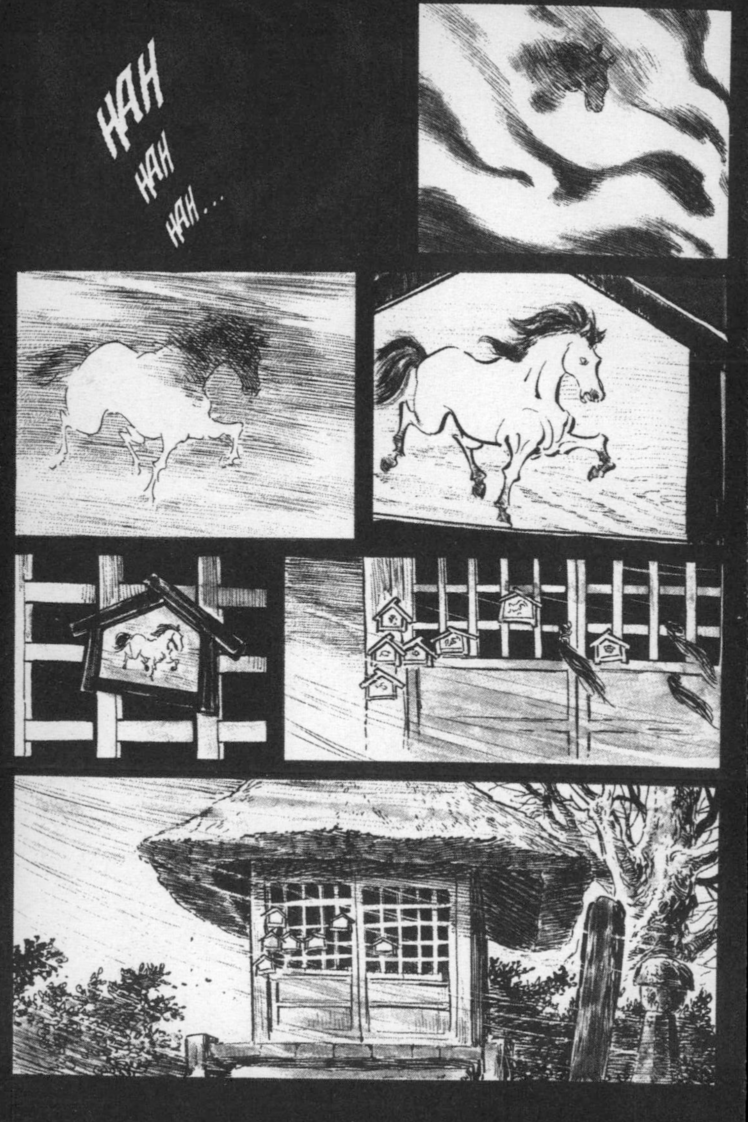
HAH
HAH
HAH...

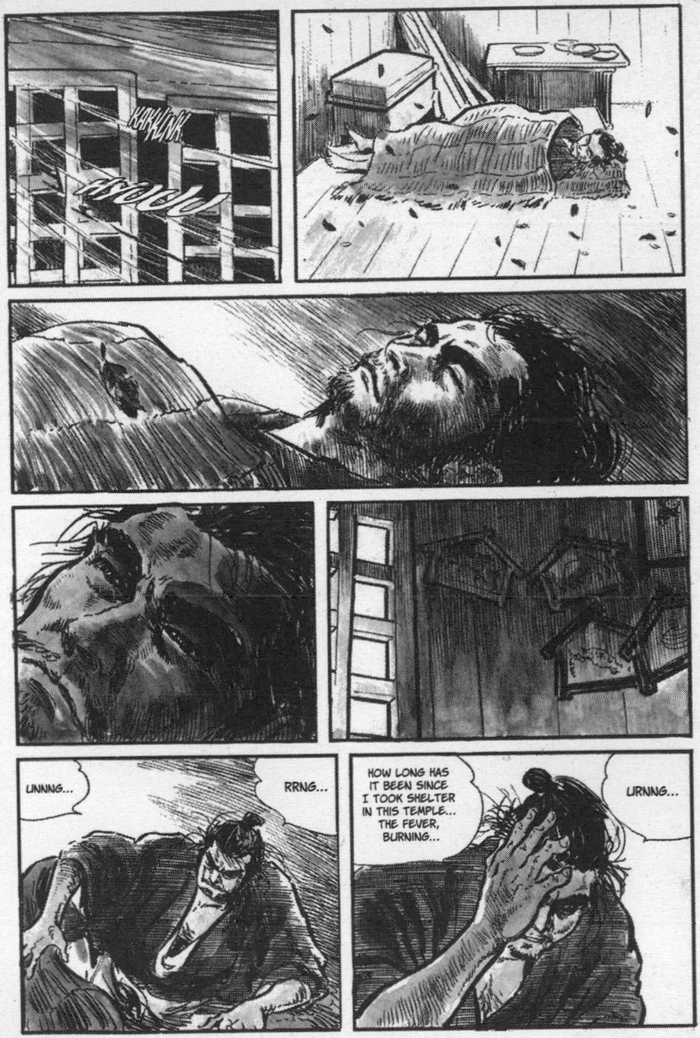
KAKLINK
UNNNG...
RRNG...
HOW LONG HAS IT BEEN SINCE I TOOK SHELTER IN THIS TEMPLE... THE FEVER, BURNING...
URNNG...

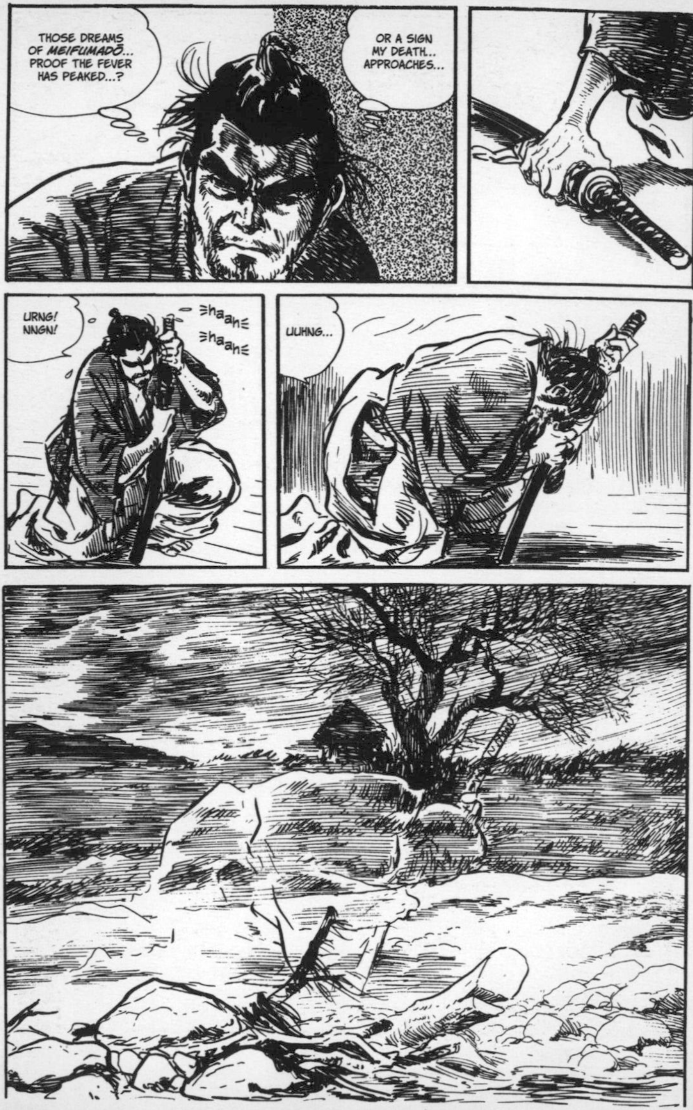
THOSE DREAMS OF *MEIFUMADŌ*... PROOF THE FEVER HAS PEAKED...?
OR A SIGN MY DEATH... APPROACHES...
URNG! NNGN!
haan
haan
UUHNG...

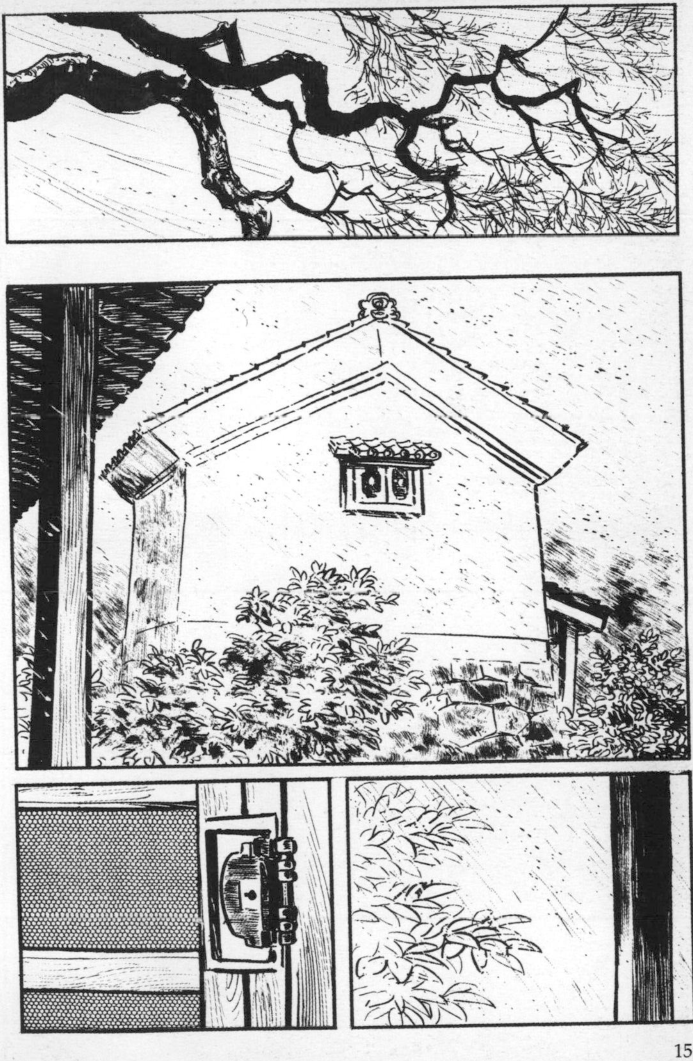

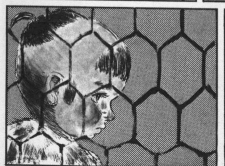

152

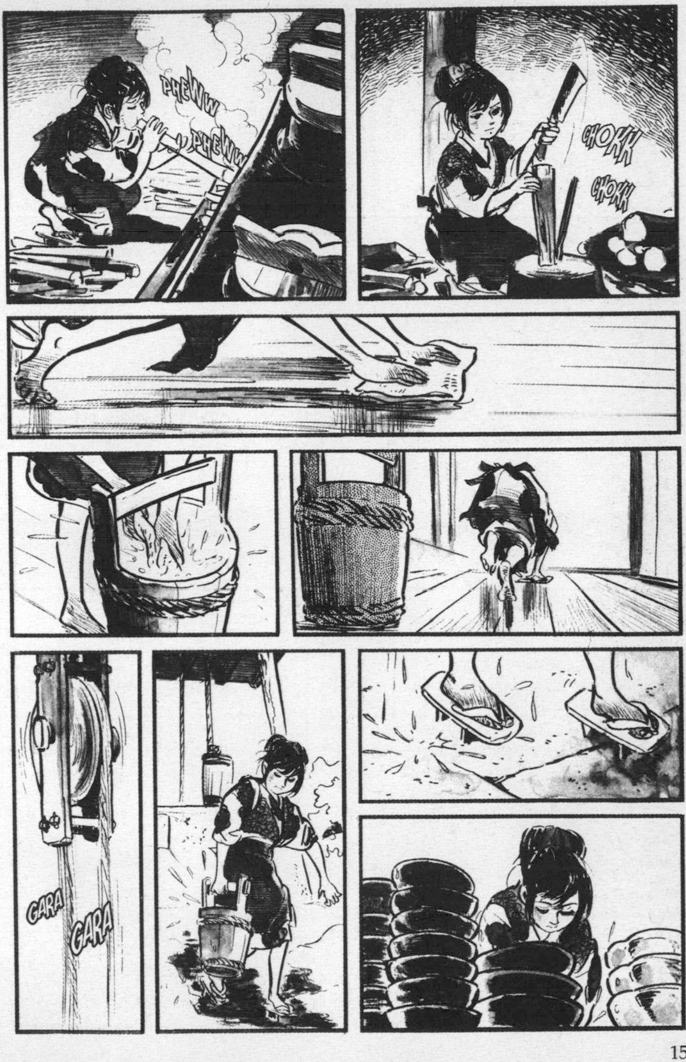
PHEWW
PHEWW
CHOKK
CHOKK
GARA
GARA

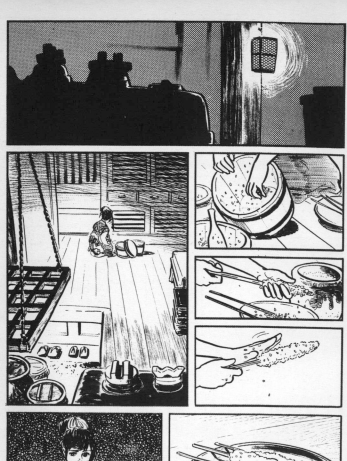

154

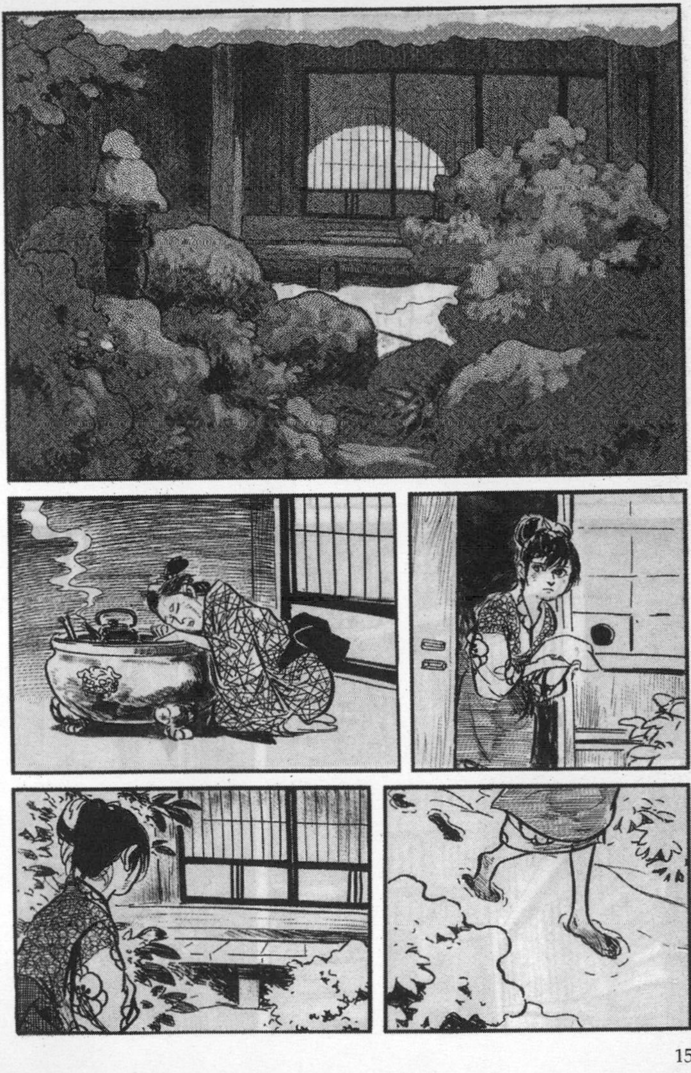

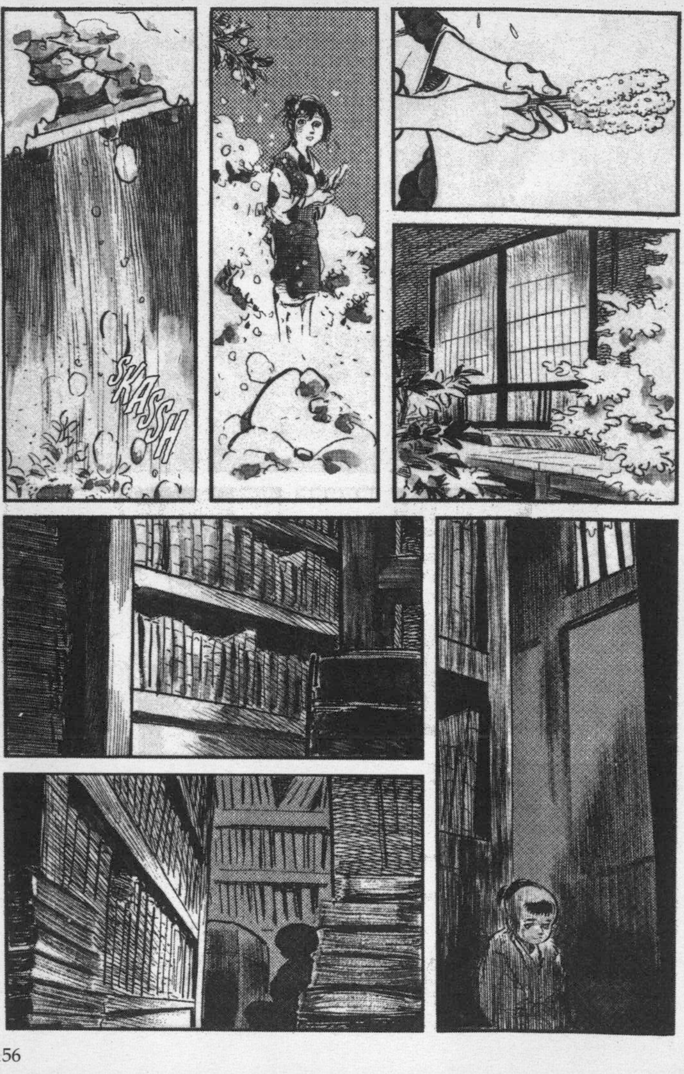
SKASSH

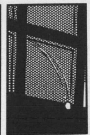

IT'S AWFUL WHAT THEY'RE DOING! TO A LITTLE CHILD LIKE YOU!

.....

YOU MUST BE SO SCARED...

I PUT SALT ON IT TO MAKE IT YUMMY. WAIT... THERE'S MORE.

IF YOUR THROAT'S DRY, HERE'S SOME SNOW...

SIS. THANK YOU, SIS.

157

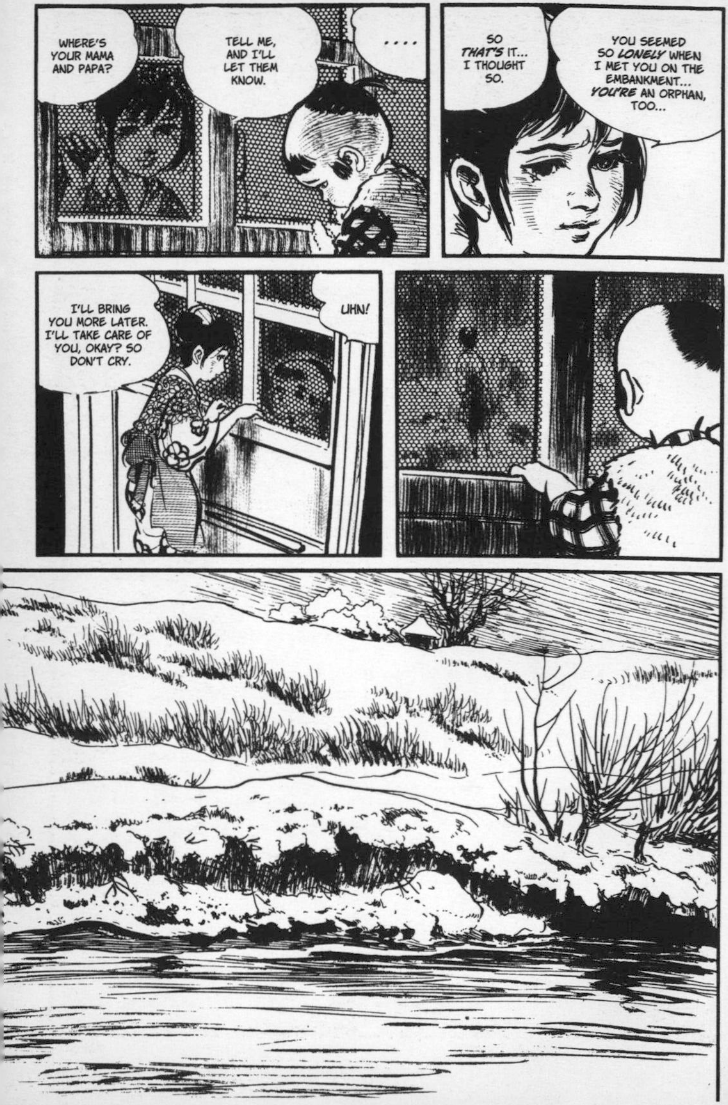
WHERE'S YOUR MAMA AND PAPA?
TELL ME, AND I'LL LET THEM KNOW.
....
SO *THAT'S* IT... I THOUGHT SO.
YOU SEEMED SO *LONELY* WHEN I MET YOU ON THE EMBANKMENT... *YOU'RE* AN ORPHAN, TOO...
I'LL BRING YOU MORE LATER. I'LL TAKE CARE OF YOU, OKAY? SO DON'T CRY.
UHN!

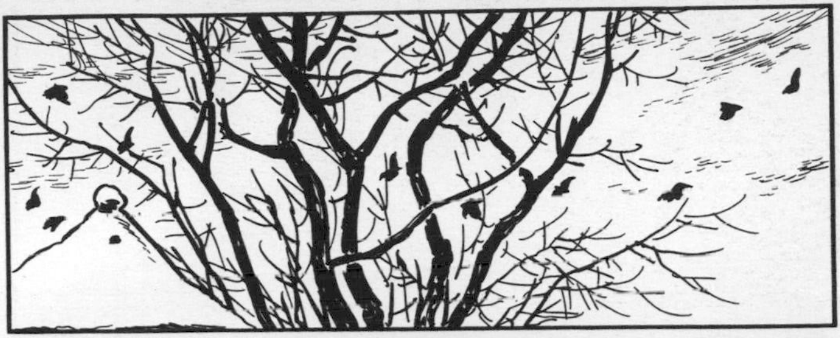

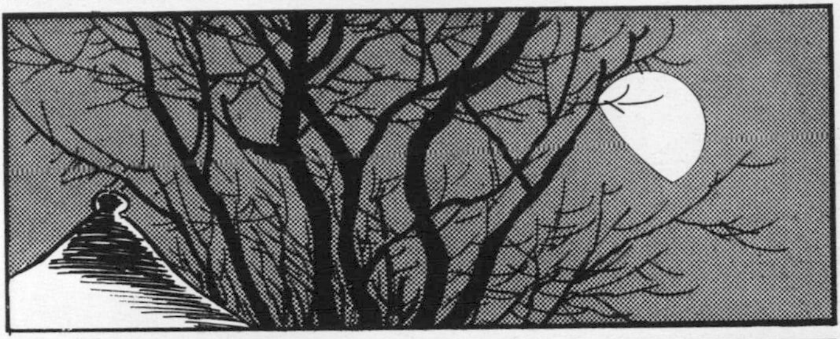

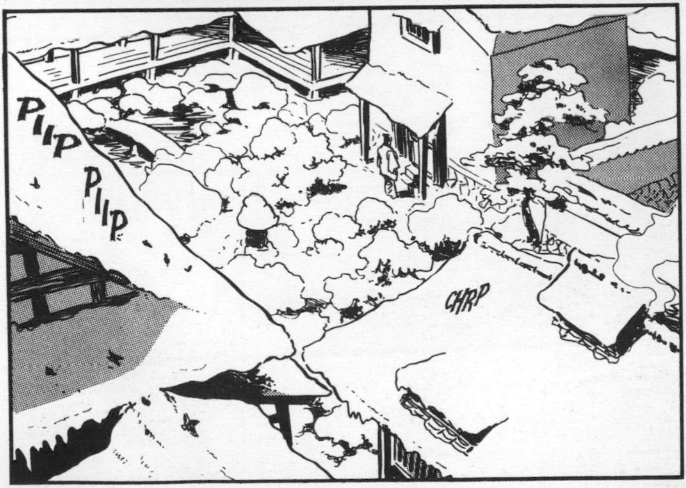
PIIP
PIIP
CHRP

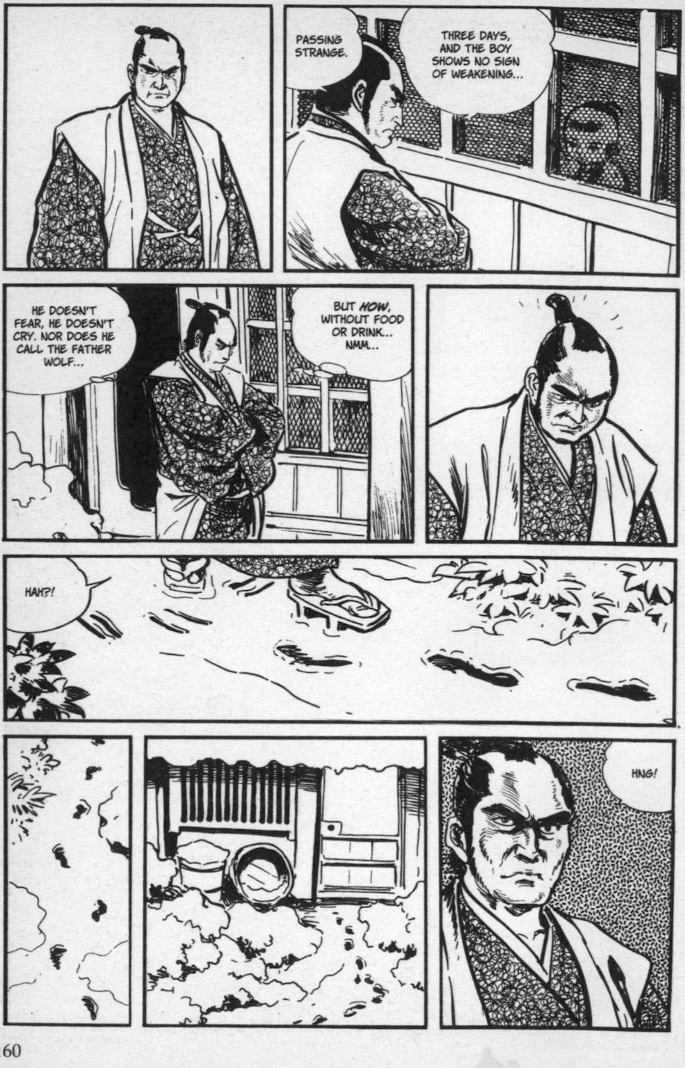
PASSING STRANGE.
THREE DAYS, AND THE BOY SHOWS NO SIGN OF WEAKENING...
HE DOESN'T FEAR, HE DOESN'T CRY. NOR DOES HE CALL THE FATHER WOLF...
BUT *HOW*, WITHOUT FOOD OR DRINK... NMM...
HAH?!
HNG!

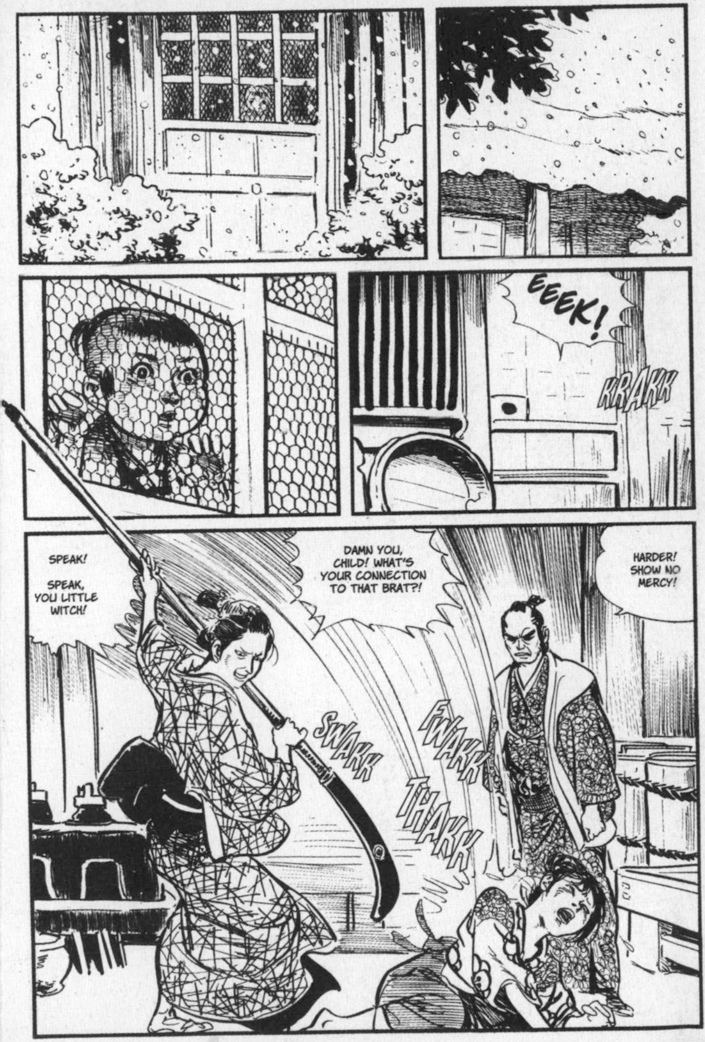
EEEK!
KRAKK
SPEAK!
SPEAK, YOU LITTLE WITCH!
DAMN YOU, CHILD! WHAT'S YOUR CONNECTION TO THAT BRAT?!
HARDER! SHOW NO MERCY!
SWAKK
FWAKK
THAKK

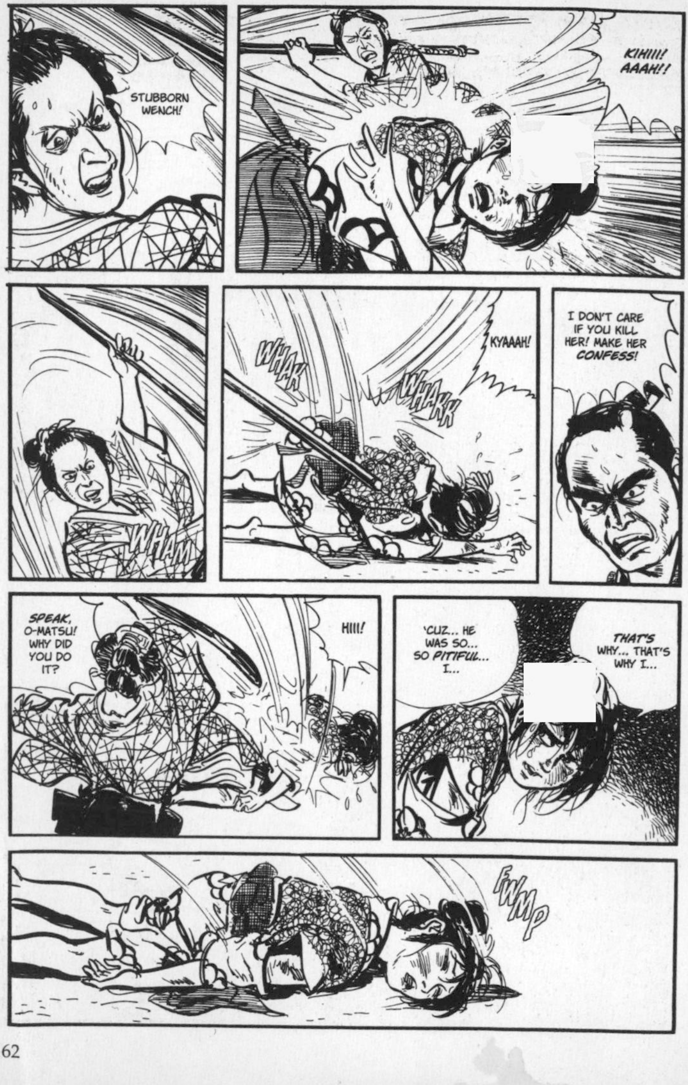
STUBBORN WENCH!
KIHIII! AAAH!!
WHAM
WHAK
KYAAAH!
WHAKK
I DON'T CARE IF YOU KILL HER! MAKE HER *CONFESS!*
SPEAK, O-MATSU! WHY DID YOU DO IT?
HIII!
'CUZ... HE WAS SO... SO *PITIFUL...* I...
THAT'S WHY... THAT'S WHY I...
FWMP

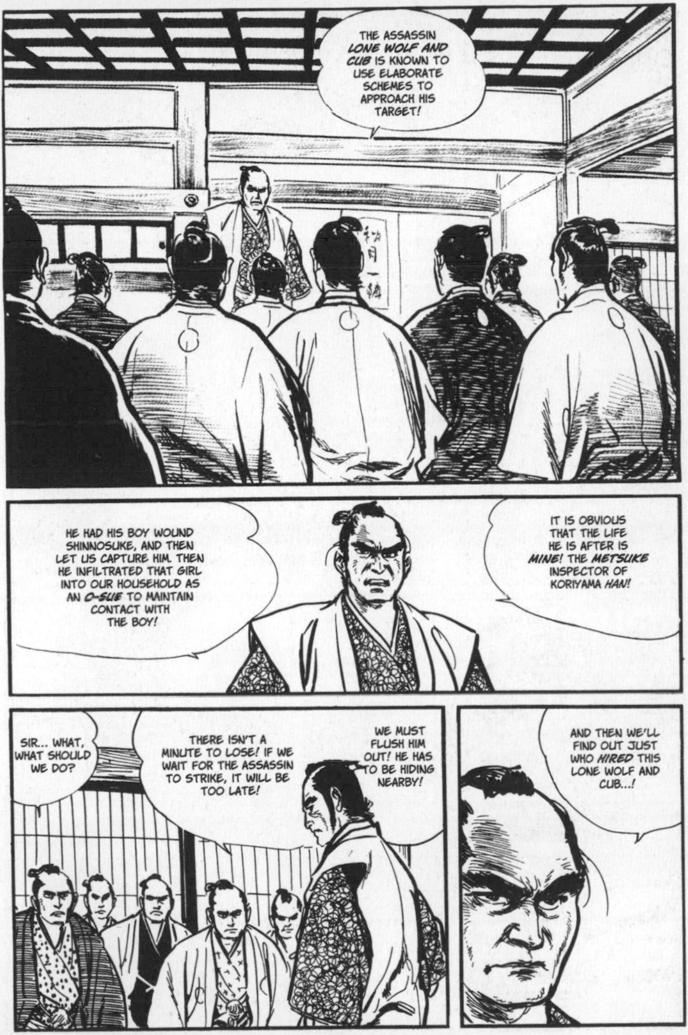
THE ASSASSIN LONE WOLF AND CUB IS KNOWN TO USE ELABORATE SCHEMES TO APPROACH HIS TARGET!
HE HAD HIS BOY WOUND SHINNOSUKE, AND THEN LET US CAPTURE HIM. THEN HE INFILTRATED THAT GIRL INTO OUR HOUSEHOLD AS AN O-SUE TO MAINTAIN CONTACT WITH THE BOY!
IT IS OBVIOUS THAT THE LIFE HE IS AFTER IS MINE! THE METSUKE INSPECTOR OF KORIYAMA HAN!
SIR... WHAT, WHAT SHOULD WE DO?
THERE ISN'T A MINUTE TO LOSE! IF WE WAIT FOR THE ASSASSIN TO STRIKE, IT WILL BE TOO LATE!
WE MUST FLUSH HIM OUT! HE HAS TO BE HIDING NEARBY!
AND THEN WE'LL FIND OUT JUST WHO HIRED THIS LONE WOLF AND CUB...!

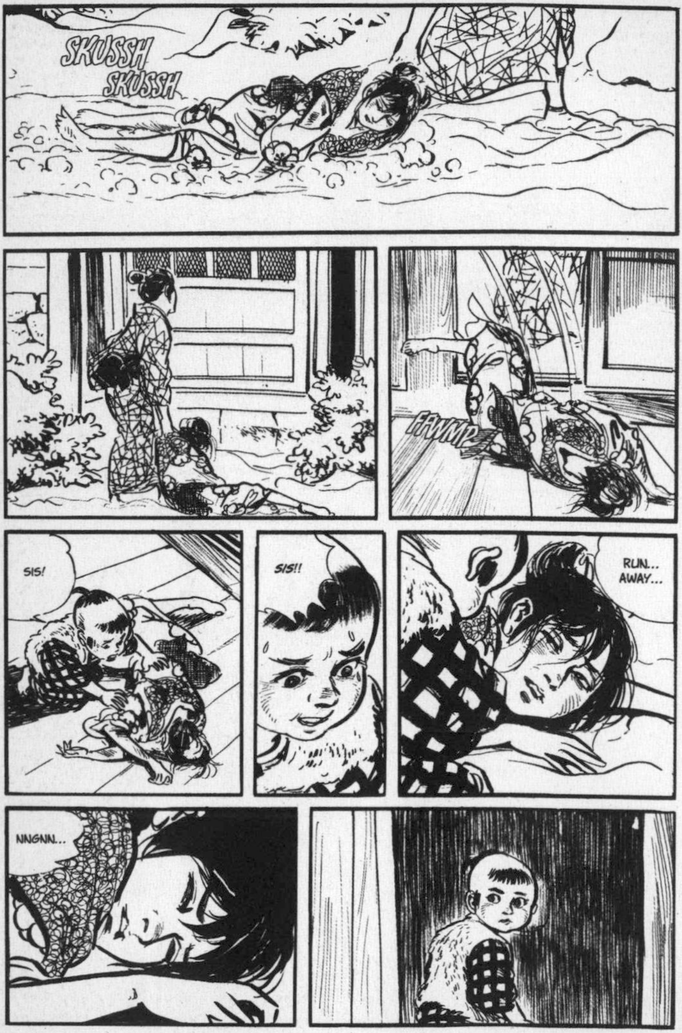
SKUSSH
SKUSSH
FFWMP
SIS!
SIS!!
RUN... AWAY...
NNGNN...

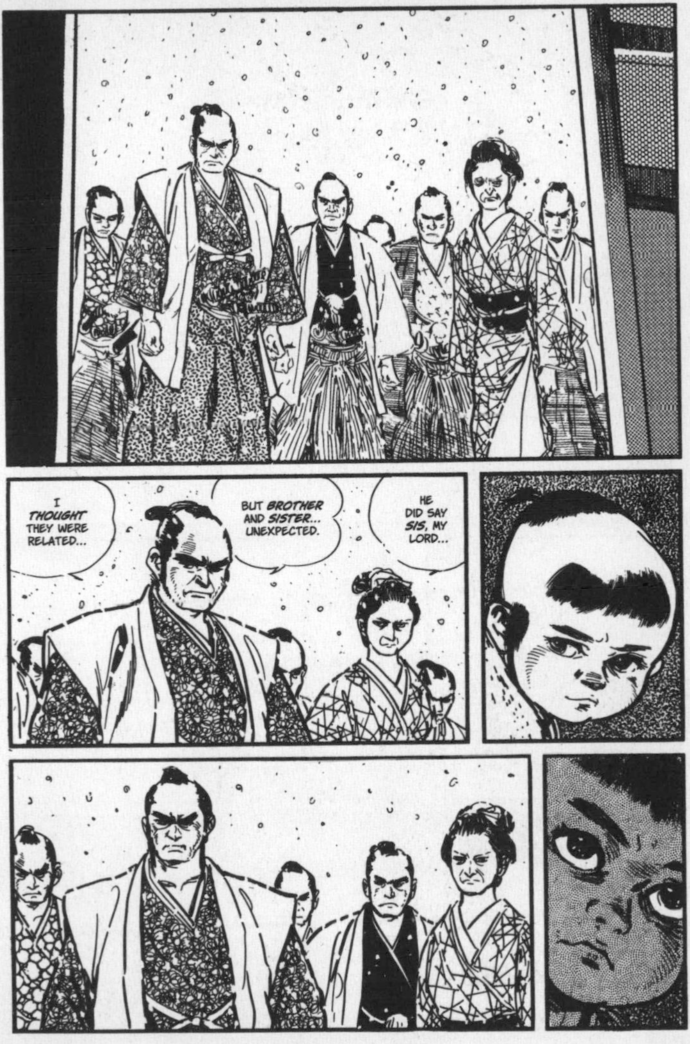
I THOUGHT THEY WERE RELATED...
BUT BROTHER AND SISTER... UNEXPECTED.
HE DID SAY SIS, MY LORD...

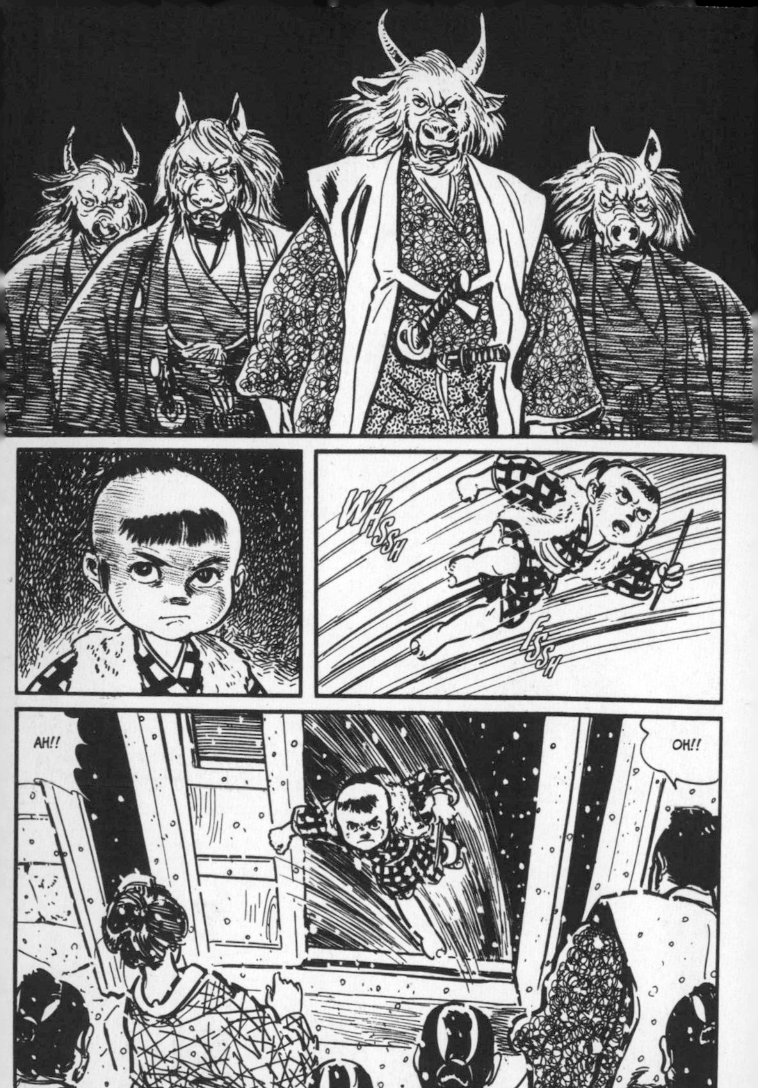
WHSSH
FSSH
AH!!
OH!!

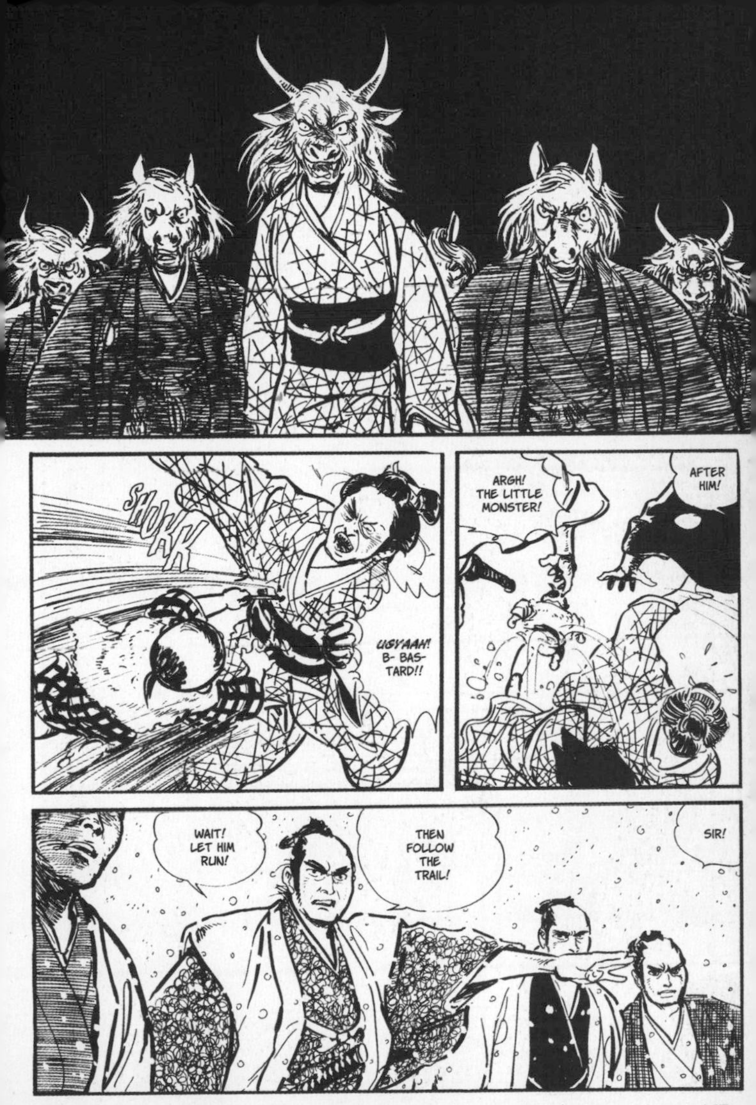
SHUKK
UGYAAH! B- BASTARD!!
ARGH! THE LITTLE MONSTER!
AFTER HIM!
WAIT! LET HIM RUN!
THEN FOLLOW THE TRAIL!
SIR!

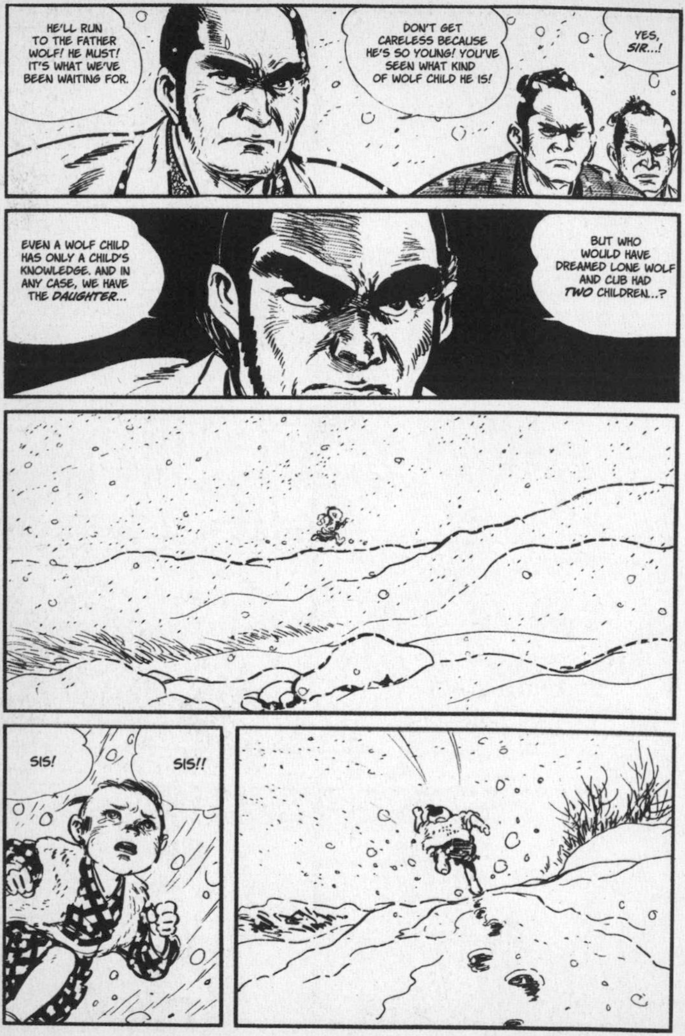
HE'LL RUN TO THE FATHER WOLF! HE MUST! IT'S WHAT WE'VE BEEN WAITING FOR.
DON'T GET CARELESS BECAUSE HE'S SO YOUNG! YOU'VE SEEN WHAT KIND OF WOLF CHILD HE IS!
YES, SIR...!
EVEN A WOLF CHILD HAS ONLY A CHILD'S KNOWLEDGE. AND IN ANY CASE, WE HAVE THE DAUGHTER...
BUT WHO WOULD HAVE DREAMED LONE WOLF AND CUB HAD TWO CHILDREN...?
SIS!
SIS!!

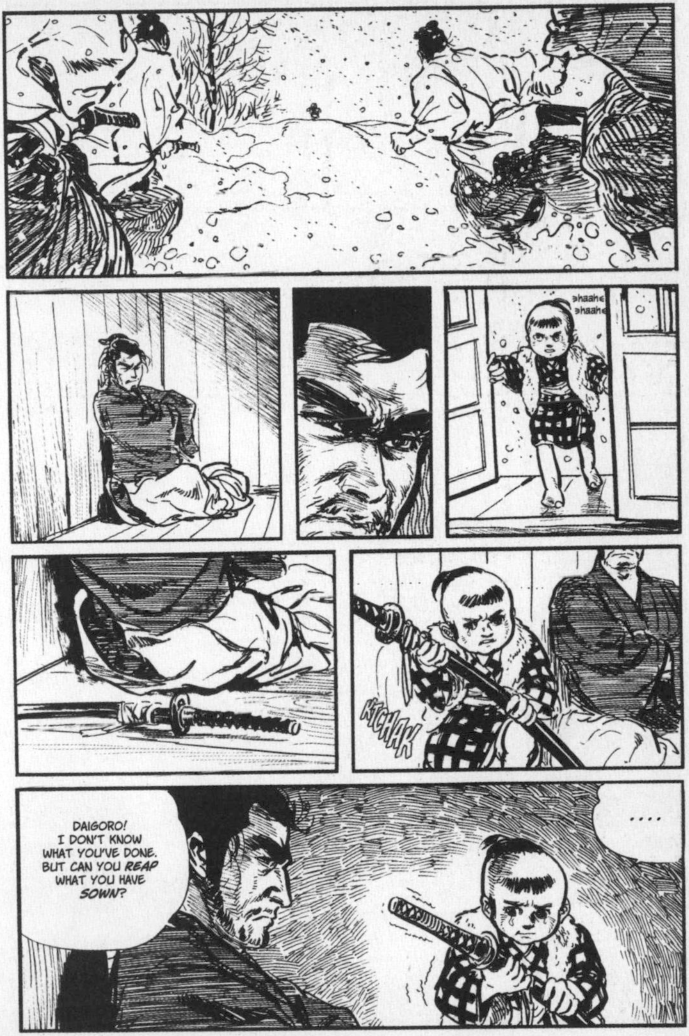
haah
haah
KTCHAK
DAIGORO! I DON'T KNOW WHAT YOU'VE DONE. BUT CAN YOU *REAP* WHAT YOU HAVE *SOWN*?
....

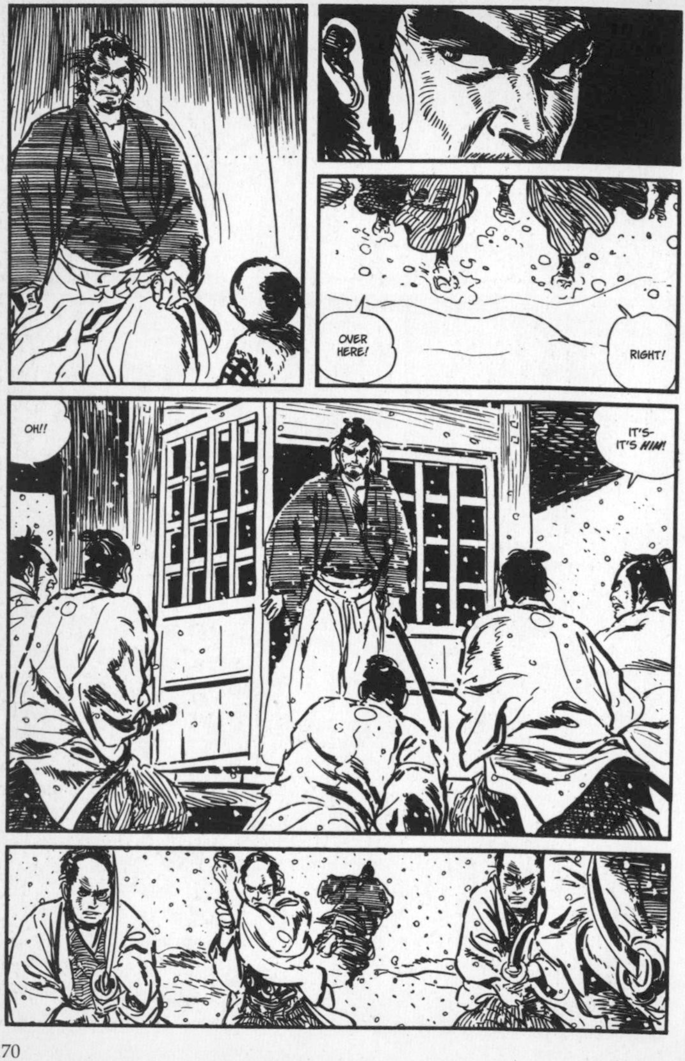
OVER HERE!
RIGHT!
OH!!
IT'S-
IT'S HIM!

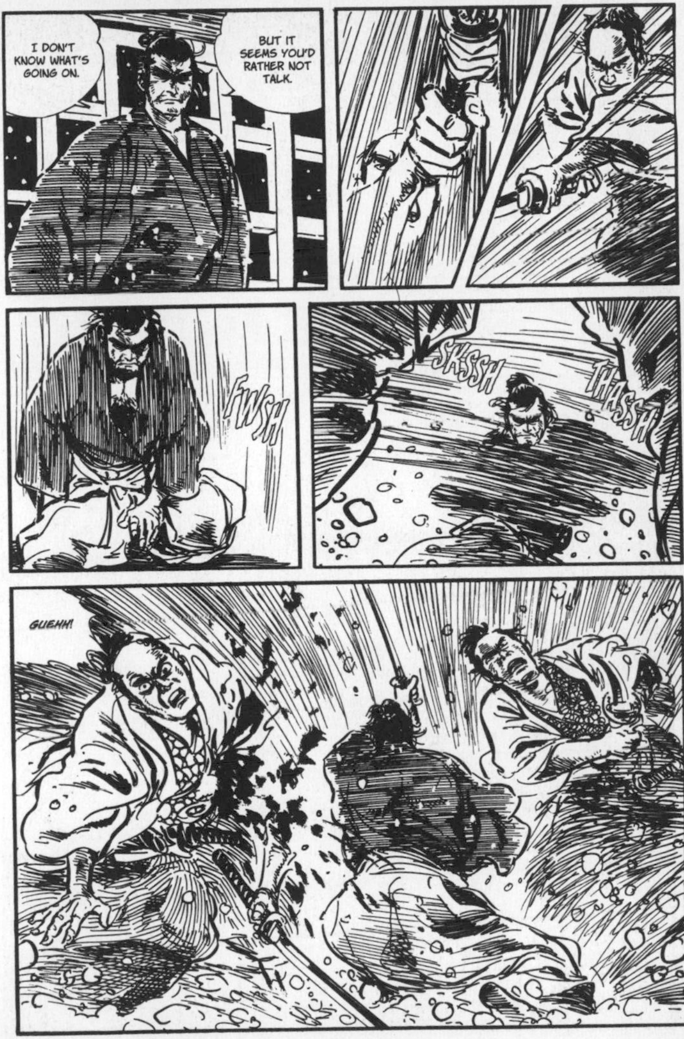
I DON'T KNOW WHAT'S GOING ON.
BUT IT SEEMS YOU'D RATHER NOT TALK.
FWSH
SKSSH
THASSH
GUEHH!

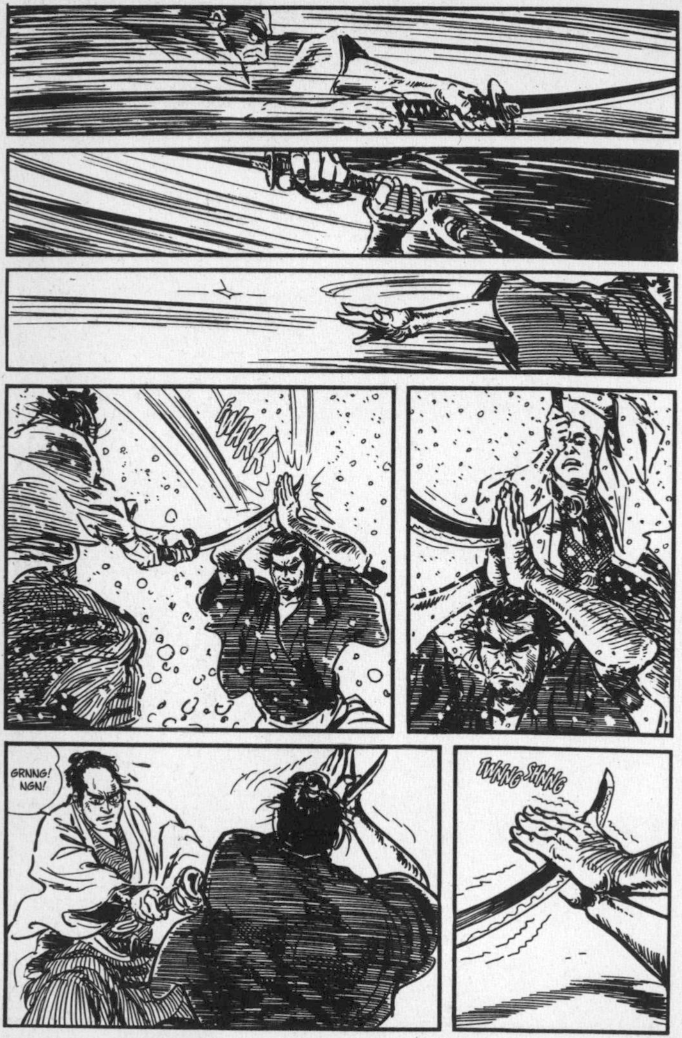
FWAKK
GRNNG! NGN!
TWNNG SHNNG

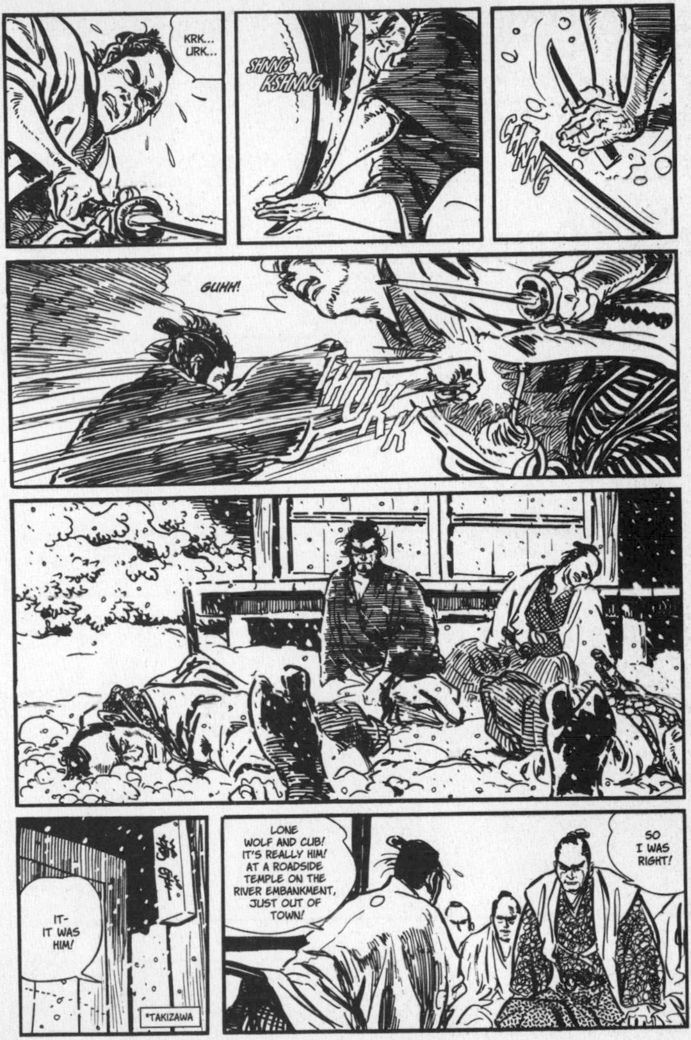
KRK... URK...
SHNNG KSHNNG
CHNNG
GUHH!
THOKK
IT- IT WAS HIM!
*TAKIZAWA
LONE WOLF AND CUB! IT'S REALLY HIM! AT A ROADSIDE TEMPLE ON THE RIVER EMBANKMENT, JUST OUT OF TOWN!
SO I WAS RIGHT!

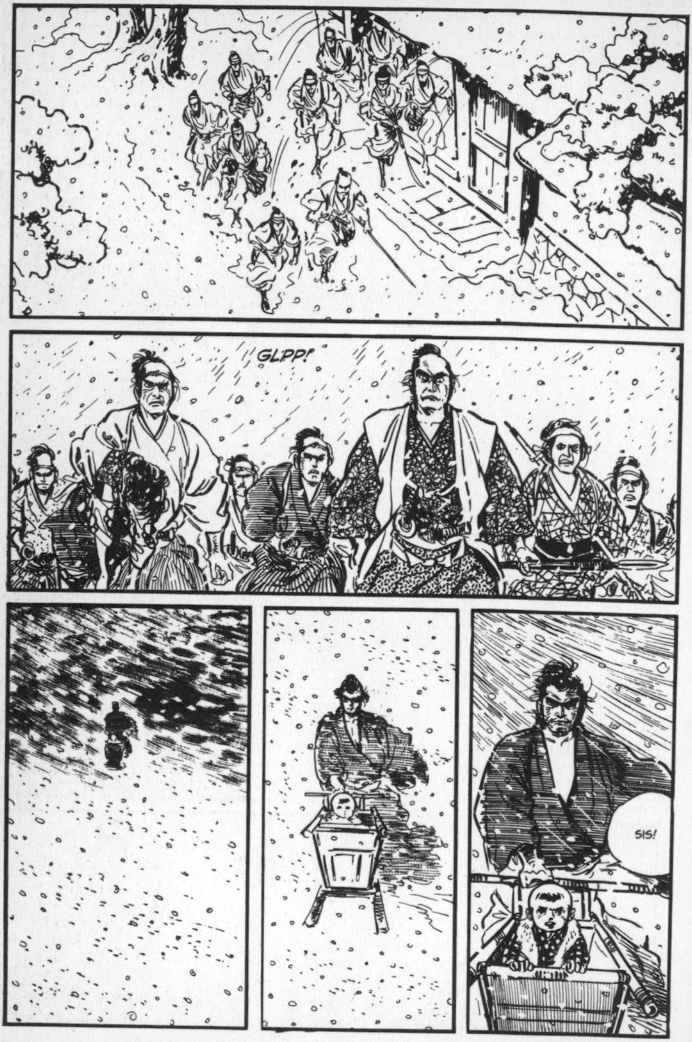
GLPP!
SIS!

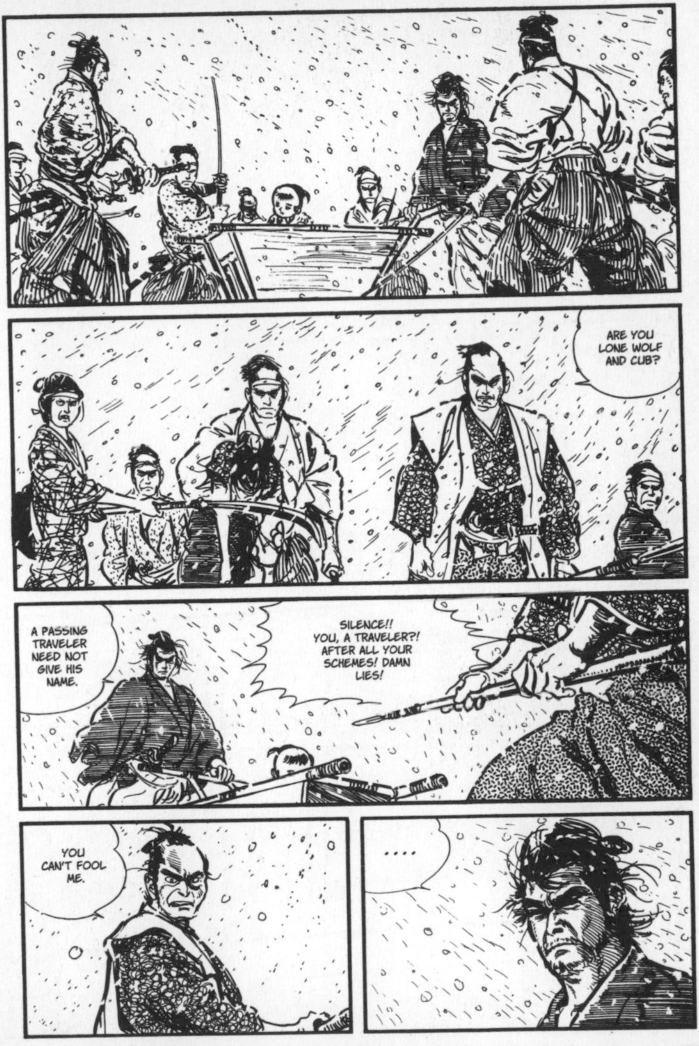
ARE YOU LONE WOLF AND CUB?
A PASSING TRAVELER NEED NOT GIVE HIS NAME.
SILENCE!! YOU, A TRAVELER?! AFTER ALL YOUR SCHEMES! DAMN LIES!
YOU CAN'T FOOL ME.
....

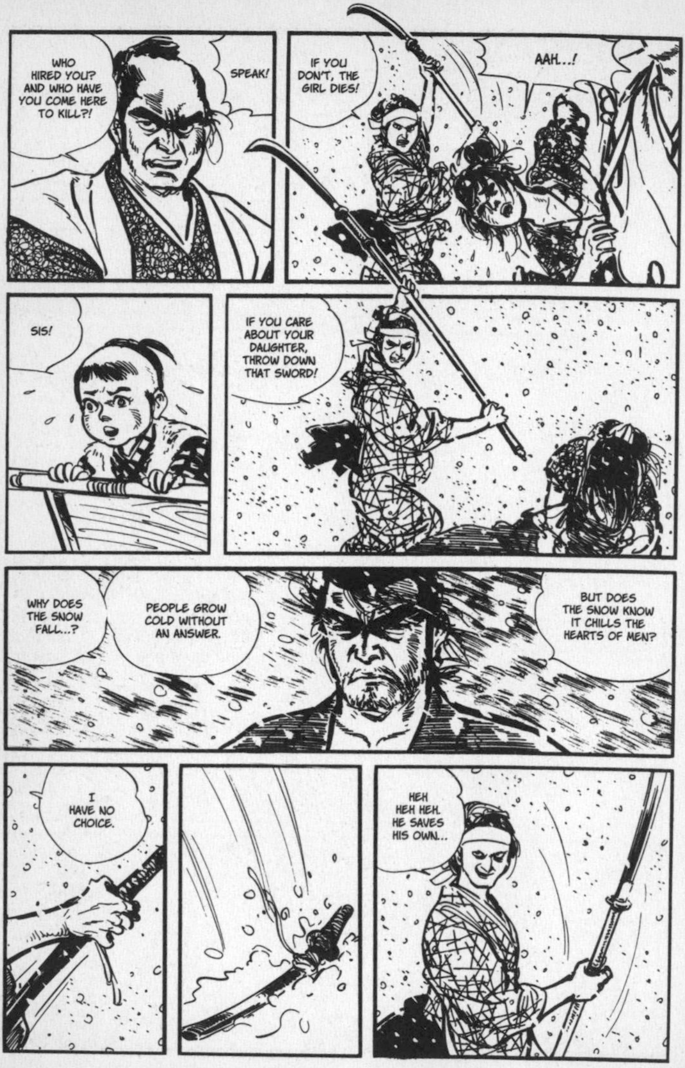
WHO HIRED YOU? AND WHO HAVE YOU COME HERE TO KILL?!
SPEAK!
IF YOU DON'T, THE GIRL DIES!
AAH...!
SIS!
IF YOU CARE ABOUT YOUR DAUGHTER, THROW DOWN THAT SWORD!
WHY DOES THE SNOW FALL...?
PEOPLE GROW COLD WITHOUT AN ANSWER.
BUT DOES THE SNOW KNOW IT CHILLS THE HEARTS OF MEN?
I HAVE NO CHOICE.
HEH HEH HEH. HE SAVES HIS OWN...

GIEHHH!!

SWHWKK

AH!!

FSH FSH

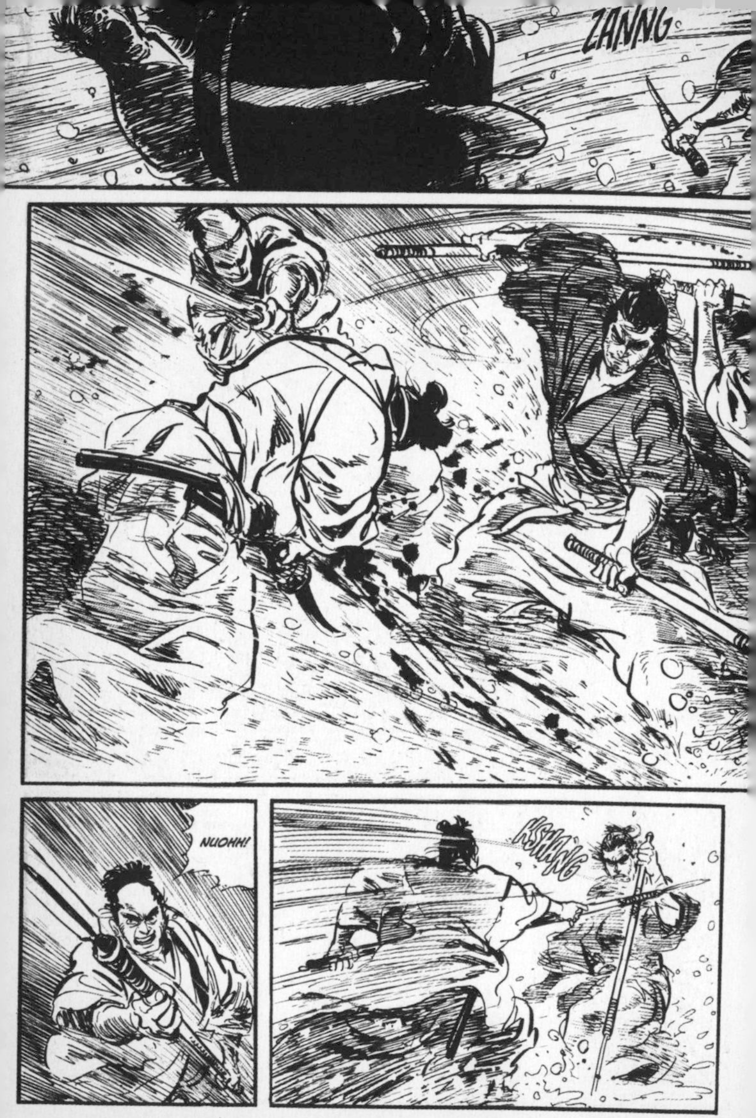
ZANNG
NUOHH!
KSHANG

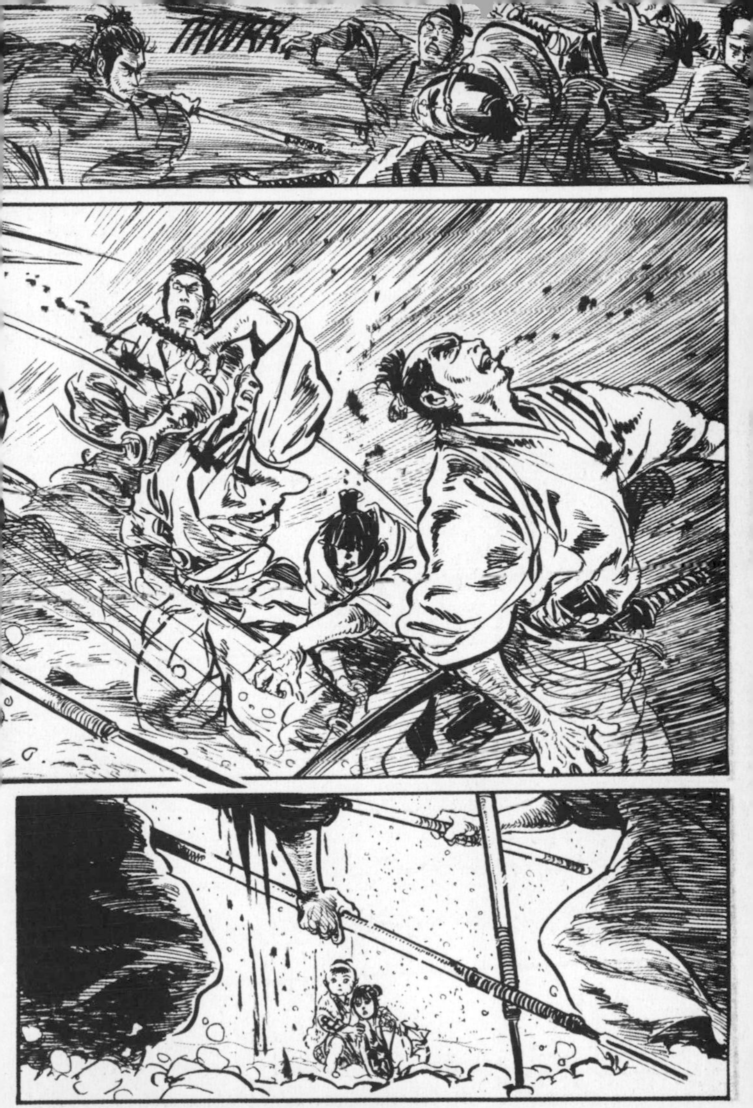
THWRR

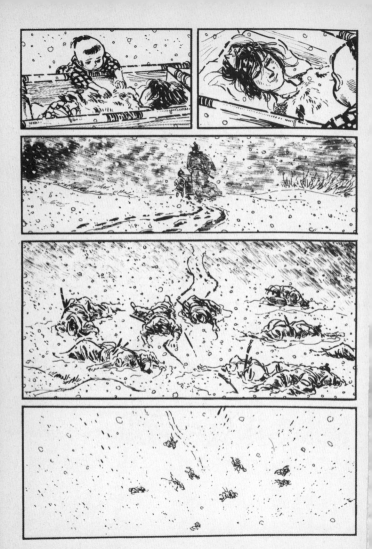

the thirteenth

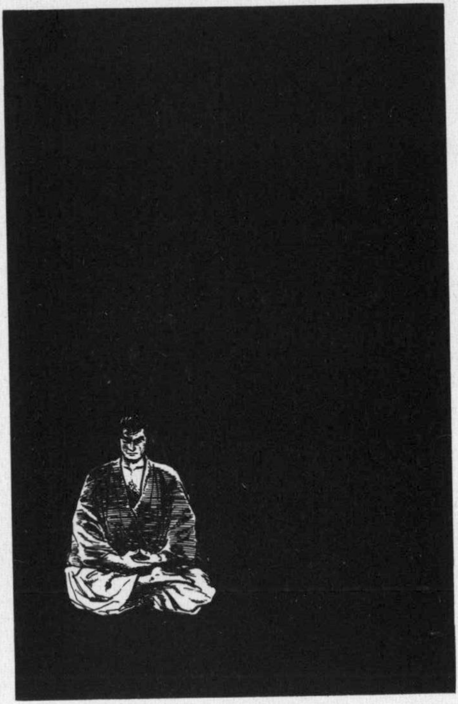

The Gateless Barrier

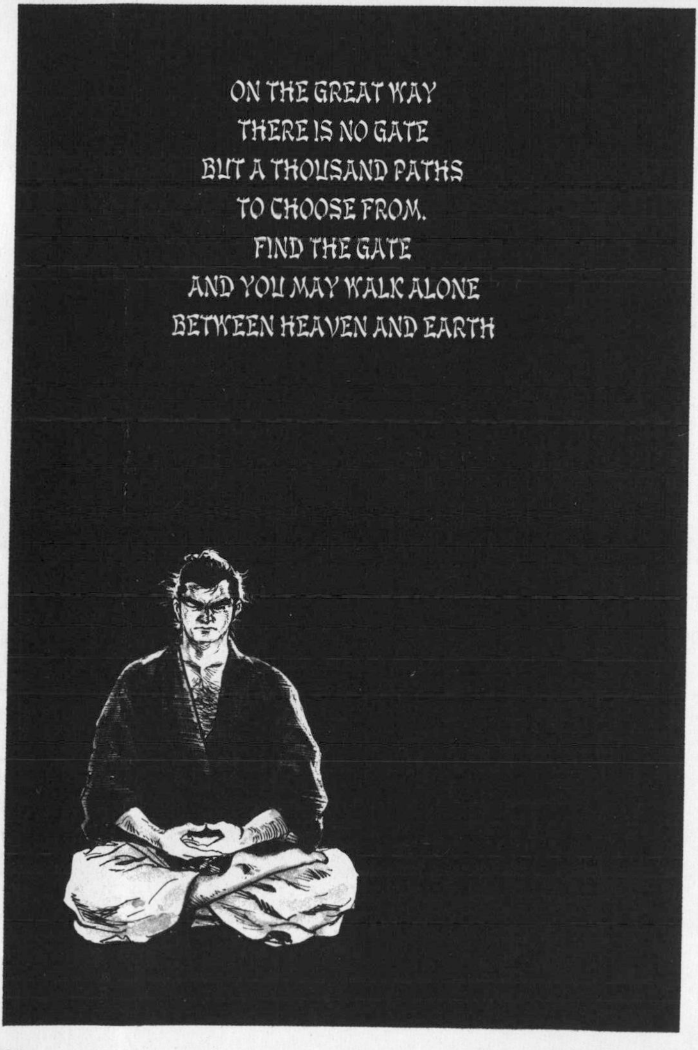
ON THE GREAT WAY
THERE IS NO GATE
BUT A THOUSAND PATHS
TO CHOOSE FROM.
FIND THE GATE
AND YOU MAY WALK ALONE
BETWEEN HEAVEN AND EARTH

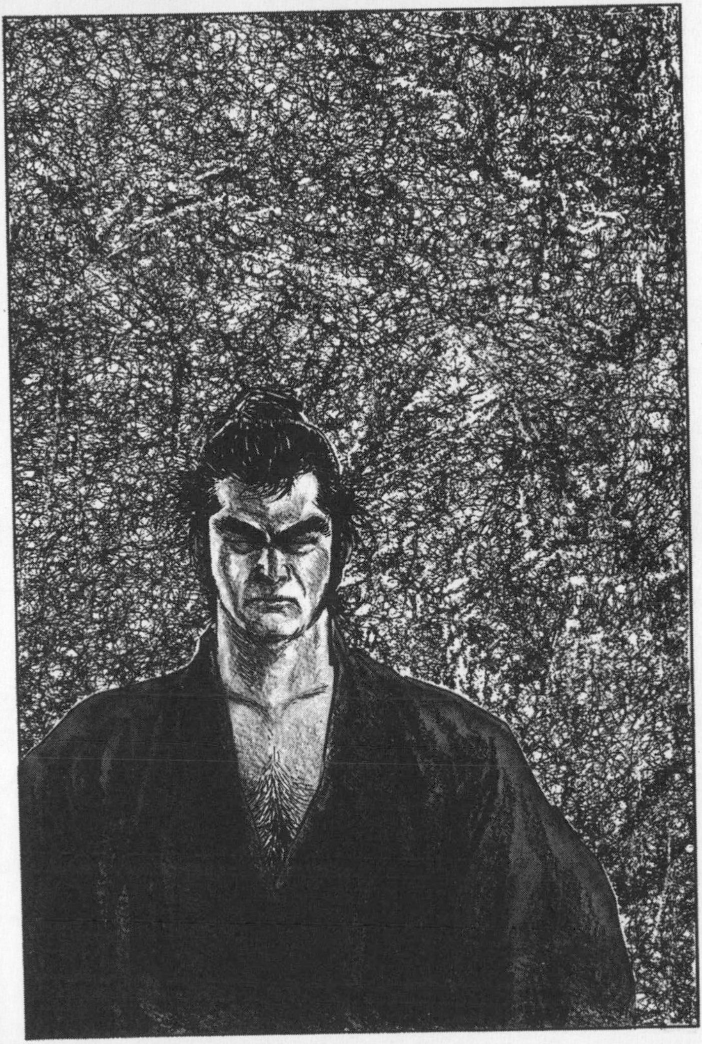

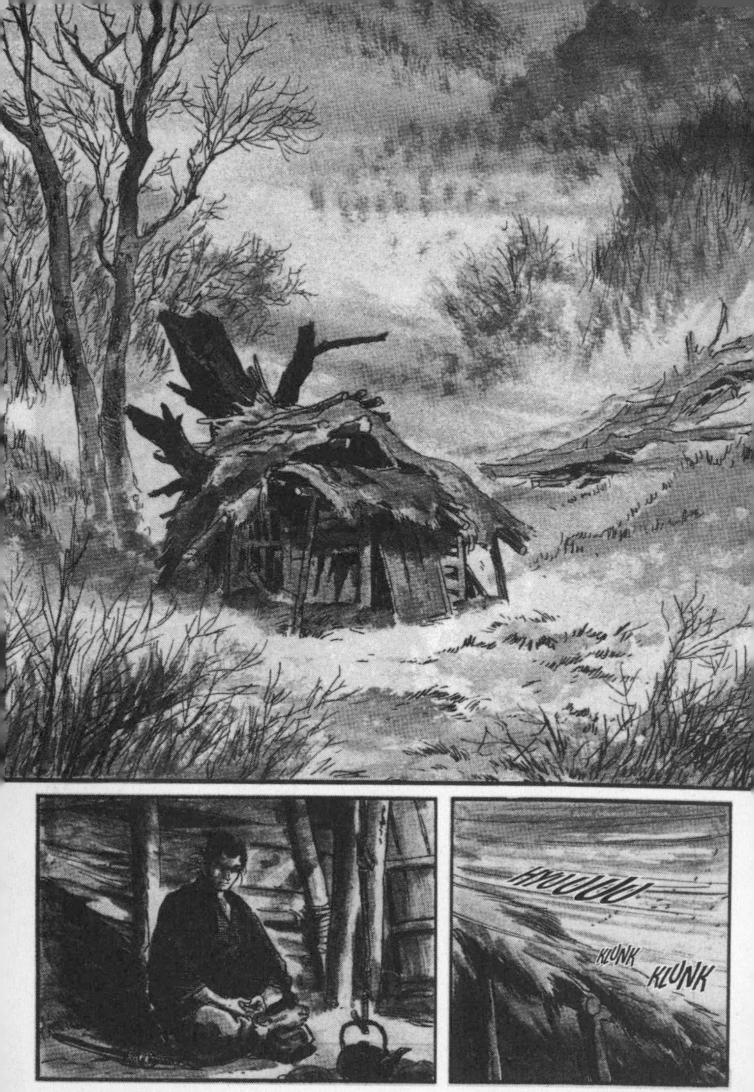
HYUUUUU
KLUNK
KLUNK

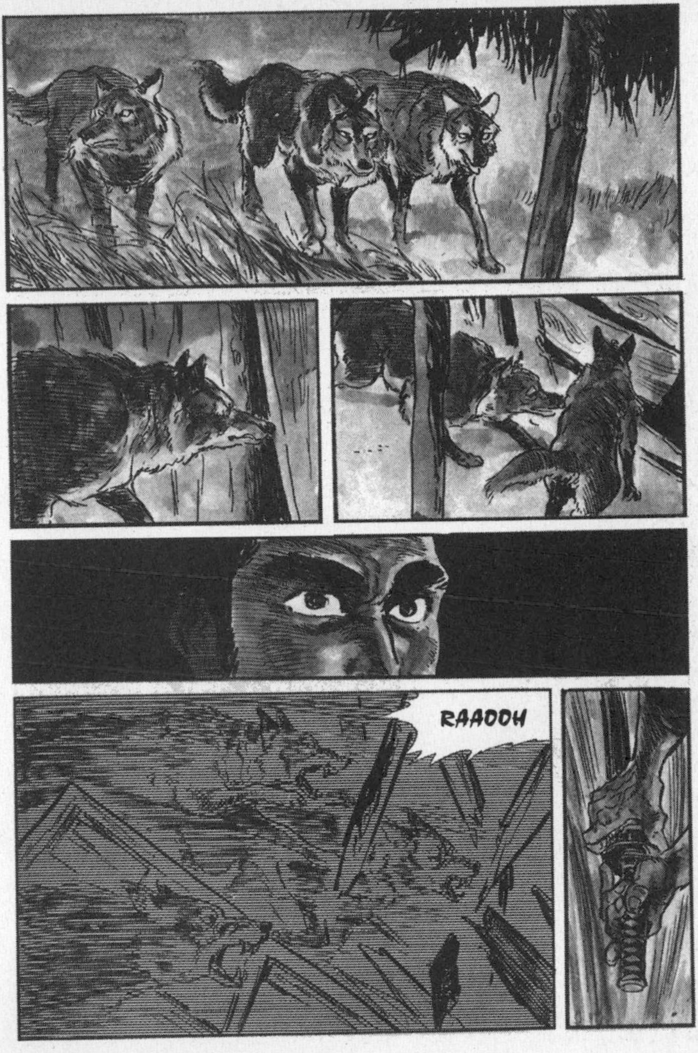
RAAOOH

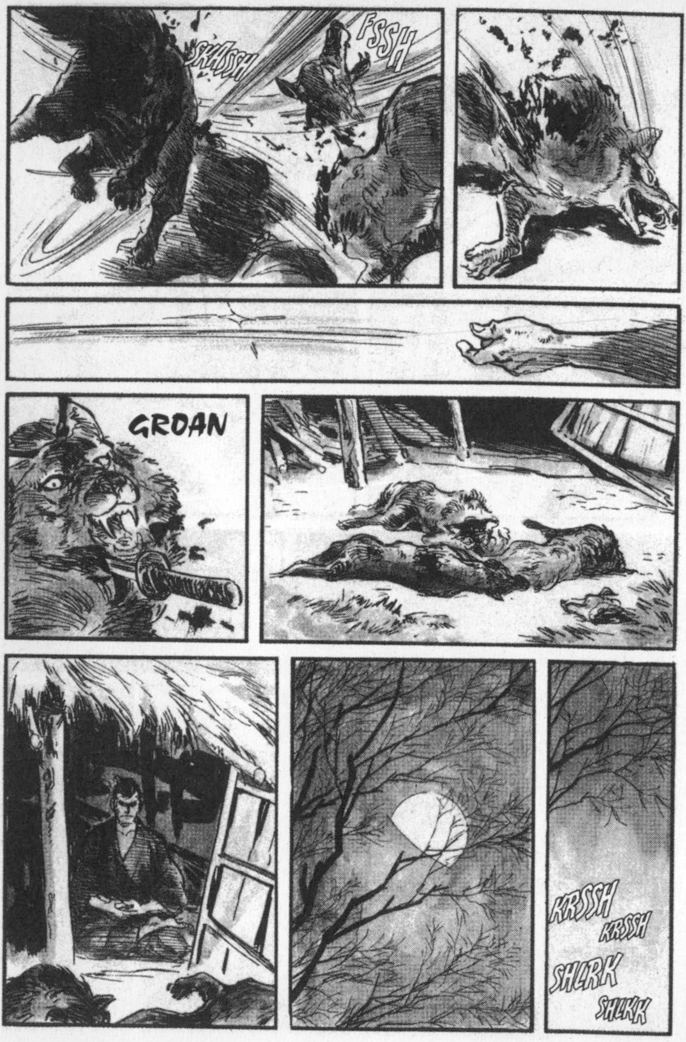
SKASSH
FSSH
GROAN
KRSSH
KRSSH
SHLRK
SHLKK

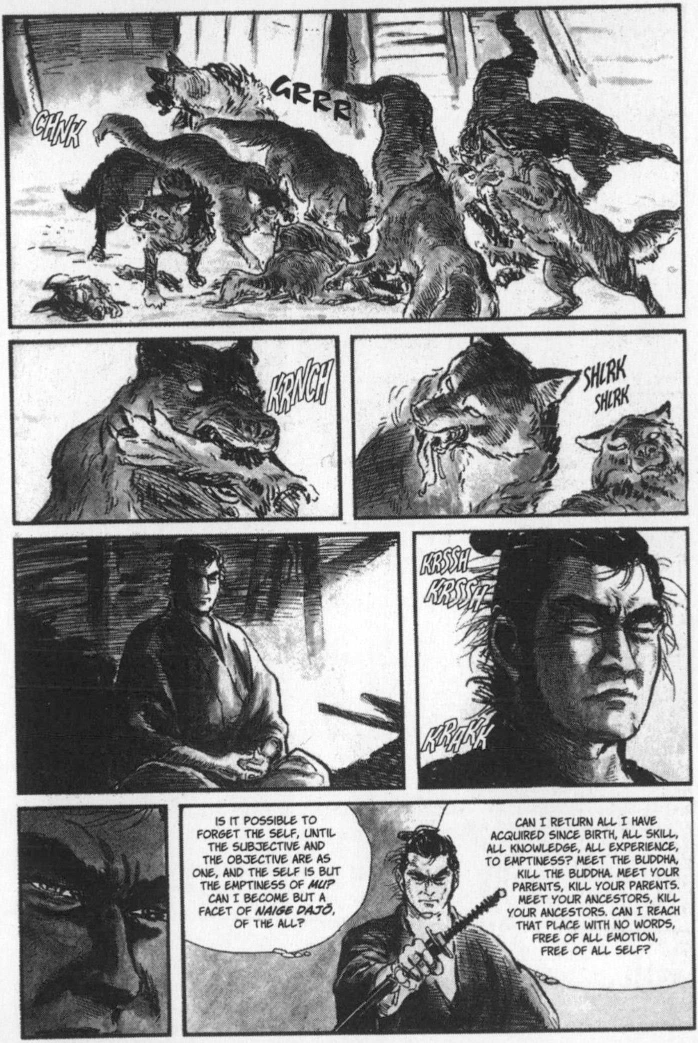
GRRR
CHNK
KRNCH
SHLRK
SHLRK
KRSSH
KRSSH
KRAKK
IS IT POSSIBLE TO FORGET THE SELF, UNTIL THE SUBJECTIVE AND THE OBJECTIVE ARE AS ONE, AND THE SELF IS BUT THE EMPTINESS OF MU? CAN I BECOME BUT A FACET OF NAIGE DAJŌ, OF THE ALL?
CAN I RETURN ALL I HAVE ACQUIRED SINCE BIRTH, ALL SKILL, ALL KNOWLEDGE, ALL EXPERIENCE, TO EMPTINESS? MEET THE BUDDHA, KILL THE BUDDHA. MEET YOUR PARENTS, KILL YOUR PARENTS. MEET YOUR ANCESTORS, KILL YOUR ANCESTORS. CAN I REACH THAT PLACE WITH NO WORDS, FREE OF ALL EMOTION, FREE OF ALL SELF?

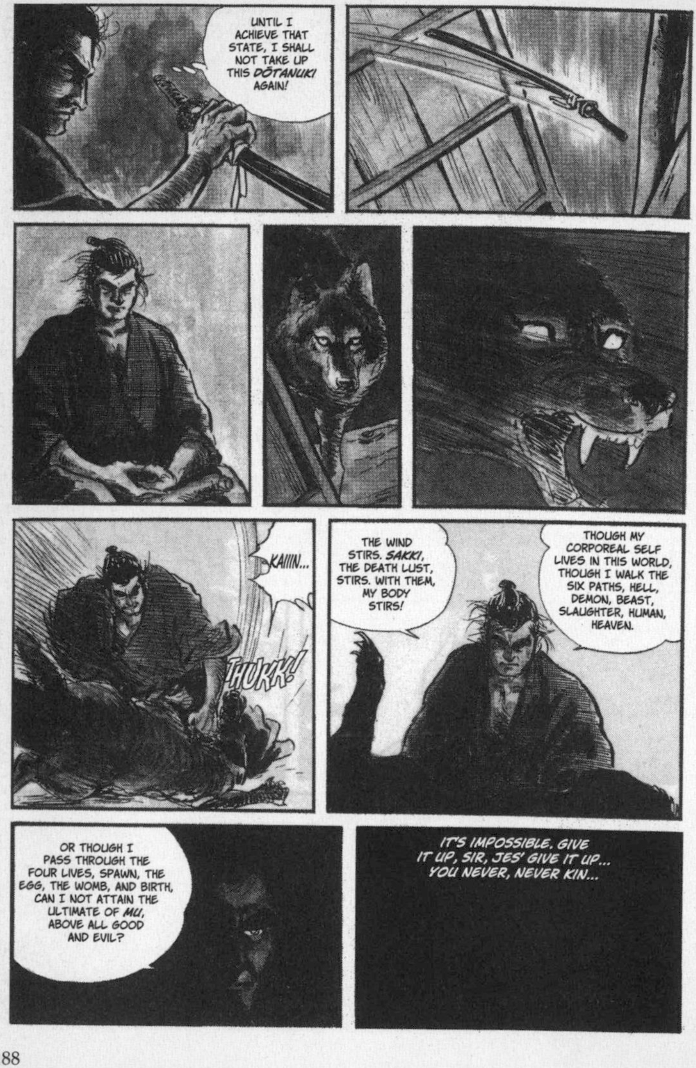
UNTIL I ACHIEVE THAT STATE, I SHALL NOT TAKE UP THIS DŌTANUKI AGAIN!
KAIIIN...
THUKK!
THE WIND STIRS. SAKKI, THE DEATH LUST, STIRS. WITH THEM, MY BODY STIRS!
THOUGH MY CORPOREAL SELF LIVES IN THIS WORLD, THOUGH I WALK THE SIX PATHS, HELL, DEMON, BEAST, SLAUGHTER, HUMAN, HEAVEN.
OR THOUGH I PASS THROUGH THE FOUR LIVES, SPAWN, THE EGG, THE WOMB, AND BIRTH, CAN I NOT ATTAIN THE ULTIMATE OF MU, ABOVE ALL GOOD AND EVIL?
IT'S IMPOSSIBLE. GIVE IT UP, SIR, JES' GIVE IT UP... YOU NEVER, NEVER KIN...

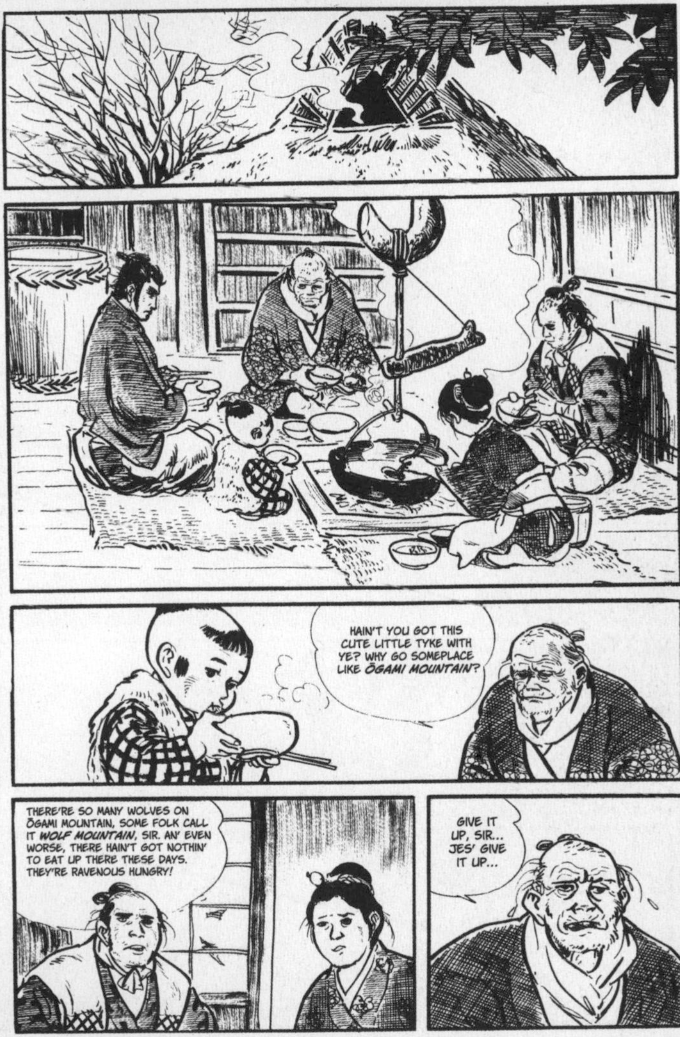
HAIN'T YOU GOT THIS CUTE LITTLE TYKE WITH YE? WHY GO SOMEPLACE LIKE ŌGAMI MOUNTAIN?
THERE'RE SO MANY WOLVES ON ŌGAMI MOUNTAIN, SOME FOLK CALL IT WOLF MOUNTAIN, SIR. AN' EVEN WORSE, THERE HAIN'T GOT NOTHIN' TO EAT UP THERE THESE DAYS. THEY'RE RAVENOUS HUNGRY!
GIVE IT UP, SIR... JES' GIVE IT UP...

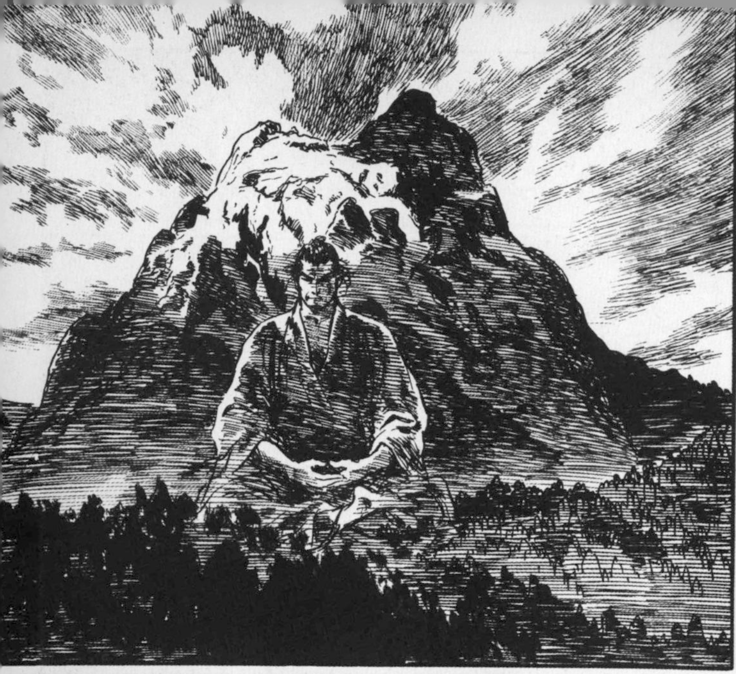

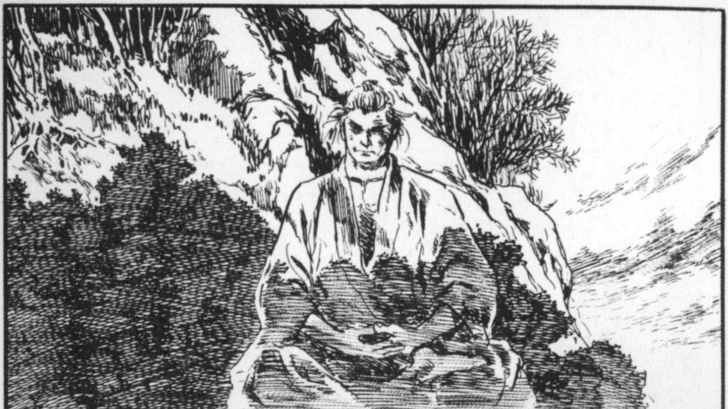

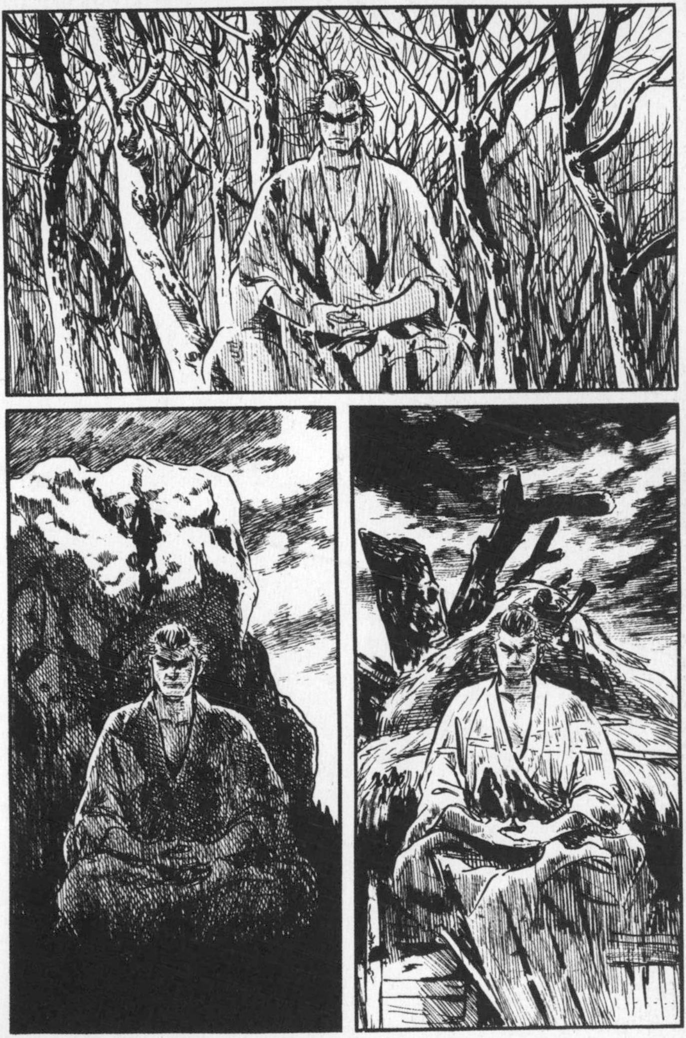

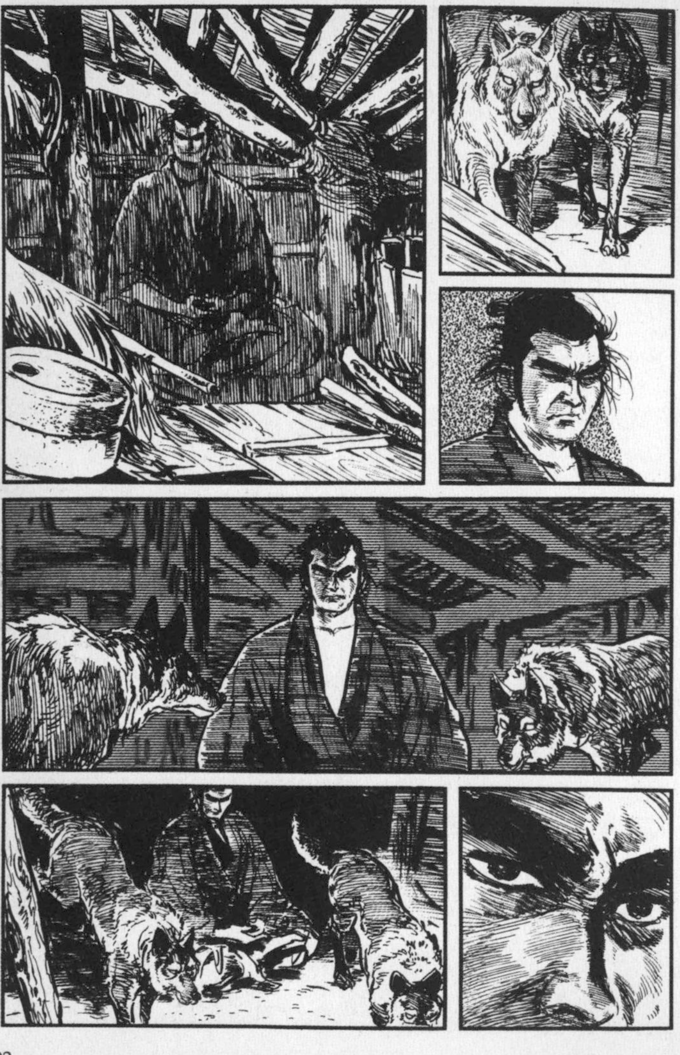

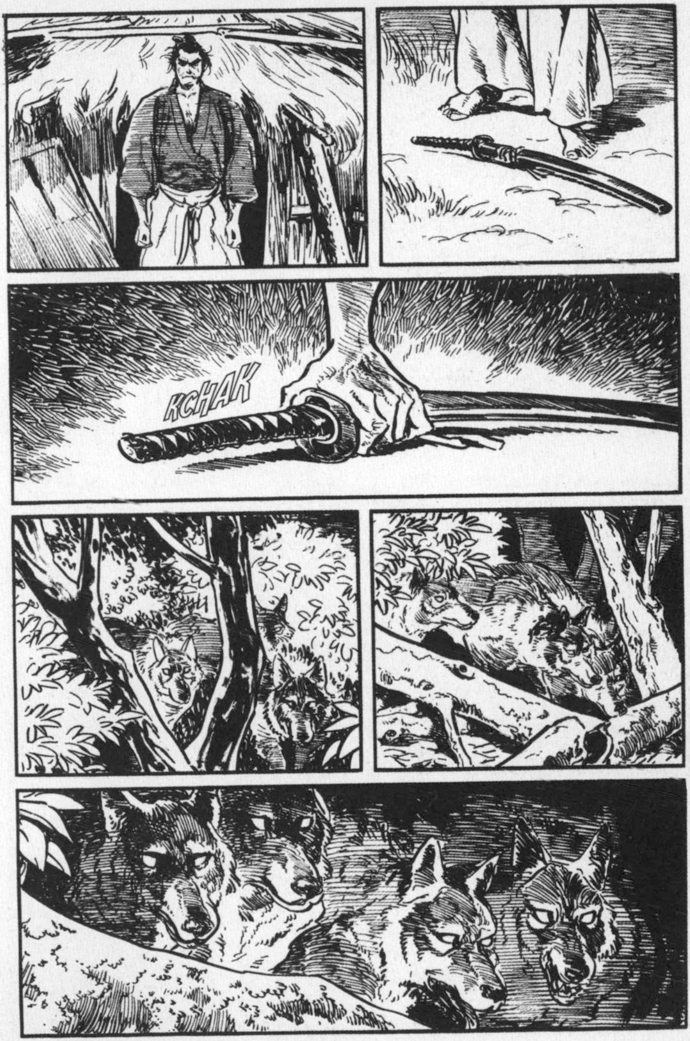
KCHAK

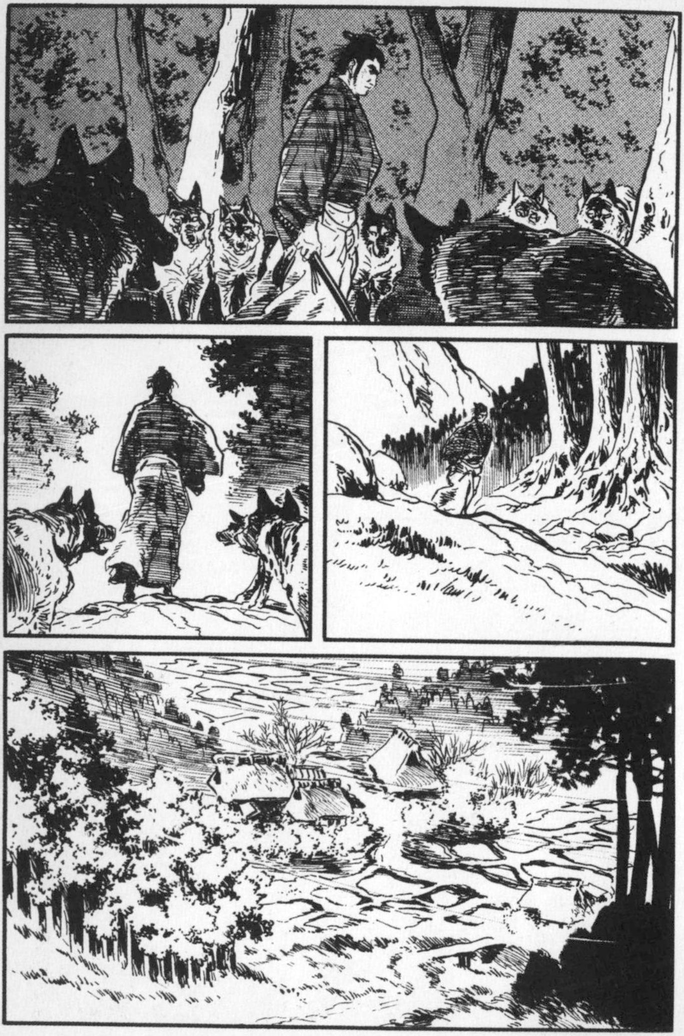

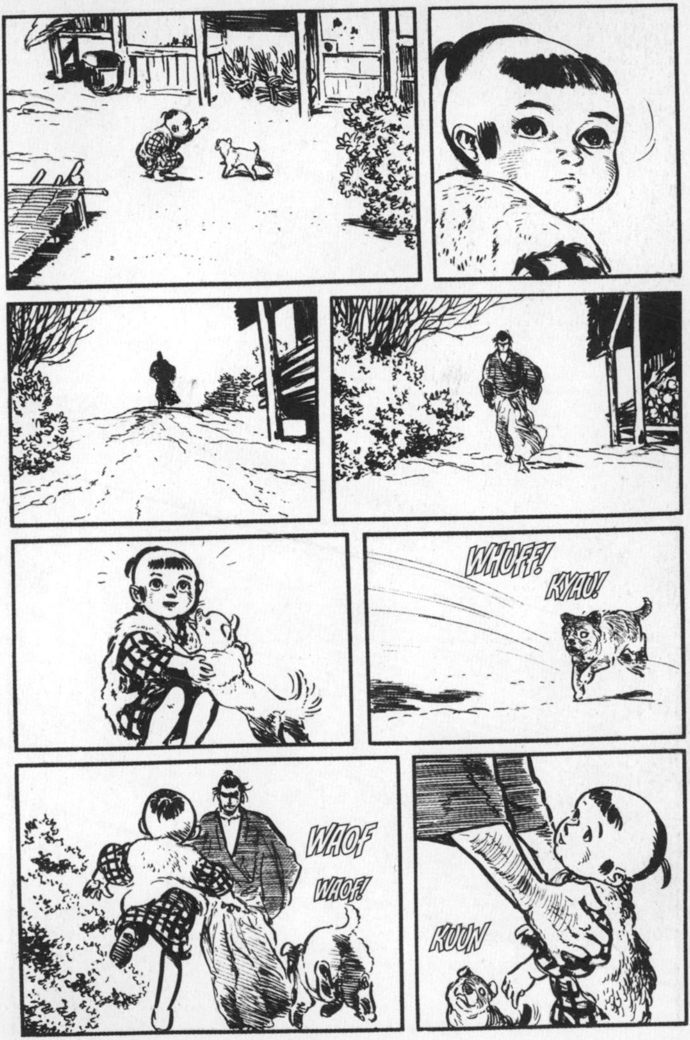
WHUFF!
KYAU!
WAOF
WAOF!
KUUN

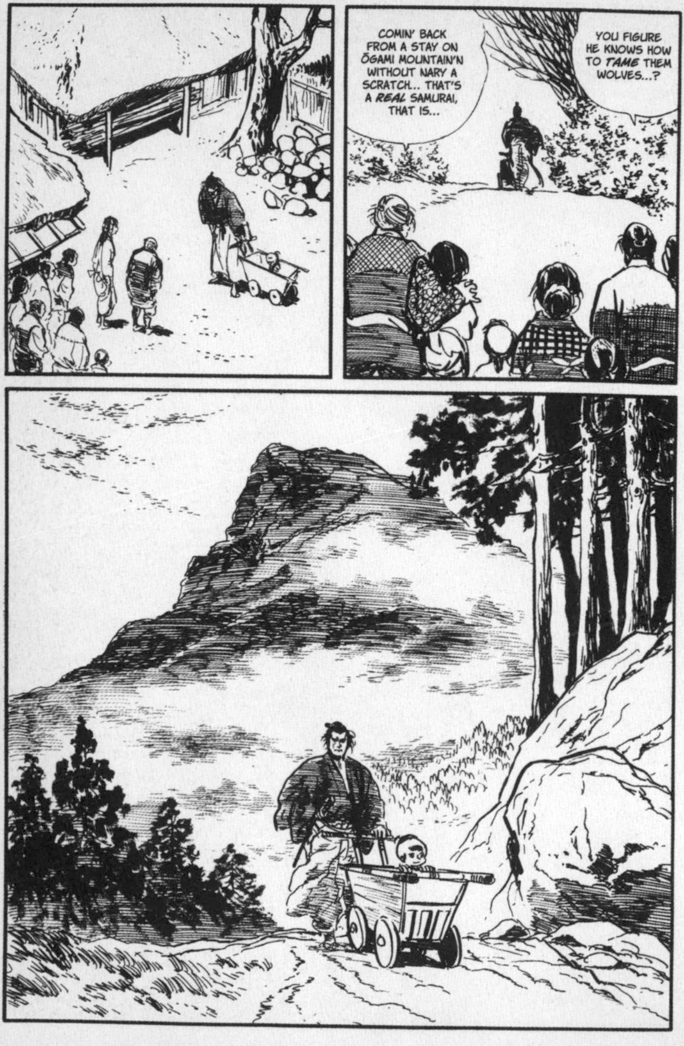
COMIN' BACK FROM A STAY ON ŌGAMI MOUNTAIN'N WITHOUT NARY A SCRATCH... THAT'S A *REAL* SAMURAI, THAT IS...
YOU FIGURE HE KNOWS HOW TO *TAME* THEM WOLVES...?

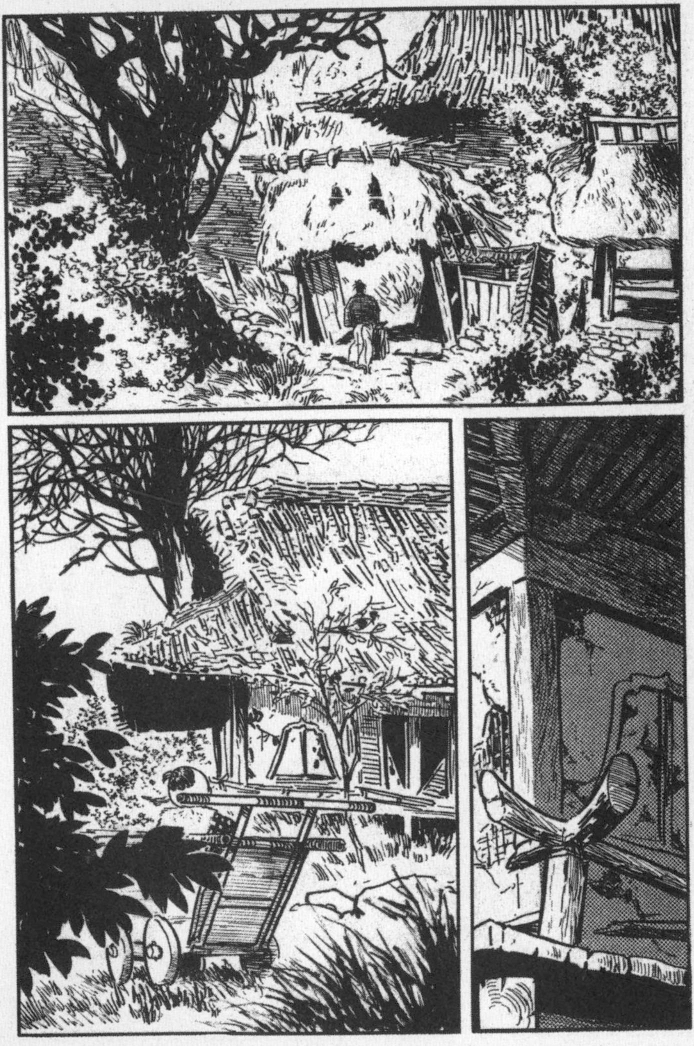

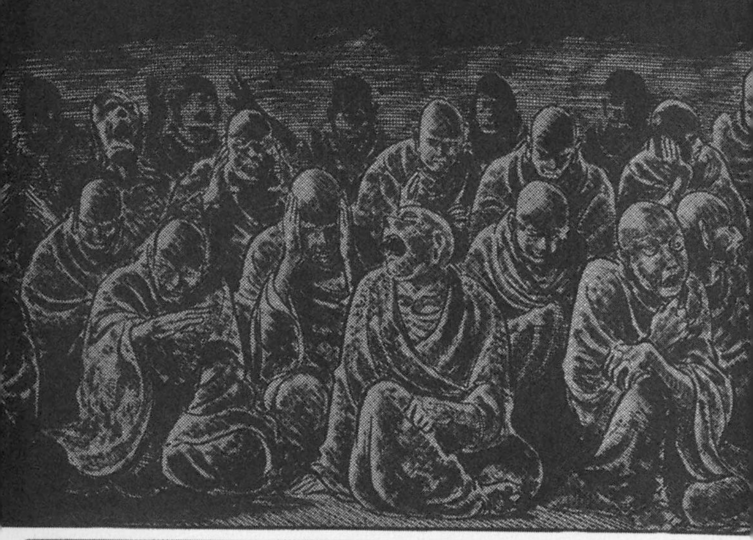

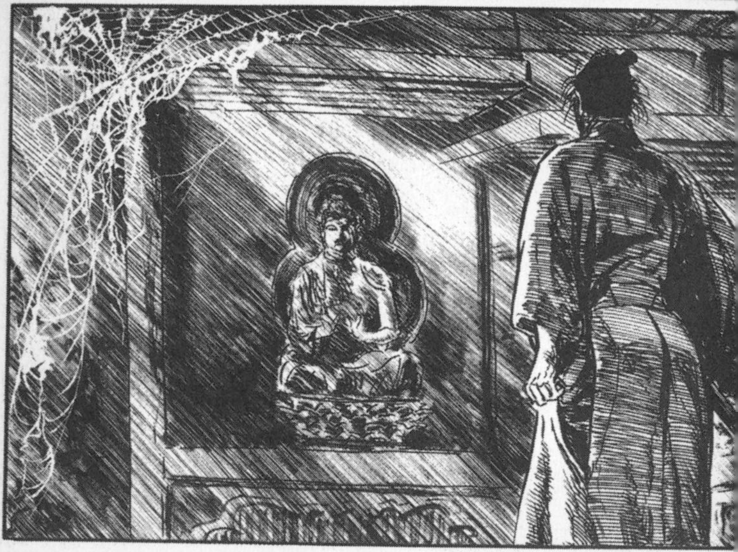

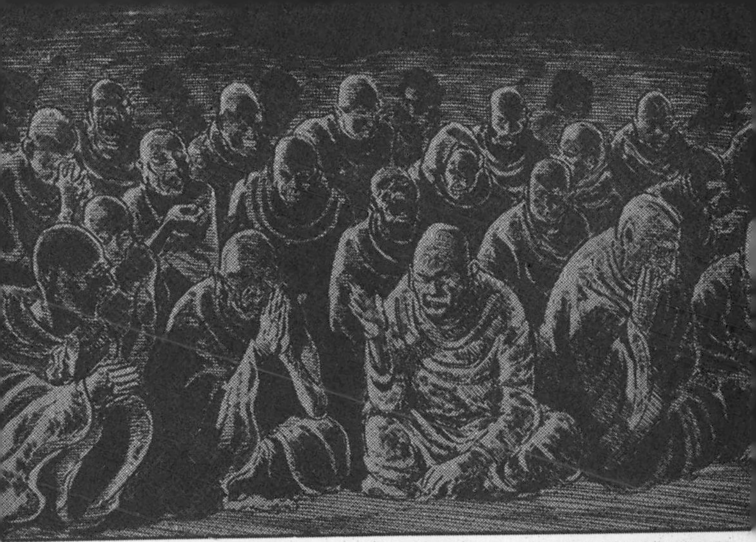

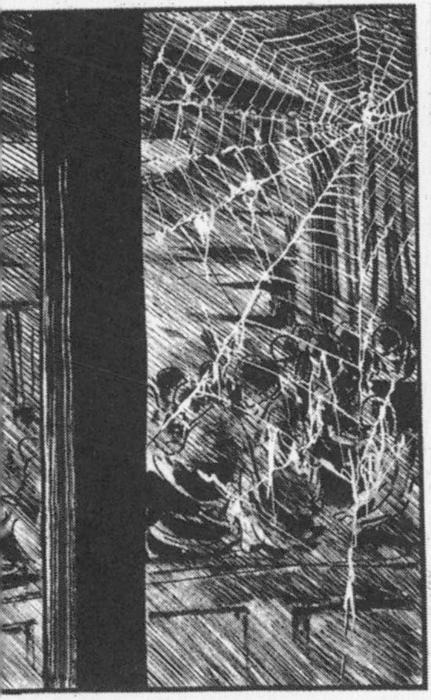

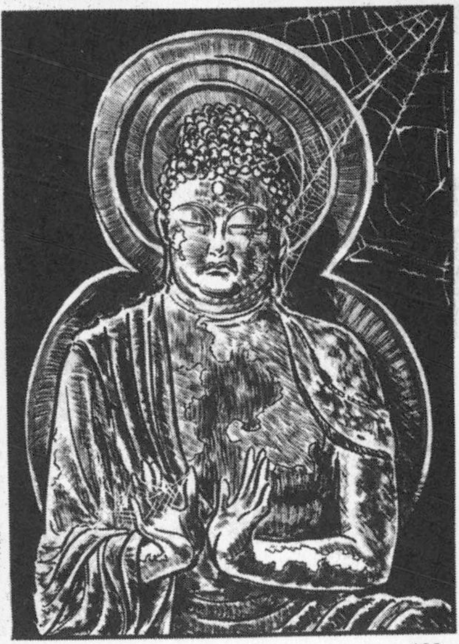

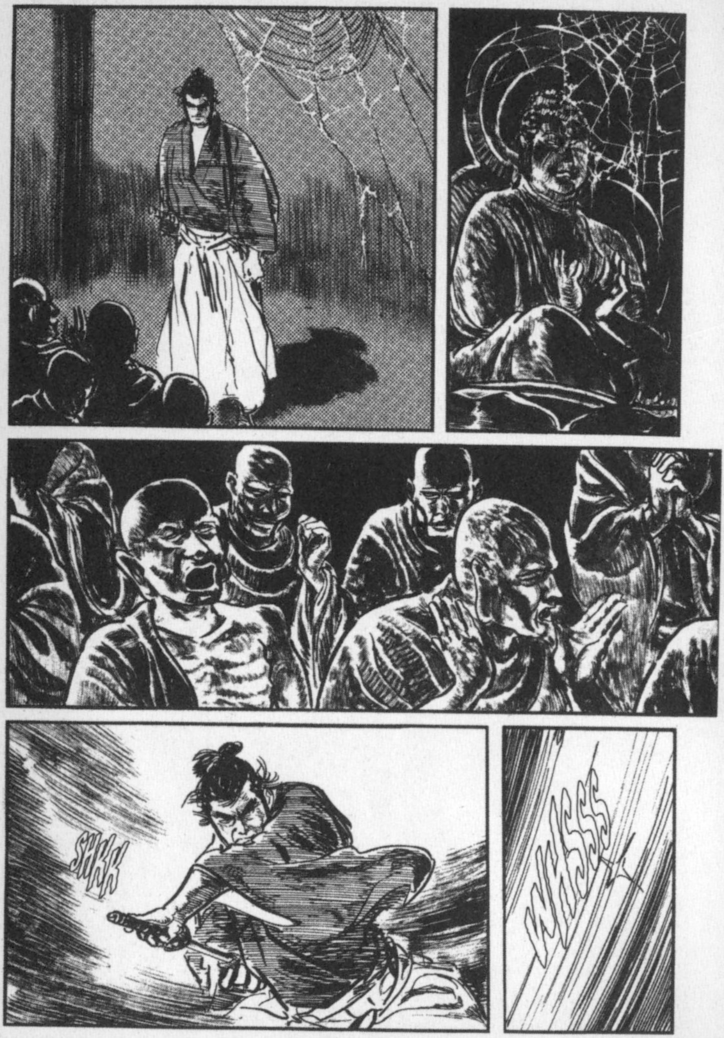
SHKK
WHSSS

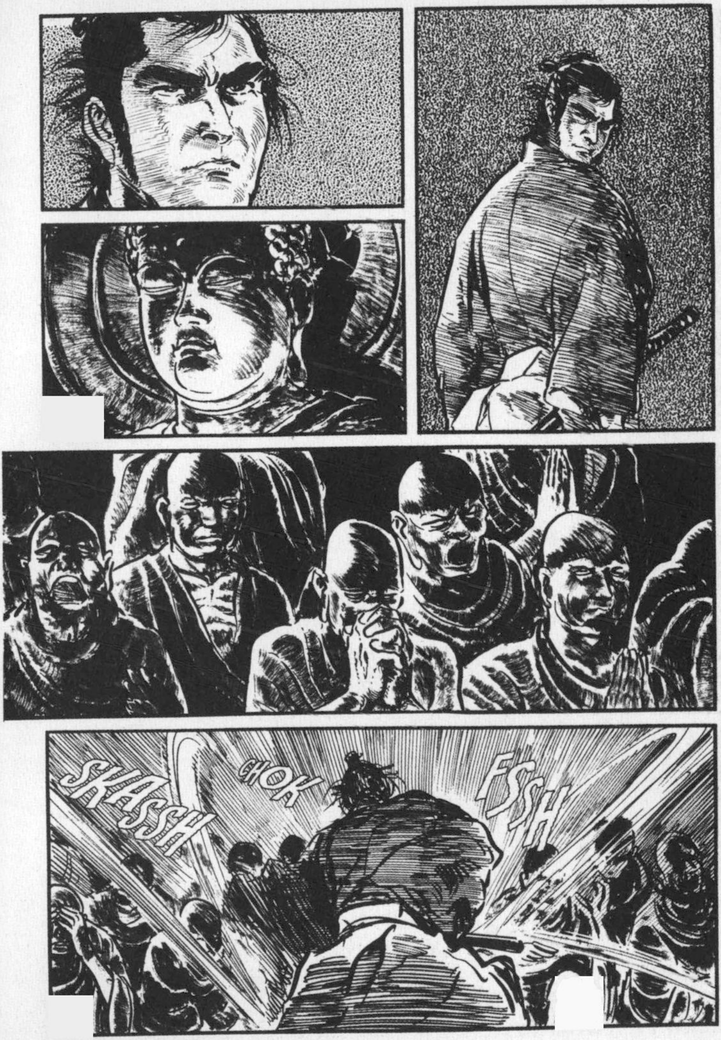
SKASSH
CHOK
FSSH

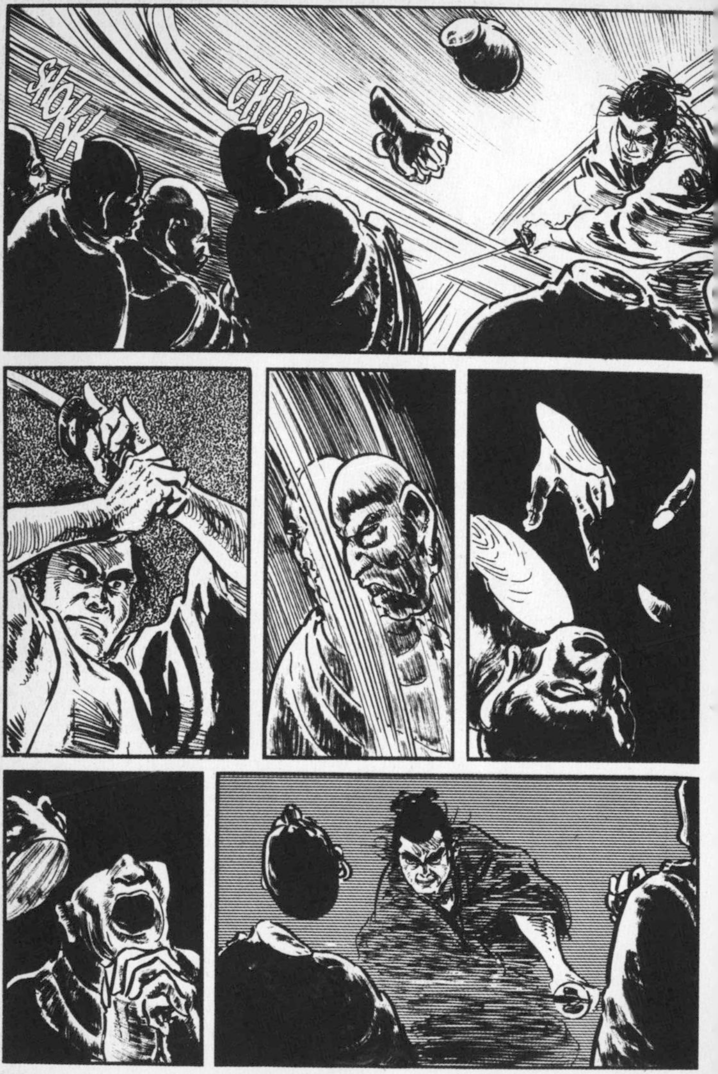
SHOKK
CHUDD

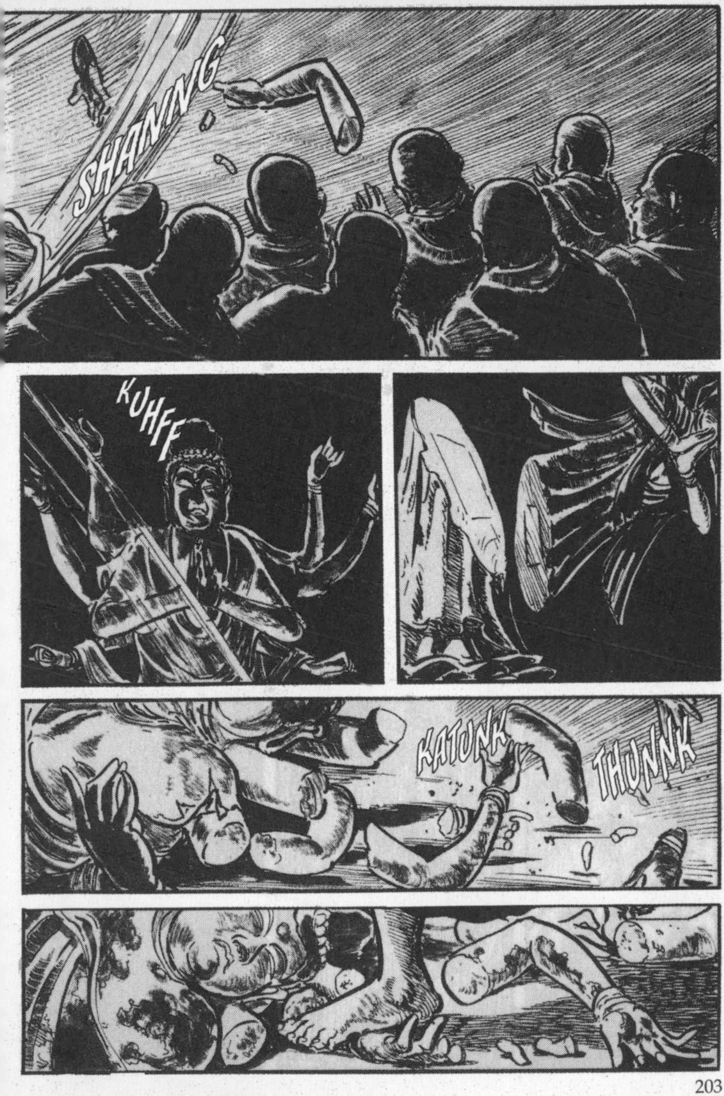
SHANNG
KUHFF
KATUNK
THUNNK

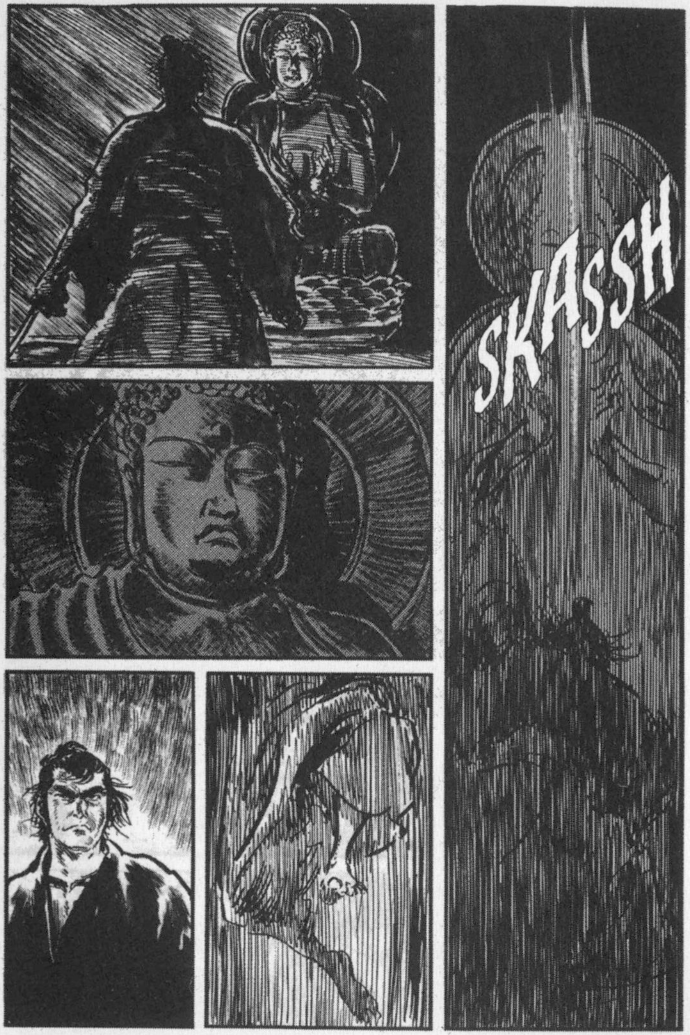
SKASSH

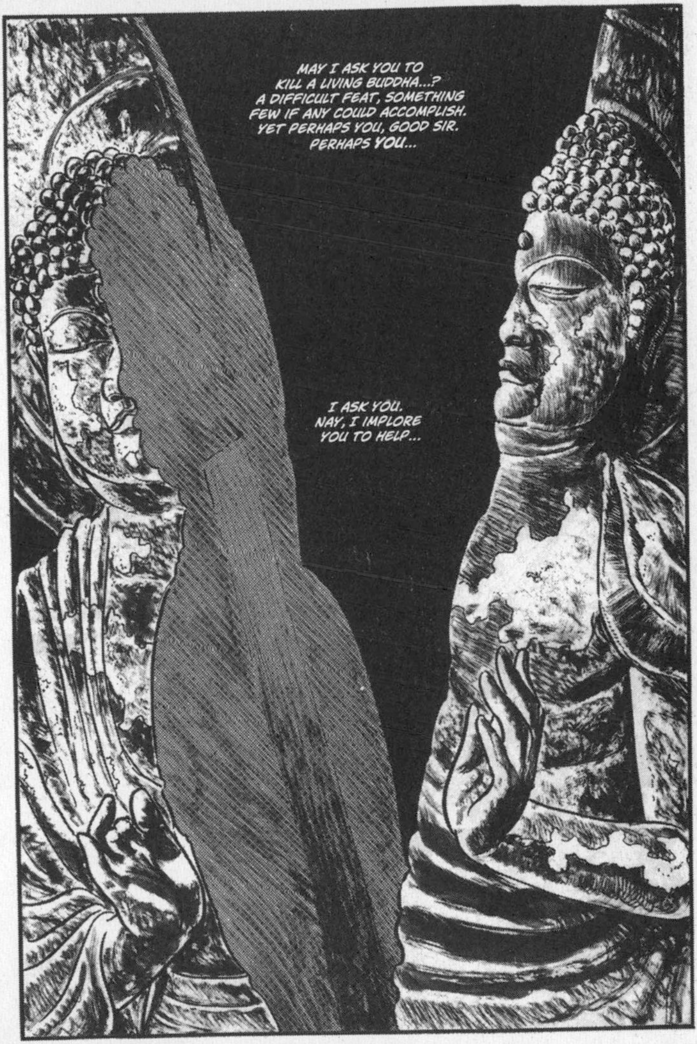
MAY I ASK YOU TO KILL A LIVING BUDDHA...? A DIFFICULT FEAT, SOMETHING FEW IF ANY COULD ACCOMPLISH. YET PERHAPS YOU, GOOD SIR. PERHAPS YOU...
I ASK YOU. NAY, I IMPLORE YOU TO HELP...

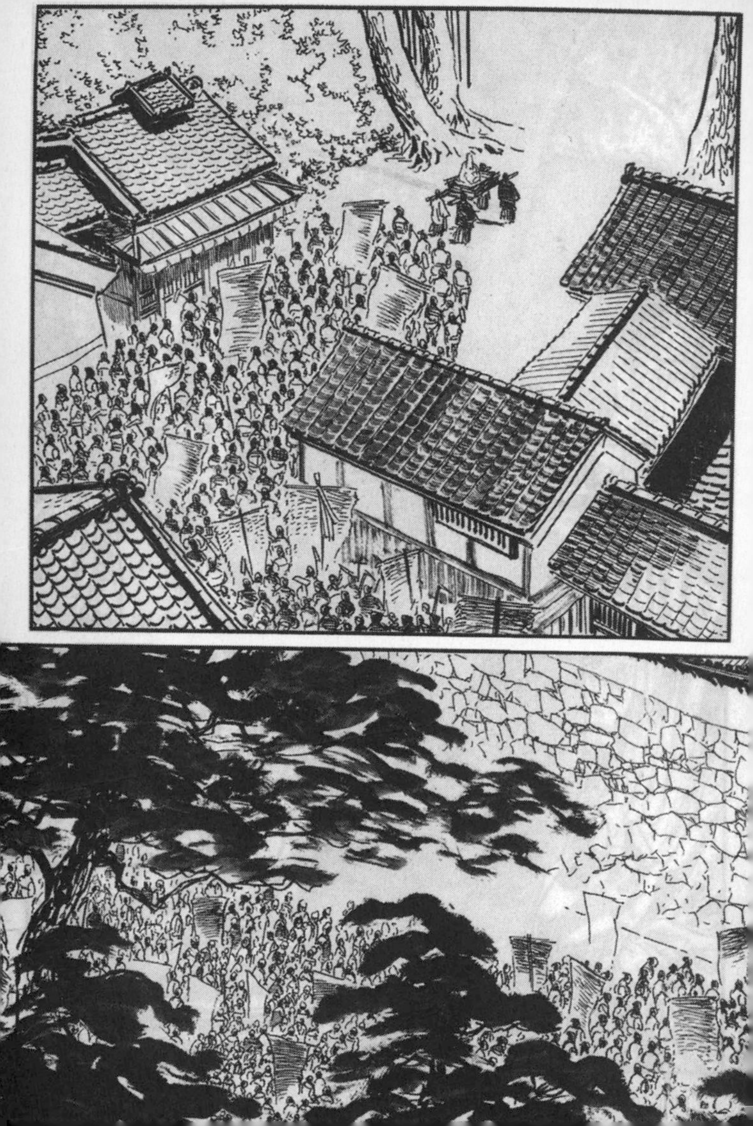

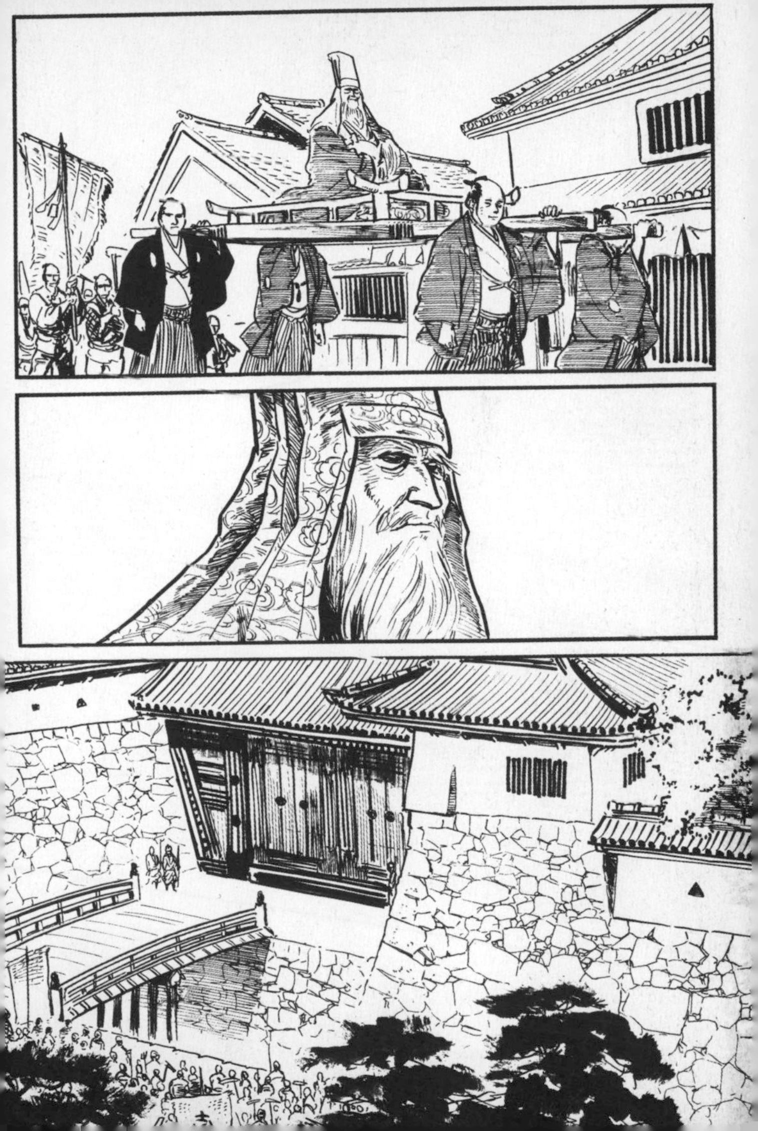

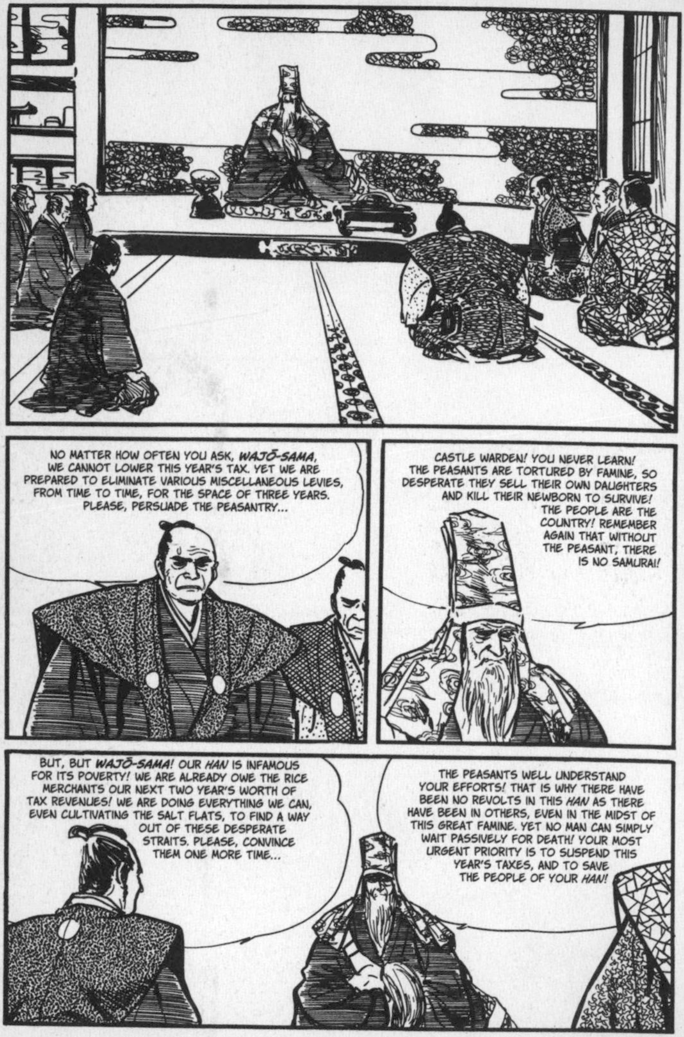

NO MATTER HOW OFTEN YOU ASK, *WAJŌ-SAMA*, WE CANNOT LOWER THIS YEAR'S TAX. YET WE ARE PREPARED TO ELIMINATE VARIOUS MISCELLANEOUS LEVIES, FROM TIME TO TIME, FOR THE SPACE OF THREE YEARS. PLEASE, PERSUADE THE PEASANTRY...
CASTLE WARDEN! YOU NEVER LEARN! THE PEASANTS ARE TORTURED BY FAMINE, SO DESPERATE THEY SELL THEIR OWN DAUGHTERS AND KILL THEIR NEWBORN TO SURVIVE! THE PEOPLE ARE THE COUNTRY! REMEMBER AGAIN THAT WITHOUT THE PEASANT, THERE IS NO SAMURAI!
BUT, BUT *WAJŌ-SAMA!* OUR *HAN* IS INFAMOUS FOR ITS POVERTY! WE ARE ALREADY OWE THE RICE MERCHANTS OUR NEXT TWO YEAR'S WORTH OF TAX REVENUES! WE ARE DOING EVERYTHING WE CAN, EVEN CULTIVATING THE SALT FLATS, TO FIND A WAY OUT OF THESE DESPERATE STRAITS. PLEASE, CONVINCE THEM ONE MORE TIME...
THE PEASANTS WELL UNDERSTAND YOUR EFFORTS! THAT IS WHY THERE HAVE BEEN NO REVOLTS IN THIS *HAN* AS THERE HAVE BEEN IN OTHERS, EVEN IN THE MIDST OF THIS GREAT FAMINE. YET NO MAN CAN SIMPLY WAIT PASSIVELY FOR DEATH! YOUR MOST URGENT PRIORITY IS TO SUSPEND THIS YEAR'S TAXES, AND TO SAVE THE PEOPLE OF YOUR *HAN!*

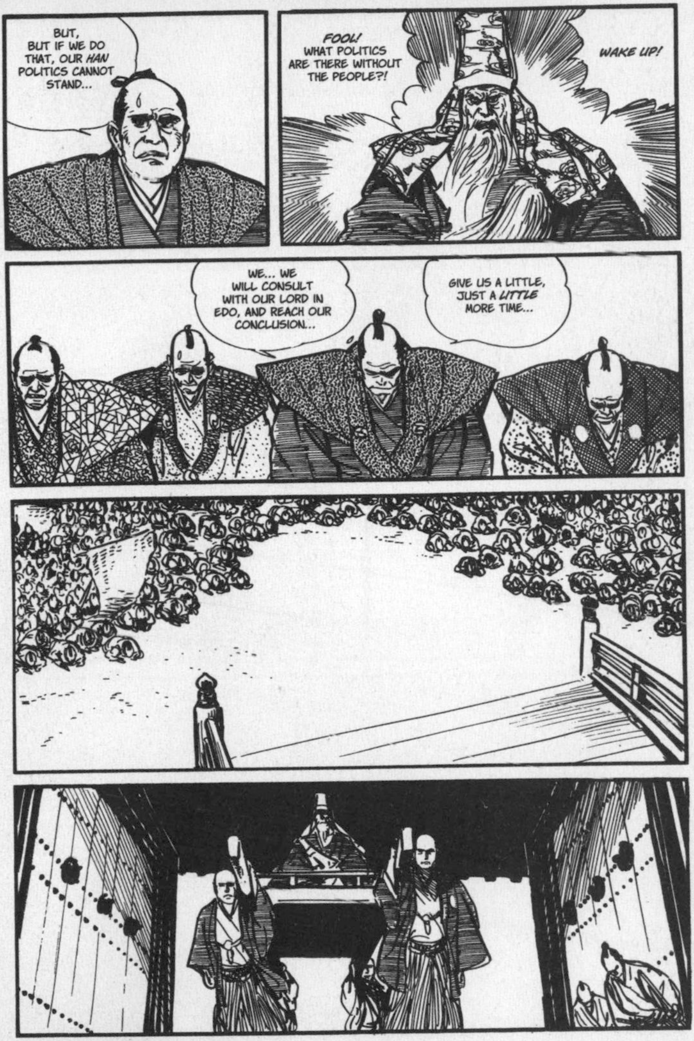
BUT, BUT IF WE DO THAT, OUR HAN POLITICS CANNOT STAND...
FOOL! WHAT POLITICS ARE THERE WITHOUT THE PEOPLE?!
WAKE UP!
WE... WE WILL CONSULT WITH OUR LORD IN EDO, AND REACH OUR CONCLUSION...
GIVE US A LITTLE, JUST A LITTLE MORE TIME...

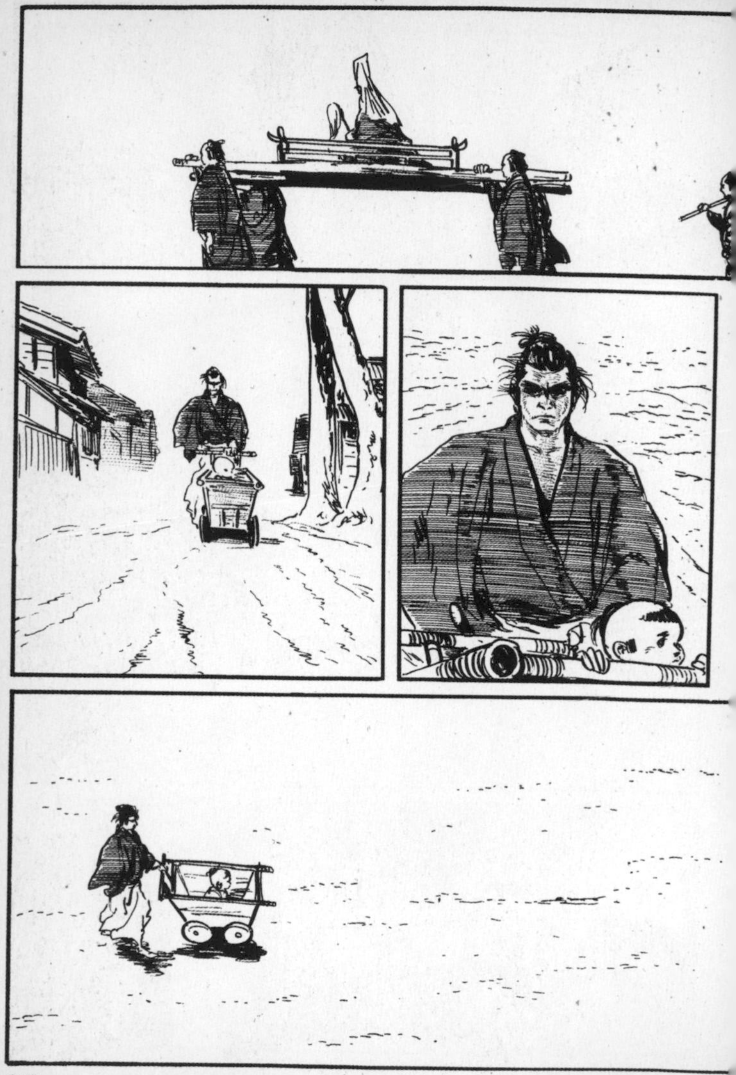

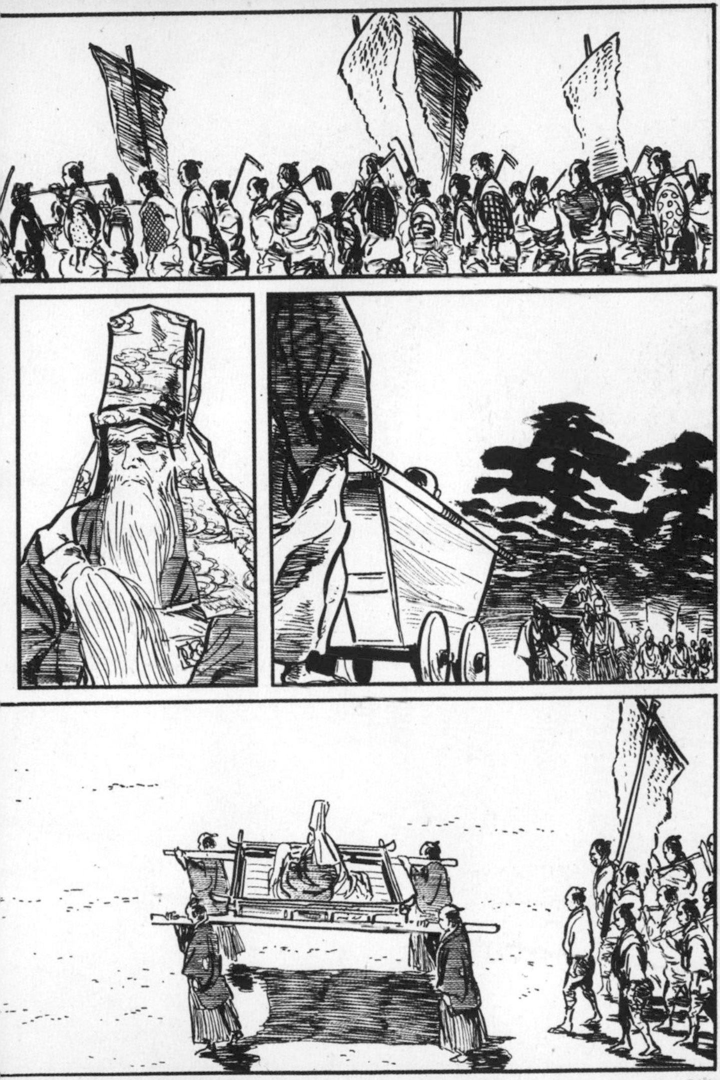

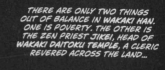

THERE ARE ONLY TWO THINGS
OUT OF BALANCE IN WAKAKI HAN.
ONE IS POVERTY. THE OTHER IS
THE ZEN PRIEST JIKEI, HEAD OF
WAKAKI DAITOKU TEMPLE, A CLERIC
REVERED ACROSS THE LAND...

JIKEI WAJŌ IS A MAN
OF THE HIGHEST MORALS
AND DEEPEST COMPASSION,
SO MUCH SO HE IS WORSHIPPED
BY OUR PEOPLE AS A LIVING
BUDDHA. EVEN OUR DAIMYŌ,
LORD HIROTAKA, RESPECTS
HIM WITH ALL HIS HEART.

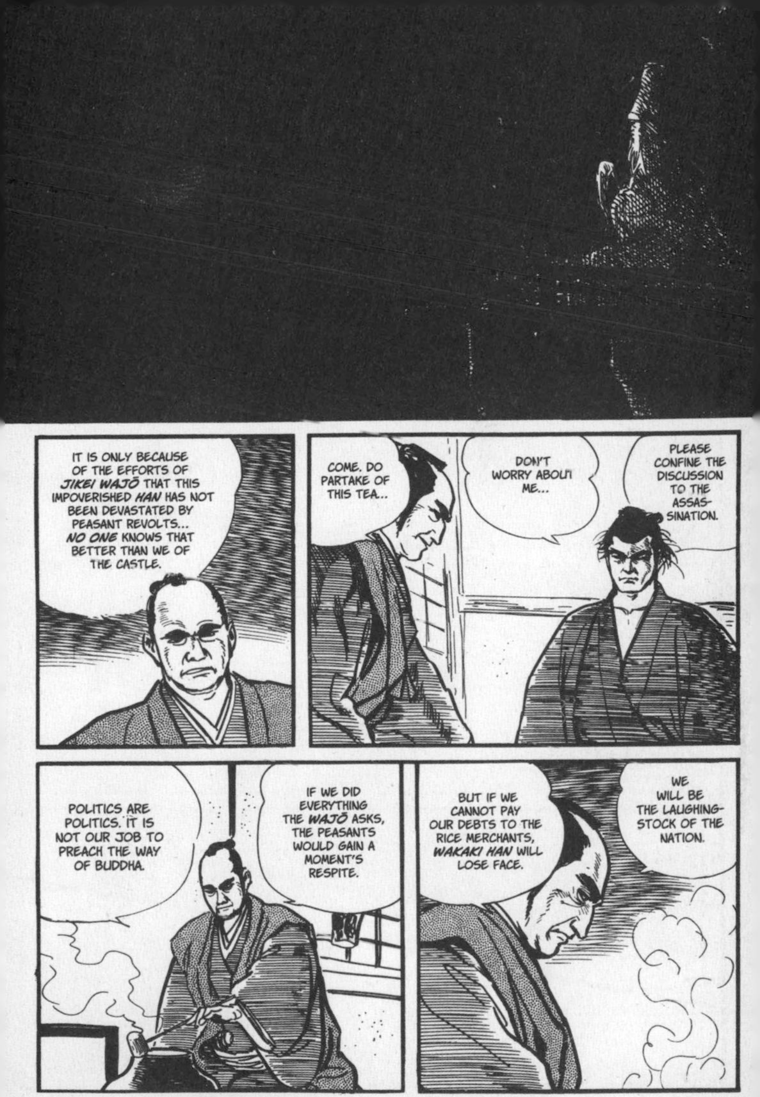
IT IS ONLY BECAUSE OF THE EFFORTS OF *JIKEI WAJŌ* THAT THIS IMPOVERISHED *HAN* HAS NOT BEEN DEVASTATED BY PEASANT REVOLTS... *NO ONE* KNOWS THAT BETTER THAN WE OF THE CASTLE.
COME. DO PARTAKE OF THIS TEA...
DON'T WORRY ABOUT ME...
PLEASE CONFINE THE DISCUSSION TO THE ASSAS-SINATION.
POLITICS ARE POLITICS. IT IS NOT OUR JOB TO PREACH THE WAY OF BUDDHA.
IF WE DID EVERYTHING THE *WAJŌ* ASKS, THE PEASANTS WOULD GAIN A MOMENT'S RESPITE.
BUT IF WE CANNOT PAY OUR DEBTS TO THE RICE MERCHANTS, *WAKAKI HAN* WILL LOSE FACE.
WE WILL BE THE LAUGHING-STOCK OF THE NATION.

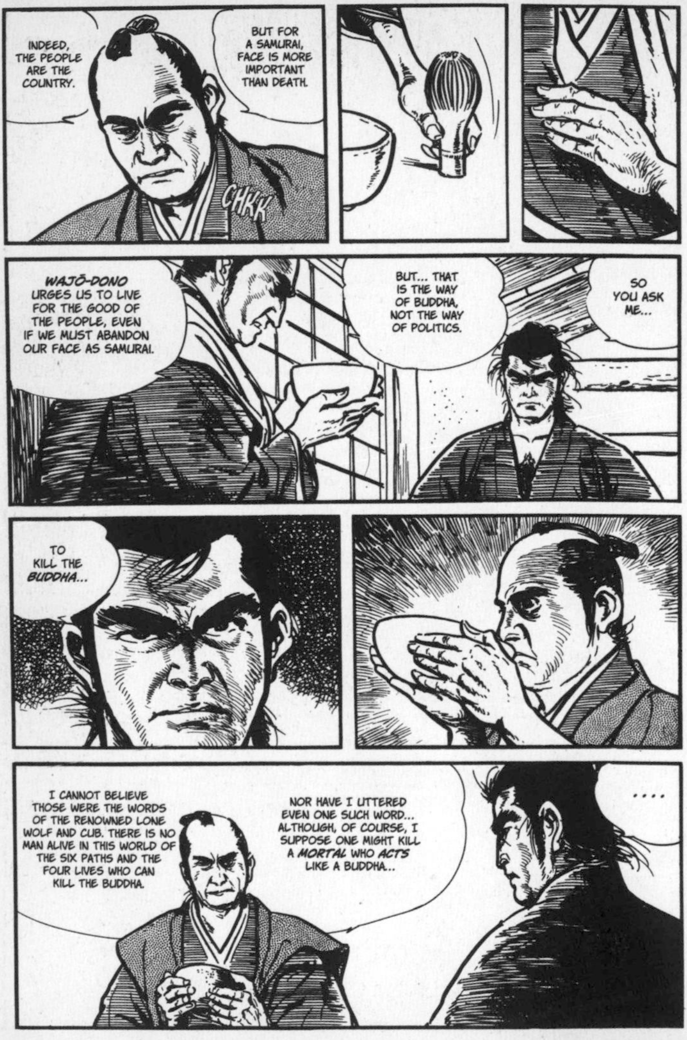
INDEED, THE PEOPLE ARE THE COUNTRY.
BUT FOR A SAMURAI, FACE IS MORE IMPORTANT THAN DEATH.
CHKK
WAJŌ-DONO URGES US TO LIVE FOR THE GOOD OF THE PEOPLE, EVEN IF WE MUST ABANDON OUR FACE AS SAMURAI.
BUT... THAT IS THE WAY OF BUDDHA, NOT THE WAY OF POLITICS.
SO YOU ASK ME...
TO KILL THE BUDDHA...
I CANNOT BELIEVE THOSE WERE THE WORDS OF THE RENOWNED LONE WOLF AND CUB. THERE IS NO MAN ALIVE IN THIS WORLD OF THE SIX PATHS AND THE FOUR LIVES WHO CAN KILL THE BUDDHA.
NOR HAVE I UTTERED EVEN ONE SUCH WORD... ALTHOUGH, OF COURSE, I SUPPOSE ONE MIGHT KILL A MORTAL WHO ACTS LIKE A BUDDHA...
....

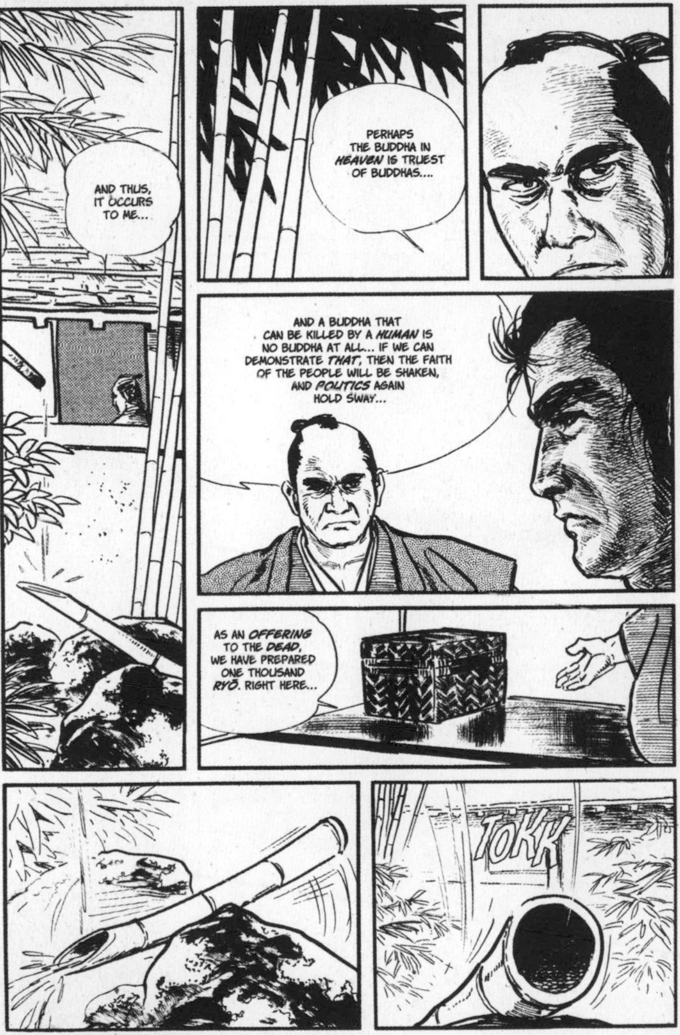
AND THUS, IT OCCURS TO ME...
PERHAPS THE BUDDHA IN *HEAVEN* IS TRUEST OF BUDDHAS....
AND A BUDDHA THAT CAN BE KILLED BY A *HUMAN* IS NO BUDDHA AT ALL... IF WE CAN DEMONSTRATE *THAT*, THEN THE FAITH OF THE PEOPLE WILL BE SHAKEN, AND *POLITICS* AGAIN HOLD SWAY...
AS AN *OFFERING* TO THE *DEAD*, WE HAVE PREPARED ONE THOUSAND *RYŌ*. RIGHT HERE...
TOKK

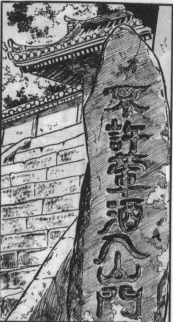

KRNNCH
KRNNCH

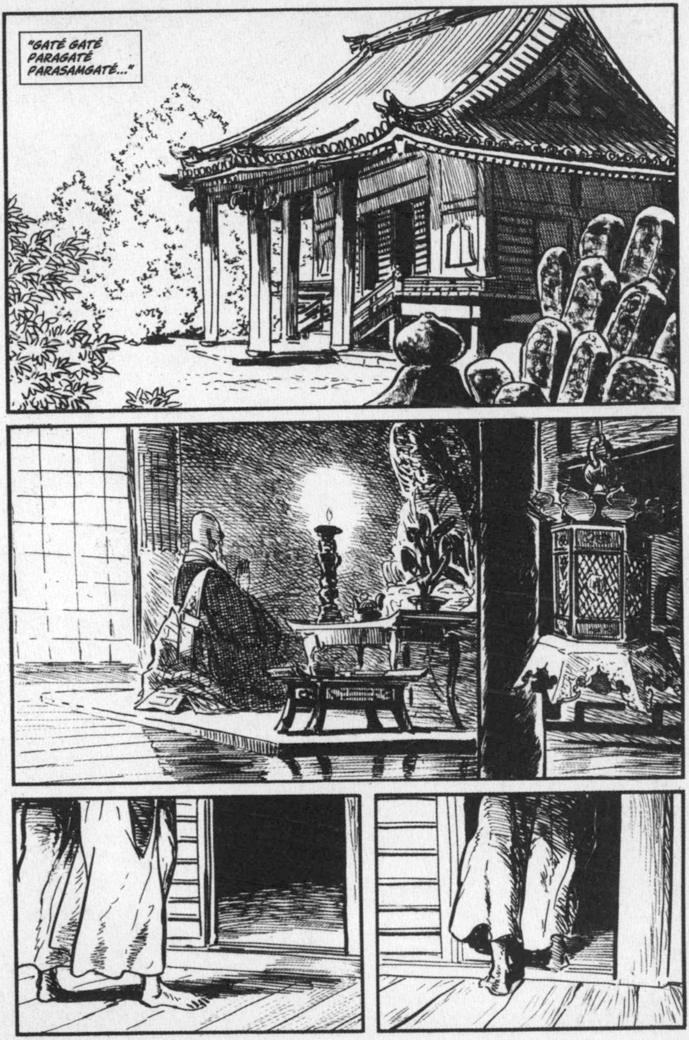
"GATÉ GATÉ
PARAGATÉ
PARASAMGATÉ..."

ASSASSIN! LONE WOLF AND CUB...

GATE GATE PARAGATE PARASAMGATE

I HAVE COME FOR YOUR LIFE.

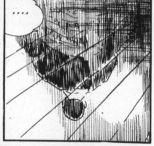

. . . .

218

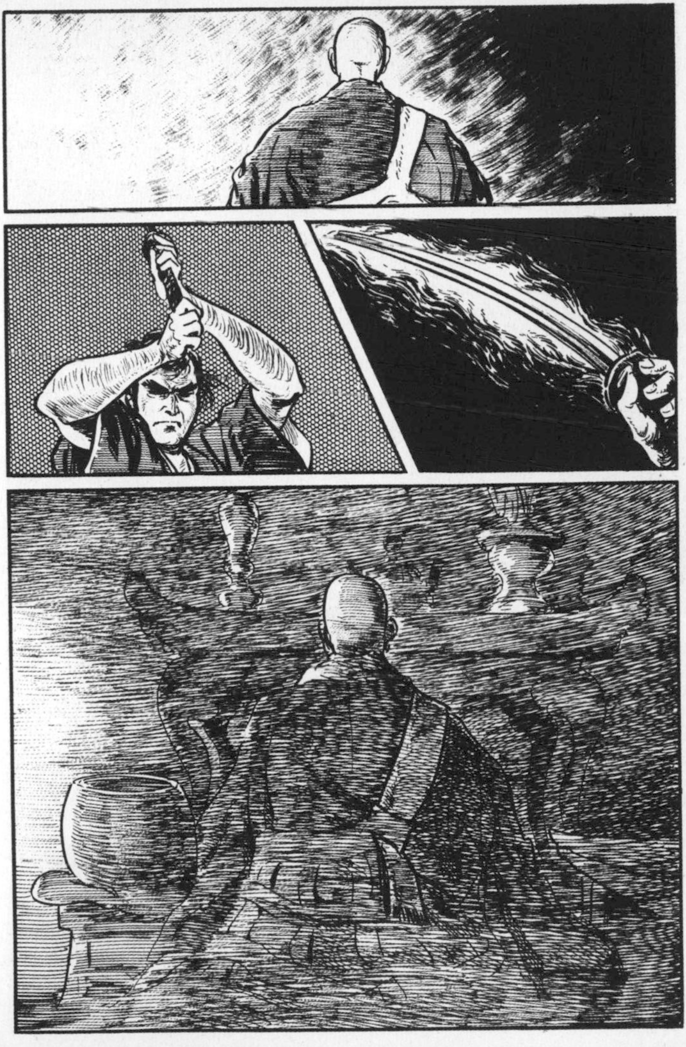

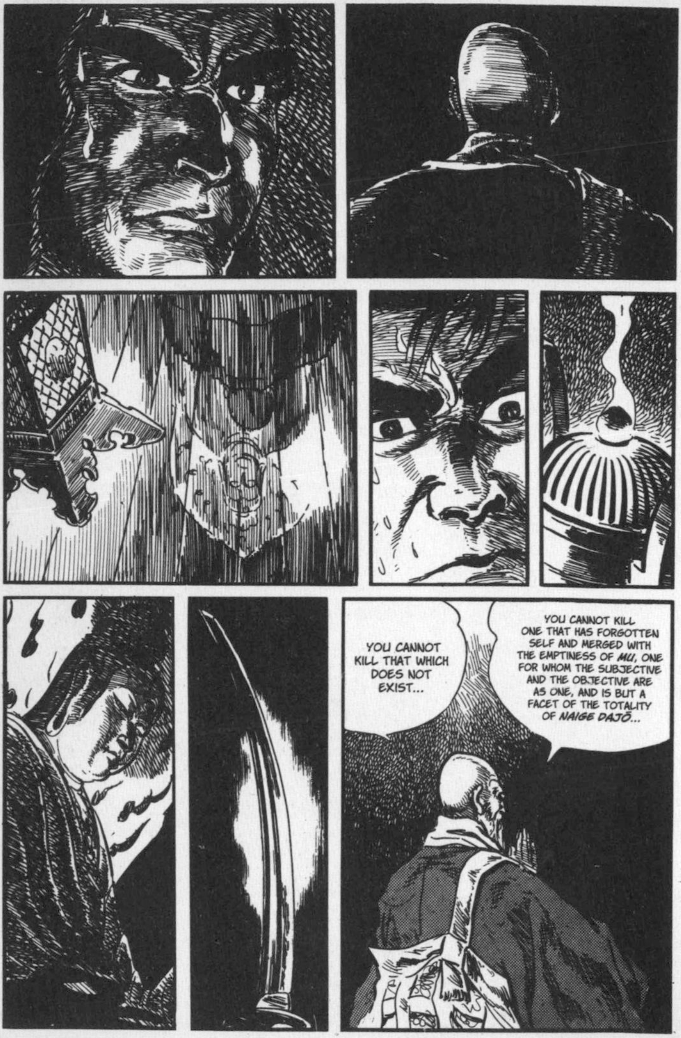
YOU CANNOT KILL THAT WHICH DOES NOT EXIST...
YOU CANNOT KILL ONE THAT HAS FORGOTTEN SELF AND MERGED WITH THE EMPTINESS OF *MU*, ONE FOR WHOM THE SUBJECTIVE AND THE OBJECTIVE ARE AS ONE, AND IS BUT A FACET OF THE TOTALITY OF *NAIGE DAJŌ*...

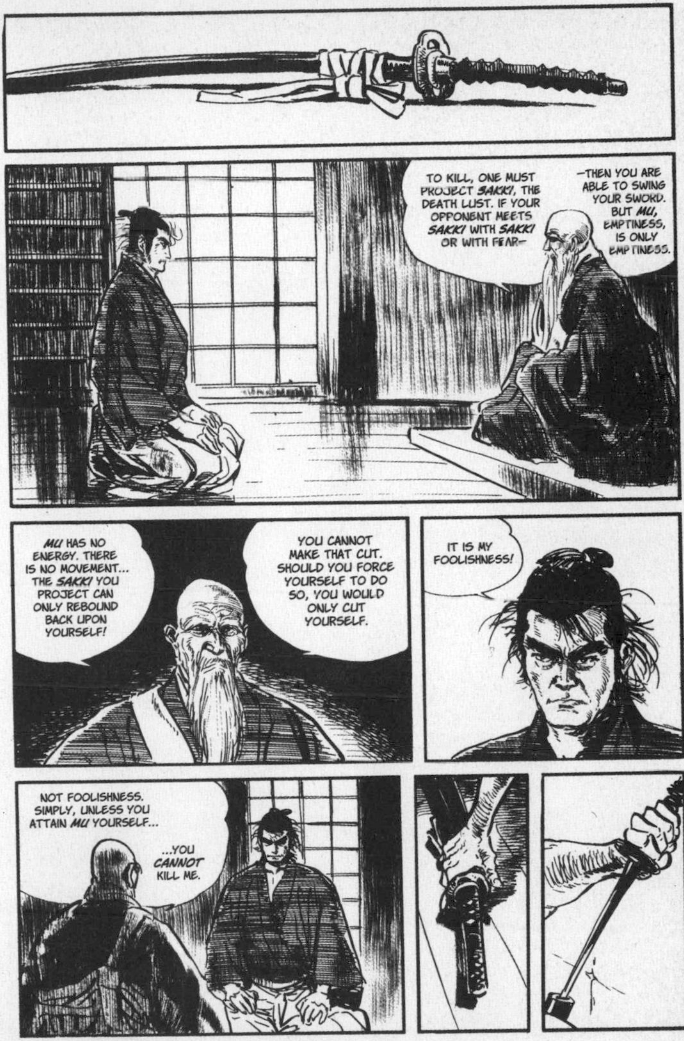
TO KILL, ONE MUST PROJECT SAKKI, THE DEATH LUST. IF YOUR OPPONENT MEETS SAKKI WITH SAKKI OR WITH FEAR—
—THEN YOU ARE ABLE TO SWING YOUR SWORD. BUT MU, EMPTINESS, IS ONLY EMPTINESS.
MU HAS NO ENERGY. THERE IS NO MOVEMENT... THE SAKKI YOU PROJECT CAN ONLY REBOUND BACK UPON YOURSELF!
YOU CANNOT MAKE THAT CUT. SHOULD YOU FORCE YOURSELF TO DO SO, YOU WOULD ONLY CUT YOURSELF.
IT IS MY FOOLISHNESS!
NOT FOOLISHNESS. SIMPLY, UNLESS YOU ATTAIN MU YOURSELF...
...YOU CANNOT KILL ME.

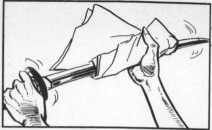

ONE WHO LIVES IN *MEIFUMADŌ* CAN CUT OPEN HIS STOMACH, EVEN BEFORE BUDDHA HIMSELF.

IF I CANNOT ASSASSINATE YOU, THEN I HAVE NO RIGHT TO WALK THE ASSASSIN'S ROAD... FORGIVE ME!

THEN *ABANDON* THAT ASSASSIN'S ROAD!

THAT I CANNOT DO. SO LONG AS I HAVE LIFE, MY QUEST WILL NOT PERMIT IT.

IF YOU TRULY CANNOT ABANDON THE ASSASSIN'S ROAD, THEN YOU MUST PERFECT *MUMON-SEKI,* THE GATELESS BARRIER.

... *MUMON-SEKI*...?!

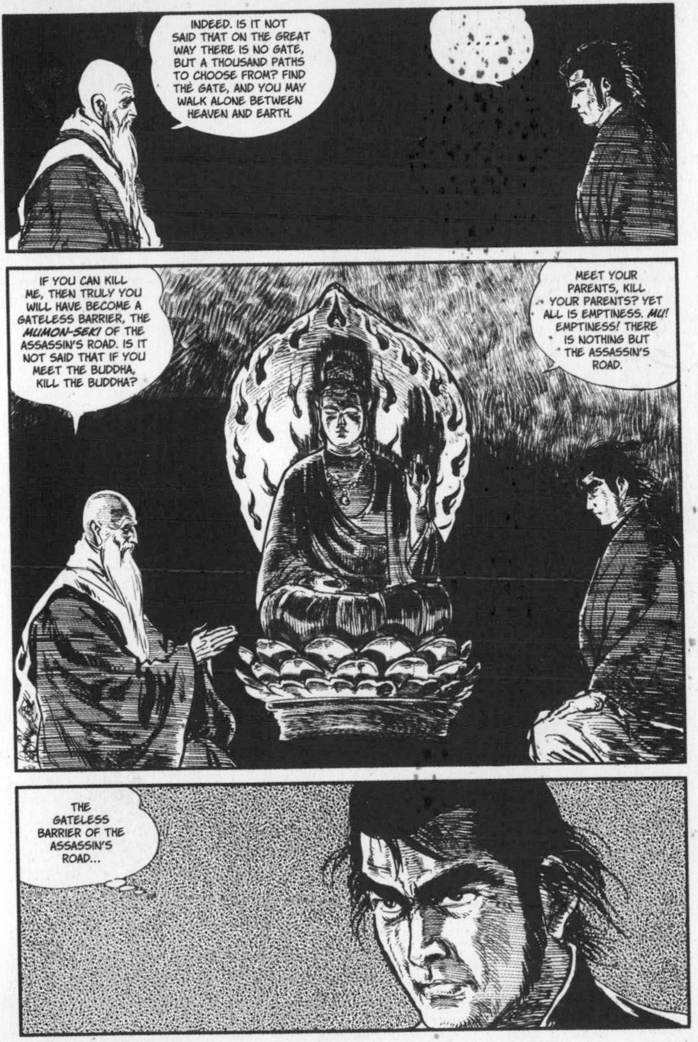
INDEED. IS IT NOT SAID THAT ON THE GREAT WAY THERE IS NO GATE, BUT A THOUSAND PATHS TO CHOOSE FROM? FIND THE GATE, AND YOU MAY WALK ALONE BETWEEN HEAVEN AND EARTH.
IF YOU CAN KILL ME, THEN TRULY YOU WILL HAVE BECOME A GATELESS BARRIER, THE *MUMON-SEKI* OF THE ASSASSIN'S ROAD. IS IT NOT SAID THAT IF YOU MEET THE BUDDHA, KILL THE BUDDHA?
MEET YOUR PARENTS, KILL YOUR PARENTS? YET ALL IS EMPTINESS. *MU!* EMPTINESS! THERE IS NOTHING BUT THE ASSASSIN'S ROAD.
THE GATELESS BARRIER OF THE ASSASSIN'S ROAD...

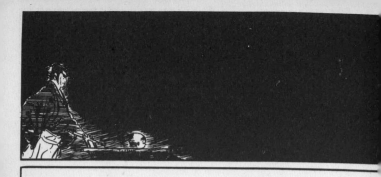

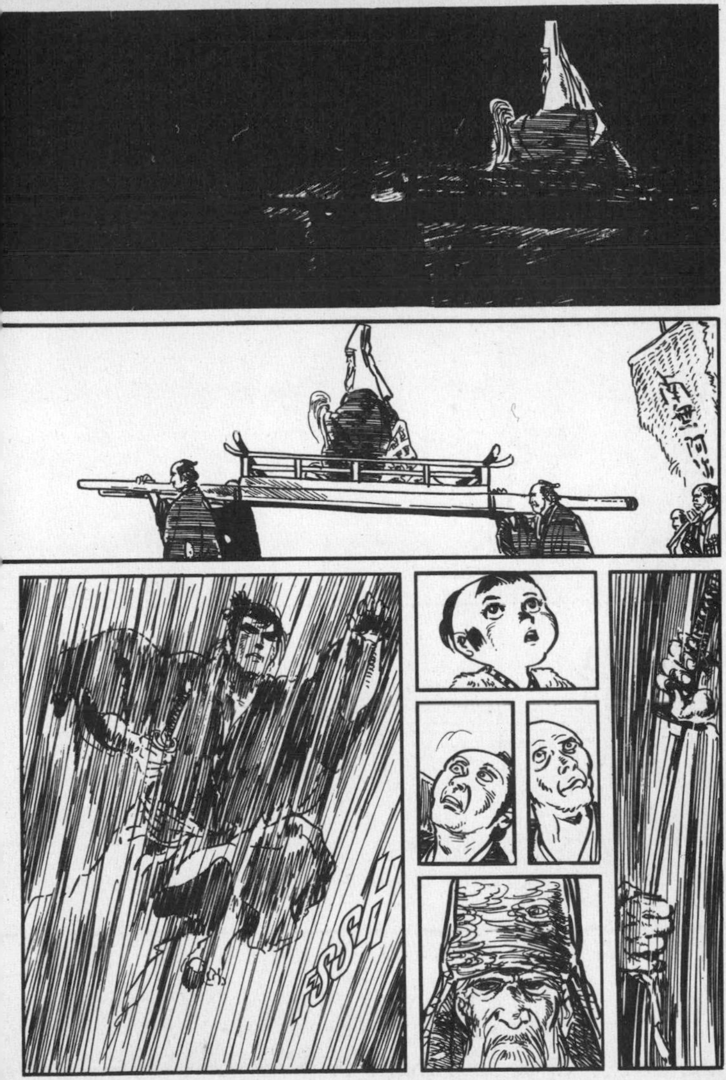
FSSH

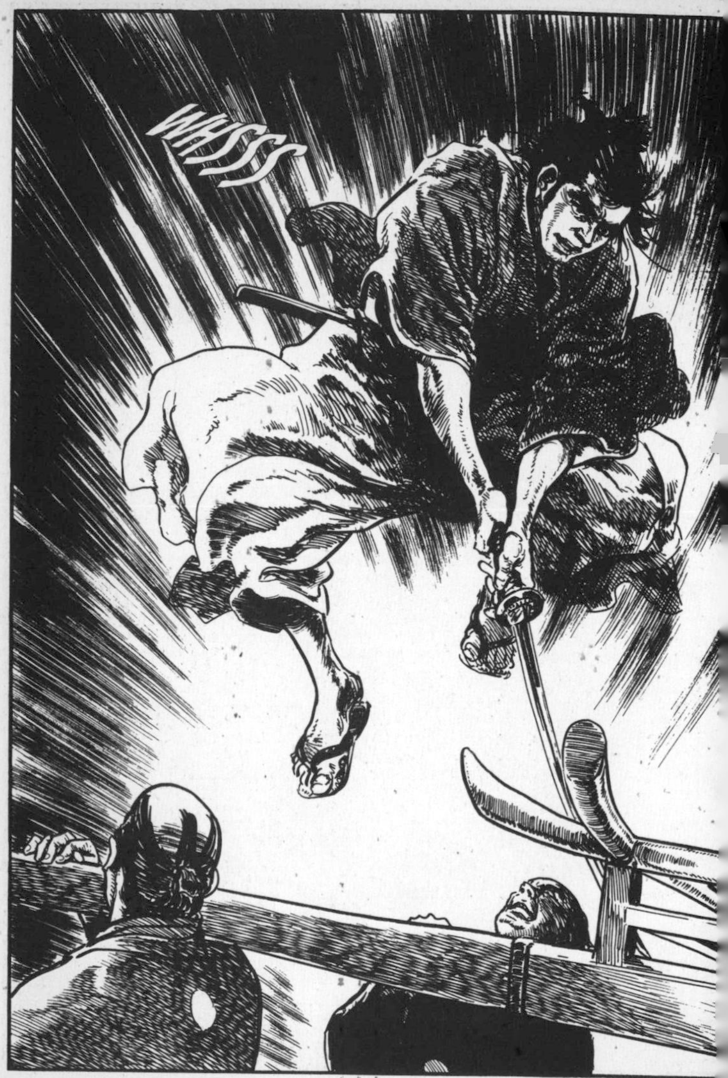
WHSSS

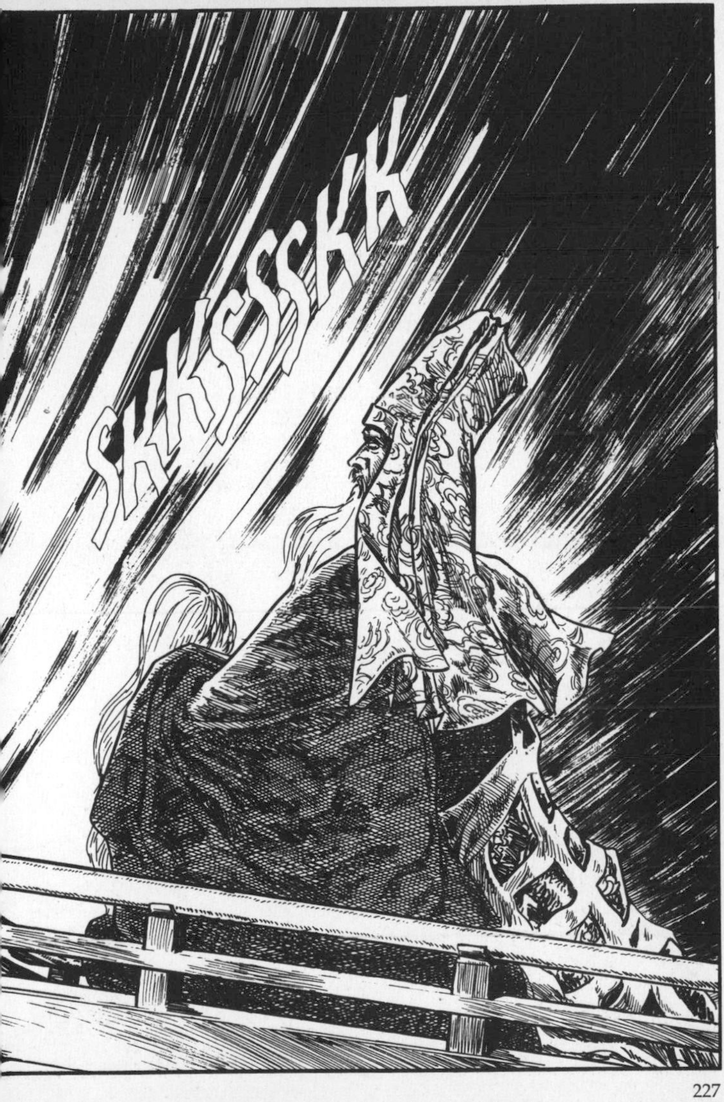
SKKSSSKK

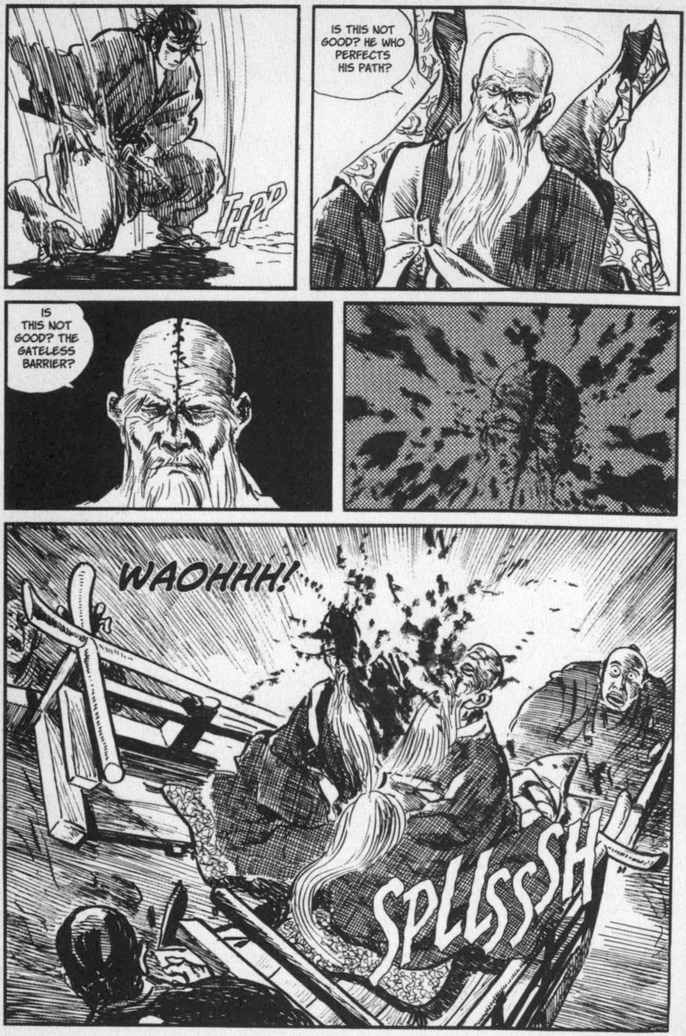
THPP
IS THIS NOT GOOD? HE WHO PERFECTS HIS PATH?
IS THIS NOT GOOD? THE GATELESS BARRIER?
WAOHHH!
SPLLSSH

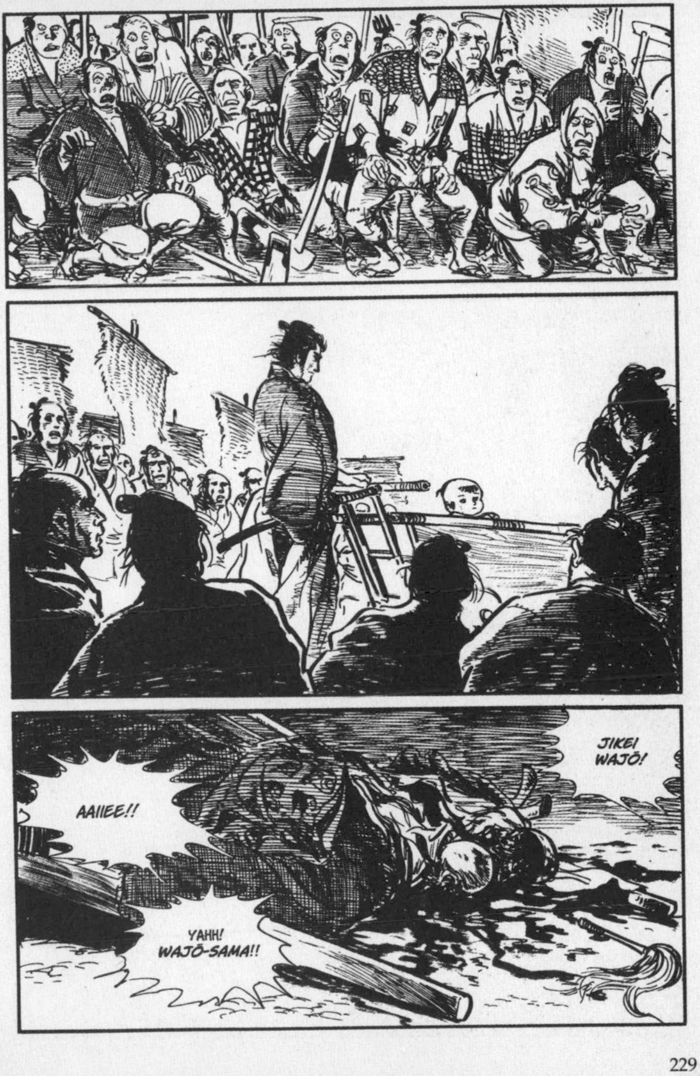
JIKEI WAJŌ!
AAIIEE!!
YAHH! WAJŌ-SAMA!!

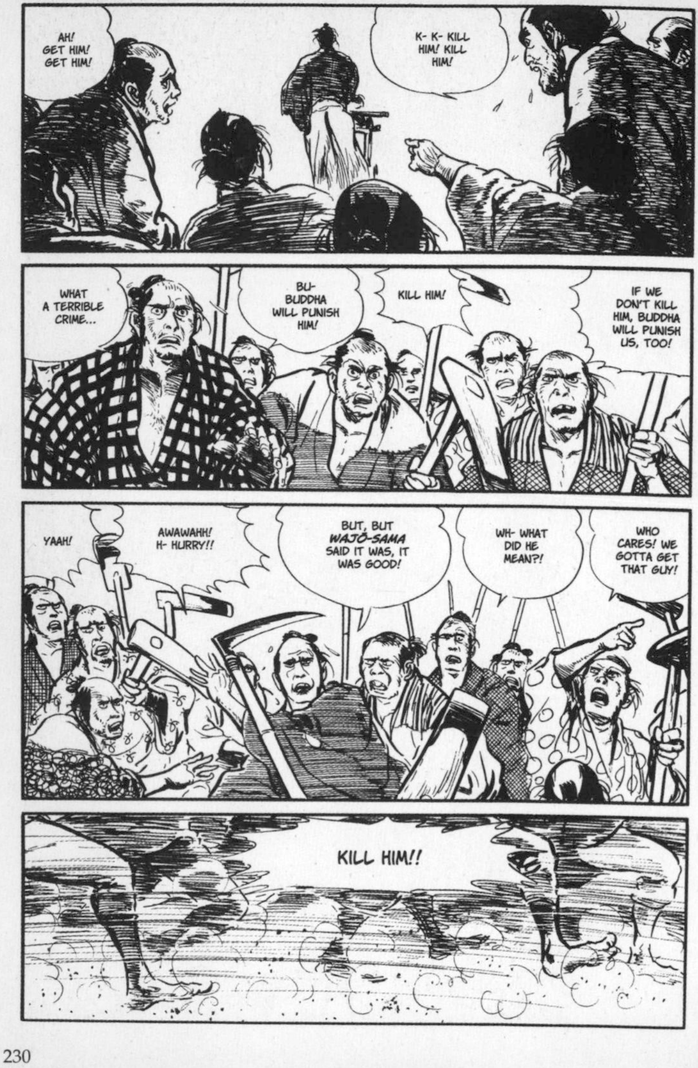
K- K- KILL HIM! KILL HIM!
AH! GET HIM! GET HIM!
IF WE DON'T KILL HIM, BUDDHA WILL PUNISH US, TOO!
KILL HIM!
BU- BUDDHA WILL PUNISH HIM!
WHAT A TERRIBLE CRIME...
WHO CARES! WE GOTTA GET THAT GUY!
WH- WHAT DID HE MEAN?!
BUT, BUT *WAJŌ-SAMA* SAID IT WAS, IT WAS GOOD!
AWAWAHH! H- HURRY!!
YAAH!
KILL HIM!!

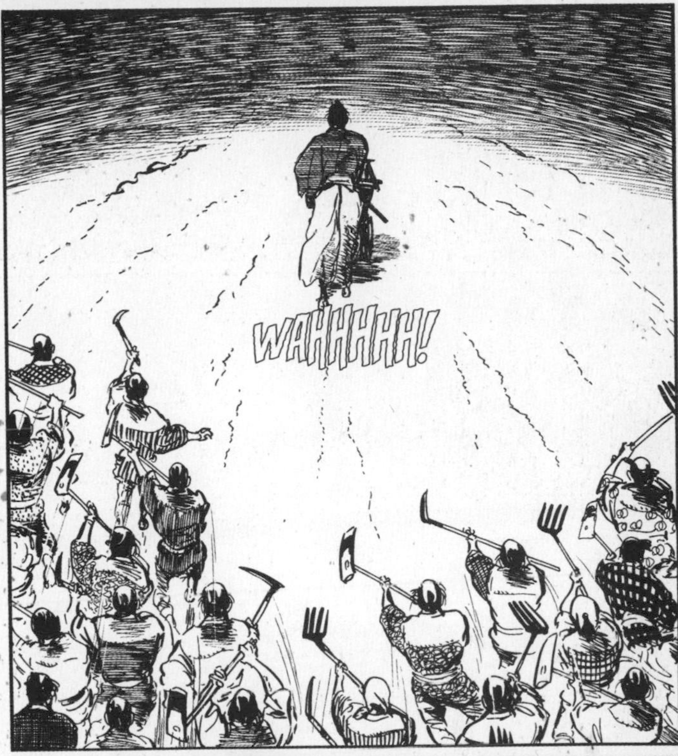
WAHHHHH!

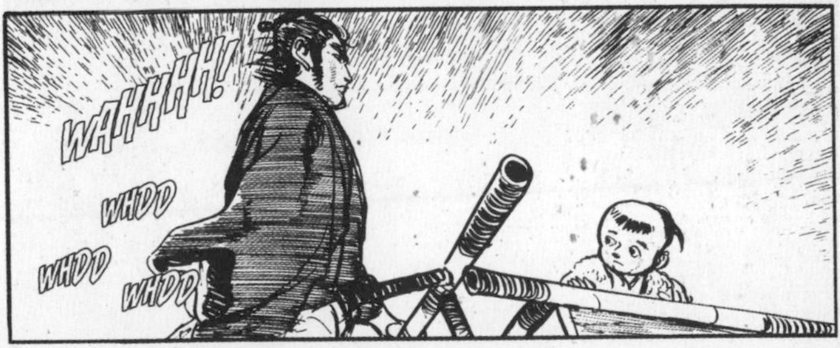
WAHHHH!
WHDD
WHDD
WHDD

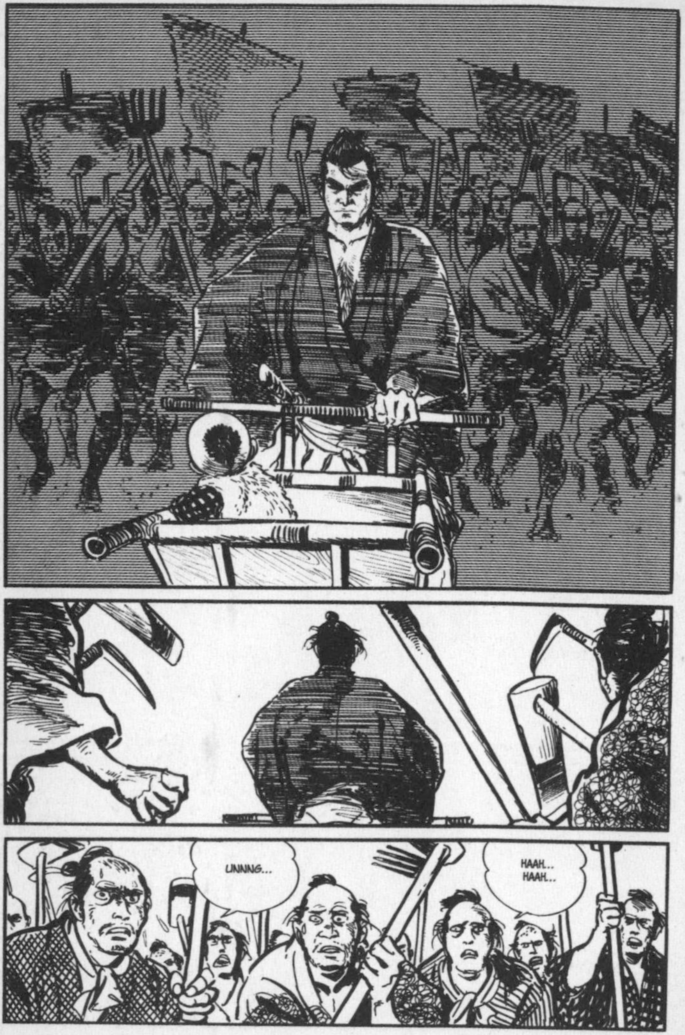
UNNNG...
HAAH... HAAH...

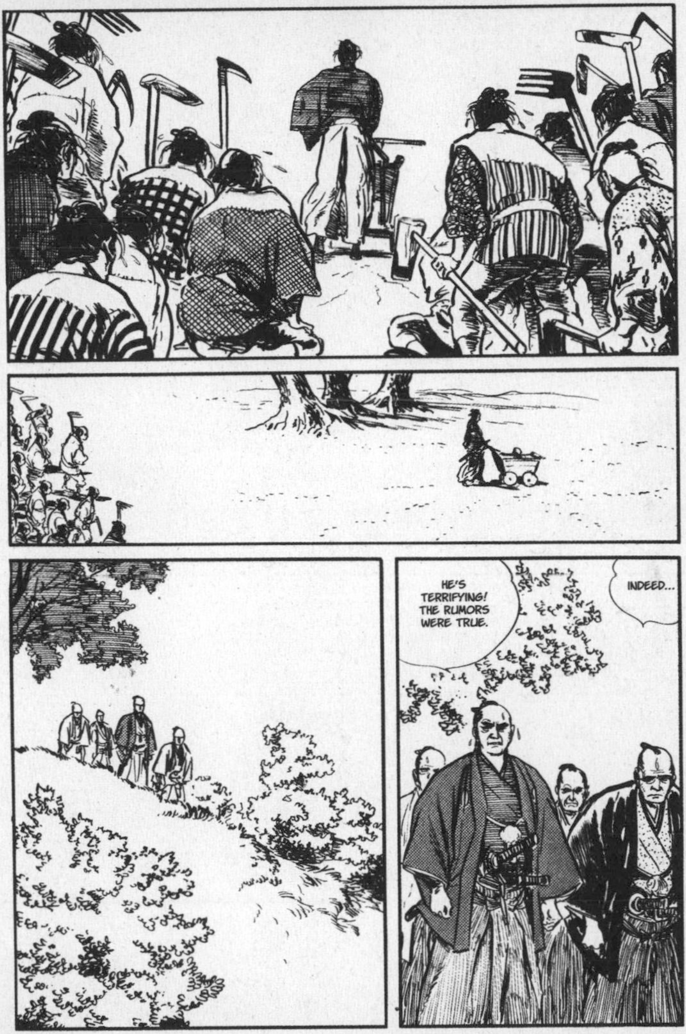
HE'S TERRIFYING! THE RUMORS WERE TRUE.
INDEED...

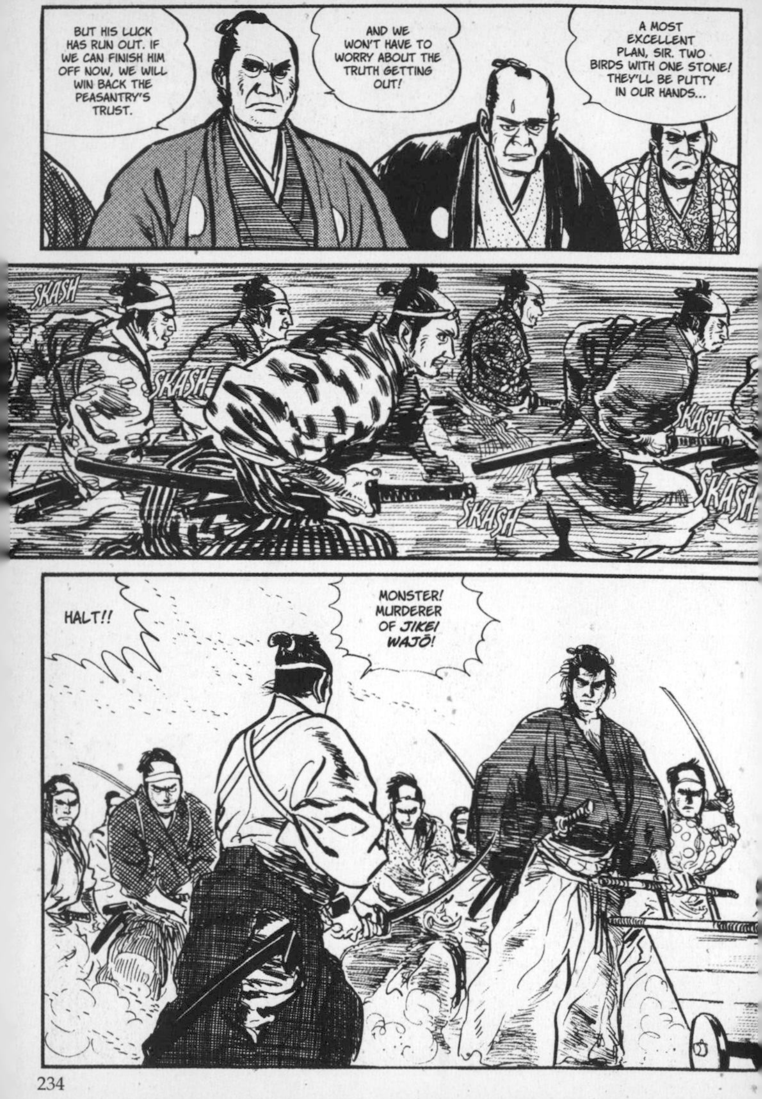
BUT HIS LUCK HAS RUN OUT. IF WE CAN FINISH HIM OFF NOW, WE WILL WIN BACK THE PEASANTRY'S TRUST.
AND WE WON'T HAVE TO WORRY ABOUT THE TRUTH GETTING OUT!
A MOST EXCELLENT PLAN, SIR. TWO BIRDS WITH ONE STONE! THEY'LL BE PUTTY IN OUR HANDS...
SKASH
SKASH
SKASH
SKASH
SKASH
HALT!!
MONSTER! MURDERER OF *JIKEI WAJŌ*!

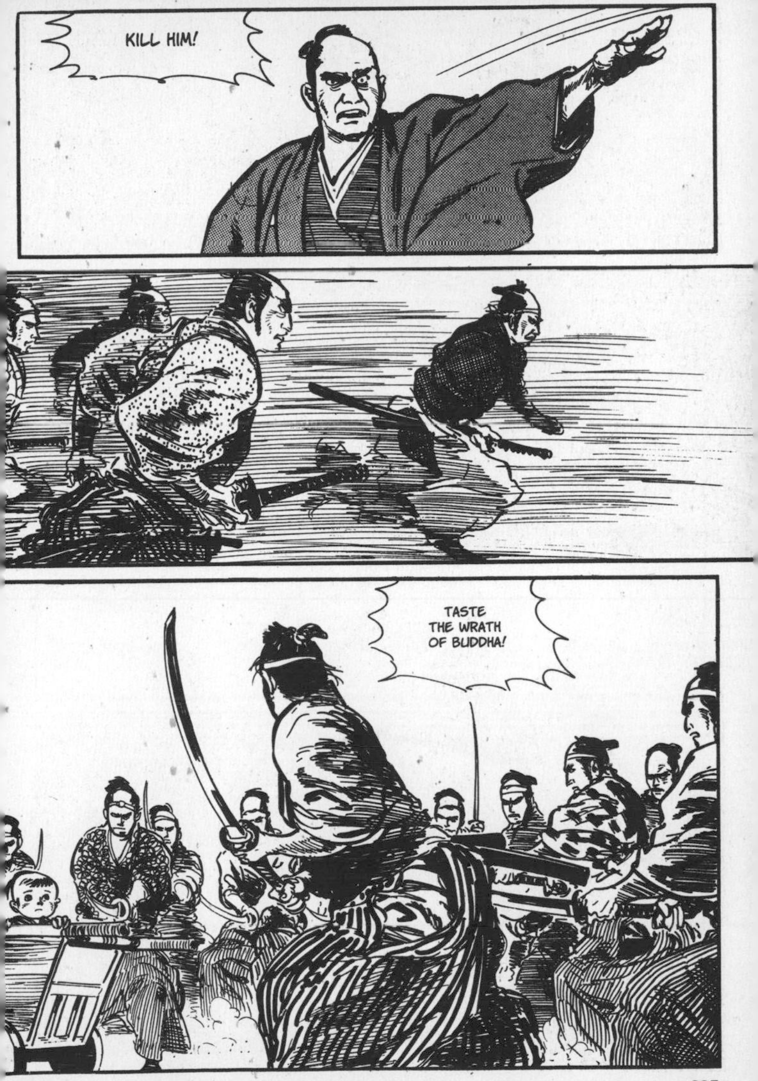
KILL HIM!
TASTE THE WRATH OF BUDDHA!

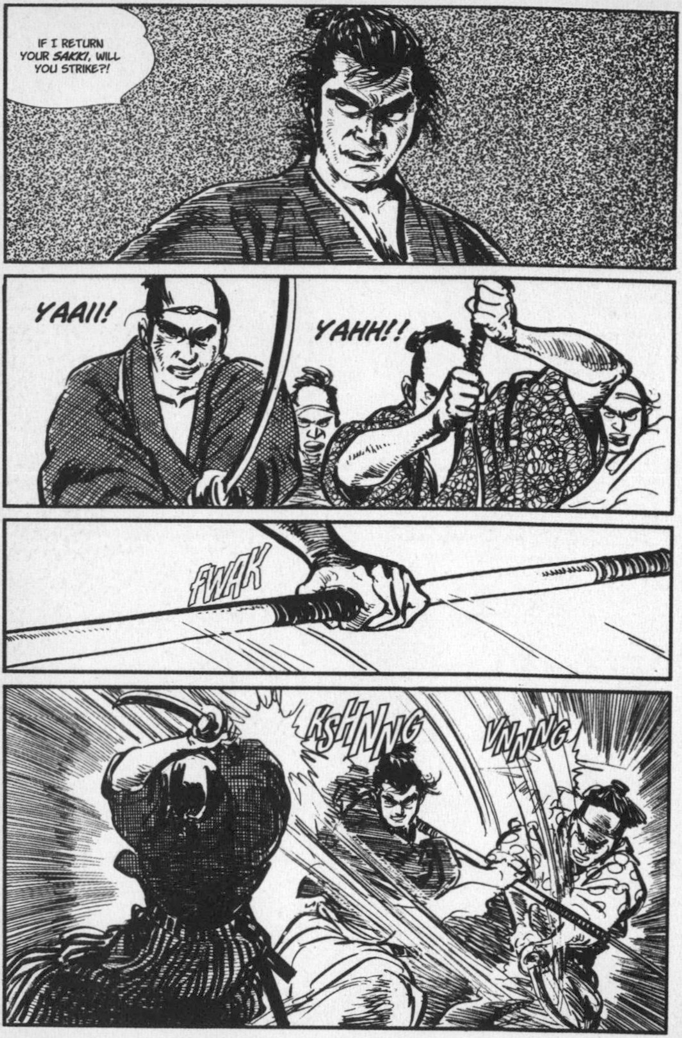
IF I RETURN YOUR *SAKKI*, WILL YOU STRIKE?!
YAAII!
YAHH!!
FWAK
KSHNNG
VNNNG

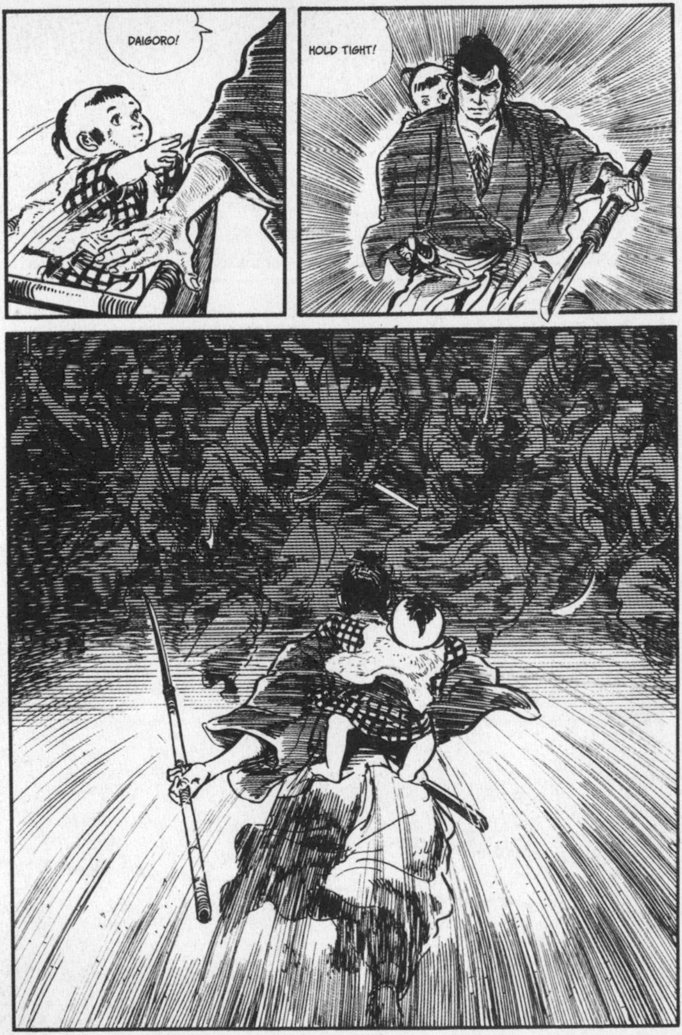
DAIGORO!
HOLD TIGHT!

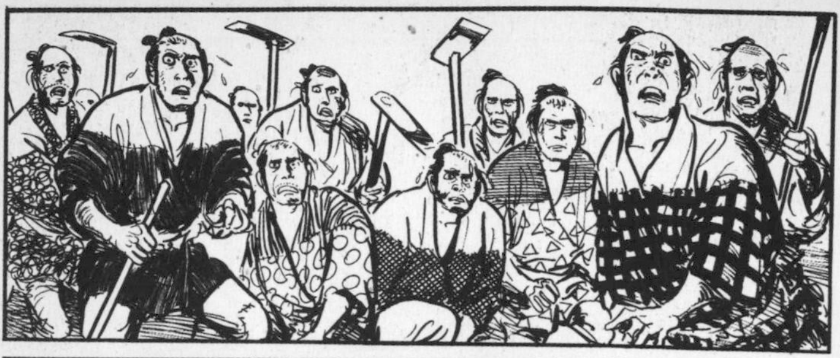
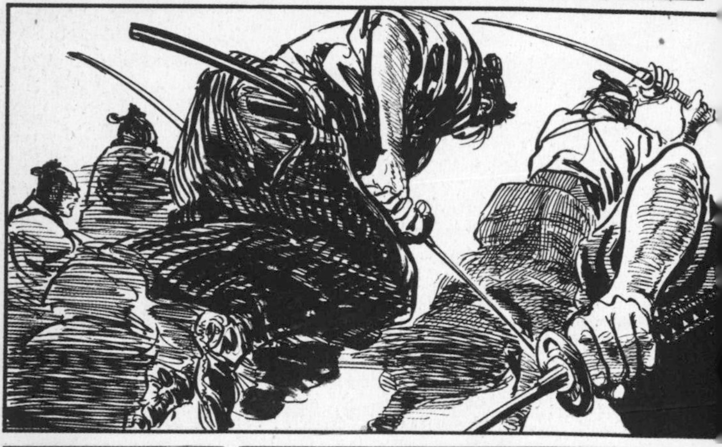
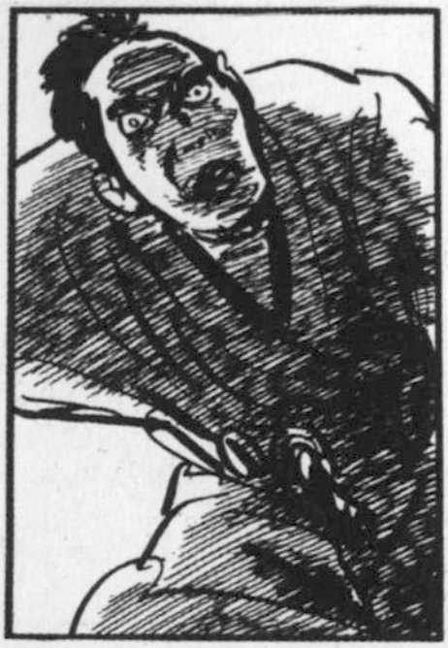
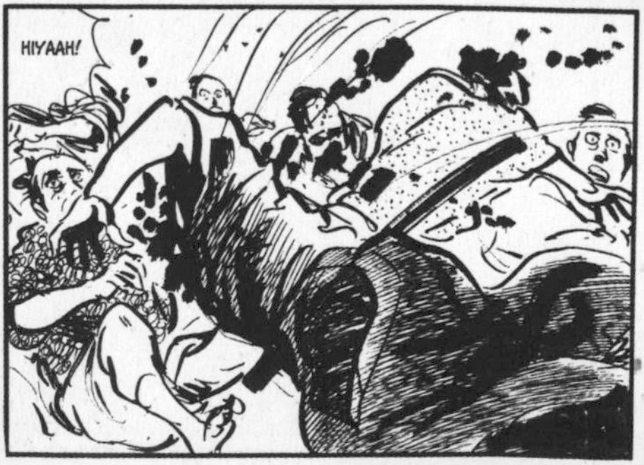
HIYAAH!

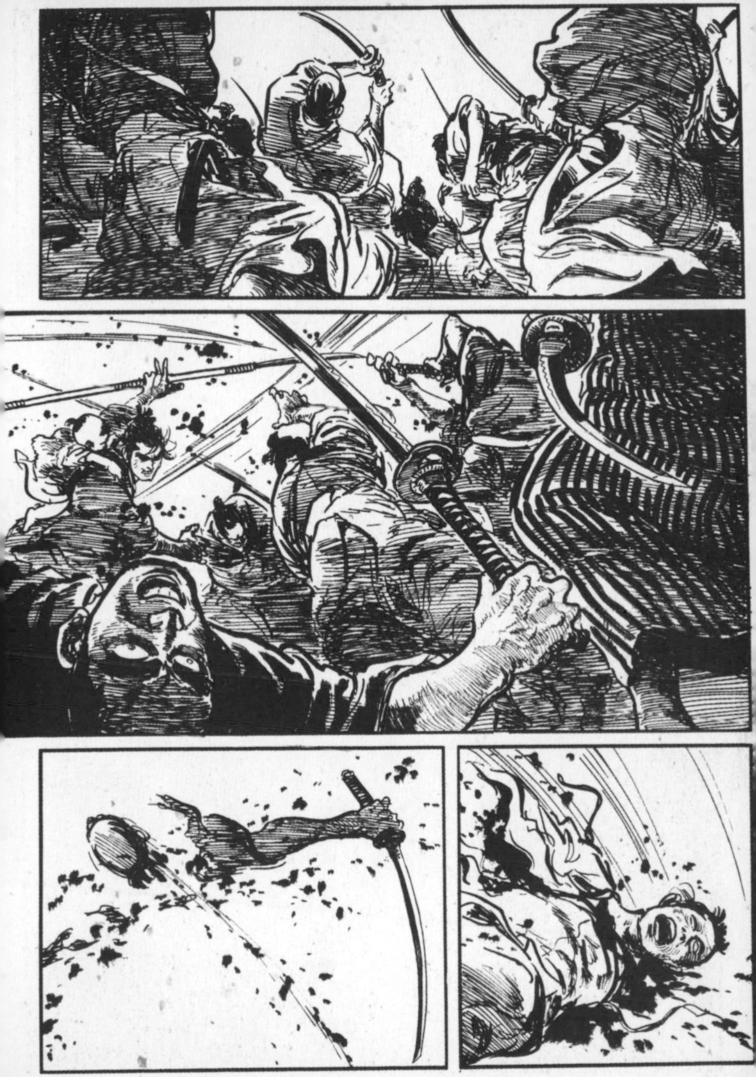

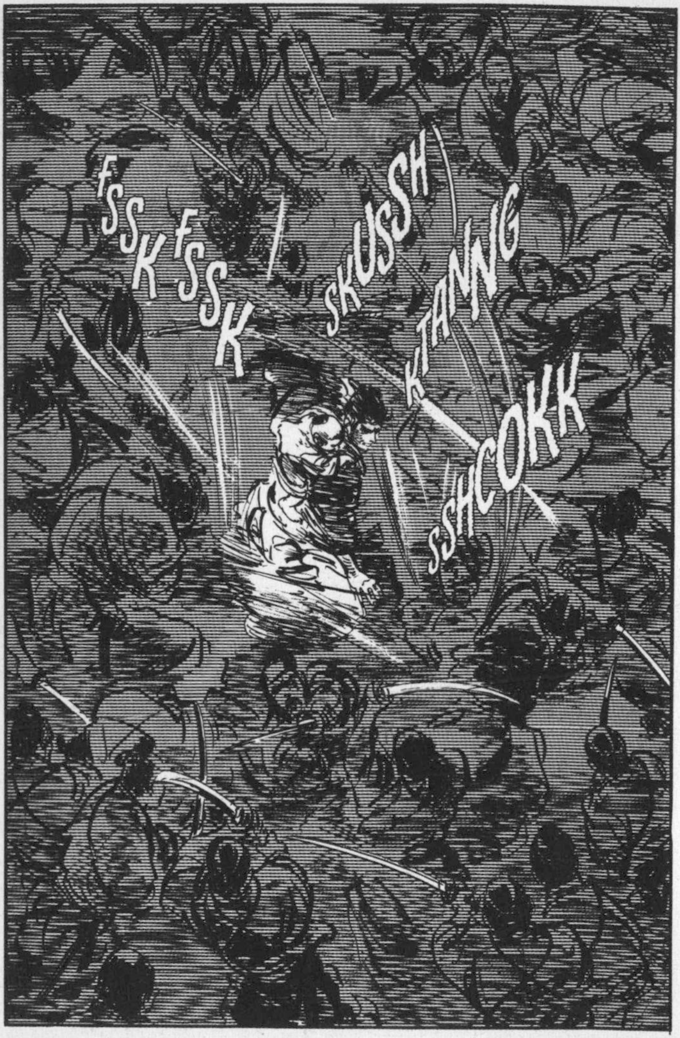
FSSK FSSK
SKUSSH
KTANNG
SSHCOKK

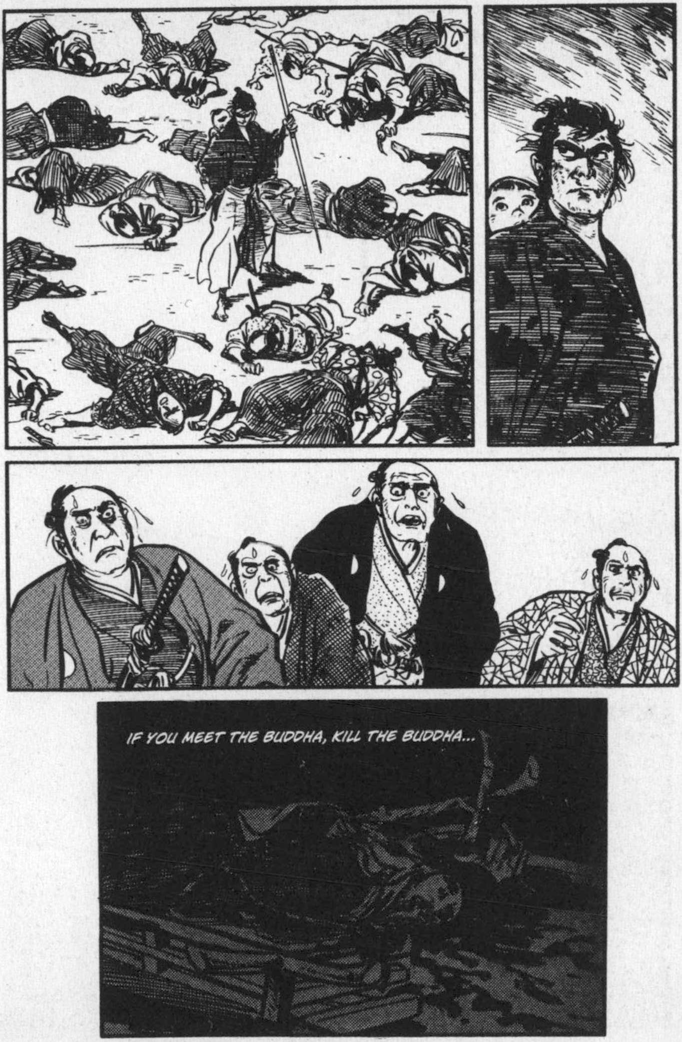

IF YOU MEET THE BUDDHA, KILL THE BUDDHA...

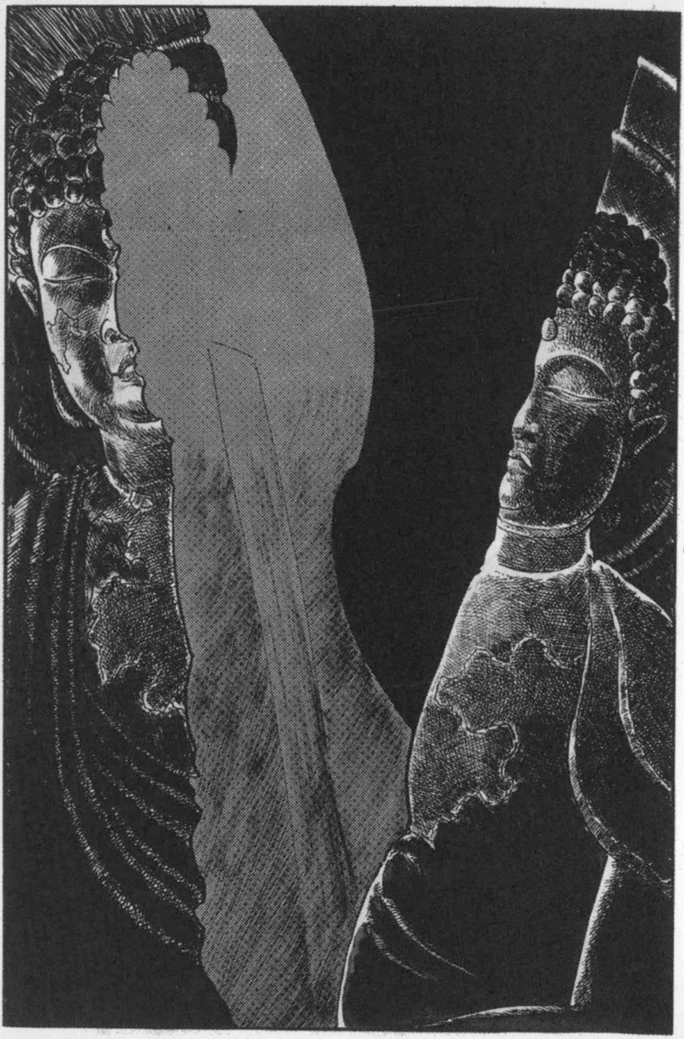

the fourteenth

Winter Flower

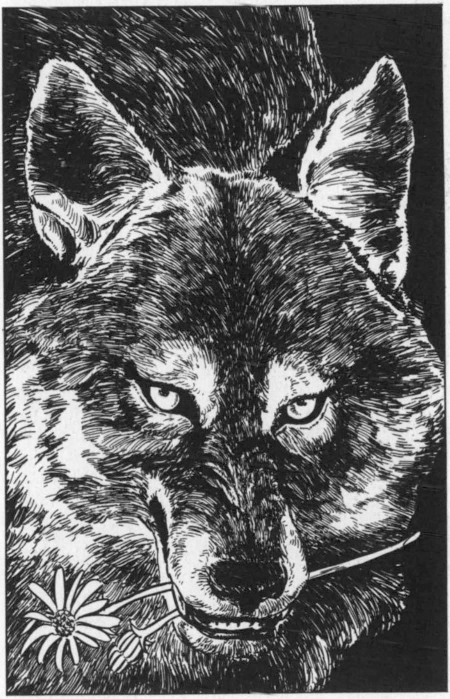

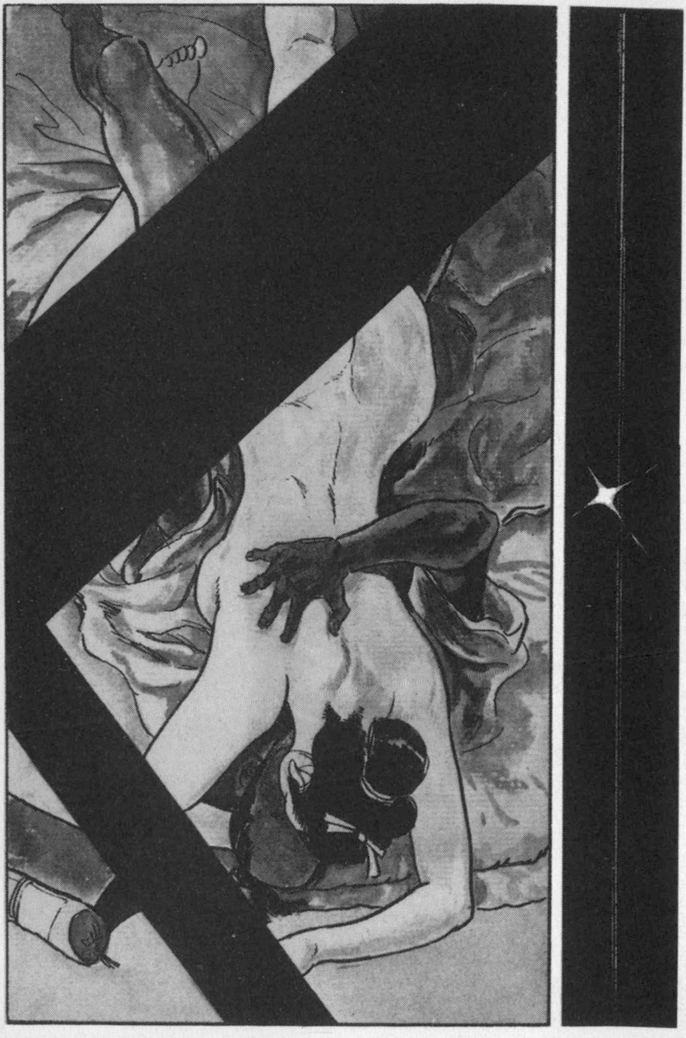

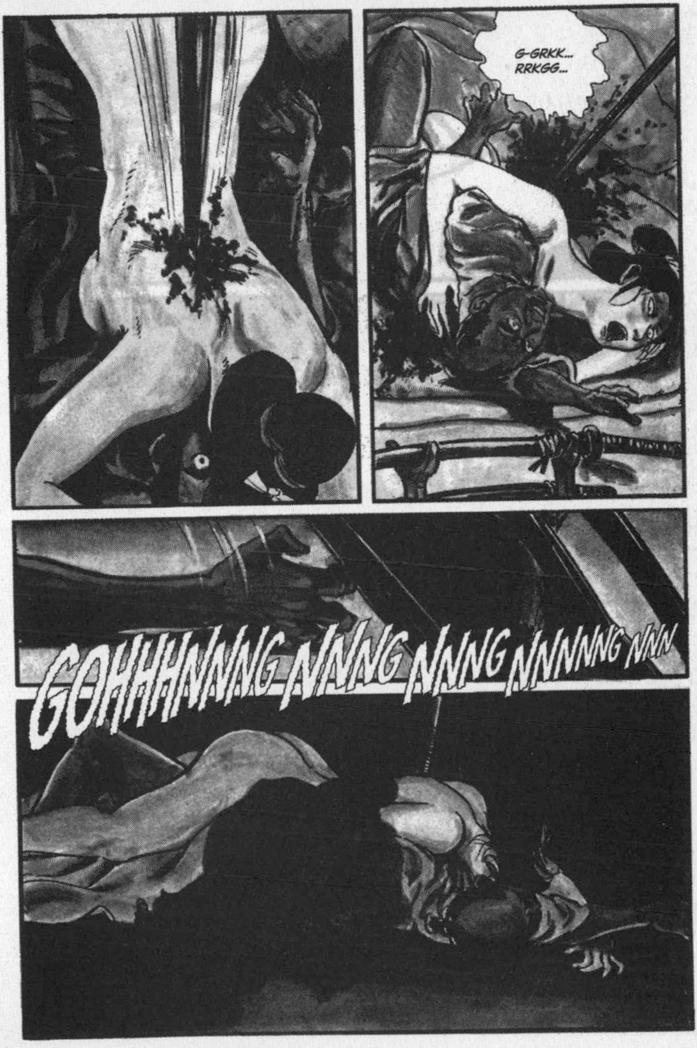
G-GRKK...
RRKGG...
GOHHHNNNG NNNG NNNG NNNNNG NNN

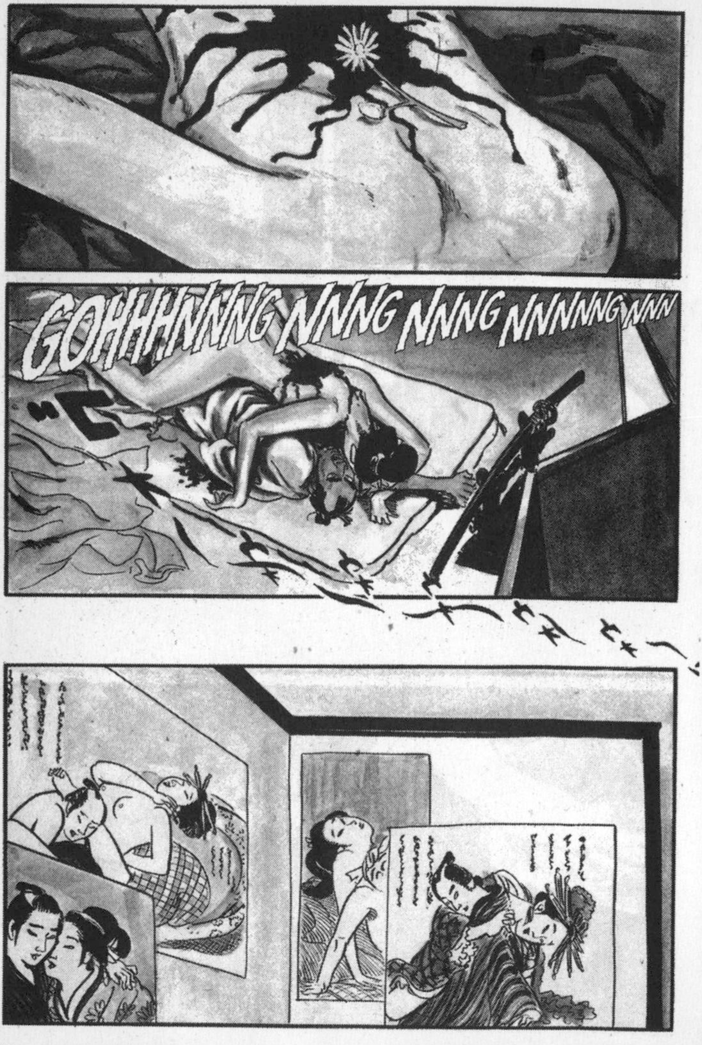
GOHHHNNNG NNNG NNNG NNNNNG NNN

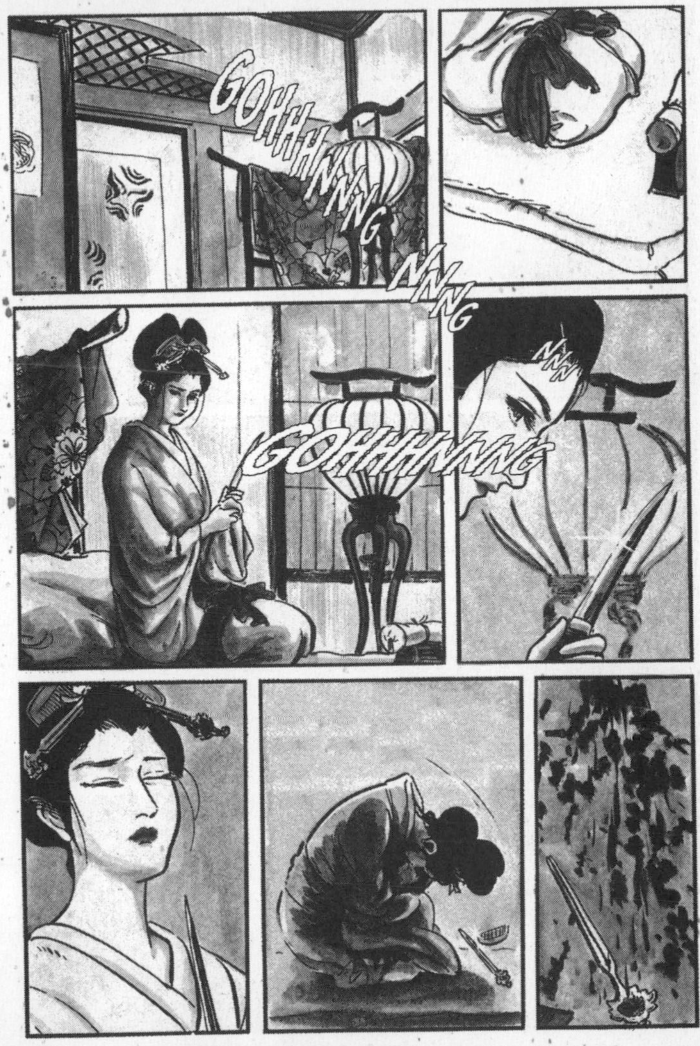
GOHHHNNNG
NNG
NNN
GOHHHNNNG

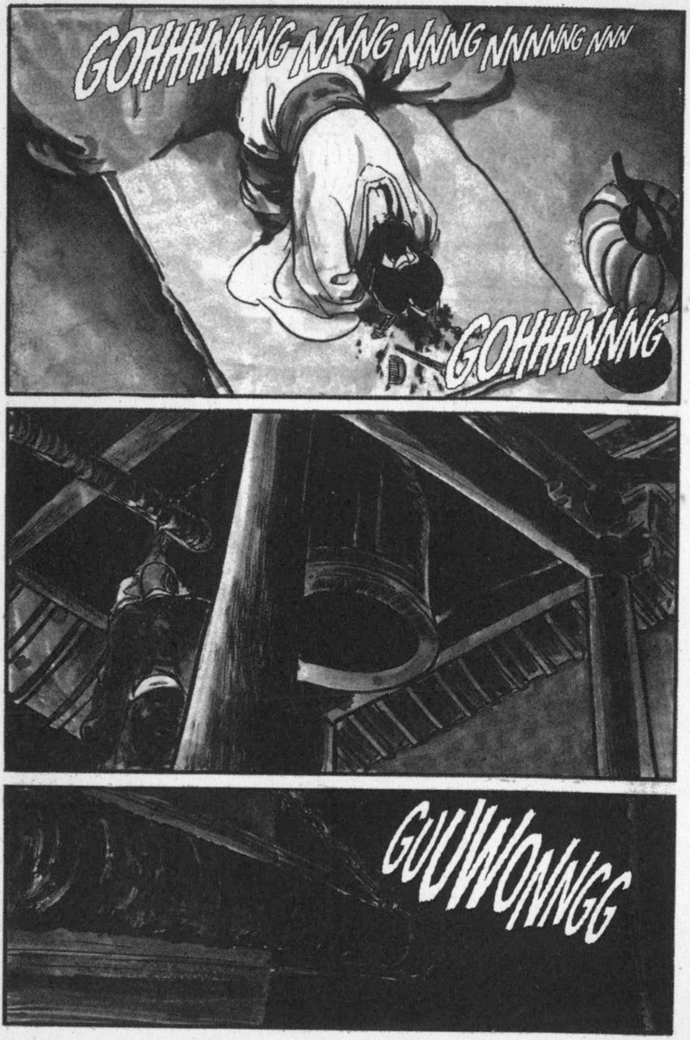
GOHHHNNNG NNNG NNNG NNNNNG NNN
GOHHHNNNG
GUUWONNGG

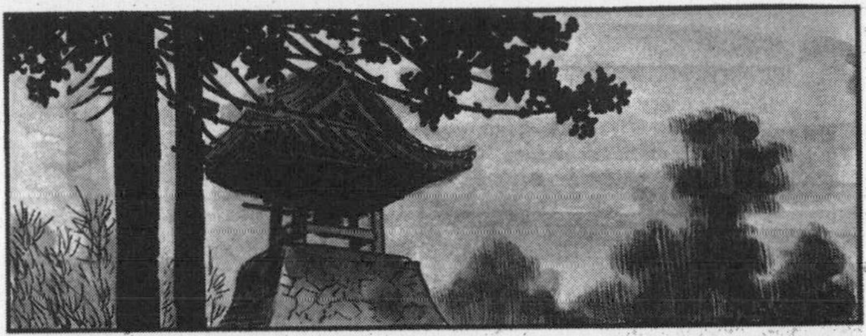
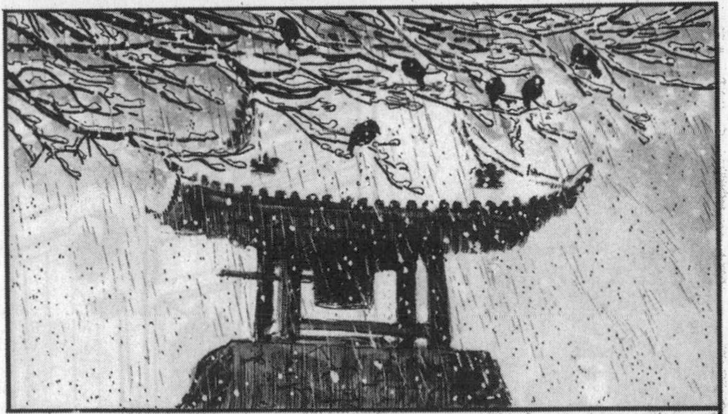
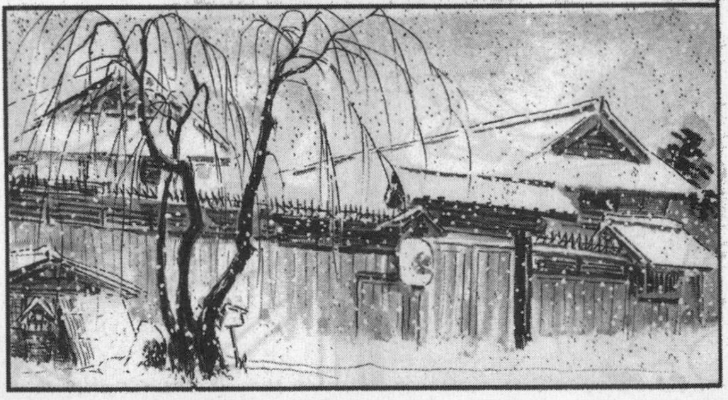

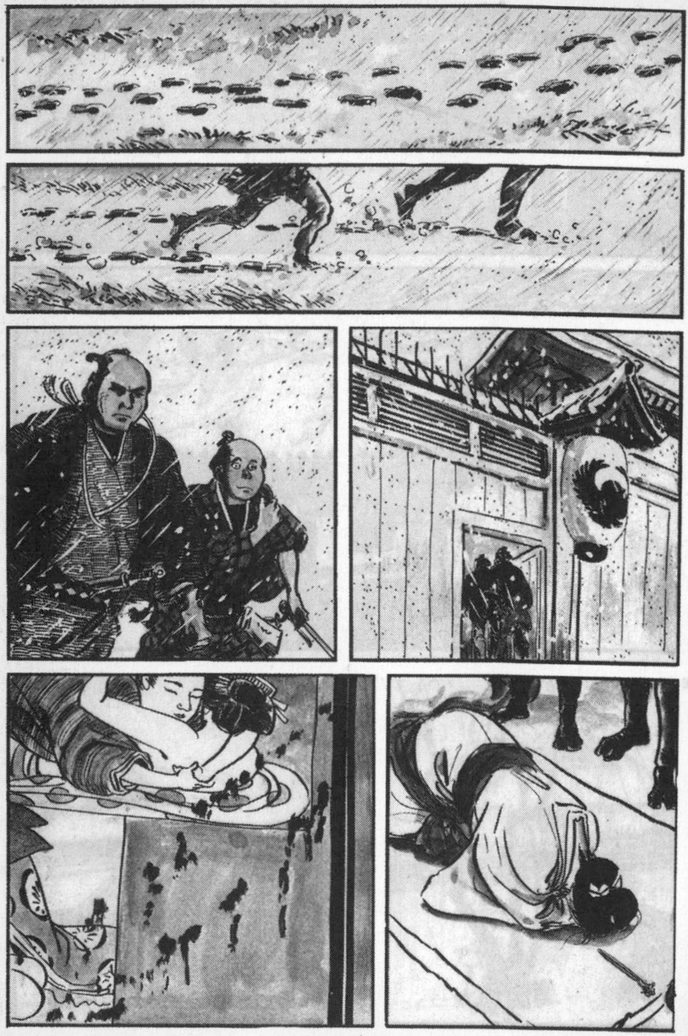

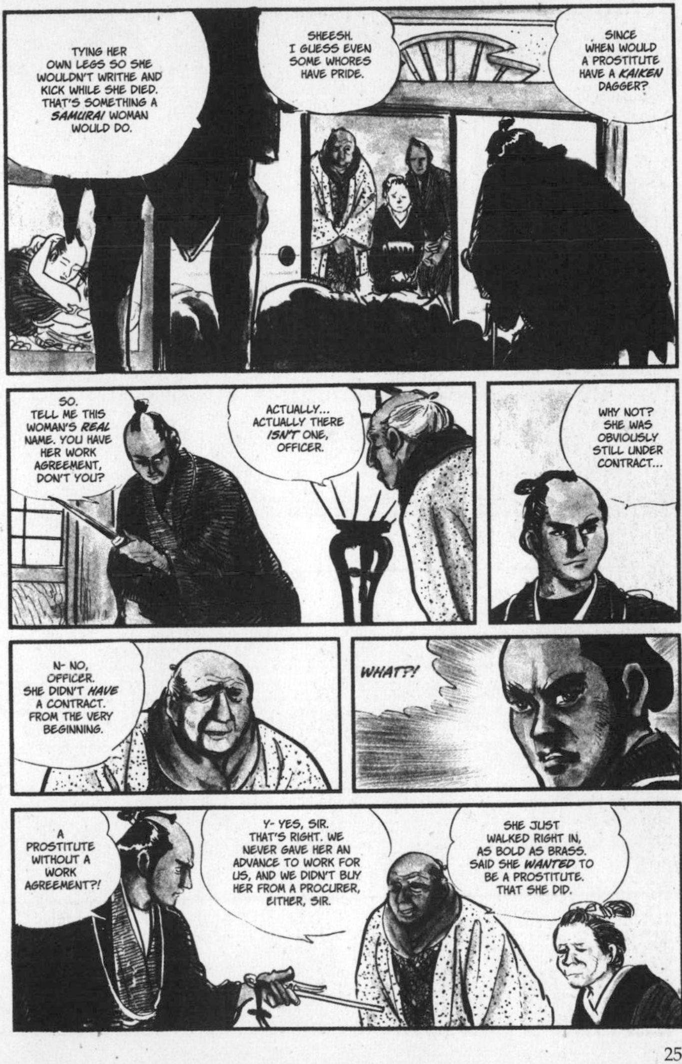
TYING HER OWN LEGS SO SHE WOULDN'T WRITHE AND KICK WHILE SHE DIED. THAT'S SOMETHING A *SAMURAI* WOMAN WOULD DO.
SHEESH. I GUESS EVEN SOME WHORES HAVE PRIDE.
SINCE WHEN WOULD A PROSTITUTE HAVE A *KAIKEN* DAGGER?
SO. TELL ME THIS WOMAN'S *REAL* NAME. YOU HAVE HER WORK AGREEMENT, DON'T YOU?
ACTUALLY... ACTUALLY THERE *ISN'T* ONE, OFFICER.
WHY NOT? SHE WAS OBVIOUSLY STILL UNDER CONTRACT...
N- NO, OFFICER. SHE DIDN'T *HAVE* A CONTRACT. FROM THE VERY BEGINNING.
WHAT?!
A PROSTITUTE WITHOUT A WORK AGREEMENT?!
Y- YES, SIR. THAT'S RIGHT. WE NEVER GAVE HER AN ADVANCE TO WORK FOR US, AND WE DIDN'T BUY HER FROM A PROCURER, EITHER, SIR.
SHE JUST WALKED RIGHT IN, AS BOLD AS BRASS. SAID SHE *WANTED* TO BE A PROSTITUTE. THAT SHE DID.

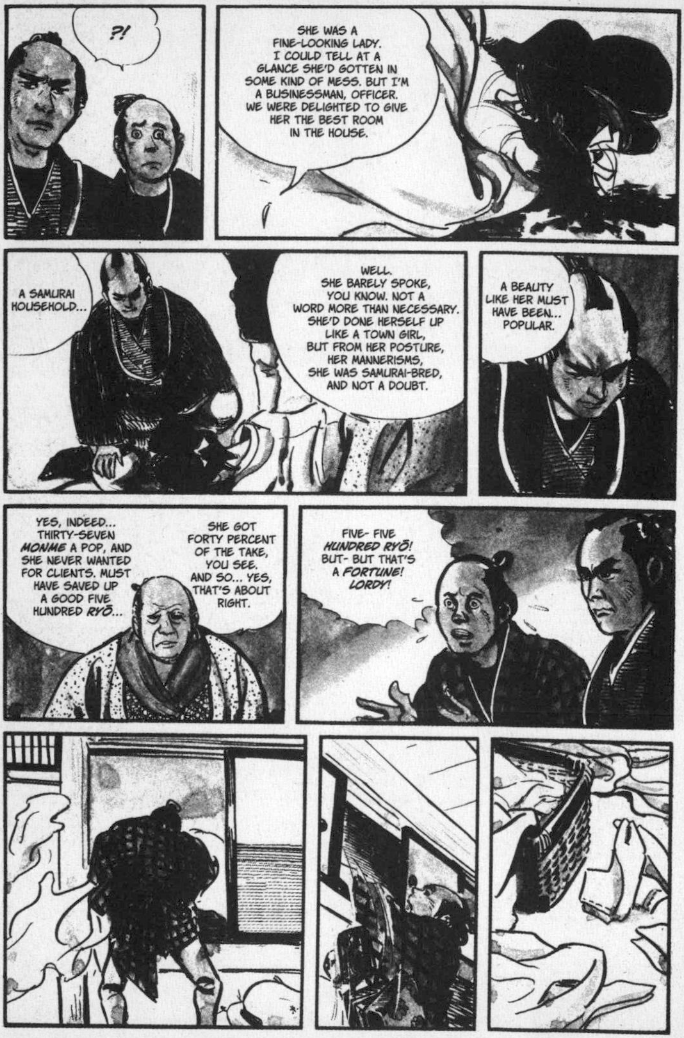
?!
SHE WAS A FINE-LOOKING LADY. I COULD TELL AT A GLANCE SHE'D GOTTEN IN SOME KIND OF MESS. BUT I'M A BUSINESSMAN, OFFICER. WE WERE DELIGHTED TO GIVE HER THE BEST ROOM IN THE HOUSE.
A SAMURAI HOUSEHOLD...
WELL. SHE BARELY SPOKE, YOU KNOW. NOT A WORD MORE THAN NECESSARY. SHE'D DONE HERSELF UP LIKE A TOWN GIRL, BUT FROM HER POSTURE, HER MANNERISMS, SHE WAS SAMURAI-BRED, AND NOT A DOUBT.
A BEAUTY LIKE HER MUST HAVE BEEN... POPULAR.
YES, INDEED... THIRTY-SEVEN *MONME* A POP, AND SHE NEVER WANTED FOR CLIENTS. MUST HAVE SAVED UP A GOOD FIVE HUNDRED *RYŌ*...
SHE GOT FORTY PERCENT OF THE TAKE, YOU SEE. AND SO... YES, THAT'S ABOUT RIGHT.
FIVE- FIVE *HUNDRED RYŌ*! BUT- BUT THAT'S A *FORTUNE*! *LORDY*!

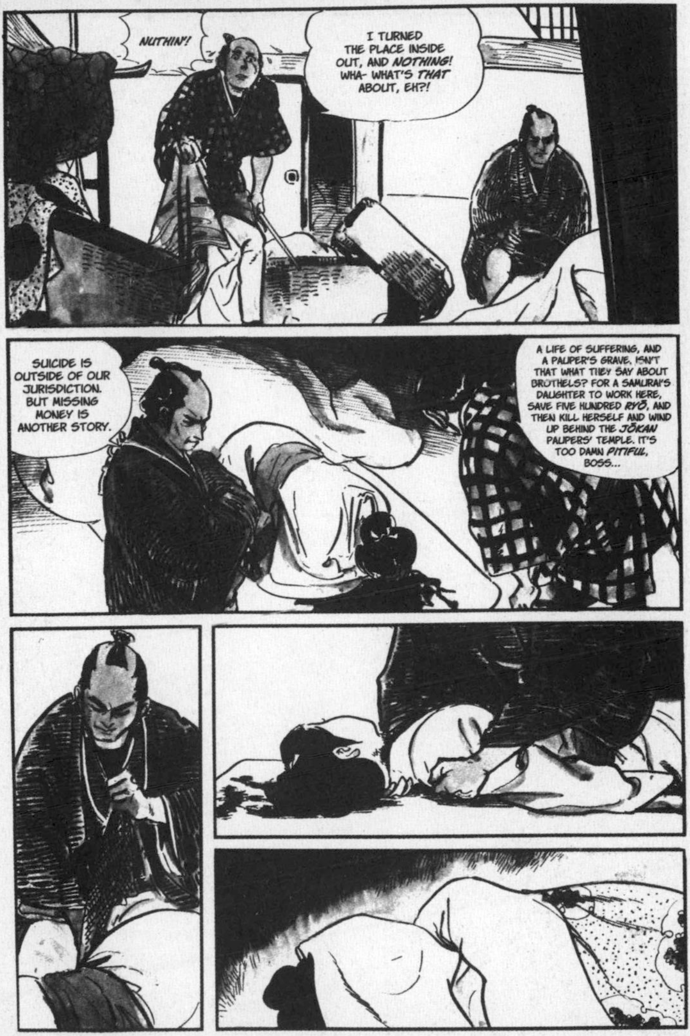
NUTHIN'!
I TURNED THE PLACE INSIDE OUT, AND NOTHING! WHA- WHAT'S THAT ABOUT, EH?!
SUICIDE IS OUTSIDE OF OUR JURISDICTION. BUT MISSING MONEY IS ANOTHER STORY.
A LIFE OF SUFFERING, AND A PAUPER'S GRAVE, ISN'T THAT WHAT THEY SAY ABOUT BROTHELS? FOR A SAMURAI'S DAUGHTER TO WORK HERE, SAVE FIVE HUNDRED RYŌ, AND THEN KILL HERSELF AND WIND UP BEHIND THE JŌKAN PAUPERS' TEMPLE. IT'S TOO DAMN PITIFUL, BOSS...

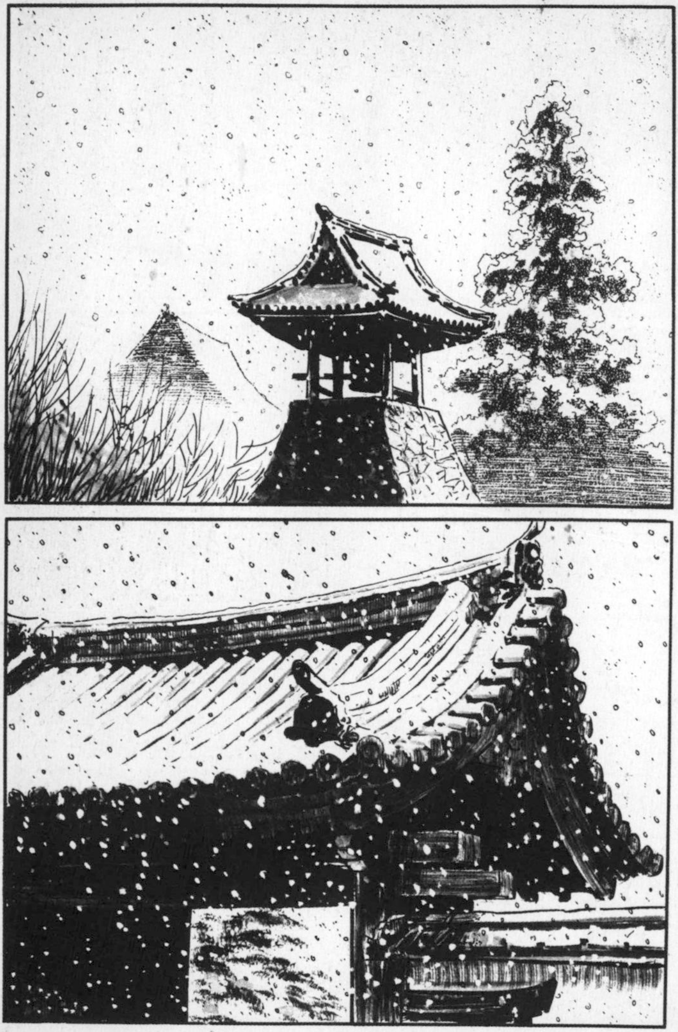

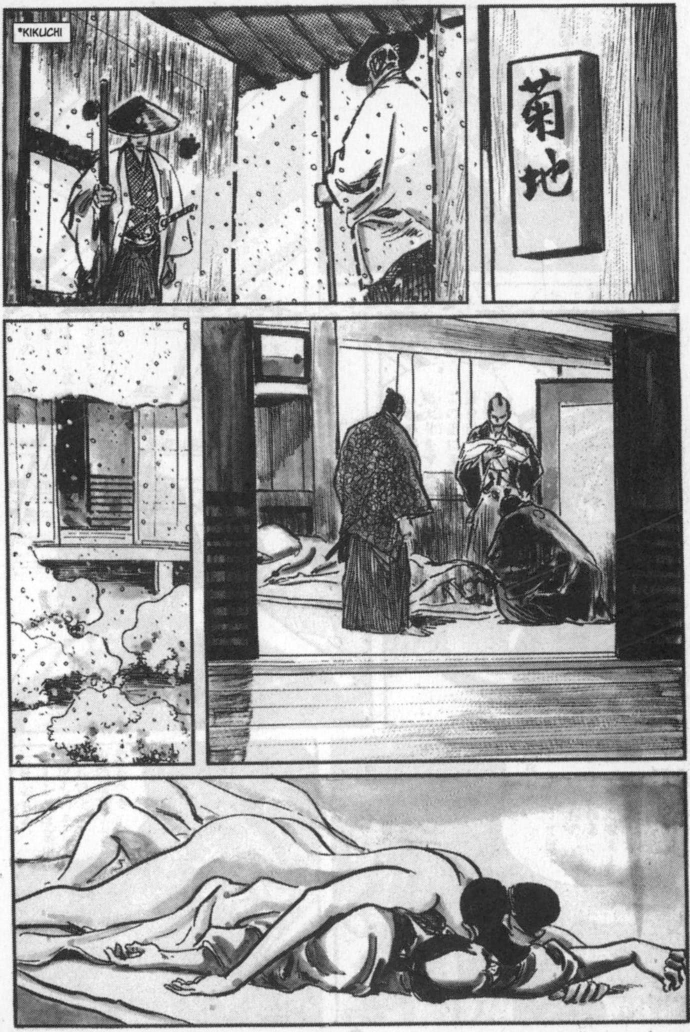
*KIKUCHI
菊地

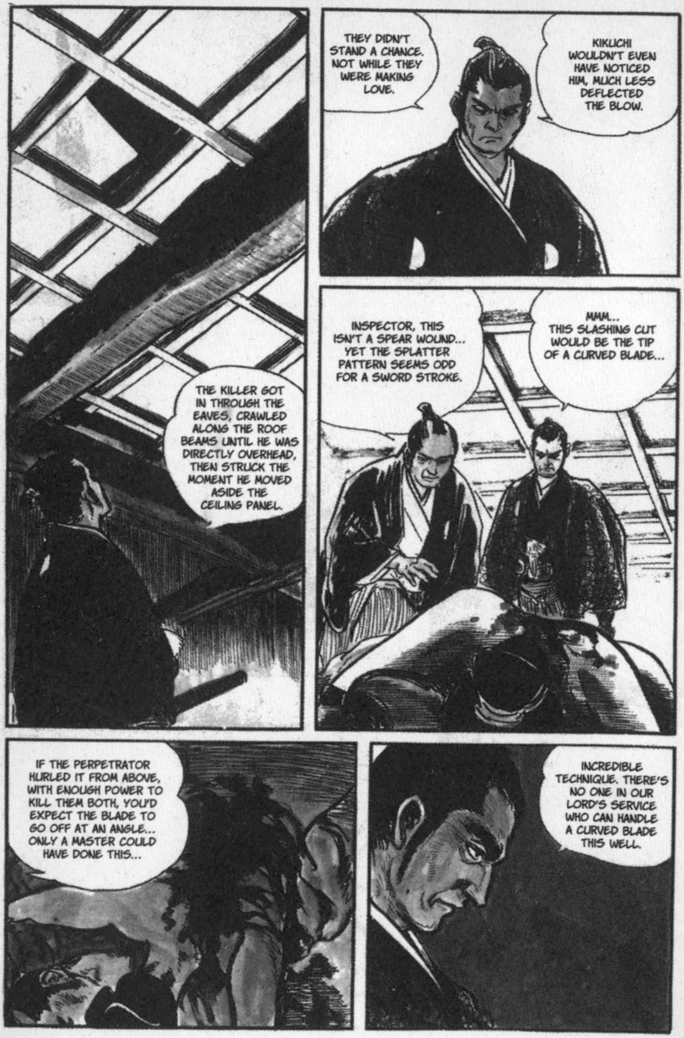
THE KILLER GOT IN THROUGH THE EAVES, CRAWLED ALONG THE ROOF BEAMS UNTIL HE WAS DIRECTLY OVERHEAD, THEN STRUCK THE MOMENT HE MOVED ASIDE THE CEILING PANEL.
THEY DIDN'T STAND A CHANCE. NOT WHILE THEY WERE MAKING LOVE.
KIKUCHI WOULDN'T EVEN HAVE NOTICED HIM, MUCH LESS DEFLECTED THE BLOW.
INSPECTOR, THIS ISN'T A SPEAR WOUND... YET THE SPLATTER PATTERN SEEMS ODD FOR A SWORD STROKE.
MMM... THIS SLASHING CUT WOULD BE THE TIP OF A CURVED BLADE...
IF THE PERPETRATOR HURLED IT FROM ABOVE, WITH ENOUGH POWER TO KILL THEM BOTH, YOU'D EXPECT THE BLADE TO GO OFF AT AN ANGLE... ONLY A MASTER COULD HAVE DONE THIS...
INCREDIBLE TECHNIQUE. THERE'S NO ONE IN OUR LORD'S SERVICE WHO CAN HANDLE A CURVED BLADE THIS WELL.

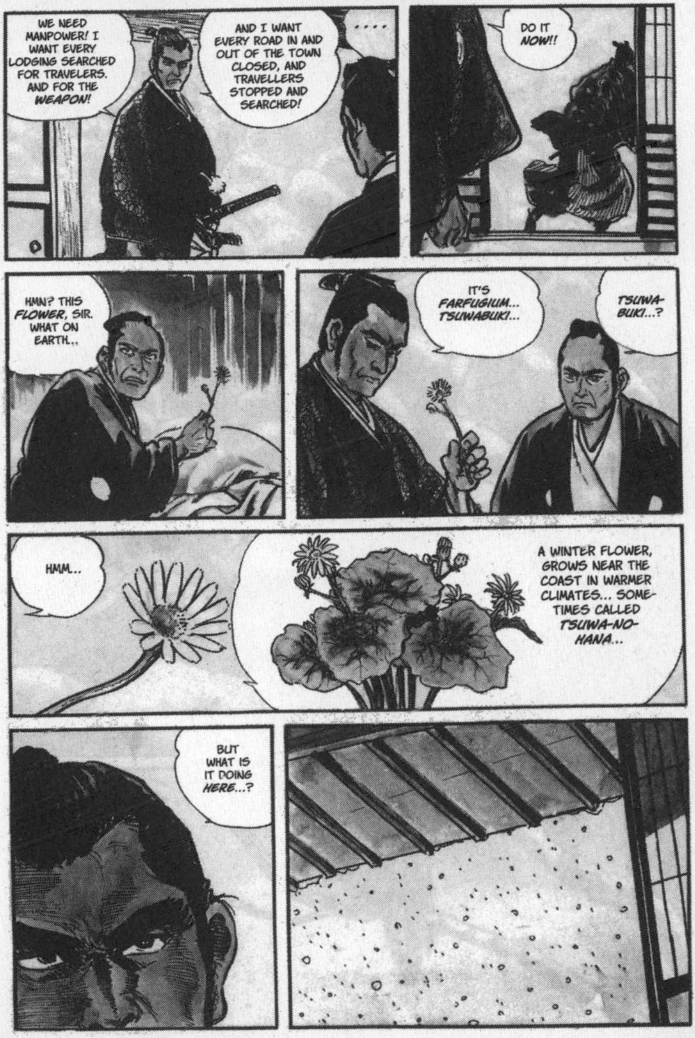
WE NEED MANPOWER! I WANT EVERY LODGING SEARCHED FOR TRAVELERS. AND FOR THE *WEAPON!*
AND I WANT EVERY ROAD IN AND OUT OF THE TOWN CLOSED, AND TRAVELLERS STOPPED AND SEARCHED!
....
DO IT *NOW!!*
HMN? THIS *FLOWER*, SIR. WHAT ON EARTH...
IT'S *FARFUGIUM... TSUWABUKI...*
TSUWA-BUKI...?
HMM...
A WINTER FLOWER, GROWS NEAR THE COAST IN WARMER CLIMATES... SOMETIMES CALLED *TSUWA-NO-HANA...*
BUT WHAT IS IT DOING *HERE...?*

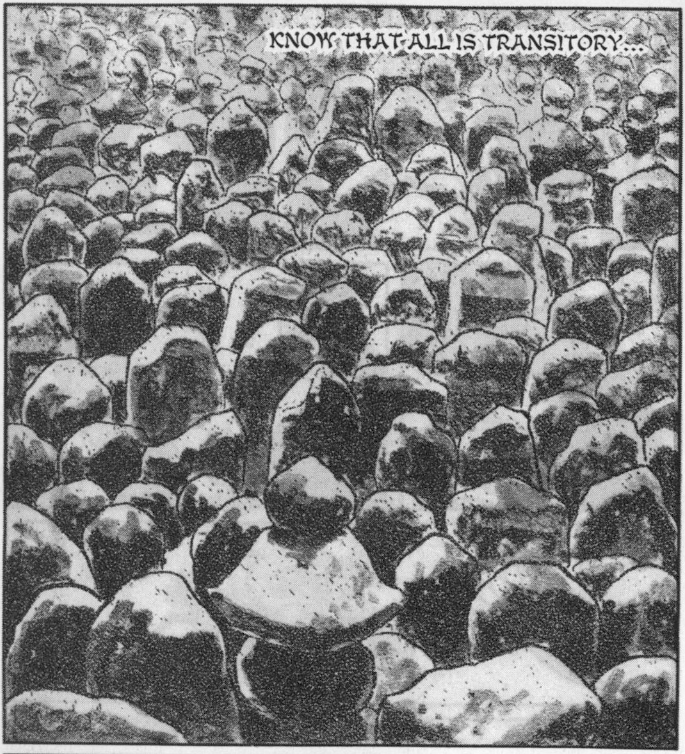
KNOW THAT ALL IS TRANSITORY...

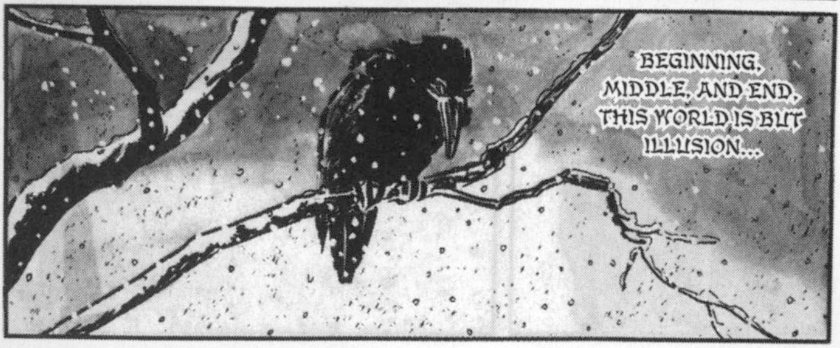
BEGINNING, MIDDLE, AND END, THIS WORLD IS BUT ILLUSION...

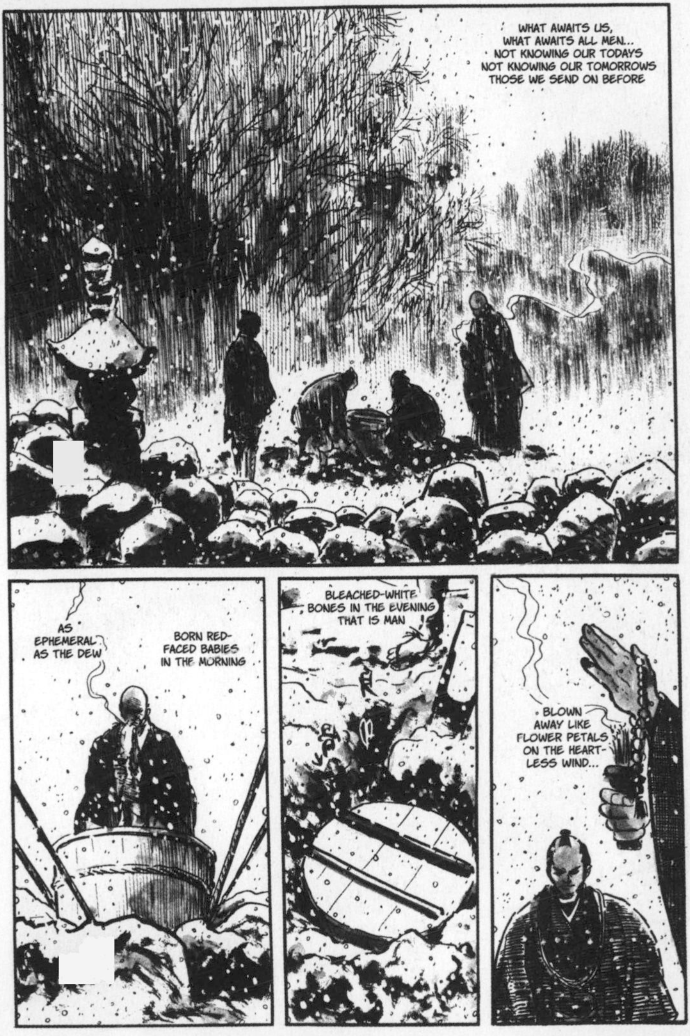
WHAT AWAITS US,
WHAT AWAITS ALL MEN...
NOT KNOWING OUR TODAYS
NOT KNOWING OUR TOMORROWS
THOSE WE SEND ON BEFORE
AS EPHEMERAL AS THE DEW
BORN RED-FACED BABIES IN THE MORNING
BLEACHED-WHITE BONES IN THE EVENING THAT IS MAN
BLOWN AWAY LIKE FLOWER PETALS ON THE HEART-LESS WIND...

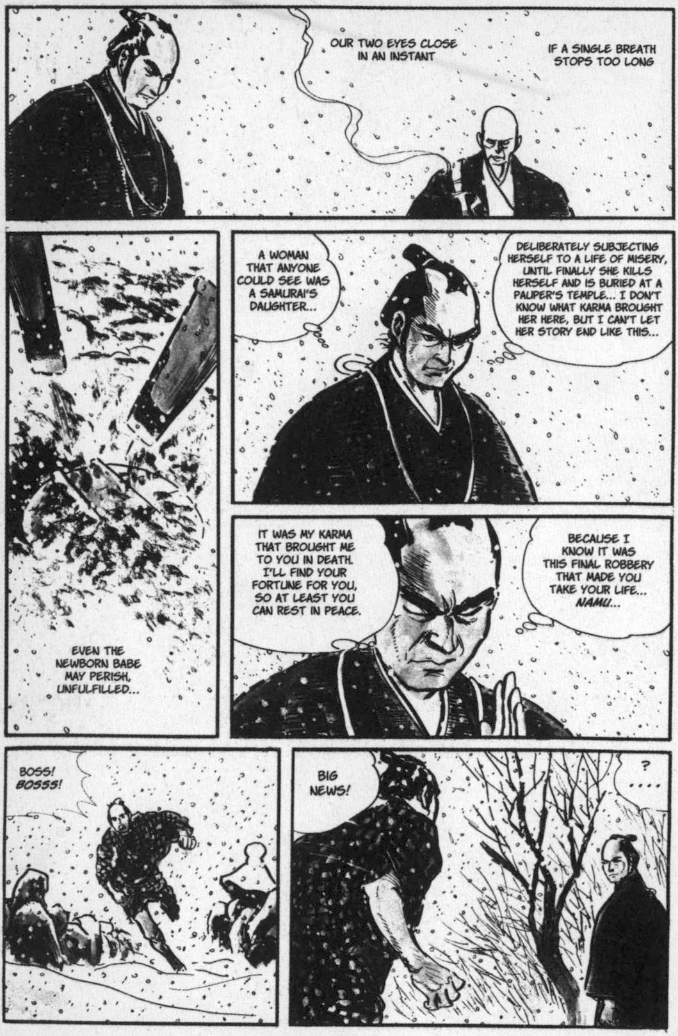
OUR TWO EYES CLOSE IN AN INSTANT
IF A SINGLE BREATH STOPS TOO LONG
EVEN THE NEWBORN BABE MAY PERISH, UNFULFILLED...
A WOMAN THAT ANYONE COULD SEE WAS A SAMURAI'S DAUGHTER...
DELIBERATELY SUBJECTING HERSELF TO A LIFE OF MISERY, UNTIL FINALLY SHE KILLS HERSELF AND IS BURIED AT A PAUPER'S TEMPLE... I DON'T KNOW WHAT KARMA BROUGHT HER HERE, BUT I CAN'T LET HER STORY END LIKE THIS...
IT WAS MY KARMA THAT BROUGHT ME TO YOU IN DEATH. I'LL FIND YOUR FORTUNE FOR YOU, SO AT LEAST YOU CAN REST IN PEACE.
BECAUSE I KNOW IT WAS THIS FINAL ROBBERY THAT MADE YOU TAKE YOUR LIFE... *NAMU*...
BOSS! *BOSSS!*
BIG NEWS!
?
....

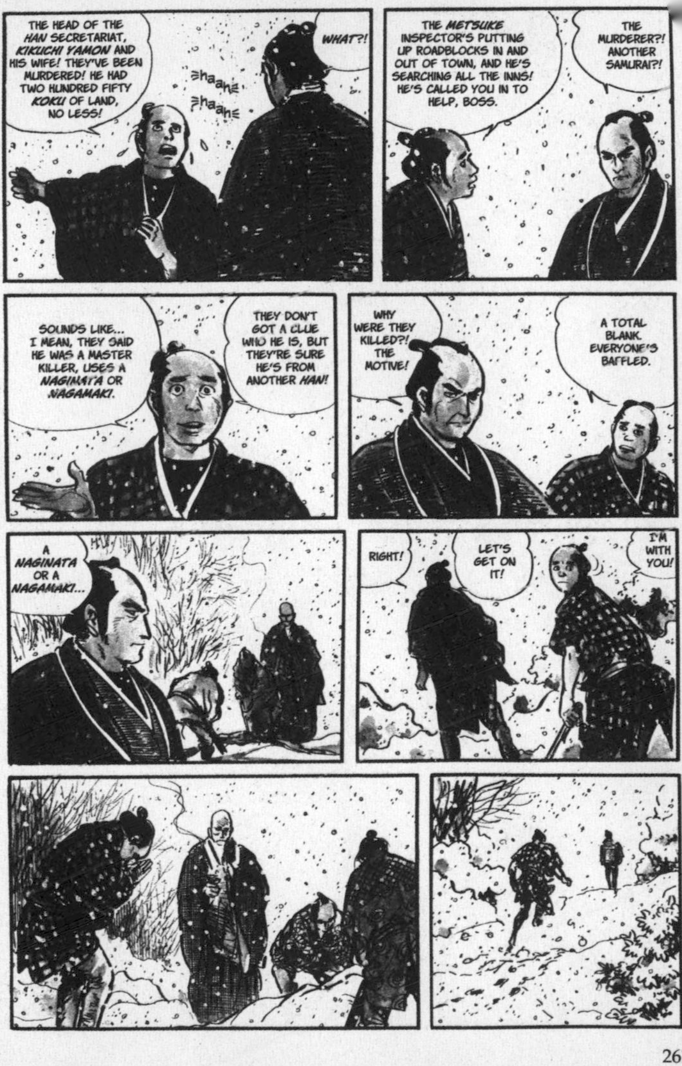
THE HEAD OF THE *HAN* SECRETARIAT, *KIKUCHI YAMON* AND HIS WIFE! THEY'VE BEEN MURDERED! HE HAD TWO HUNDRED FIFTY *KOKU* OF LAND, NO LESS!
haah
haah
WHAT?!
THE *METSUKE* INSPECTOR'S PUTTING UP ROADBLOCKS IN AND OUT OF TOWN, AND HE'S SEARCHING ALL THE INNS! HE'S CALLED YOU IN TO HELP, BOSS.
THE MURDERER?! ANOTHER SAMURAI?!
SOUNDS LIKE... I MEAN, THEY SAID HE WAS A MASTER KILLER, USES A *NAGINATA* OR *NAGAMAKI*.
THEY DON'T GOT A CLUE WHO HE IS, BUT THEY'RE SURE HE'S FROM ANOTHER *HAN*!
WHY WERE THEY KILLED?! THE MOTIVE!
A TOTAL BLANK. EVERYONE'S BAFFLED.
A *NAGINATA* OR A *NAGAMAKI*...
RIGHT!
LET'S GET ON IT!
I'M WITH YOU!

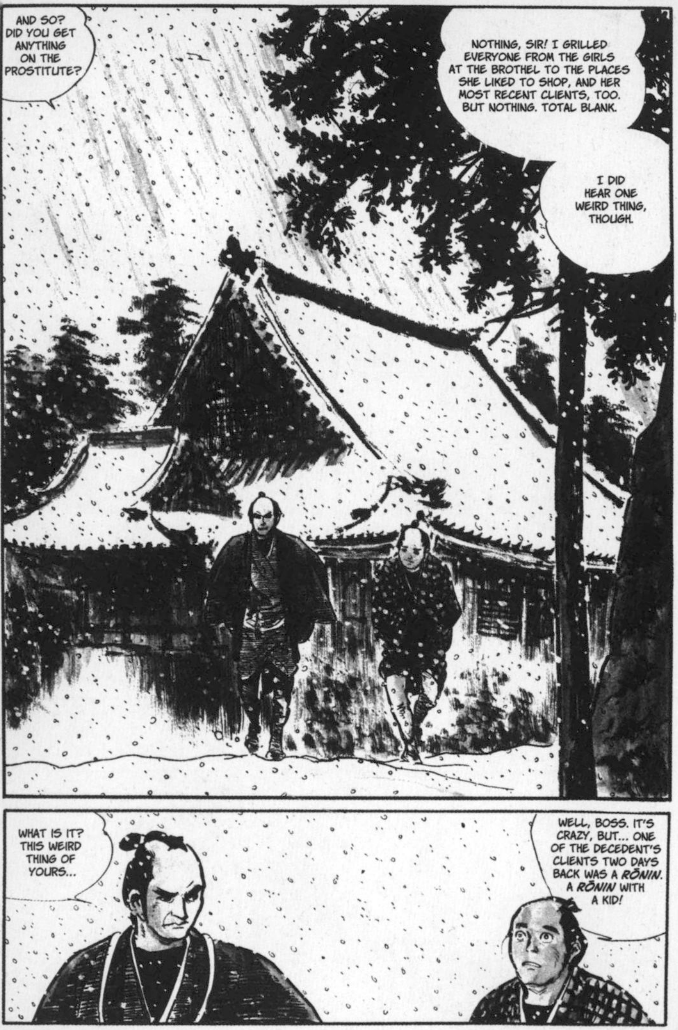
AND SO? DID YOU GET ANYTHING ON THE PROSTITUTE?
NOTHING, SIR! I GRILLED EVERYONE FROM THE GIRLS AT THE BROTHEL TO THE PLACES SHE LIKED TO SHOP, AND HER MOST RECENT CLIENTS, TOO. BUT NOTHING. TOTAL BLANK.
I DID HEAR ONE WEIRD THING, THOUGH.
WHAT IS IT? THIS WEIRD THING OF YOURS...
WELL, BOSS. IT'S CRAZY, BUT... ONE OF THE DECEDENT'S CLIENTS TWO DAYS BACK WAS A *RŌNIN*. A *RŌNIN* WITH A KID!

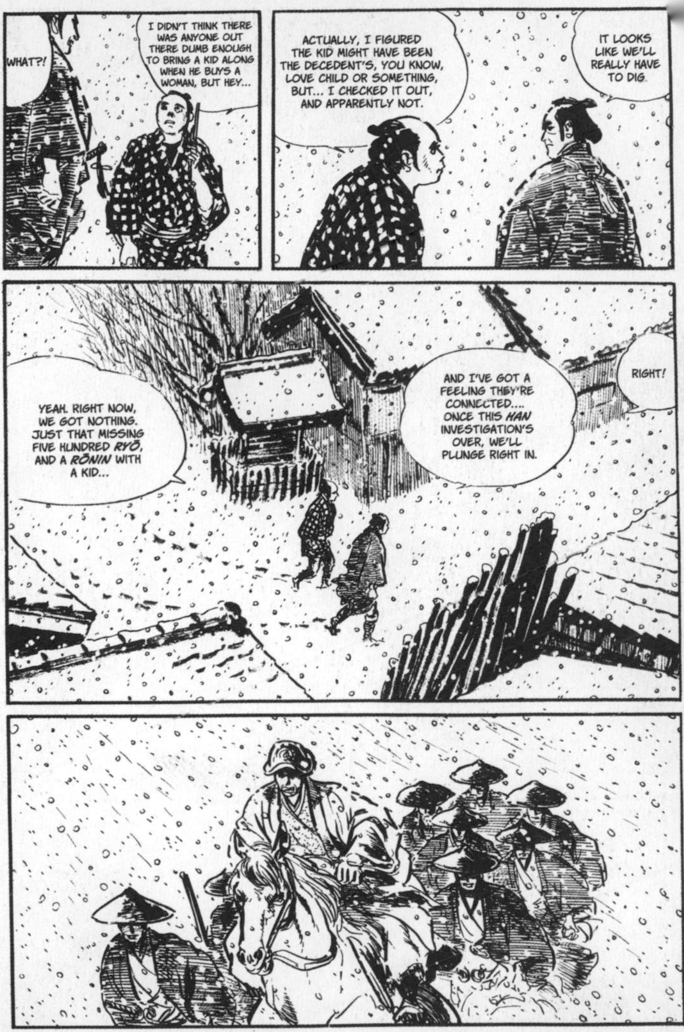
WHAT?!
I DIDN'T THINK THERE WAS ANYONE OUT THERE DUMB ENOUGH TO BRING A KID ALONG WHEN HE BUYS A WOMAN, BUT HEY...
ACTUALLY, I FIGURED THE KID MIGHT HAVE BEEN THE DECEDENT'S, YOU KNOW, LOVE CHILD OR SOMETHING, BUT... I CHECKED IT OUT, AND APPARENTLY NOT.
IT LOOKS LIKE WE'LL REALLY HAVE TO DIG.
YEAH. RIGHT NOW, WE GOT NOTHING. JUST THAT MISSING FIVE HUNDRED *RYŌ*, AND A *RŌNIN* WITH A KID...
AND I'VE GOT A FEELING THEY'RE CONNECTED.... ONCE THIS *HAN* INVESTIGATION'S OVER, WE'LL PLUNGE RIGHT IN.
RIGHT!

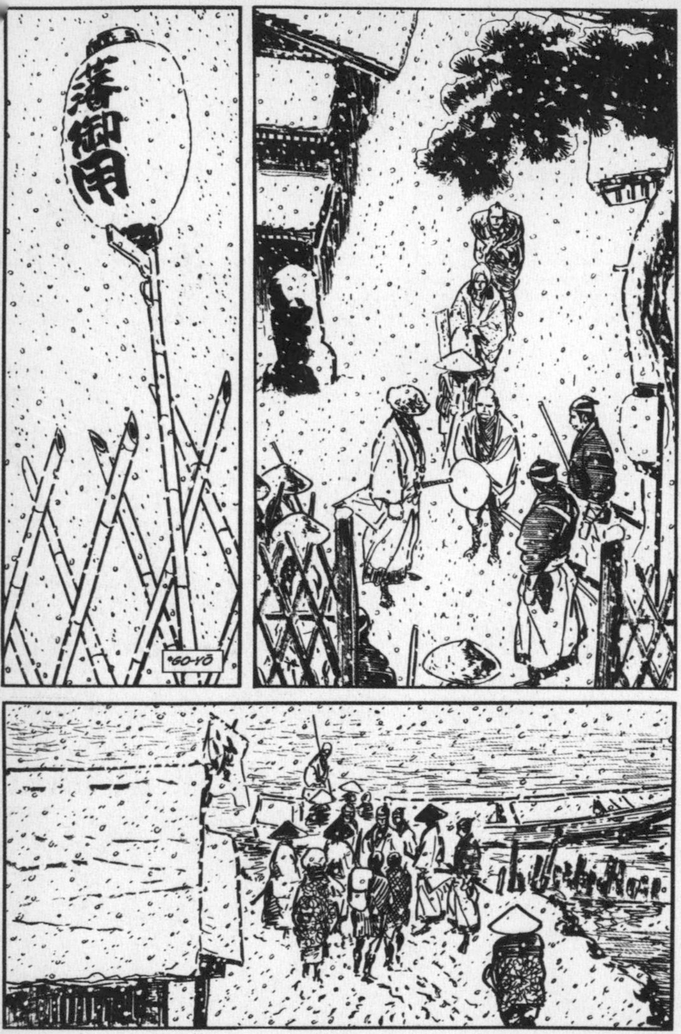
藩御用
*GO-YŌ

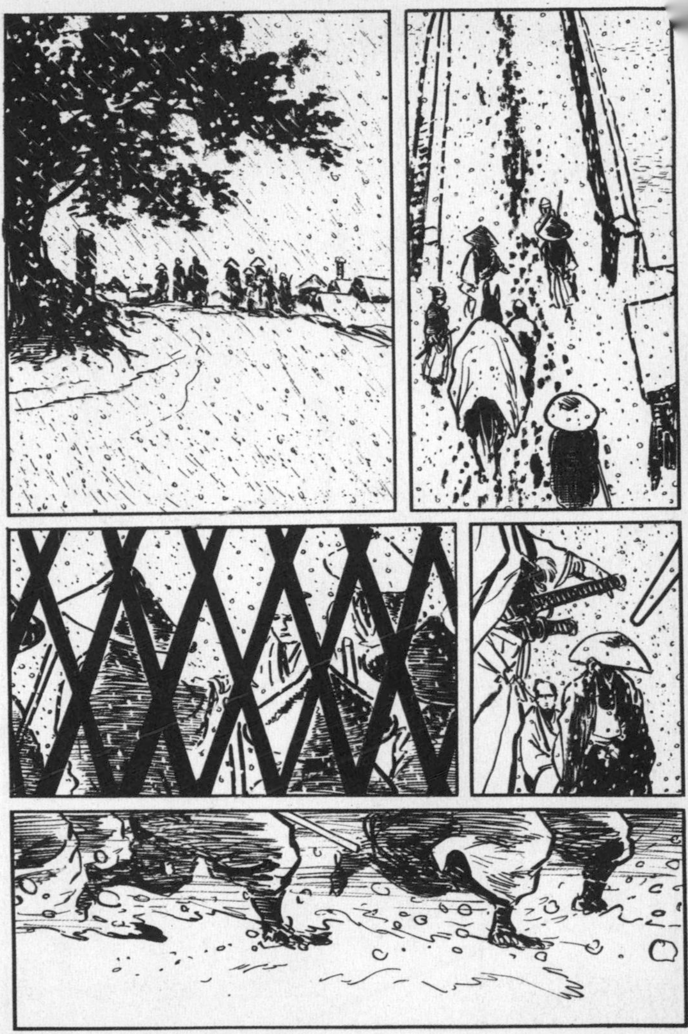

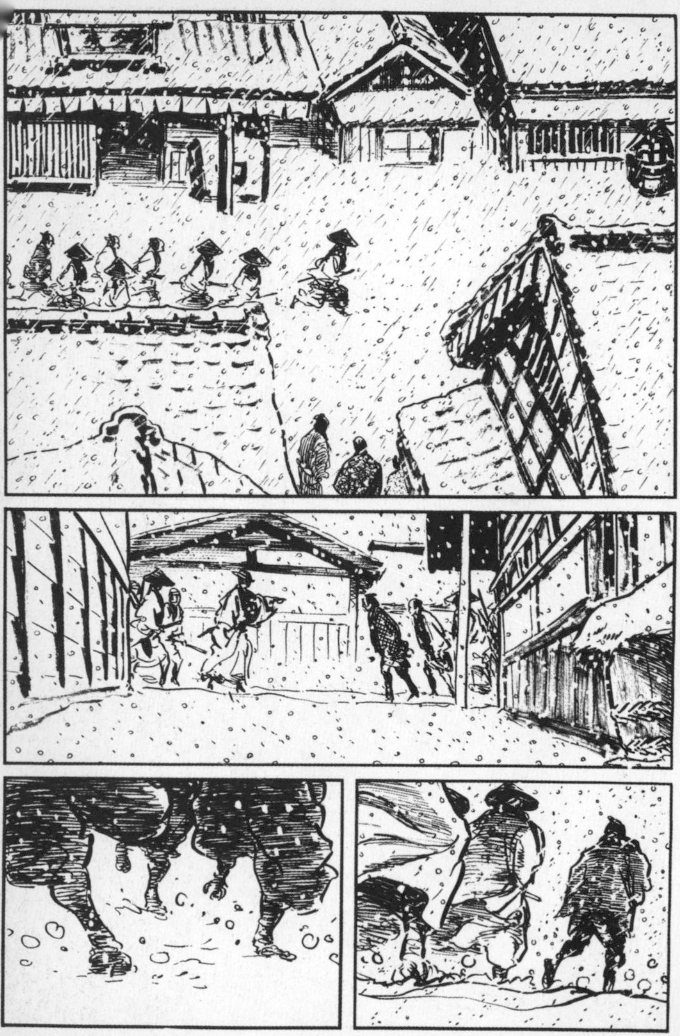

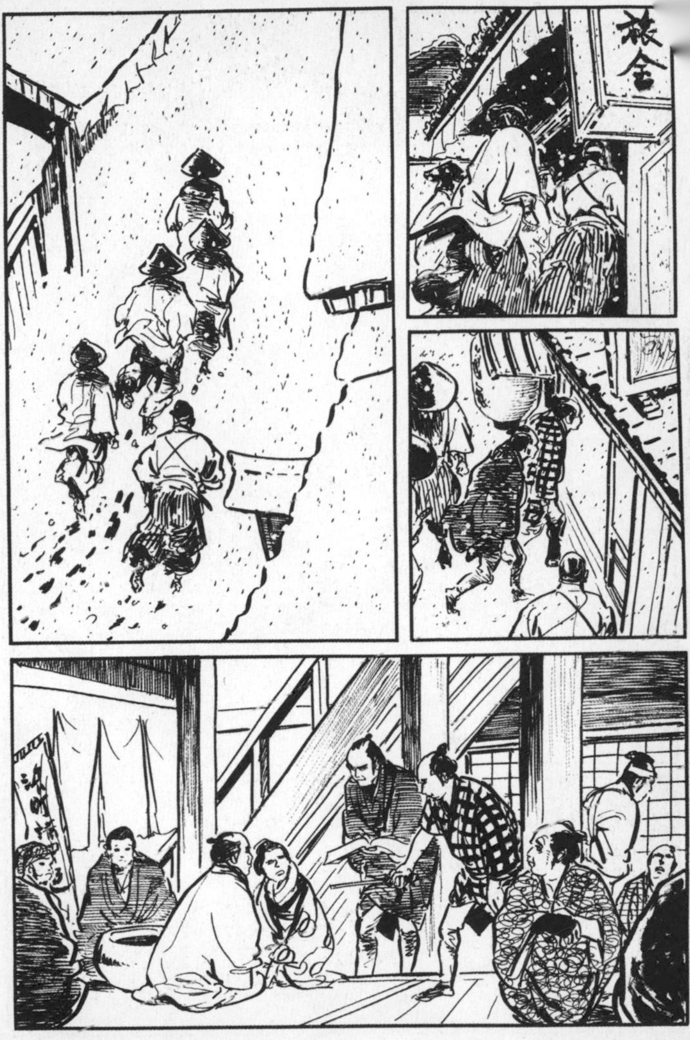
旅舎

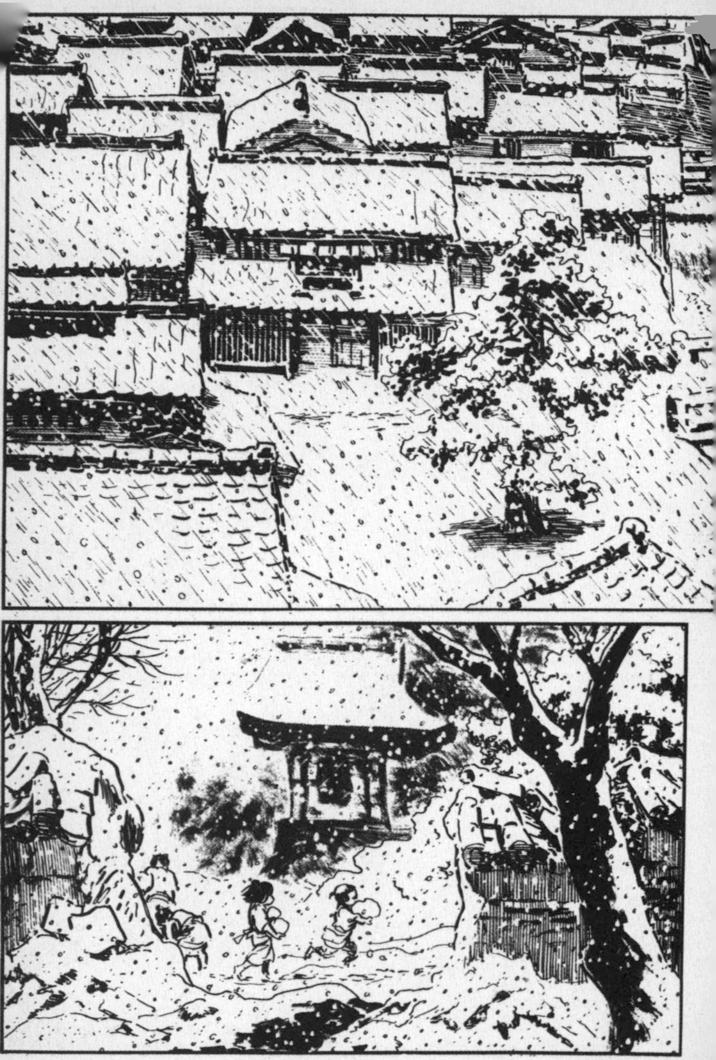

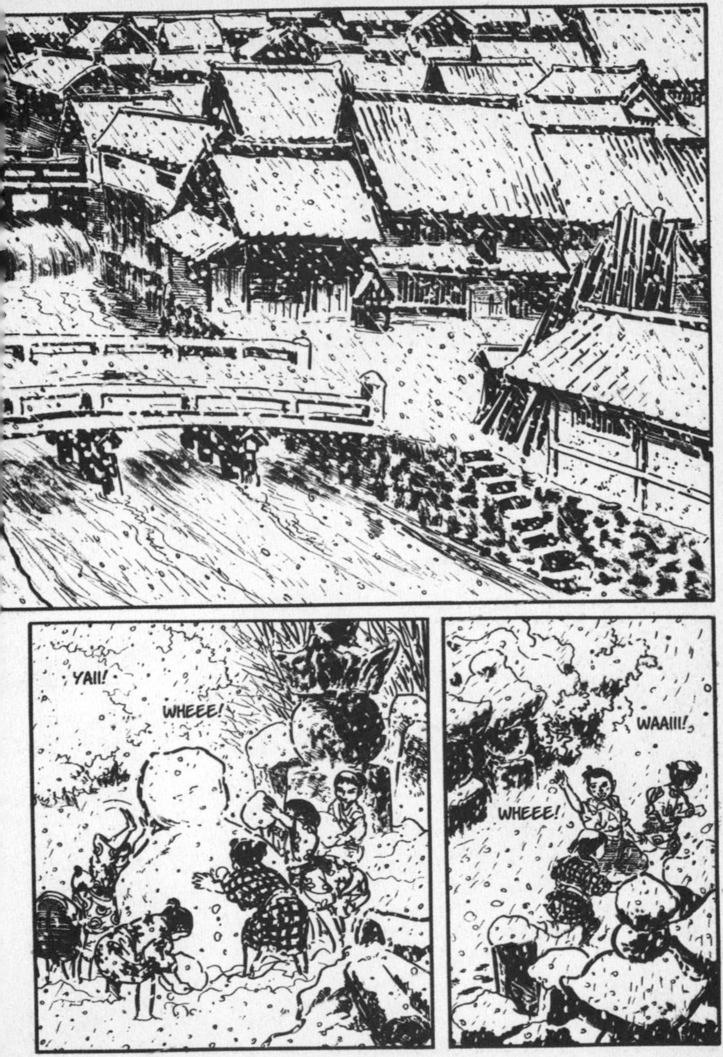
YAII!
WHEEE!
WAAIII!
WHEEE!

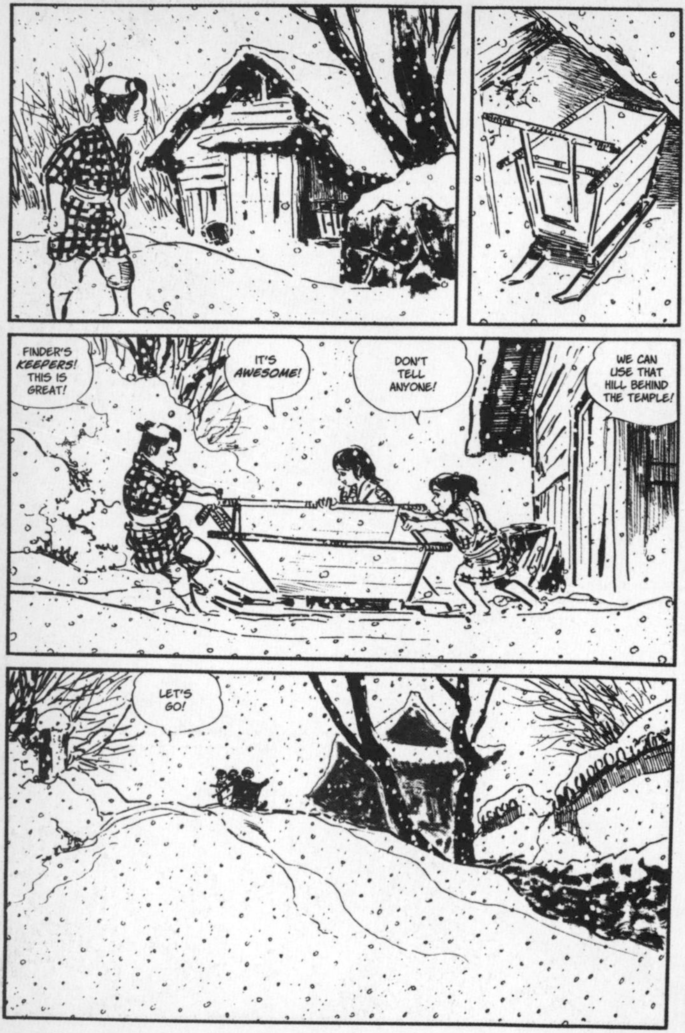
FINDER'S *KEEPERS!* THIS IS GREAT!
IT'S *AWESOME!*
DON'T TELL ANYONE!
WE CAN USE THAT HILL BEHIND THE TEMPLE!
LET'S GO!

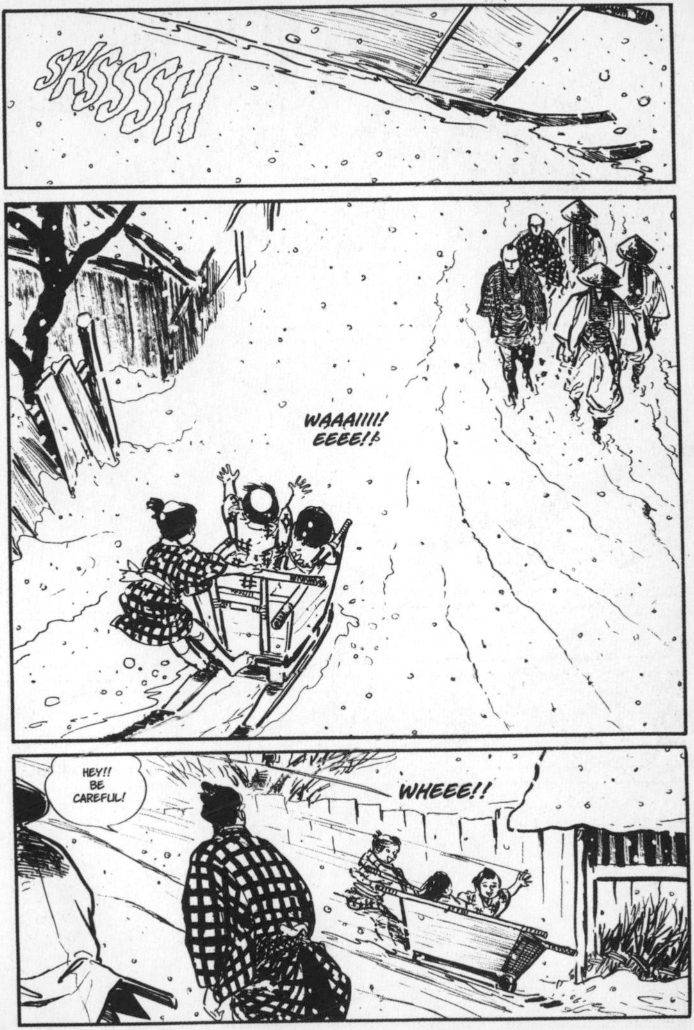
SKSSSH
WAAAIIII! EEEE!!
HEY!! BE CAREFUL!
WHEEE!!

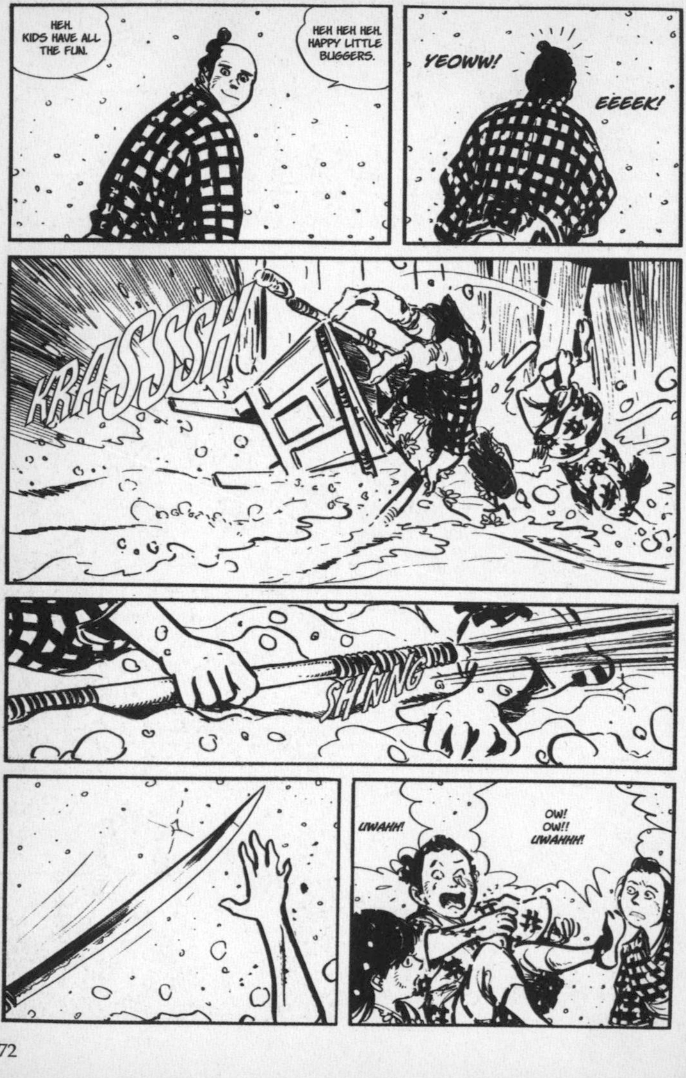
HEH. KIDS HAVE ALL THE FUN.
HEH HEH HEH. HAPPY LITTLE BUGGERS.
YEOWW!
EEEEK!
KRASSSH
SHING
UWAHH!
OW! OW!! UWAHHH!

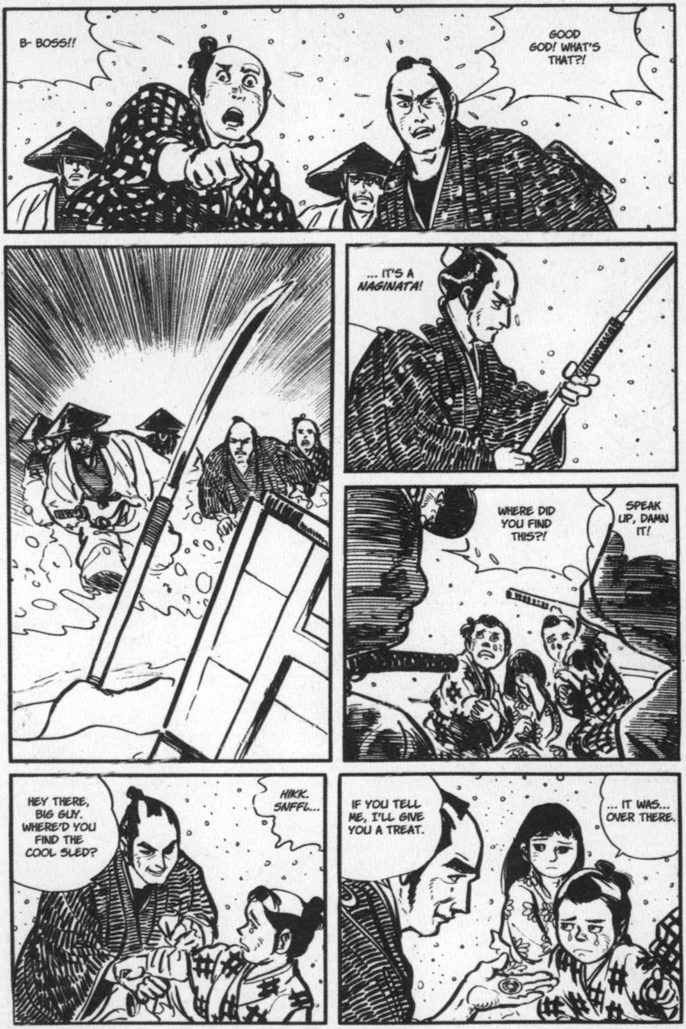
B- BOSS!!
GOOD GOD! WHAT'S THAT?!
... IT'S A NAGINATA!
WHERE DID YOU FIND THIS?!
SPEAK UP, DAMN IT!
HEY THERE, BIG GUY. WHERE'D YOU FIND THE COOL SLED?
HIKK. SNFFL...
IF YOU TELL ME, I'LL GIVE YOU A TREAT.
... IT WAS... OVER THERE.

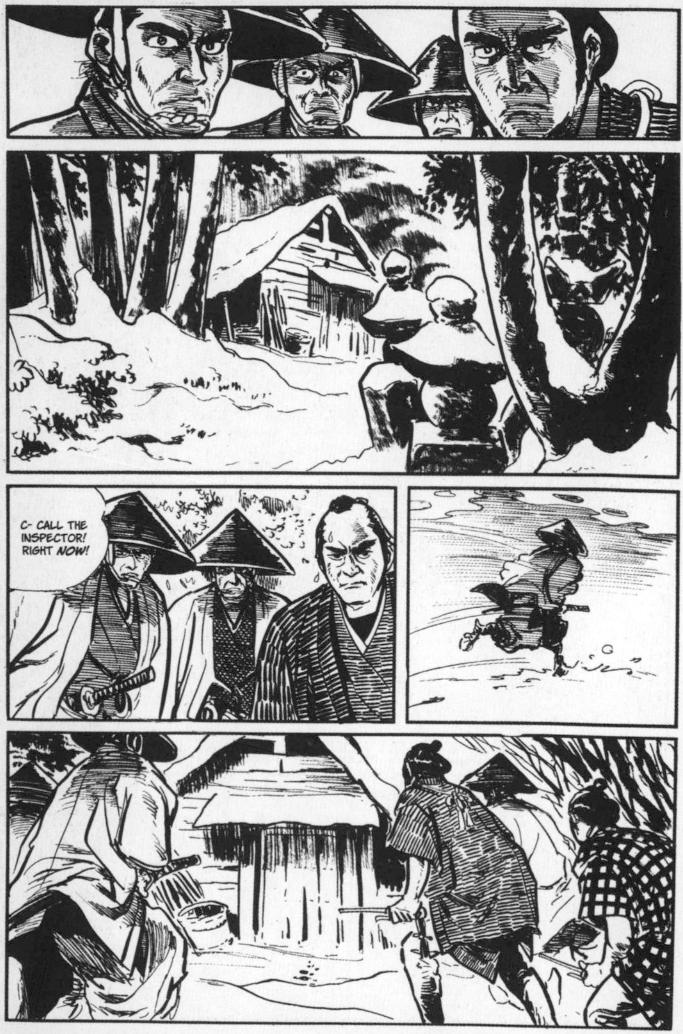
C- CALL THE INSPECTOR! RIGHT NOW!

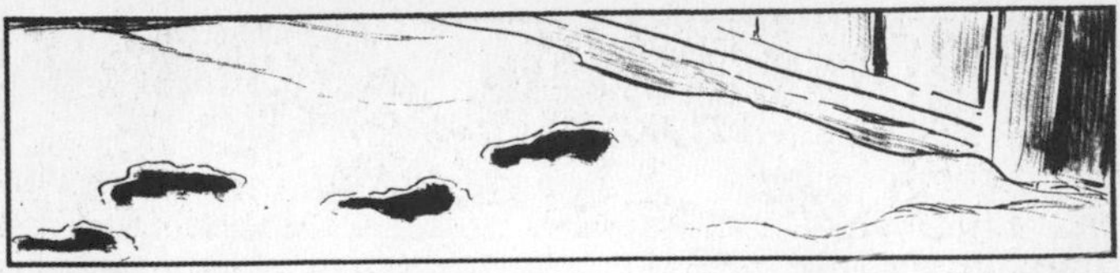
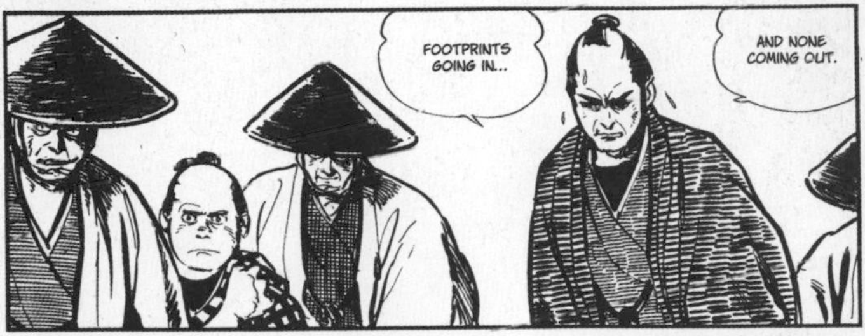
FOOTPRINTS GOING IN...
AND NONE COMING OUT.
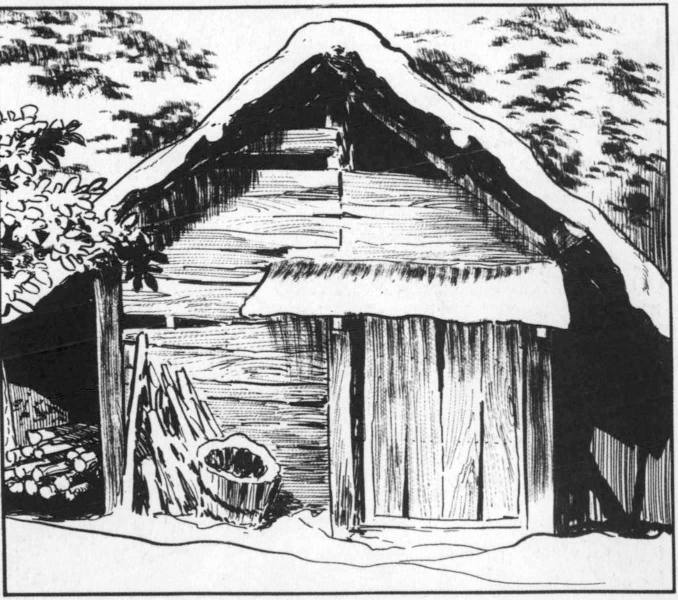

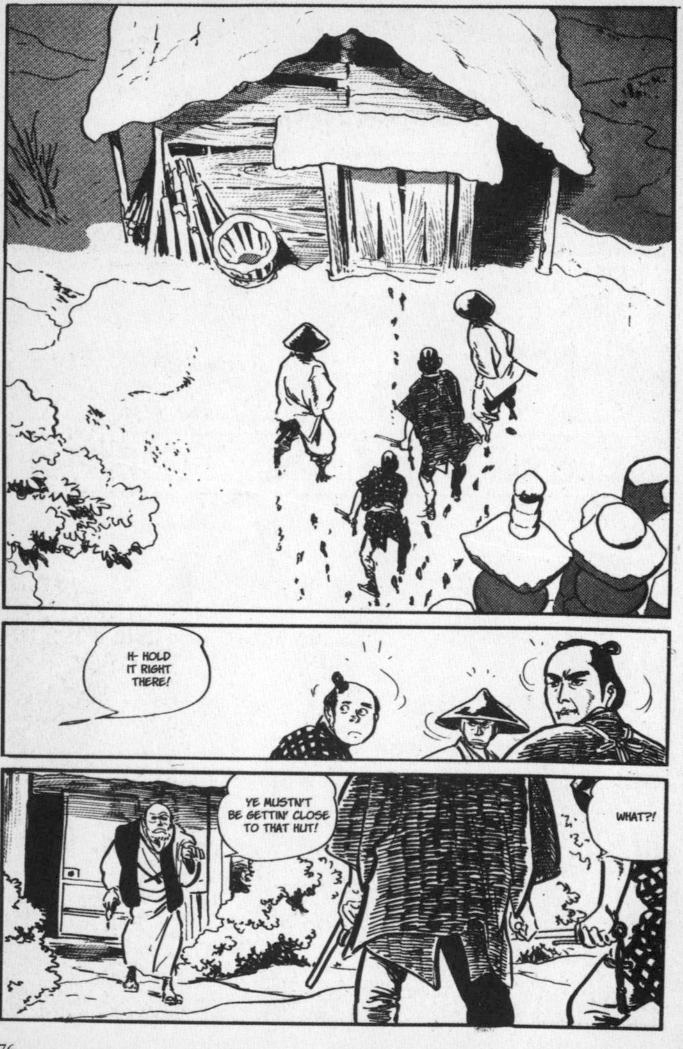
H- HOLD IT RIGHT THERE!
YE MUSTN'T BE GETTIN' CLOSE TO THAT HUT!
WHAT?!

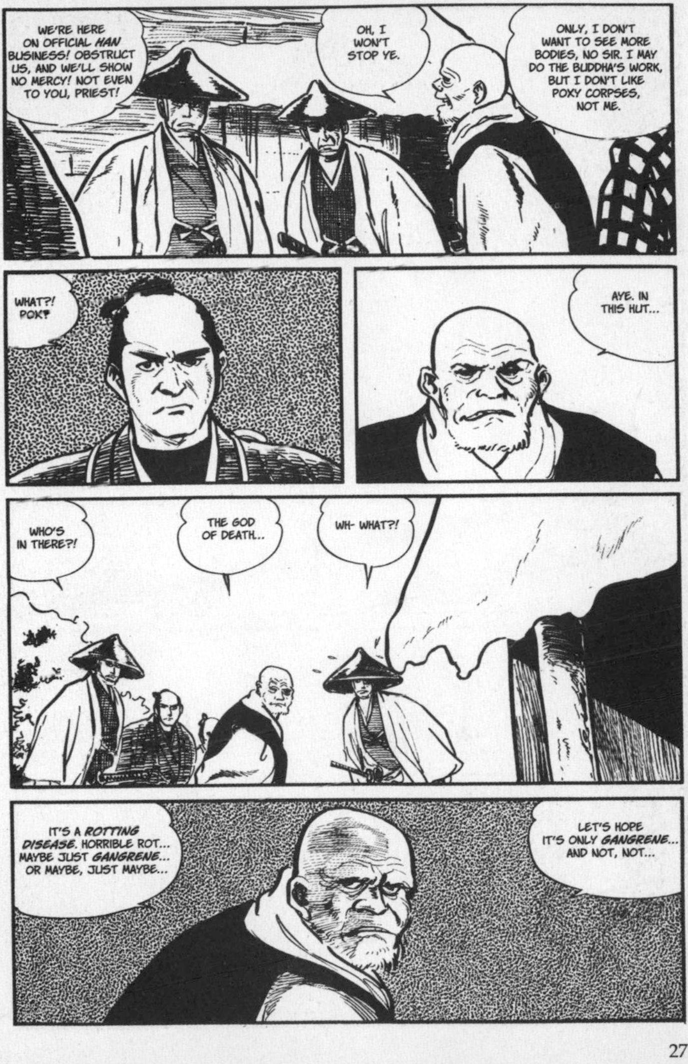
WE'RE HERE ON OFFICIAL *HAN* BUSINESS! OBSTRUCT US, AND WE'LL SHOW NO MERCY! NOT EVEN TO YOU, PRIEST!
OH, I WON'T STOP YE.
ONLY, I DON'T WANT TO SEE MORE BODIES, NO SIR. I MAY DO THE BUDDHA'S WORK, BUT I DON'T LIKE POXY CORPSES, NOT ME.
WHAT?! POX?
AYE. IN THIS HUT...
WHO'S IN THERE?!
THE GOD OF DEATH...
WH- WHAT?!
IT'S A *ROTTING DISEASE*. HORRIBLE ROT... MAYBE JUST *GANGRENE*... OR MAYBE, JUST MAYBE...
LET'S HOPE IT'S ONLY *GANGRENE*... AND NOT, NOT...

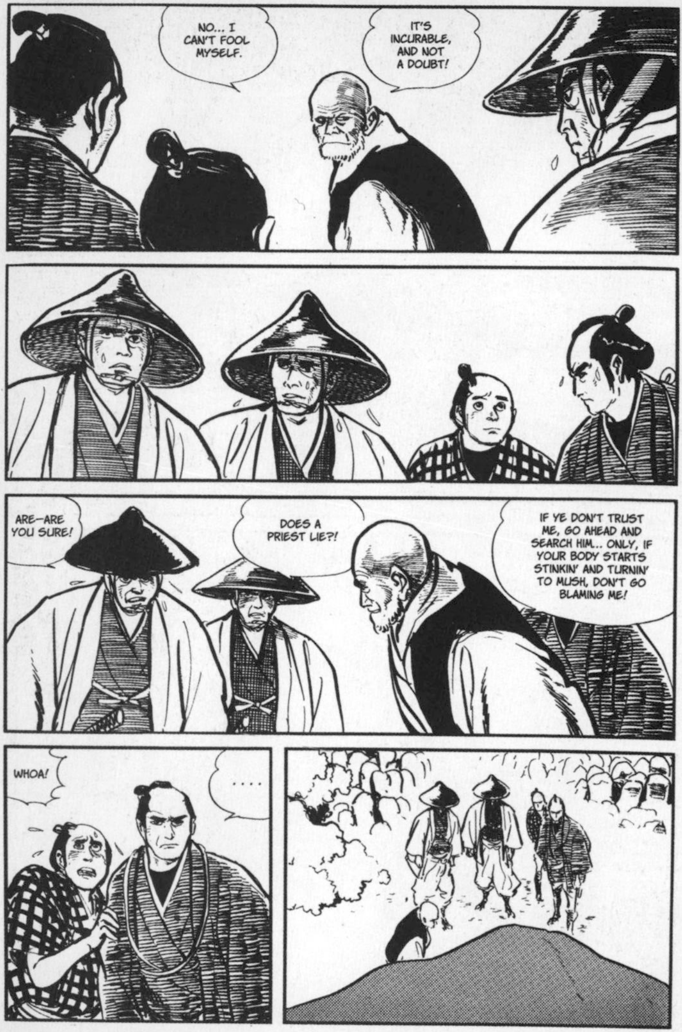
NO... I CAN'T FOOL MYSELF.
IT'S INCURABLE, AND NOT A DOUBT!
ARE—ARE YOU SURE!
DOES A PRIEST LIE?!
IF YE DON'T TRUST ME, GO AHEAD AND SEARCH HIM... ONLY, IF YOUR BODY STARTS STINKIN' AND TURNIN' TO MUSH, DON'T GO BLAMING ME!
WHOA!
....

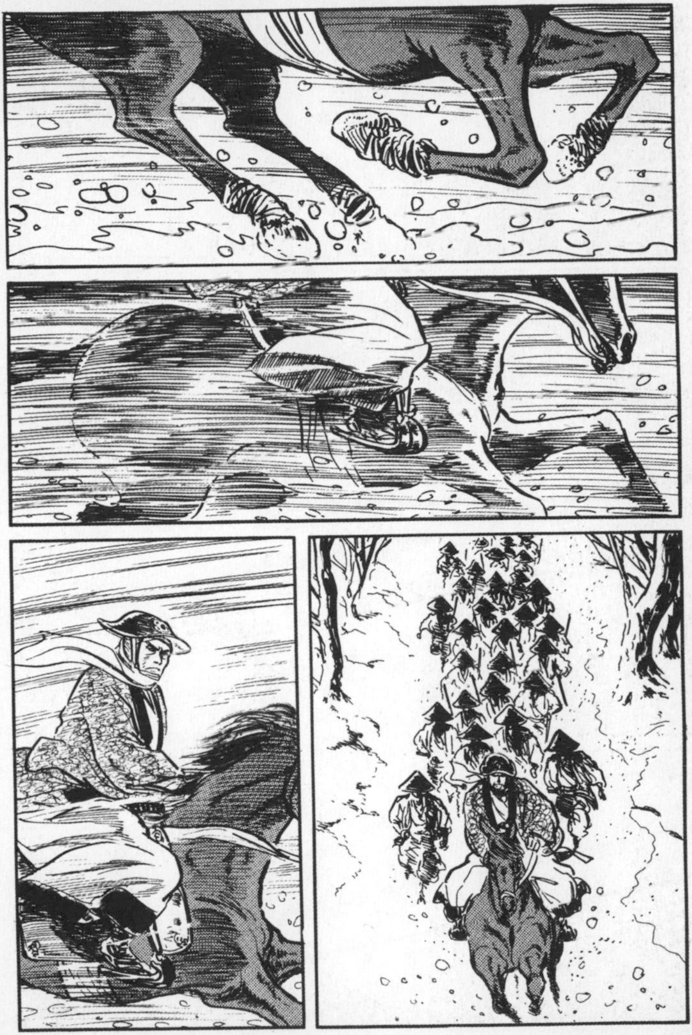

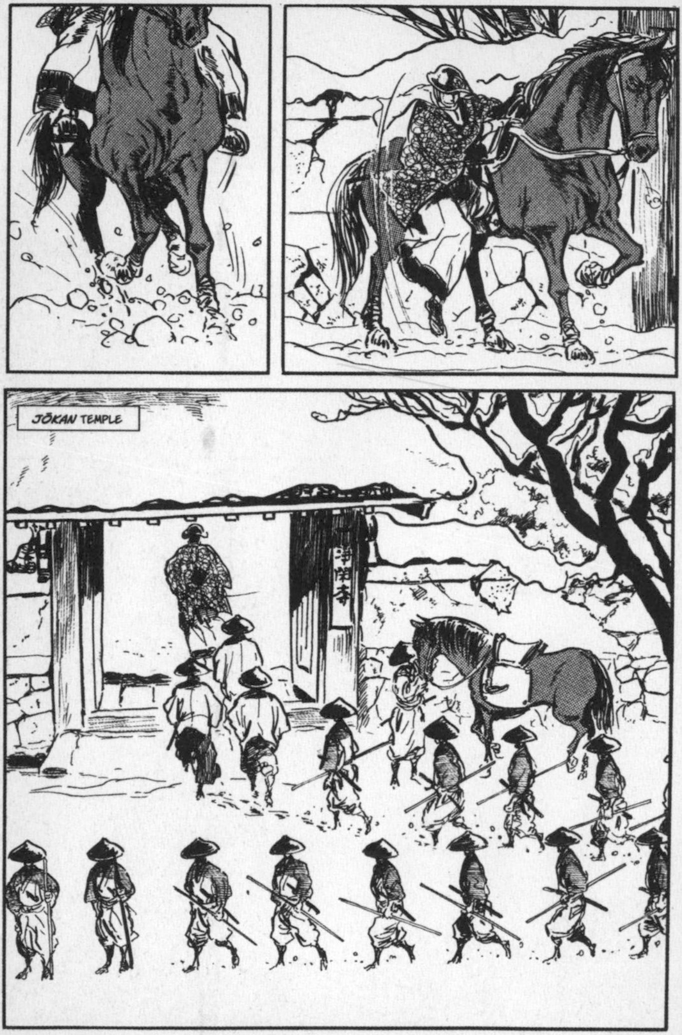
JŌKAN TEMPLE

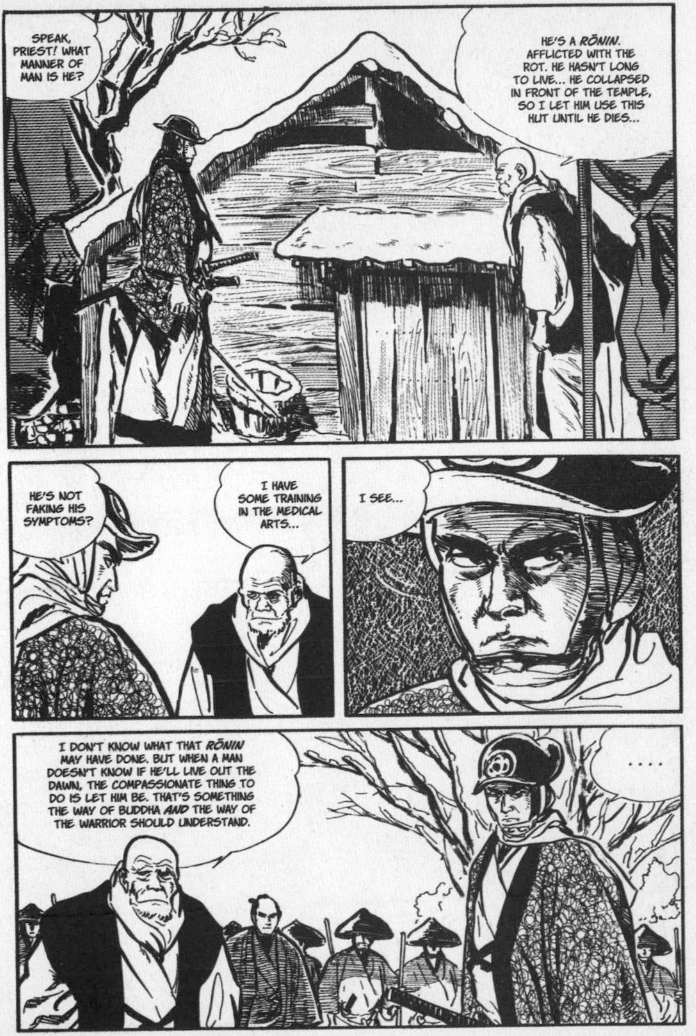
SPEAK, PRIEST! WHAT MANNER OF MAN IS HE?
HE'S A *RŌNIN*. AFFLICTED WITH THE ROT. HE HASN'T LONG TO LIVE... HE COLLAPSED IN FRONT OF THE TEMPLE, SO I LET HIM USE THIS HUT UNTIL HE DIES...
HE'S NOT FAKING HIS SYMPTOMS?
I HAVE SOME TRAINING IN THE MEDICAL ARTS...
I SEE...
I DON'T KNOW WHAT THAT *RŌNIN* MAY HAVE DONE. BUT WHEN A MAN DOESN'T KNOW IF HE'LL LIVE OUT THE DAWN, THE COMPASSIONATE THING TO DO IS LET HIM BE. THAT'S SOMETHING THE WAY OF BUDDHA *AND* THE WAY OF THE WARRIOR SHOULD UNDERSTAND.
....

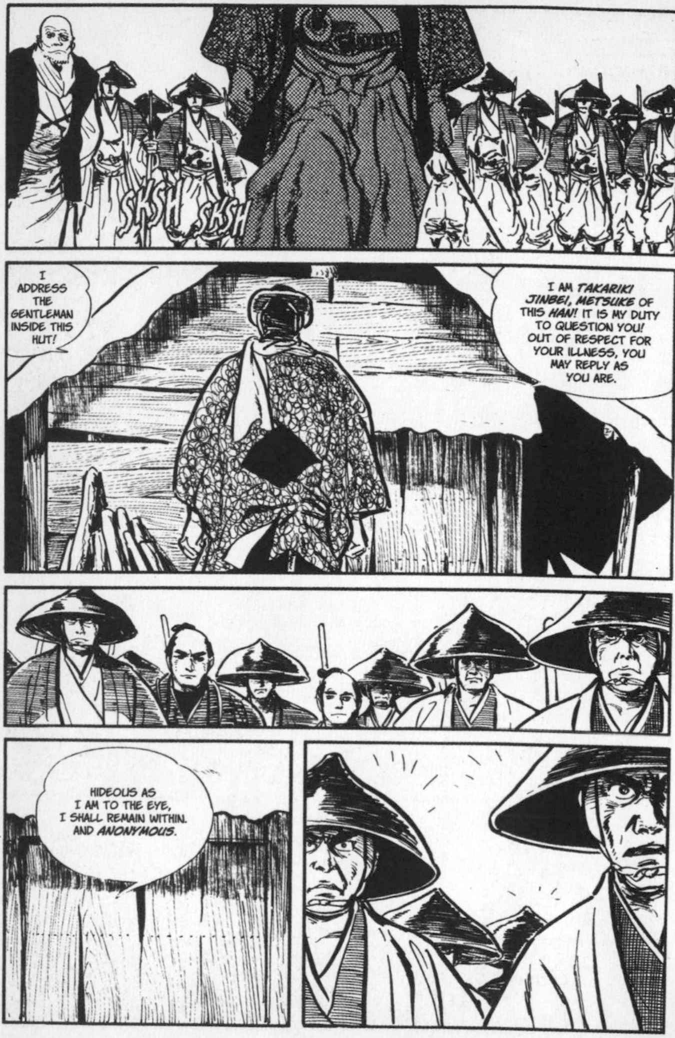
SKSH SKSH
I ADDRESS THE GENTLEMAN INSIDE THIS HUT!
I AM *TAKARIKI JINBEI, METSUKE* OF THIS *HAN!* IT IS MY DUTY TO QUESTION YOU! OUT OF RESPECT FOR YOUR ILLNESS, YOU MAY REPLY AS YOU ARE.
HIDEOUS AS I AM TO THE EYE, I SHALL REMAIN WITHIN. AND *ANONYMOUS*.

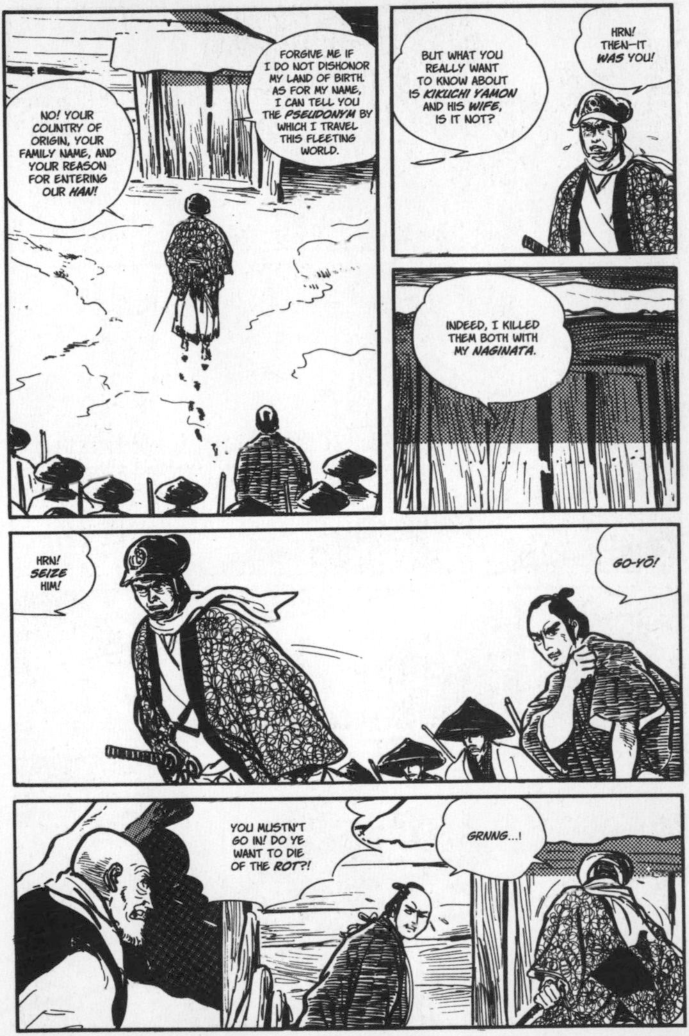
NO! YOUR COUNTRY OF ORIGIN, YOUR FAMILY NAME, AND YOUR REASON FOR ENTERING OUR HAN!
FORGIVE ME IF I DO NOT DISHONOR MY LAND OF BIRTH. AS FOR MY NAME, I CAN TELL YOU THE PSEUDONYM BY WHICH I TRAVEL THIS FLEETING WORLD.
BUT WHAT YOU REALLY WANT TO KNOW ABOUT IS KIKUCHI YAMON AND HIS WIFE, IS IT NOT?
HRN! THEN—IT WAS YOU!
INDEED, I KILLED THEM BOTH WITH MY NAGINATA.
HRN! SEIZE HIM!
GO-YŌ!
YOU MUSTN'T GO IN! DO YE WANT TO DIE OF THE ROT?!
GRNNG...!

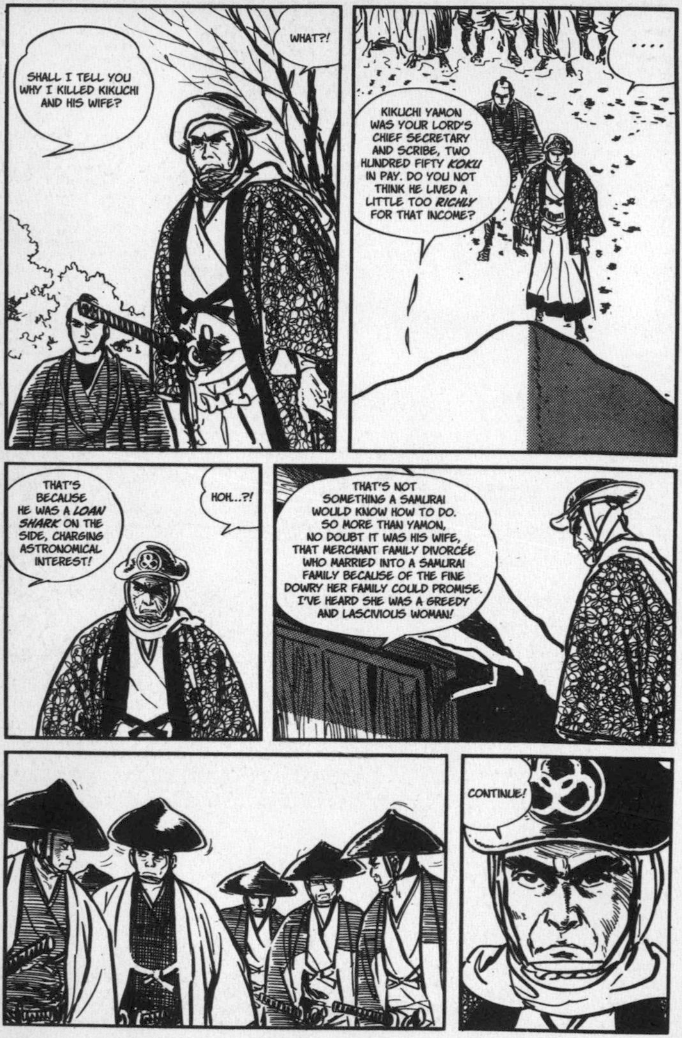
SHALL I TELL YOU WHY I KILLED KIKUCHI AND HIS WIFE?
WHAT?!
KIKUCHI YAMON WAS YOUR LORD'S CHIEF SECRETARY AND SCRIBE, TWO HUNDRED FIFTY *KOKU* IN PAY. DO YOU NOT THINK HE LIVED A LITTLE TOO *RICHLY* FOR THAT INCOME?
....
THAT'S BECAUSE HE WAS A *LOAN SHARK* ON THE SIDE, CHARGING ASTRONOMICAL INTEREST!
HOH..?!
THAT'S NOT SOMETHING A SAMURAI WOULD KNOW HOW TO DO. SO MORE THAN YAMON, NO DOUBT IT WAS HIS WIFE, THAT MERCHANT FAMILY DIVORCÉE WHO MARRIED INTO A SAMURAI FAMILY BECAUSE OF THE FINE DOWRY HER FAMILY COULD PROMISE. I'VE HEARD SHE WAS A GREEDY AND LASCIVIOUS WOMAN!
CONTINUE!

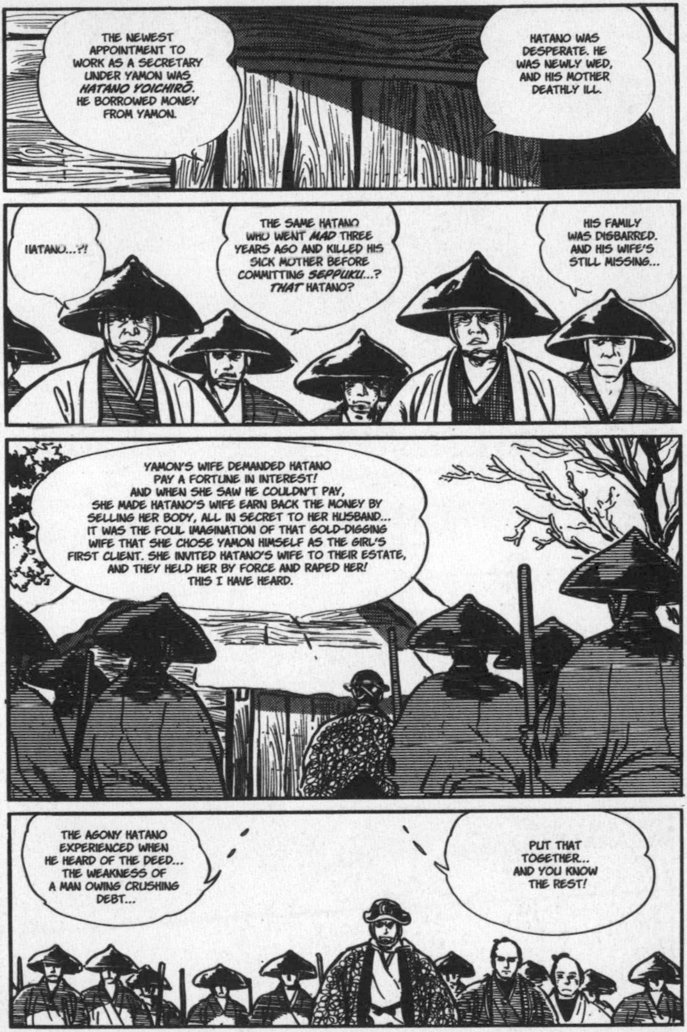
THE NEWEST APPOINTMENT TO WORK AS A SECRETARY UNDER YAMON WAS *HATANO YOICHIRŌ*. HE BORROWED MONEY FROM YAMON.
HATANO WAS DESPERATE. HE WAS NEWLY WED, AND HIS MOTHER DEATHLY ILL.
HATANO...?!
THE SAME HATANO WHO WENT *MAD* THREE YEARS AGO AND KILLED HIS SICK MOTHER BEFORE COMMITTING *SEPPUKU*...? *THAT* HATANO?
HIS FAMILY WAS DISBARRED. AND HIS WIFE'S STILL MISSING...
YAMON'S WIFE DEMANDED HATANO PAY A FORTUNE IN INTEREST! AND WHEN SHE SAW HE COULDN'T PAY, SHE MADE HATANO'S WIFE EARN BACK THE MONEY BY SELLING HER BODY, ALL IN SECRET TO HER HUSBAND... IT WAS THE FOUL IMAGINATION OF THAT GOLD-DIGGING WIFE THAT SHE CHOSE YAMON HIMSELF AS THE GIRL'S FIRST CLIENT. SHE INVITED HATANO'S WIFE TO THEIR ESTATE, AND THEY HELD HER BY FORCE AND RAPED HER! THIS I HAVE HEARD.
THE AGONY HATANO EXPERIENCED WHEN HE HEARD OF THE DEED... THE WEAKNESS OF A MAN OWING CRUSHING DEBT...
PUT THAT TOGETHER... AND YOU KNOW THE REST!

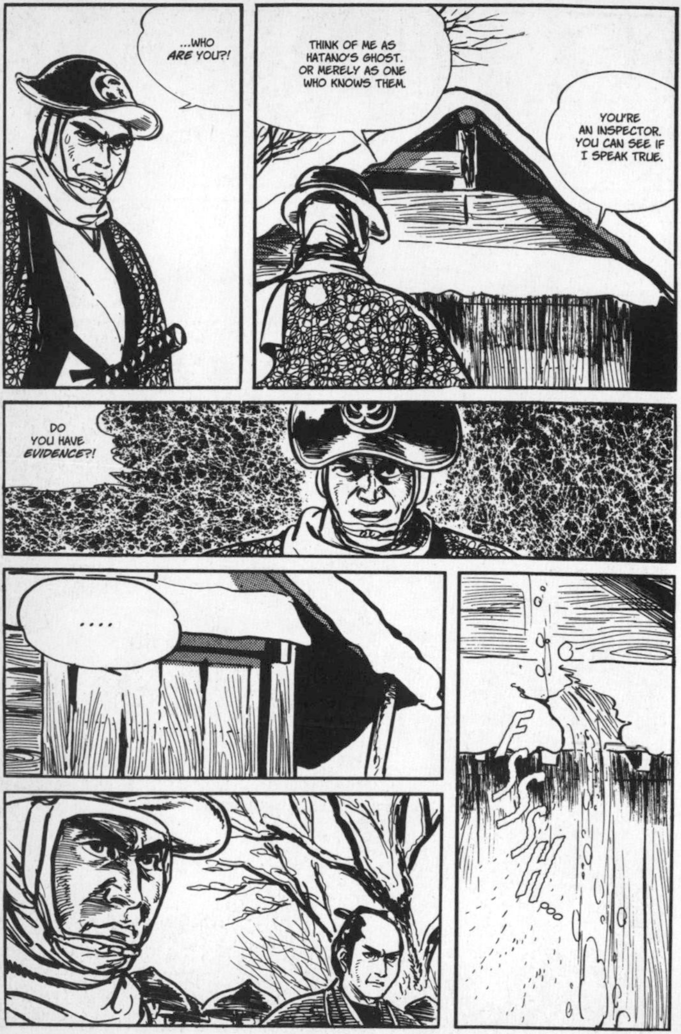
...WHO *ARE* YOU?!
THINK OF ME AS HATANO'S GHOST. OR MERELY AS ONE WHO KNOWS THEM.
YOU'RE AN INSPECTOR. YOU CAN SEE IF I SPEAK TRUE.
DO YOU HAVE *EVIDENCE*?!
....
FSSH

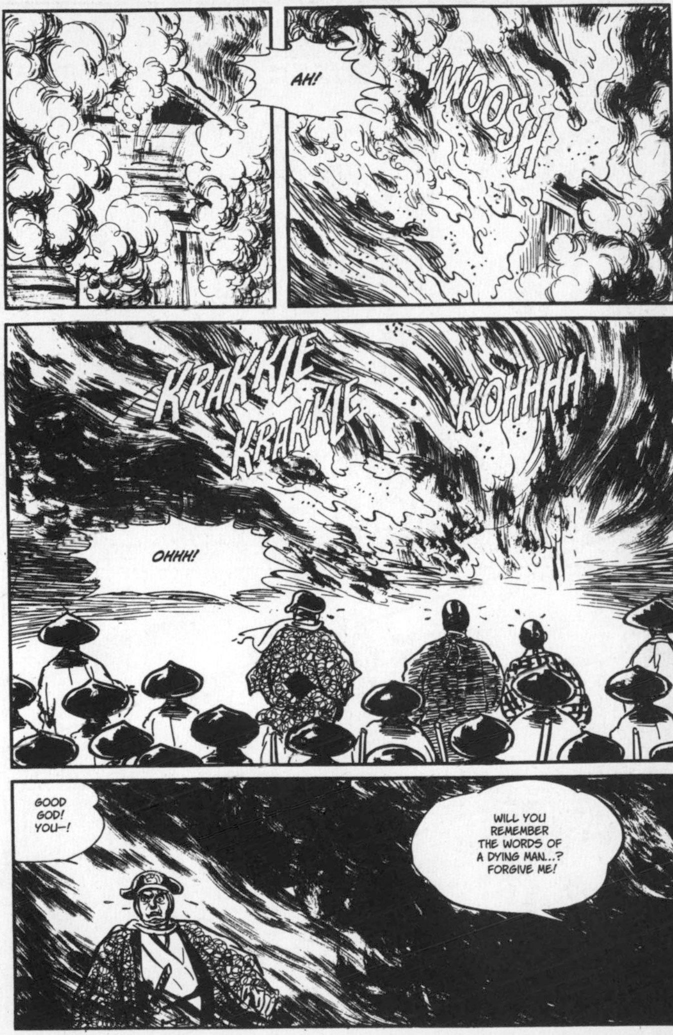
AH!
WOOSH
KRAKKLE
KRAKKLE
KOHHHH
OHHH!
GOOD GOD! YOU—!
WILL YOU REMEMBER THE WORDS OF A DYING MAN...? FORGIVE ME!

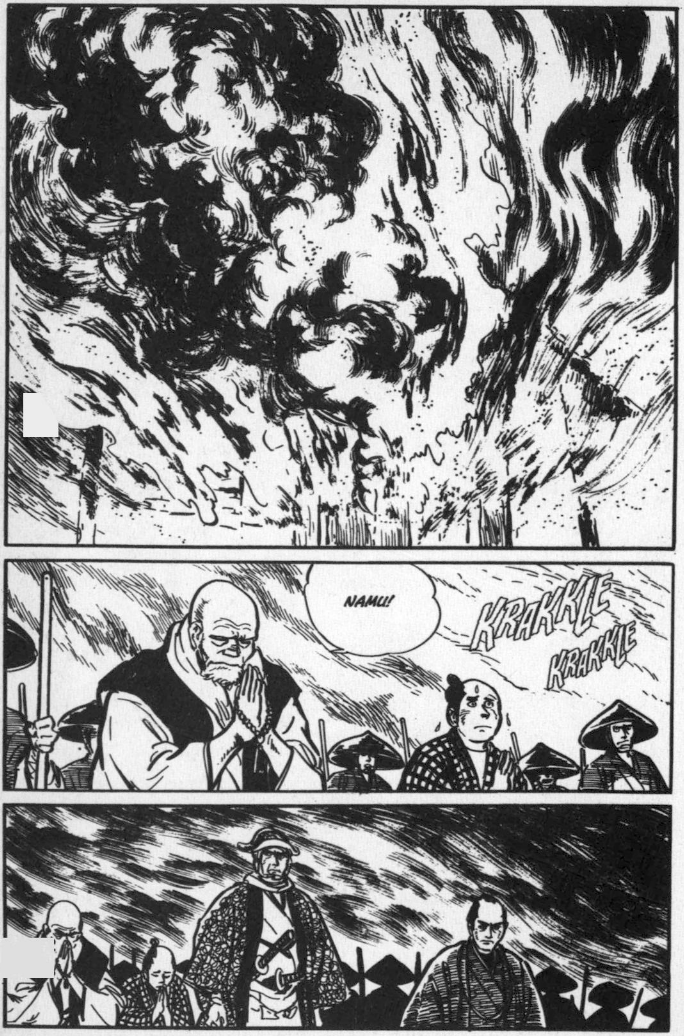
NAMU!
KRAKKLE
KRAKKLE

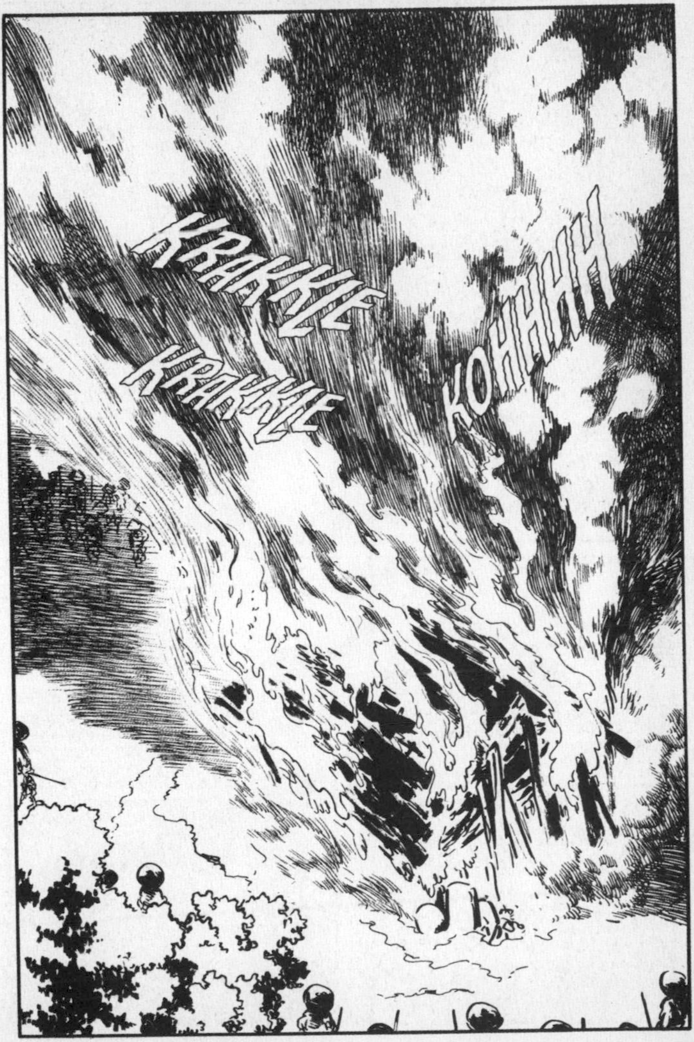
KRAKKLE
KRAKKLE
KOHHHH

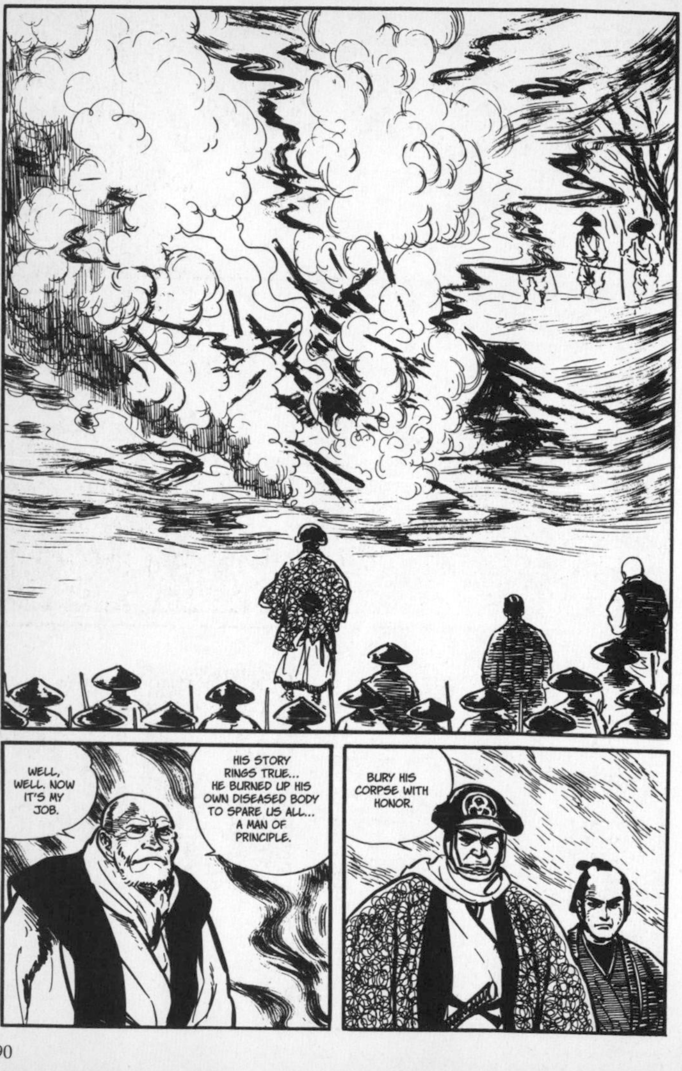
WELL, WELL. NOW IT'S MY JOB.
HIS STORY RINGS TRUE... HE BURNED UP HIS OWN DISEASED BODY TO SPARE US ALL... A MAN OF PRINCIPLE.
BURY HIS CORPSE WITH HONOR.

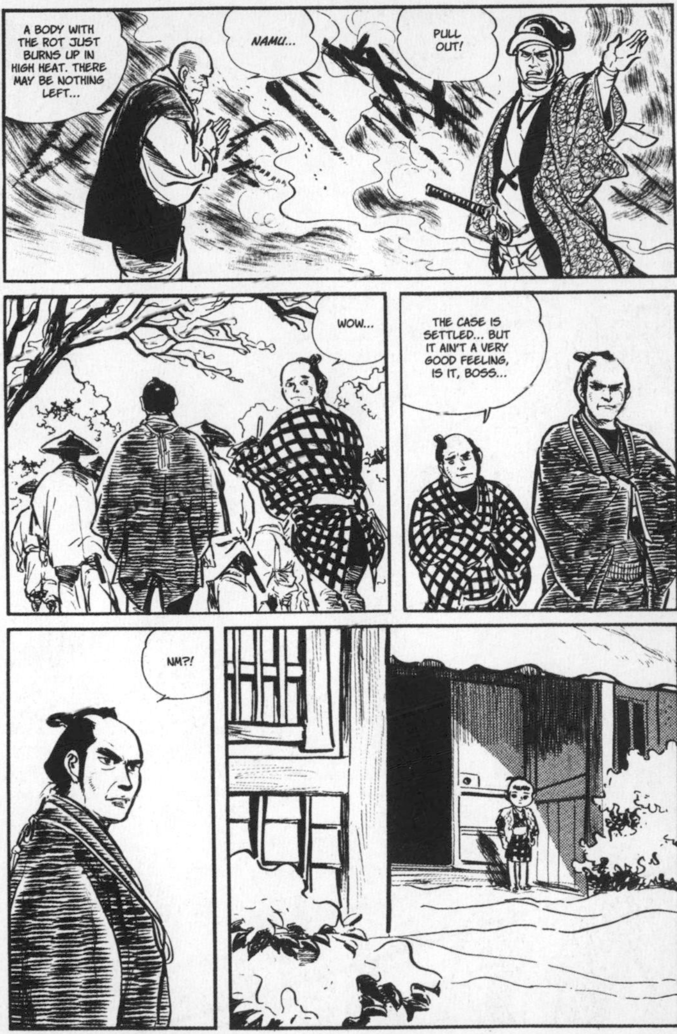
A BODY WITH THE ROT JUST BURNS UP IN HIGH HEAT. THERE MAY BE NOTHING LEFT...
NAMU...
PULL OUT!
WOW...
THE CASE IS SETTLED... BUT IT AIN'T A VERY GOOD FEELING, IS IT, BOSS...
NM?!

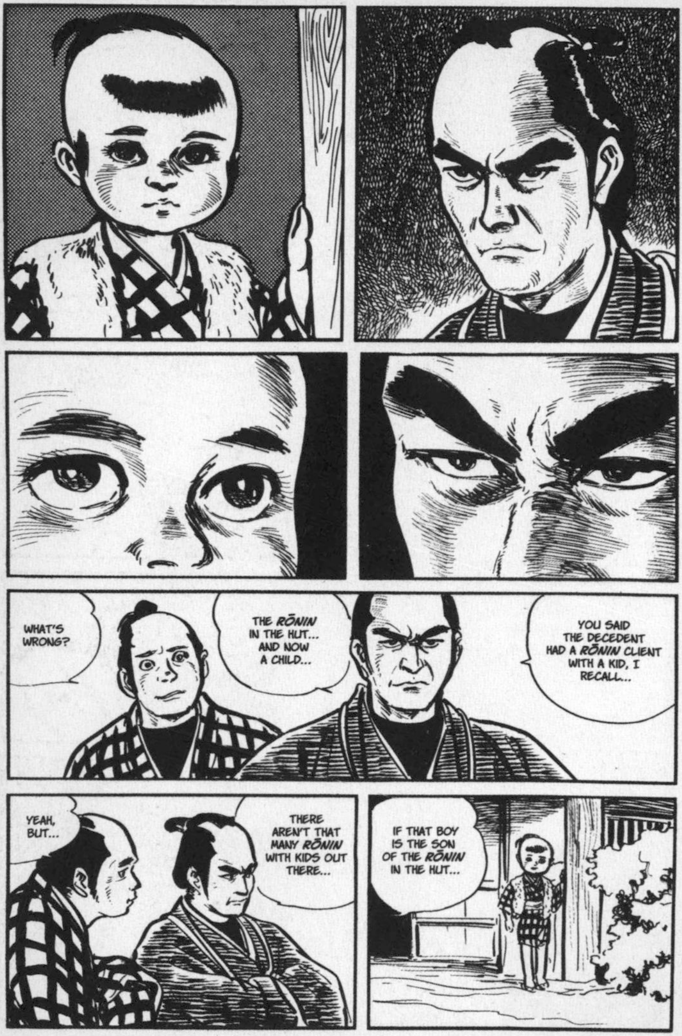
WHAT'S WRONG?
THE RŌNIN IN THE HUT... AND NOW A CHILD...
YOU SAID THE DECEDENT HAD A RŌNIN CLIENT WITH A KID, I RECALL...
YEAH, BUT...
THERE AREN'T THAT MANY RŌNIN WITH KIDS OUT THERE...
IF THAT BOY IS THE SON OF THE RŌNIN IN THE HUT...

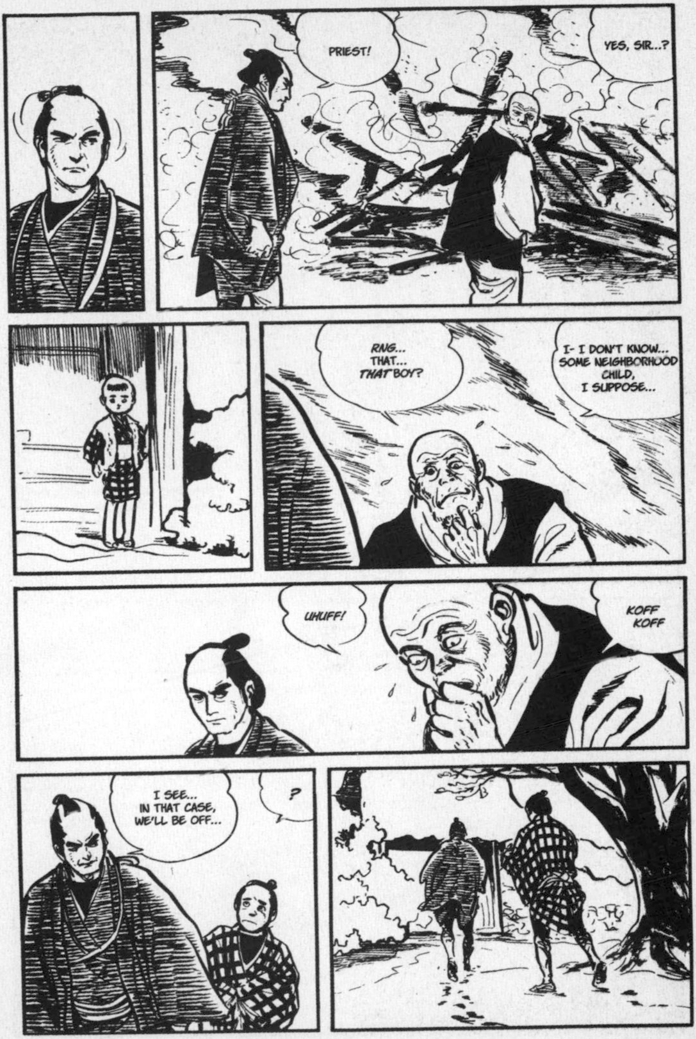
PRIEST!
YES, SIR...?
RNG... THAT... *THAT* BOY?
I- I DON'T KNOW... SOME NEIGHBORHOOD CHILD, I SUPPOSE...
UHUFF!
KOFF KOFF
I SEE... IN THAT CASE, WE'LL BE OFF...
?

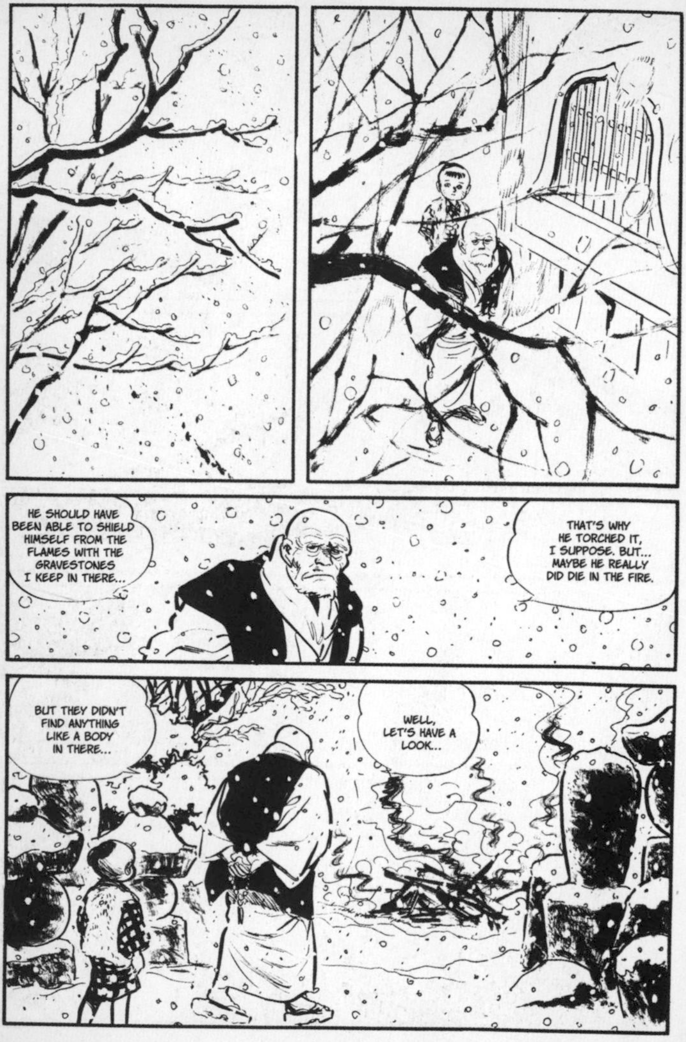
HE SHOULD HAVE BEEN ABLE TO SHIELD HIMSELF FROM THE FLAMES WITH THE GRAVESTONES I KEEP IN THERE...
THAT'S WHY HE TORCHED IT, I SUPPOSE. BUT... MAYBE HE REALLY DID DIE IN THE FIRE.
BUT THEY DIDN'T FIND ANYTHING LIKE A BODY IN THERE...
WELL, LET'S HAVE A LOOK...

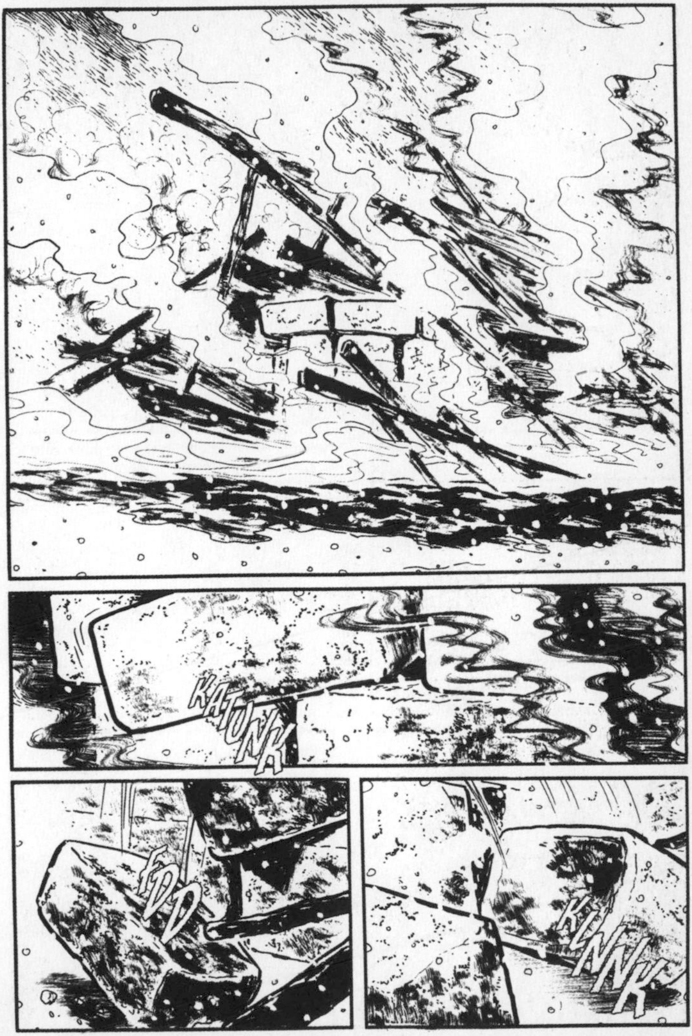
KATUNK
KLNNK

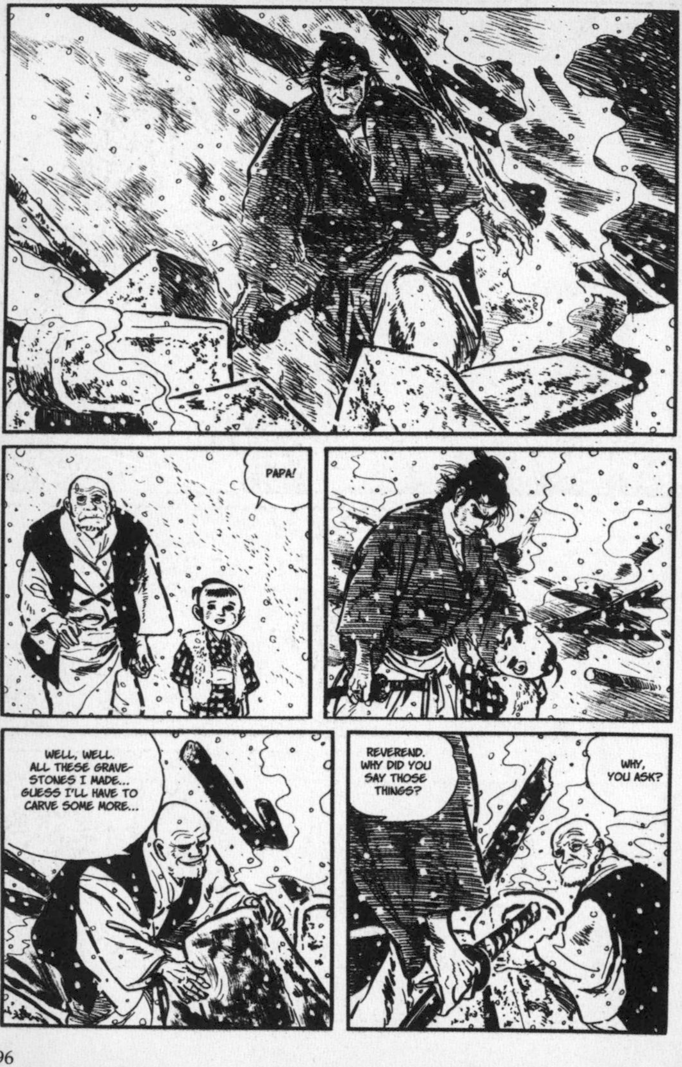
PAPA!
WELL, WELL. ALL THESE GRAVE-STONES I MADE... GUESS I'LL HAVE TO CARVE SOME MORE...
REVEREND. WHY DID YOU SAY THOSE THINGS?
WHY, YOU ASK?

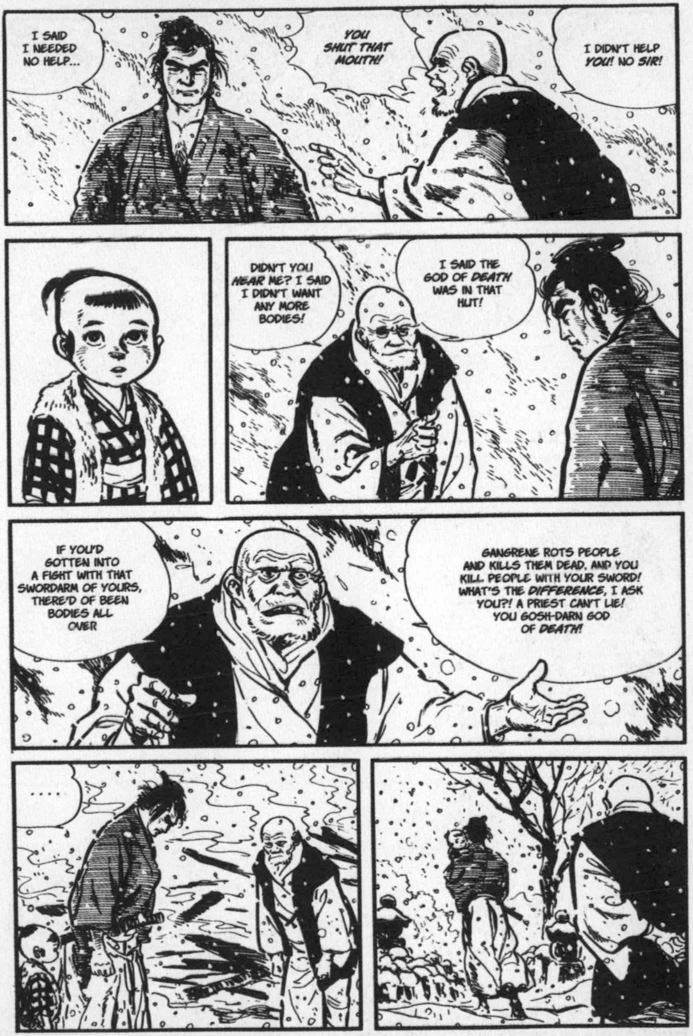

I SAID I NEEDED NO HELP...
YOU SHUT THAT MOUTH!
I DIDN'T HELP YOU! NO SIR!
DIDN'T YOU HEAR ME? I SAID I DIDN'T WANT ANY MORE BODIES!
I SAID THE GOD OF DEATH WAS IN THAT HUT!
IF YOU'D GOTTEN INTO A FIGHT WITH THAT SWORDARM OF YOURS, THERE'D OF BEEN BODIES ALL OVER
GANGRENE ROTS PEOPLE AND KILLS THEM DEAD. AND YOU KILL PEOPLE WITH YOUR SWORD! WHAT'S THE DIFFERENCE, I ASK YOU?! A PRIEST CAN'T LIE! YOU GOSH-DARN GOD OF DEATH!
....

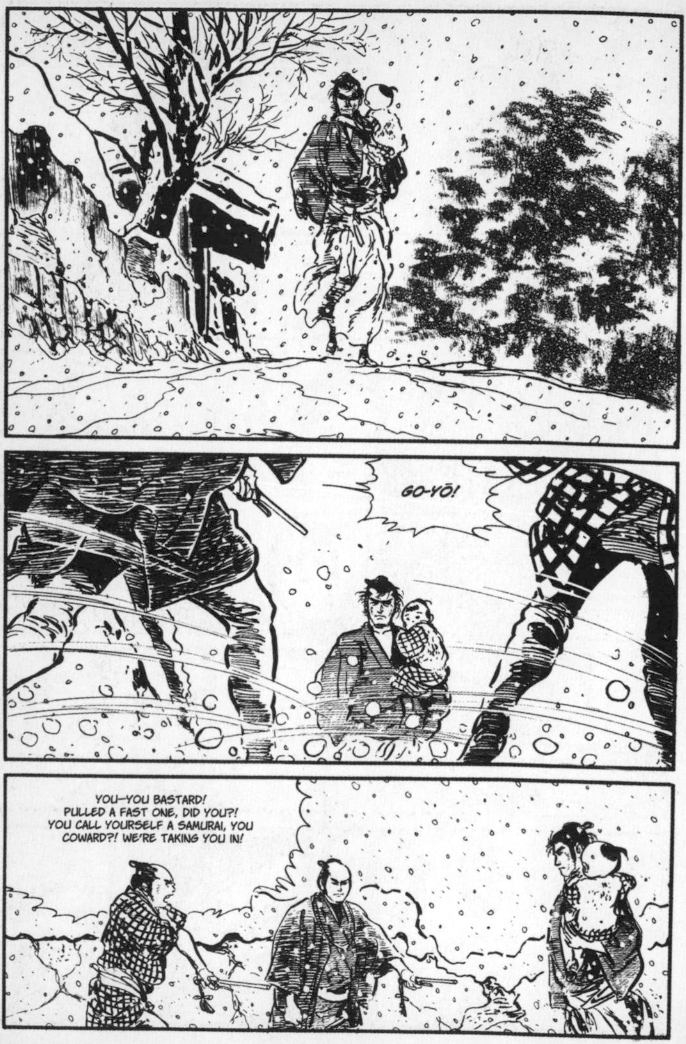
GO-YŌ!
YOU—YOU BASTARD! PULLED A FAST ONE, DID YOU?! YOU CALL YOURSELF A SAMURAI, YOU COWARD?! WE'RE TAKING YOU IN!

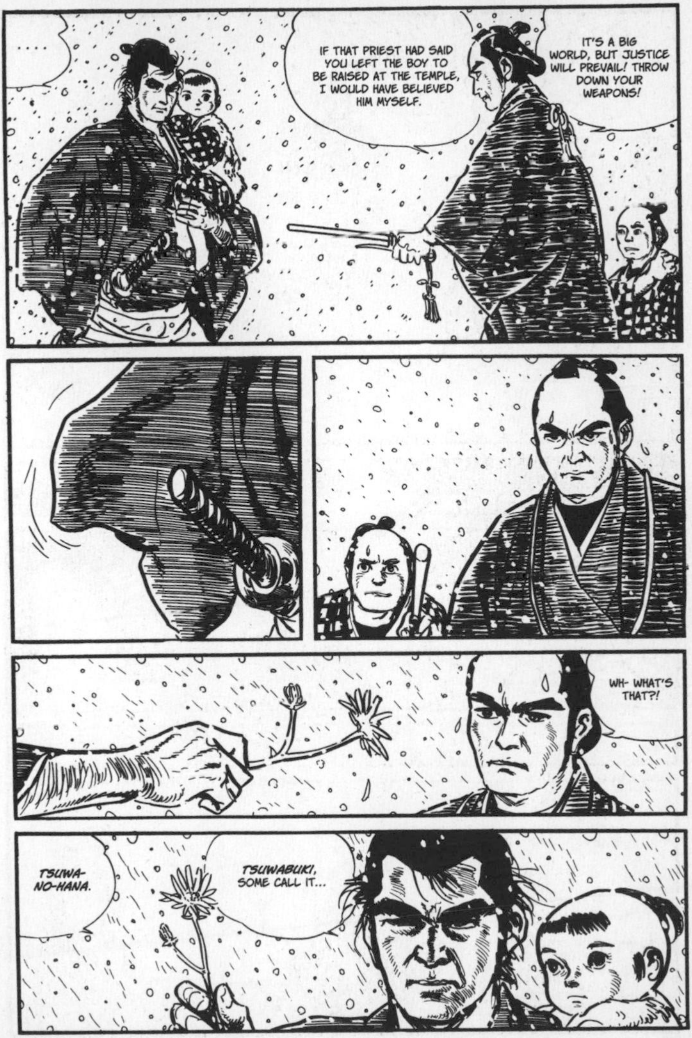

. . . .
IF THAT PRIEST HAD SAID YOU LEFT THE BOY TO BE RAISED AT THE TEMPLE, I WOULD HAVE BELIEVED HIM MYSELF.
IT'S A BIG WORLD, BUT JUSTICE WILL PREVAIL! THROW DOWN YOUR WEAPONS!
WH- WHAT'S THAT?!
TSUWA-NO-HANA.
TSUWABUKI, SOME CALL IT...

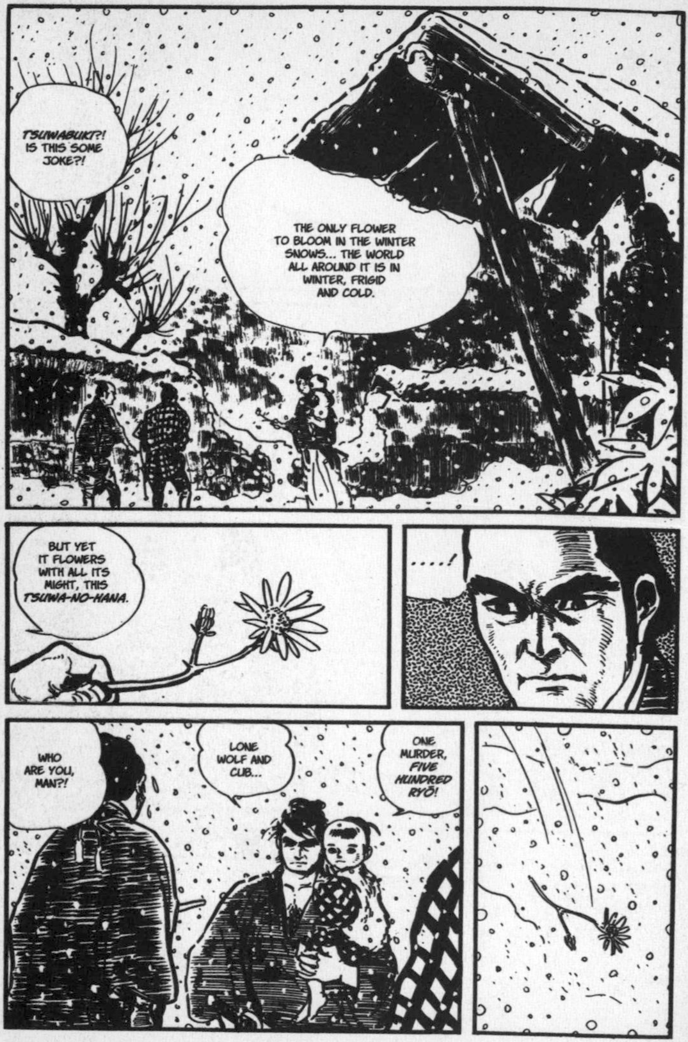
TSUWABUKI?! IS THIS SOME JOKE?!
THE ONLY FLOWER TO BLOOM IN THE WINTER SNOWS... THE WORLD ALL AROUND IT IS IN WINTER, FRIGID AND COLD.
BUT YET IT FLOWERS WITH ALL ITS MIGHT, THIS TSUWA-NO-HANA.
....!
WHO ARE YOU, MAN?!
LONE WOLF AND CUB...
ONE MURDER, FIVE HUNDRED RYŌ!

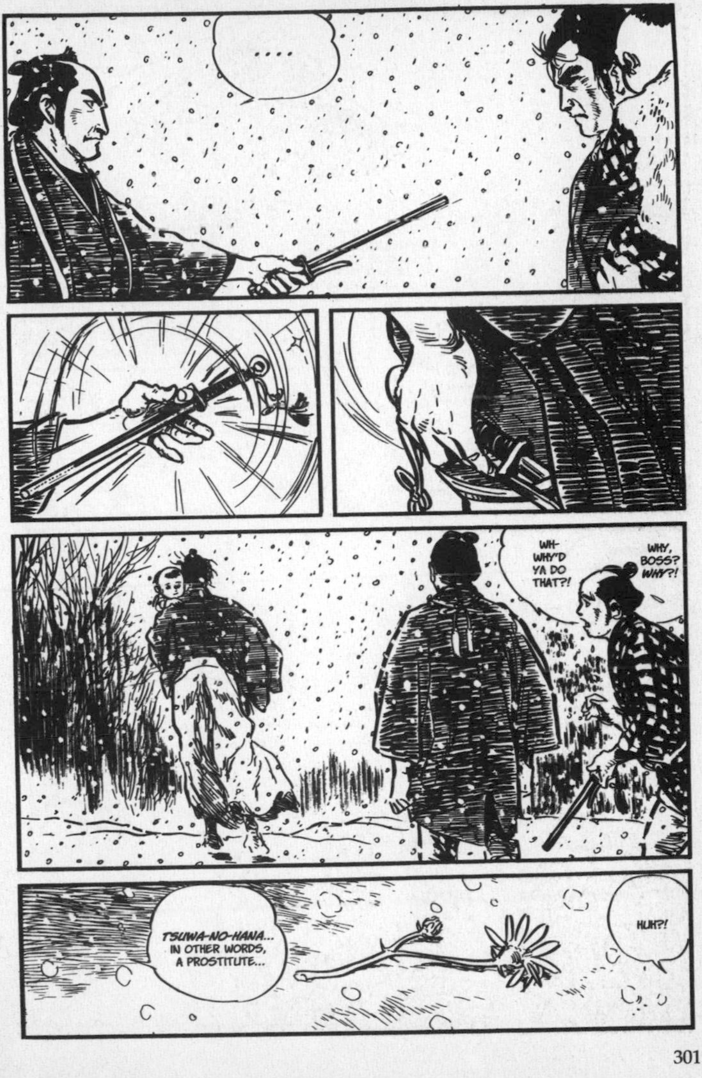
....
WH-WHY'D YA DO THAT?!
WHY, BOSS? WHY?!
TSUWA-NO-HANA... IN OTHER WORDS, A PROSTITUTE...
HUH?!

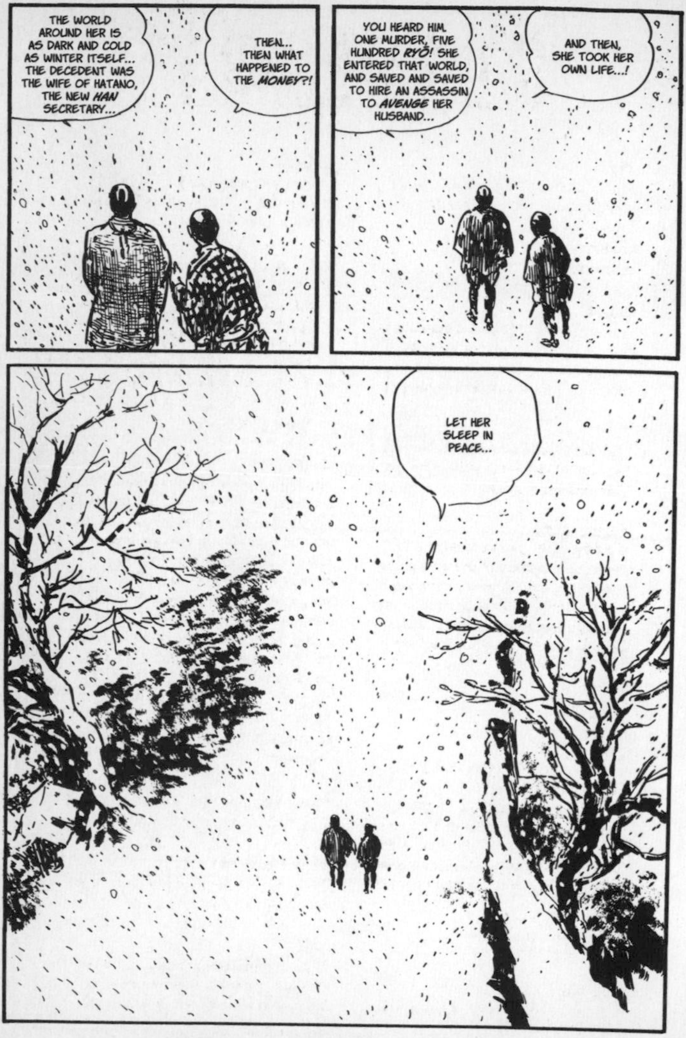
THE WORLD AROUND HER IS AS DARK AND COLD AS WINTER ITSELF... THE DECEDENT WAS THE WIFE OF HATANO, THE NEW *HAN* SECRETARY...
THEN... THEN WHAT HAPPENED TO THE *MONEY*?!
YOU HEARD HIM. ONE MURDER, FIVE HUNDRED *RYŌ*! SHE ENTERED THAT WORLD, AND SAVED AND SAVED TO HIRE AN ASSASSIN TO *AVENGE* HER HUSBAND...
AND THEN, SHE TOOK HER OWN LIFE...!
LET HER SLEEP IN PEACE...

LONE WOLF AND CUB BOOK TWO: THE END
TO BE CONTINUED

GLOSSARY

cho
Old unit of measurement. Approximately 109 meters (119 yards).

daimyo
A feudal lord.

dono
A term of respect for a higher-ranking official or aristocrat. A more common term of respect among civilians is *sama*, indicating more respect than the most common *san*.

Edo
The capital of medieval Japan and the seat of the shogunate. The site of modern-day Tokyo.

"Gaté gaté paragaté parasamgaté"
The closing mantra of *Prajnaparamita Hridaya, The Heart of Perfect Wisdom Sutra*, one of the central texts of Zen Buddhism. The sutra is in Sanskrit, and is chanted today in Zen temples around the world.

gomen
"Forgive me."

go-yo
Literally, "official business." Police and posses carried *"go-yo"* lanterns when searching for criminals, identifying themselves as law enforcers. A shouted *"Go-yo!"* could be the Edo equivalent of "Halt! Police!" for a *metsuke*, or "Make way!" for an official procession.

han
A feudal domain.

hanshi
Samurai in the service of a *han*.

kaiken
A dagger kept inside the *kimono* for self-defense. Common among the wives and daughters of samurai.

kaishaku
A second. In the rite of *seppuku*, a samurai was allowed death with honor by cutting his own abdomen. After the incision was complete, the second would perform *kaishaku*, severing the samurai's head for a quick death. The second was know as a *kaishakunin*.

karo
Elders, usually the senior advisor to a *daimyo*, the lord of a *han*. Since the *daimyo* was required to alternate each year between life in his castle in the *han* and his residence in Edo, the capital and seat of the Tokugawa shogunate, there was usually an *Edo-karo* (Edo elder) and a *kuni-karo* (*han* elder), who would administer affairs in Edo of in the *han* when their lord was away.

ken
Old unit of measure. Approximately five feet.

kimeban
Boards on which prison rules were written.

kogi kaishakunin
The Shogun's official executioner and *kaishkunin* (see *kaishaku*).

koku
A bale of rice. The traditional measure of a *han's* wealth, a measure of its agricultural land and productivity.

makura-sagashi

Literally, a pillow searcher. A wandering thief who preyed on other travelers, stealing their valuables from under their pillows while they slept.

meido

The afterlife. The land after death. Believed to be a place of darkness. Only a few Buddhist sects described a division between heaven and hell.

meifumado

The Buddhist Hell. The way of demons and damnation.

metsuke

Inspector. A post combining the functions of chief of police and chief intelligence officer.

monme

Unit of currency. Worth 1/60th of a *ryo* gold piece.

mu

Nothingness. A crucial concept in Zen Buddhism, and a goal of all the martial arts. Clearing the mind of all extraneous thoughts and connections, to exist wholly in the moment, freed of all attachment to life and the world around you.

naginata

A two-handed weapon taller than a man, with a long, curved blade. The less-common *nagamaki* was similar, with a shorter shaft and longer blade.

namu

From the Sanskrit *"namas"*: "take refuge in the Buddha." A common prayer for the dead.

o-bangashira

The supreme commander of a *han*'s standing guard (or *ban*) of samurai, charged to protect the lord and castle.

Ogami Mountain

Mountain of the great gods. The Chinese characters are different from those used in Itto Ogami's own name, "to pray, to perceive, to see," but have a similar pronunciation. It is also a play on *"okami,"* or "wolf."

ri

Old unit of measurement. Approximately 4 kilometers (2.5 miles).

ronin

A masterless samurai. Literally, "one adrift on the waves." Members of the samurai caste who have lost their masters through the dissolution of *han*, expulsion for misbehavior, or other reasons. Prohibited from working as farmers or merchants under the strict Confucian caste system imposed by the Tokugawa shogunate, many impoverished *ronin* became "hired guns" for whom the code of the samurai was nothing but empty words.

ryo

A gold piece.

seppuku

The right to kill oneself with honor to atone for failure, or to follow one's master into death. Only the samurai class was allowed this glorious but excruciating